MILITARY RULE IN CHILE

DICTATORSHIP AND OPPOSITIONS

Edited by
J. Samuel Valenzuela
and Arturo Valenzuela

THE JOHNS HOPKINS UNIVERSITY PRESS   BALTIMORE AND LONDON

Originally published, 1986
Johns Hopkins Paperbacks edition, 1987

The Johns Hopkins University Press
701 West 40th Street
Baltimore, Maryland 21211
The Johns Hopkins Press Ltd., London

LIBRARY OF CONGRESS CATALOGING-IN-PUBLICATION DATA

Main entry under title:

Military rule in Chile.

Includes index.
1. Chile—Politics and government—1970–   —Addresses,
essays, lectures. 2. Civil-military relations—Chile—Addresses,
essays, lectures. 3. Authoritarianism—Chile—Addresses,
essays, lectures. 4. Chile—Economic conditions—1970–
—Addresses, essays, lectures. I. Valenzuela, J. Samuel (Julio
Samuel) II. Valenzuela, Arturo, 1944–
JL2681.M45   1985   983'.0647   85-9797
ISBN 0-8018-3154-7 (alk. paper)
ISBN 0-8018-3563-1 (pbk.)

Contents

Tables

Preface

While the literature on President Salvador Allende's short-lived (1970–73) Popular Unity coalition government is voluminous and continues to grow, there is a dearth of work on the military regime which has ruled Chile for over a decade. Allende and his coalition partners attracted world attention by promising to move the nation towards socialism while respecting democratic procedures and adhering strictly to existing legal norms. That seemed like a bold and unusual experiment, and academic as well as other observers from Europe and the United States, some skeptical and some enthusiastic, flocked to Santiago to study its course. When, on 11 September 1973, the armed forces put a brutal end to the leftist government, most subsequent international attention focused on the authorities' serious violations of human rights. Aside from expressing their concerns over this issue, a majority of the social scientists who studied Allende's Chile have focused their research on other areas.

This book represents an effort to right the imbalance. Admittedly, studying an authoritarian regime is more difficult, and certainly more disheartening, than analyzing a democratic one. And yet, the task is necessary, not only because of the longevity of the military regime, but also because it has instituted changes that are much more far reaching (although in a conservative, even reactionary way) than those which the Popular Unity government had attempted. Allende's administration was mostly an extension, although with a more leftist program, of the policies of the recent past, while the military regime represents a radical departure.

This volume has been long in the making. It was conceived by the editors in mid-1974, when they collaborated on a paper (presented at the International Sociological Association meetings in Toronto) offering an early overall assessment and characterization of the military regime. It was clear by then that there would be no rapid return to democracy, and that the authorities had visions of generating a new economy and society as well as a sharply different polity. Such attempts in a nation of long-standing democratic institutions and vigorous traditions deserved careful attention and study.

The book was set in motion in 1979, when General Pinochet celebrated his sixth anniversary as head of state, the equivalent of one presidential term according to the constitution in force until 1973. The Latin America Program of Woodrow Wilson International Center for Scholars in Washington generously offered support for a special workshop on Chilean authoritarian rule. The workshop, "Six Years of Military Rule in Chile," was convened for May 15 to 17, 1980. Invited scholars (most of them Chileans, since it is they who have produced the principal studies of the period) presented papers on various aspects of Chilean society, economy, and state organization.

The papers included in this collection, none of which deal directly with the well-known issue of human rights violations, were all first written for the Wilson Center discussions. The editors asked the authors to place a heavy emphasis on description; we wanted to know what has happened in Chile, and not only how one should interpret what has occurred. We also noted that we wished to steer clear of the catastrophic style found in some writings on Chile, since declamations often stand in lieu of analysis. To be sure, all papers were revised after the meeting, but with the exception of the paper by Alejandro Foxley (whom we specifically asked for an update, given the extent of the economic downturn in 1982–83) and some minor changes in the others, all the essays were finished by the end of 1982. They therefore antedate the political crisis the regime faced during 1983 with the remarkable resurgence of popular mobilization against the government. The papers were originally written during the most triumphant moments for the regime, when its economic policy was touted internationally as a success, when new and important projects such as social security, educational, and labor law reforms were set in motion, and when the internal opposition was disillusioned by General Pinochet's success in consolidating his power and by its own apparent inability to reach a broader public. That the essays here can be published today without major alterations is a tribute to their more permanent value.

Many persons have aided us in the difficult process of producing this volume. Our thanks go, in particular, to Abraham Lowenthal, Alexander Wilde, and the Wilson Center staff, who contributed so much to our highly successful workshop. We wish to extend our special appreciation to Peter Hakim, of the Inter-American Foundation, for his interest in the project. Nina Serafino, Esperanza Oteo, Hugo Castillo, Juan Allende, Willian Ilgin, Josefina Tyriakian, and others helped with the translations; to them our thanks also. Scott Bradner of the Computer-Based Laboratory at Harvard University and Susan Ishikawa provided word processing assistance. Pamela Palma and Carolyn Moser also provided invaluable assistance in the preparation of the final draft. Henry Tom, of Johns Hopkins University

Press, merits a note of appreciation for his patience in awaiting the manuscript.

We would also like to thank the participants of the Wilson Center workshop, whose comments and suggestions were most helpful for the authors' revisions of their papers. Excluding the names of those whose papers we publish here, the participants were Patricio Chaparro, David Collier, Jaime Crispi, Rafael Echeverría, Tom Farer, Albert Fishlow, Carlos Fortín, Edmundo Fuenzalida, Federico Gil, Peter Hakim, Jorge Heine, Ronald Hellman, Fred Levy, Juan Linz, Abraham Lowenthal, Rolf Lüders, Barbara Mauger, Kenneth Maxwell, Claudio Orrego Vicuña, Karen Remmer, Philippe Schmitter, Christopher Scott, Dudley Seers, Paul Sigmund, Alfred Stepan, Jorge Tapia Videla, Anthony D. Tillett, Laurence Whitehead, Alexander Wilde, Manfred Wilhemy, Peter Winn, and José Zalaquett.

Finally, a note of appreciation to Patricio Chaparro, Francisco Cumplido, Rafael Echeverría, and especially, to Carlos Fortín and Daniel Levy, for contributing papers for this project which, given space limitations as it was scaled down by publishing constraints to one volume, we were in the end regretfully unable to publish. It is our loss. As always Raimundo Valenzuela provided many suggestions which improved the quality of the papers, as did an anonymous reader for Johns Hopkins University Press.

MILITARY RULE IN CHILE

Introduction

*J. Samuel Valenzuela and
Arturo Valenzuela*

The 1973 military coup which overthrew the government of President
Salvador Allende initiated a period that constitutes a sharp departure from
past Chilean history and experience. Chileans had long prided themselves
on their democratic institutions and procedures. Chilean democracy was
among the first to emerge and was one of the most long-standing in the
world, a record which stood in stark contrast to that of the rest of Latin
America. From the 1830s until 1973 all of the nation's chief executives had
been elected to their office (with literate male suffrage provisions since
1874), although there were short-lived exceptions in the turbulent years of
1891, 1924, and 1932.

As a result, few political leaders and observers believed, even during
the chaotic years of the Popular Unity government, in the possibility of a
military coup. Moreover, those who held this belief expected the ensuing
authorities to sponsor a new round of political negotiations, and to rapidly
set the nation back on its constitutionally mandated electoral schedule and
traditions of political accommodation. Instead, a remarkably durable military regime emerged from the ruins of La Moneda, the Chilean presidential
palace destroyed by Air Force bombs on that Tuesday, 11 September.

General Augusto Pinochet, who became the head of state after leading
the troops against the president, would preside over the nation for a longer
period of time than any of his predecessors, including three nineteenth-
century presidents who were elected to two consecutive five-year terms.

The military regime has proven to be a harsh dictatorship, among the
most repressive in South America. The expanded and centrally unified
political police tortures its detainees as a matter of course, and many individuals have been killed, jailed, or forced into exile.

The Congress, the centerpiece of the Chilean democracy, was closed
permanently for the first time since its formation after the country's independence from Spain. Political parties, which had structured politics for
generations and served as the fundamental channels for representation and
control, were banned or their activities severely circumscribed. The

national labor federation was dissolved, and union leaders were imprisoned or exiled. Electoral registries were burned, and all national elections, except for highly irregular and self-serving plebiscites, were suspended. The political independence of the judicial system and of the comptroller general's office have been questionable since the coup, even though these institutions have retained some of their autonomy. Freedom of the press has similarly been curbed, with many organs closed outright and others subject to censorship or self-censorship. The nation's universities, which had long enjoyed political autonomy and academic freedom, have been run by special rectors, usually from military ranks, appointed directly by the head of state. Many professors and students have been summarily dismissed.

Democratic procedures have been abrogated in local government. Mayors are appointed directly by the president. Municipal councils, with a tradition going back to colonial times, have been abolished in favor of appointed advisory boards. Individual citizens and organized groups, long accustomed to addressing congressmen and administration functionaries with their varied petitions, have found the military authorities to be inaccessible and quick to resort to repressive measures to deal with public expressions of discontent.

The only serious countervailing force to the regime has been the Roman Catholic Church, which by initiative of the archbishop of Santiago set up an agency to monitor human rights abuses and provide legal aid. Parishes and church organs have also served as umbrella organizations for opposition community groups and surviving elements from the political parties and labor movement.

Significant as it is, the abrupt change from democracy to dictatorship is not the only change the country has experienced in over a decade of military rule. The authorities also attempted to institute the most far-reaching transformations in the economic and social order of any government in this century. At least until the severe deterioration of the Chilean economy in 1982, these transformations were pursued with single-minded determination.

The dramatic changes were engineered by a group of technocrats, known as the Chicago boys, who gave the Chilean regime a distinct ideological flavor as their influence spread throughout the administrative structure of the state. Professing a commitment to freedom and the free market economy, the young technicians (many of whom were actually trained at the University of Chicago) argued that authoritarianism was required to prevent the continued spread of collectivist ideologies and programs. The dictatorship, in their view, was simply a convenient means to rapidly introduce the necessary reforms that would allow Chileans to experience, for the first time ever, a "truly" open society, a society where entrepreneurship could flourish unbridled and where individual opportunity would undermine the "foreign" socialist doctrines of Chile's political class. Government spokesmen explicitly argued that economic progress under a consumer-oriented free market economy would render obsolete the traditional political loyalties of the Chilean people.

In this conception a totally "free market" is one in which individuals with greater resources can dominate, one in which the strong backing of an impervious state is required to prevent the distorting influences of collective action and the political pressure of individuals of lesser market capacity. In the view of government advisers some democracies, such as those in Scandinavia, generate a society more "closed" to individual choice than does a government inspired by the liberal principles they uphold, even if it is a dictatorship. And, in a democratic context, without the repressive apparatus of the state, it would have been impossible for the authorities to stand up to the pressures of organized groups such as parties, professional associations, labor unions, and business associations in implementing the rules and regulations required for an "open society."[1]

Thus, in the name of free market liberalism the regime was impervious to most of the protests of affected groups and individuals, making full use of its monopoly of power to implement its new programs. Virtually no aspect of Chilean society was left untouched. The protectionist industrial policies of the late 1920s were abruptly eliminated on the assumption that Chile's economy could develop only by being exposed to the rigors of international competition. Such competition would force inefficient firms and enterprises out of business and encourage Chileans to specialize in products in which the country has a comparative advantage. Many enterprises in the state sector were sold at below market prices to private investors, leading to a significant concentration of economic power in the hands of a few individuals with access to capital, foreign and domestic, able to purchase the firms. The agrarian reform process was terminated. At least a third of the land was returned to former owners, and land assigned to cooperatives passed gradually into individual holdings. The national health service was scaled down and much of the health care delivery system privatized, as was the bulk of the state-sponsored social insurance scheme.

Regime Characterization

A significant question confronting the study of any nondemocratic regime is its overall characterization. The recent literature on the military governments of Argentina, Brazil, Chile, and Uruguay by Latin American scholars has contained a lively debate on whether or not these regimes should be considered a new form of fascism.[2] To some authors the fascist label seems appropriate because both the European interwar and the Latin American military regimes are dictatorships which stress nationalism and the objective of forging a new, purified order. Both also favor the consolidation of industrial capitalism, resort frequently to the repression of opponents with security organizations enjoying marked degrees of autonomy, and add to their visceral antisocialism and communism a profound mistrust of independently organized working-class movements.

There are, however, several key differences between European fascism and contemporary Latin American authoritarianism which render the term less than useful in describing the latter. By contrast with European fascism the Latin American dictatorships acquired power through coups and not mass movements, explicitly rejecting the option of sponsoring official parties or mass organizations. With the partial exception of the Peruvian case during the Velasco period, they also resisted the temptation to manipulate or direct social organizations from the state, an important feature of European fascism even if it was not fully implemented, especially in the Italian case. Finally, while European fascism had some anti-oligarchic elements to its discourse, the Latin American Southern Cone dictatorships have largely avoided such discourse.

It is also inappropriate to characterize the Latin American dictatorships of the sixties and seventies as corporatist or functionalist. While they occasionally made use of corporatist rhetoric, no serious attempt was made to create formal mechanisms of representation for societal groups defined along functional lines. Nowhere has this been clearer than in Chile. The March 1974 "Declaration of Principles" does draw from integralist conceptions in Catholic social doctrine, and the activities of the National Secretariat of Women or the National Secretariat of Youth have provided the government with something of a corporatist cast. But these organizations have been insignificant, and the whole thrust of the Chilean regime has been to exclude organized groups from any policy-making role in the name of social and economic liberalism. Indeed, the Pinochet government has gone farther than any government in Chilean history in rooting out the few corporatist features of Chilean politics, such as the representation of professional associations and business and labor groups in government decision-making bodies. Schemes on paper for functional representation at the local level have never really been implemented, and local politics has continued to be characterized by a highly vertical and authoritarian pattern of authority, closely paralleling the military chain of command.

Juan Linz's well-known designation of nondemocratic and nonmobilizing regimes as "authoritarian" is far more useful than either the fascist or corporatist labels in characterizing the Latin American dictatorships.[3] The distinctive feature of authoritarian regimes according to Linz is the separation they create between the state and civil society. This contrasts with totalitarian regimes, where the state seeks to permeate and control society, and democratic regimes, where mechanisms of representation allow for state accountability to society.

This separation between state and society is quite clear in the Latin American cases, with Chile constituting the most extreme example. The authorities have sought to break the conduits through which groups and individuals have gained access to policy-making circles, leaving them to their own devices or repressing them for noncompliance with official directives.

And yet, in reflecting on the experience of military government in Brazil, Linz was struck at how much less institutionalized it was than Franco's Spain, his paradigmatic case.[4] This led him to characterize Brazil as an authoritarian situation rather than an authoritarian regime. In Linz's terms, Chile can also be thought of as an authoritarian situation. In Chile decision-making circles are extremely circumscribed. Though the 1980 Constitution provides a framework for a future political order with a specific timetable for regime transition, the same document gives Pinochet extraordinary power until the Constitution is fully implemented in 1989. The Constitution does give the junta, made up of the commanders-in-chief of each of the branches of the armed forces, some jurisdiction in legislative matters. But executive authority is paramount, and when Pinochet persuades his fellow military commanders to go along with various policy initiatives, five men determine the fate of national policy in the time that it takes to write and sign a decree law.

It should be noted that the Chilean variant of an authoritarian situation is probably characterized by a greater degree of ideological coherence than Linz ascribes to authoritarian regimes. Linz argues that authoritarian regimes are more likely to have "distinctive mentalities," as opposed to fully articulated ideological schema.[5] In Chile, however, the neoliberalism or ultraliberalism which marked the regime at least through its first ten years was more than simply an attitude or frame of mind or even an attempt to dress up a deep-seated anti-Communism. It was an elaborate "system of thought" with specific intellectual exponents.[6] And while it is likely that many, if not most, military officers and civil servants have had no use for the ideology (which means that belief in it is by no means a condition for serving in government positions), the neoliberal framework does appear in government documents and in the speeches Pinochet and other junta members as justification for policy innovations.

Guillermo O'Donnell's notion of the bureaucratic authoritarian state adds further to an understanding of the Chilean case.[7] The Chilean regime is staffed by individuals who have a technocratic orientation and are employed by complex civilian and military organizations. It emerged as a reaction to popular mobilization and a perceived threat of socialist transformations in a society fraught with difficulties in its imperfect but extensive industrial economy.

Chile, however, would have to be understood as a case of failed bureaucratic authoritarianism. The military rulers have not succeeded in forging an alliance between the state, multinationals, and local business interests, an alliance which, according to the original formulation of the model, would provide the necessary dynamism to impel the economy to a new level of investment and growth. While local entrepreneurs were able to obtain large amounts of foreign financing, they invested little in productive activities. And very little foreign investment materialized outside of the mining sector. No "deepening" of the productive apparatus, in O'Donnell's term, took place. Instead, the opening of the Chilean economy to world competition inflicted a severe blow to the country's industrial base, so that after almost twelve years of military rule there has not been substantial economic growth.

Both the Linz and O'Donnell characterizations are ideal typical ones. Although inspired by particular cases, they are designed to describe a class of regimes that share common features. Individual cases within that class have additional characteristics peculiar to them. The extreme neoliberal ideology of the Chilean regime may be its most prominent feature, but there are others as well.

The most salient of these is the manner in which the armed forces have participated in the government. Certainly, from the head of state and military junta down, officers in active service and retired officers have occupied the most important governmental positions, including a majority of cabinet ministries, the directorships of key state enterprises, the posts of regional intendants, and even the rectorships of universities. Moreover, many of the civilians in government have close family ties to important officers.

It would thus be correct to characterize the Chilean dictatorship as a military regime, but this label would not point to its distinctiveness. When compared with Argentina, Brazil, and Uruguay, what is unusual in the Chilean case is the preeminent position occupied by the Chilean president. General Pinochet simultaneously holds the offices of president of the republic, supreme commander, and commander-in-chief of the Army. Because of the highly disciplined and vertical nature of the Chilean military, Pinochet was able to use his position as commander of the most important military service (with a virtual monopoly over the promotion process) to persuade his fellow commanders to designate him president, a designation which was then ratified in a plebiscite and in the 1980 Constitution.

Unlike his counterparts in other Southern Cone countries, Pinochet does not serve at the pleasure of the military high command, though disciplined support from the armed forces constitutes the fundamental pillar of his authority. Unlike his Argentine counterparts, who were retired officers, Pinochet has remained in active duty, exercising day-to-day supervision over the most vertical military institution in the Western Hemisphere.

Nor have the Chilean generals constituted a deliberative body advising or pressing the government for particular measures and policies. Military officers while in government service do not take orders from their superiors in the institution; they are subject to their immediate governmental superior even if he is a civilian minister, or if an officer is a cabinet officer, to Pinochet himself. And Pinochet has been very careful not to allow military officers to achieve too much prominence, promptly replacing those who attained a measure of visibility. In Chile there has been a clear separation between governmental power and military power. The Chilean regime is one of the military, though not by the military.[8]

The Chilean situation cannot be understood without reference to the enormous power that General Pinochet has concentrated in himself, and it is therefore more proper to characterize the regime as the "dictatorship of the commander-in-chief of the armed forces" than as a military one per se. The importance of the head of state, the length of his tenure in office, and the lack of institutional controls over his actions make the Chilean authoritarian situation closer to that of the personalist authoritarian governments which were common in Latin America in earlier periods. The source of personal power has nothing to do with individual charisma or, for that matter, with the political culture; it is simply a product of the highly professional and hierarchical character of the Chilean armed forces, which allows its top officer to dictate to his subordinates and which prescribes the apoliticism of the officer corps. Ironically, the professionalism of the Chilean military and its apoliticism, which contributed in a significant way to the longevity of Chilean democracy, is a principal obstacle to an early transition to democratic rule.

The Essays in This Book

Although it is impossible to be fully comprehensive in one volume, the papers contained herein are designed to provide the reader with an overall view of the Chilean dictatorship's policies, their results, and the reaction and opposition which they have generated.

The first three essays deal with economic and social policy. Alejandro Foxley's contribution presents a general examination of the course of economic policy over the last decade and of its highly negative results: a lack of economic growth, high unemployment, a sharper concentration of ownership of enterprises and banks, a more regressive distribution of income. As the author notes, the Chilean experience is important since it represents a test case for the purest application of the most orthodox laissez-faire economic model. The unprecedentedly thorough and swift opening up of the Chilean market to the international economy merited further treatment. The second paper in this book, by Ricardo Ffrench-Davis, explores in critical detail all of its consequences. Finally, the similarly remarkable reduction of the size of the state, the wholesale divestiture of enterprises under its control, and the attempt to decentralize and even privatize the social institutions which have been an important part of its mission are the object of Pilar Vergara's article. Taken together, these three chapters cover the central focus of the regime's attempts to radically transform Chilean economy and society as a prelude to a new politics.

The next paper, written by Genaro Arriagada, covers the most sensitive aspect of the dictatorship: its military policy. Arriagada reviews the norms through which, step by step, General Pinochet forged his advance from a *primum inter pares* presidency of the military junta to his preeminent position as head of state and of the armed forces. He shows, in addition, the extensive changes which have been made in the process of military promotions and retirements, which greatly enhance Pinochet's ability to name officers loyal to him to top-ranking positions.

Manuel Antonio Garretón broadens the discussion with a perceptive interpretive essay on the course followed by the military regime. He examines its evolution as containing two somewhat overlapping phases, that of containment, and that of attempts at institutionalizing both its own rule as well as the broader changes it seeks to instill in the society following the neoliberal blueprint. He also discusses the problems faced by the opposition forces in organizing to confront the regime. Garretón argues that the regime has become more institutionalized than this introduction suggests, but the difference is mainly a semantic one. While there has been, particularly with the 1980 Constitution, some codification in legal norms of Pinochet's unipersonal power, we expect to see evidence that these rules have effectively bound him to follow fixed procedures, and that they generate broader arenas of policy discussion and review within the regime.

The editors' paper on party oppositions follows Garretón's essay. Advocates of the government have repeatedly stated that the parties of the recent past will not reemerge once the government's program of transformations is in place. This is an argument to which many observers in Chile have given some credence, as can be seen in this volume in aspects of both Vergara's and Garretón's papers. We contradict this notion and argue that the Chilean party system is very likely to reemerge in the event of a redemocratization, given the strong roots it had in the society. Nonetheless, whether or not specific party labels and organizations (as opposed to new ones which seek to appeal to the same tendencies of opinion and political self-identification in the electorate) will reemerge depends to a large degree on the survival of groups of militants who are able to retain the party labels and organizations. To do so they must have some level of activity, which occurs by maintaining contacts between the militants and their sympathizers, even if only on a social basis, as well as by a transfer of a large part of militant actions to the organizations of civil society.

The chapter by Manuel Barrera and Samuel Valenzuela further expands the discussion of the opposition by examining the course followed by the labor movement since 1973. They note how and why the various ideological and political strands of the movement came closer together in a common effort of opposition after being bitterly divided at the inception of the regime. The authors also discuss the various changes in the authorities' labor policies and examine the so-called Labor Plan, which has been presented by the government as one of its principal achievements. The labor movement leadership has taken a key role in the development of the protest movements which began on 11 May 1983, and it has become one of the most important voices in demanding an end to the dictatorship.

One of the principal institutions providing spaces for opposition activity in Chile has been the Catholic church. As the widely held colloquial expression has it, the church has provided an "umbrella" for all sorts of groups to weather the storm produced by the regime. Brian Smith's article provides a detailed analysis of the manner in which the church evolved to assume this role in the years since the coup d'état. From a position of ambiguous reception of the military takeover, the church has become one of the most forceful critics of the human rights violations by the authorities.

The final paper, by Heraldo Muñoz, discusses the military government's foreign policy. During this period, Chile has been isolated from the international community as never before. All small nations exert their diplomatic influence principally through multinational institutions such as the United Nations and the Organization for American States, and in these corridors Chilean diplomacy was formerly widely respected. This was mainly the result of the prestige that surrounded the representatives from a respected democracy as well as the fact that the foreign service was staffed by highly trained career officers. After the military coup, Muñoz argues, Chilean foreign policy abandoned its pragmatic style to adopt an ideological (anti-Communist and anti-Soviet) and praetorian one. Many foreign diplomatic missions were given to individuals outside the foreign service, including retired military officers, and these envoys have had to represent a nation whose government has been viewed widely as one of the worst offenders of human rights. Consequently, Chilean diplomacy has suffered considerable reverses in its sphere of action. The United Nations has voted yearly to condemn the human rights violations, foreign statesmen avoid accepting official visits and inviting the Chilean head of state, and international bodies have lent sympathetic attention to the nation's neighbors in territorial disputes.

Looking to the Future

One of the paradoxes of authoritarian situations (but not necessarily of authoritarian regimes) is that they appear to be fragile despite the fact that they can be very durable. The perception of fragility stems, as Juan Linz notes, basically from the inadequacy of their legitimating formulae.[9] This leads many people, even many of those working for the state, to think of the regime as a temporary arrangement, and raises questions regarding the appropriateness of the provisions for succession in power should the head of state resign, be incapacitated, or die. The future therefore appears much more open-ended than that of a democracy, where the broadly accepted political procedures lead to the sense that the electoral mechanism will continue to provide for an orderly transfer of power. The lack of institution-alization of the policy-making process and therefore its haphazard course, also emphasizes the impression of temporality, as does the fact that the authorities themselves make constant references to a future political order which will be different. Moreover, the government appears fragile once public expressions of discontent begin to mount, leading to the notion that its support in the population is not as widespread as the authorities claim. But the evident durability of many of these authoritarian situations stems simply from the fact that in the last analysis they need only to have the support and commitment of a very small minority: the armed forces, the security services, and key civil servants and technicians. From the rest of the population, they only require obedience to laws and regulations (includ-ing, of course, the tax provisions). The relatively high levels of repression serve to ensure that they retain this obedience.[10]

The government of Augusto Pinochet has been extraordinarily durable but seems particularly fragile. The key to its endurance is Pinochet's proven capacity to command the armed forces, especially his own service, and the security apparatus. The fragility has been underscored by the development of broad-based protest movements in 1983.

There is no doubt that as of 1983 the quiescence of the population, which the authorities had interpreted as support, ended. The government's project of generating a "new mentality" among Chileans that would corres-pond to the society that its policies were fashioning has been effectively contradicted by the events. The "foundational" aspects of its self-appointed mission have largely yielded to a caretaker attitude of attempt-ing simply to diffuse the challenges to the regime. Within the governing circles new disagreements have come to light, particularly over the course of economic policy. The dramatic collapse of economic activity in 1982–83 has led some individuals in or close to the regime to call for a change of direction away from the orthodox framework; they have argued that the disenchantment with the regime is merely the result of the difficulties people face as a result of the crisis, and that a reactivation of the economy will lead to greater acceptance, even support, for the regime. However, such a result, even if the economy were to turn around, seems unlikely. The mushrooming of protests may have been aided by the penury caused by the economic crisis, but they have since acquired a logic of their own, becoming a purely political problem for the regime. Protest movements generate their own dynamics and history, from which there is no turning back: the movements may even quiet down, but the memory of participation in them, and of the repression perpetrated by the security forces to still them, will not permit a change of attitudes in many quarters in favor of the regime.

The current situation is therefore principally one of stalemate. On the one hand, the government can no longer hope to implement successfully its program of transformations leading to a new society. On the other, the protest movement and the opposition cannot put an end to the dictatorship in the short run without the intervention of the armed forces—or a graceful decision by General Pinochet to yield power to a figure committed to a democratic restoration. It is not impossible that the regime could end quickly, unexpectedly, taking all observers by surprise; such is the nature of authoritarian situations. In these circumstances, the strength of the political forces pledged to restore democracy in Chile and the relatively broad consensus which the opposition has forged in opposition to the regime could permit a redemocratization of the polity. And yet, for the short-term, foreseeable future, only an escalation of violence seems in store for the nation, with each violent act making a return to the democracy that once was the pride of Chileans more and more difficult and unlikely.

Notes

1. Although the "Chicago boy" label has been affixed to Pinochet's advisers, it is not fully accurate to argue that their intellectual mentor was Milton Friedman, the Nobel laureate in economics from the University of Chicago. Their views come closer to those of Friedrich Hayek, who was also awarded the Nobel prize.

2. For a recent review of the literature on this point see Helgio Trindade, "La cuestión del fascismo en América Latina," *Desarrollo Económico* 23, no. 91 (October–December 1973).

3. Juan Linz, "An Authoritarian Regime: Spain," in Erik Allardt and Stein Rokkan, eds., *Mass Politics* (New York: Free Press, 1969). See also his comprehensive essay "Totalitarian and Authoritarian Regimes," in Nelson Polsby and Fred Greenstein, eds., *The Handbook of Political Science,* vol. 3 (Reading, Mass.: Addison Wesley Press, 1975).

4. Juan Linz, "The Future of an Authoritarian Situation or the Institutionalization of an Authoritarian Regime: The Case of Brazil," in Alfred Stepan, ed., *Authoritarian Brazil: Origins, Policies, and Future* (New Haven: Yale University Press, 1983).

5. Linz, "An Authoritarian Regime," pp. 255 and 257–59.

6. In "An Authoritarian Regime," p. 257, Linz paraphrases the distinction between ideologies and mentalities developed by Theodor Geiger to explain his argument. According to Linz, for Geiger ideologies "are systems of thought more or less intellectually elaborated and organized, often in written form, by intellectuals, pseudo-intellectuals, or with their assistance." Mentalities, by

contrast, "are ways of thinking and feeling, more emotional than rational, which provide non-codified ways of reacting to situations."

7. Guillermo O'Donnell, "Reflections on the Patterns of Change in the Bureaucratic-Authoritarian State," *Latin American Research Review* 13, no. 1 (1978).

8. Arturo Valenzuela, "Prospects for the Pinochet Regime in Chile," *Current History* 84, no. 499 (February 1985): 77–80, 89–90.

9. Linz, "The Future of an Authoritarian Situation."

10. Comments by Phillippe Schmitter and Juan Linz at the workshop "Six Years of Military Rule in Chile," held at the Woodrow Wilson International Center for Scholars, May 1980.

The Neoconservative Economic Experiment in Chile

Alejandro Foxley

This essay examines and evaluates the economic policies applied by the Chilean military government during the 1973–82 period. These policies constitute a radicalized version of the monetarist approaches that were popular in Latin America during the 1950s.

Radicalism refers to two main aspects of the new policies. The first one is the predisposition to apply tough "shock treatment" policies when other, more gradual approaches have failed. Shock is administered even when its consequences are a long, deep recession, high rates of unemployment, and deterioration in the distribution of income. These negative results can be sustained because of the political context in which the policies are applied. Second, radicalism refers also to the stronger component of structural and institutional change in the stabilization policies of the 1970s and 1980s. The idea is that if all other formulas to stabilize the economy have failed, there must be something very wrong with the essential functioning of the economic system and of the political system as well. Until this is corrected, long-term price stability and equilibrium in the balance of payments will not be possible. This kind of reasoning in fact has a strong structuralist flavor.

Proposed structural changes have a distinct free market orientation. The main elements are (1) a policy of privatization of economic activities accompanied by a withdrawal of the state from its regulatory and developmental functions, (2) an opening up of the economy to international trade and financial flows, and (3) free market policies as regards price determination and capital markets. Institutional changes refer to modifications in labor legislation, social security reform, the development of new private schemes for the provision of social services, and regional decentralization. In the political sphere, institutional changes may include, as in Chile, drafting a new constitution that drastically modifies the main political institutions and decision-making processes.

The economic policies in Argentina after 1976 and in Chile and Uruguay after 1973 share this emphasis on long-run structural and institutional changes although they differ in the timing and the intensity of the proposed changes. Of the three, Chile is the country where these neoconservative policies and reforms have been applied in a more radical and consistent fashion. In this sense it is close to being a test of "the pure case," almost a laboratory experiment.

The analysis here will center on three aspects: macroeconomic policies and performance, short-term stabilization policies and the various phases that can be identified in the stabilization program, and the impact of structural changes in the Chilean economy.

TABLE I.I   Macroeconomic Indicators, Chile

Year	GDP rate of change (1)	Consumer price index[a] (2)	Fiscal deficit (% of GDP) (3)	Nontraditional exports (4)	Net capital inflows[b] (5)	Balance of payments (6)	Gross reserves (7)
					(millions of 1977 US$)[c]		
1970	2.1	36.1	2.7	232.4	517.4	201.8	891.0
1974	1.0	369.2	10.5	274.6	264.2	−66.7	408.8
1975	−12.9	343.3	2.6	403.3	260.3	−373.9	331.0
1976	3.5	197.9	2.3	509.7	214.4	446.1	667.5
1977	9.9	84.2	1.8	589.2	572.0	113.0	685.1
1978	8.2	37.2	0.8	652.0	1,725.2	631.2	1,245.5
1979	8.3	38.9	−1.7	894.7	1,763.7	822.1	1,957.4
1980	7.8	31.2	−3.1	983.5	2,219.7	872.4	2,943.1
1981	5.7[d]	9.5	−1.6	n.d.	3,316.4	48.7	2,659.0
1982	−14.3[e]	20.7	2.4	n.d.	928.5	−829.7	1,839.8

[a] Changes in consumer prices from December to December.
[b] Autonomous credits and direct investment.
[c] Deflated by the index of external prices.
[d] Provisional.
[e] Estimated.

Sources: (1) Banco Central, "Cuentas nacionales nuevas," in *Indicadores económicos y sociales,* 1960–82, 1983. (2) R. Cortázar and J. Marshall, "Indice de precios al consumidor en Chile, 1970–1978," *Colección Estudios CIEPLAN,* no. 4 (November 1980); for 1979–82, Instituto Nacional de Estadística (INE). (3) Banco Central, *Indicadores económicos y sociales,* 1983. (4–7) R. Ffrench-Davis, "Indice de precios externos para calcular el valor real del commercio internacional de Chile, 1952–1980," *Notas Técnicas CIEPLAN,* no. 32 (June 1981). Also: (4) Ffrench-Davis, "Origen y destino de las exportaciones chilenas, 1965–1980," ibid., no. 19 (May 1981). (5–7) Ffrench-Davis, "El experimento monetarista en Chile: Una síntesis crítica," *Colección Estudios CIEPLAN,* no. 9 (December 1982) and later updates.

Results of the Stabilization Program

The Chilean monetarist experiment was credited from the late seventies until as late as 1982 by international observers with having led to an "economic miracle." The basis for this hasty conclusion is summarized in Table 1.1 As this table indicates, between 1977 and 1981 the Chilean economy showed relatively high rates of gross domestic product growth, inflation diminished substantially between 1974 and 1982, and the fiscal deficit disappeared between 1978 and 1981. There was a considerable growth of nontraditional exports and, until 1981, a strong net inflow of capital.

These indicators, however, do not reflect the full economic reality of the period. Table 1.2 should also be examined for a better assessment. Its figures show a drop of the gross domestic product per capita over the full 1974–82 period. The 1974–82 period also shows a 25% decrease in the rate of investment with respect to the 1960s, a stagnation in employment, and an increase in the rate of unemployment from an average of 6.5% in the 1960s to an average of 17.6% in the 1970s.[1]

The results appear even more negative when the information contained in Table 1.3 is added to the picture. A very sharp reversal in the external sector began in 1981, as can be appreciated from the large deficit in the current account shown in the table. The excessive external indebted-

TABLE 1.2 Other Macroeconomic Variables, Chile

Indicator	1960–70	1974–82
Average growth of GDP	4.2	1.6
Production of goods (agriculture, fishing, mining, manufacturing, construction)	4.0	0.1
Production of services (electricity, gas, water, transport, commerce)	4.3	3.5
GDP per capita	2.1	−0.14
Rate of investment	20.2	15.6
Total employment	2.1	0.1–0.8[a]
Rate of unemployment	6.5	13.4–17.6[b]

[a] Corresponds to two estimates of total employment in 1982, one according to the Instituto Nacional de Estadística (INE), and the other according to the Universidad de Chile.

[b] Official unemployment rate and unemployment rate including the state-run emergency make-work programs, the Plan de Empleo Mínimo (PEM) and the Programa de Ocupación de Jefes de Hogar (POJH).

Source: Banco Central, Indicadores económicos y sociales, 1960–82, 1983. This publication contains newly revised national account figures.

TABLE 1.3   Economic and Social Indicators, Chile

Year	GDP per capita (1)	Current account balance (millions of 1977 US$)[a] (2)	Ratio of debt service to exports[b] (3)	Rate of investment[c] (4)	Total employment (1970 = 100) (5)
1970	100.0	−166.2	27.0	20.4	100.0
1974	95.9	−255.8	35.1	17.4	100.7
1975	82.1	−533.7	55.6	15.4	96.2
1976	83.6	158.5	52.7	12.7	97.9
1977	90.2	−551.0	52.8	13.3	101.6
1978	96.0	−964.5	58.7	14.5	105.4
1979	102.2	−933.6	50.8	15.6	108.4
1980	108.3	−1,382.3	47.7	17.6	113.5
1981	112.6	−3,347.7	70.8	19.1	117.4
1982	94.8	−1,696.1	88.5	14.1	106.9

[a] Deflated by the index of external prices. See Ffrench-Davis, "Indice de precios externos," 1981.
[b] Quotient of gross credit plus net interest outflows by the export of nonfinancial goods and services.
[c] Gross fixed capital formation as % of GDP.
[d] Index of real wages and salaries calculated from INE figures.
Sources: (1) Banco Central, *Indicadores económicos y sociales, 1960-82.* (2) Ffrench-Davis, "El experimento monetarista en Chile," 1982. (3) Ffrench-Davis, "Deuda externa y liberalización financiera en Chile: El experimento monetarista en 1973-82," (CIEPLAN mimeo, 1983). (4) for 1970-79, Banco Central, *Cuentas nacionales de Chile,* 1960, 1980; for 1980-82, Banco Central, *Boletín Mensual,* May 1983. (5-8) Dirección de presupuestos, *Exposición sobre el estado de la hacienda pública,* October 1982; Banco Central, *Indicadores económicos y sociales, 1960-82,* 1983. Also: (6) for population estimates, INE. (10) R. Cortázar, "Desempleo, probreza y distribución: Chile, 1970-82," *Apuntes CIEPLAN,* no. 34 (June 1982). (11) A. Foxley and D. Raczynski, "Grupos vulnerables en situaciones recesivas: El caso de los niños y jóvenes en Chile" (CIEPLAN mimeo, 1983).

ness is clearly reflected in the fact that the debt service payments reached almost 90% of exports in 1982.

Table 1.3 also shows the sharp increase in unemployment, which in 1982 rose to 26% of the labor force. The income distribution indicators are equally negative. Real wages and salaries dropped almost 40% between 1974 and 1976 with respect to their 1970 levels, which by the end of 1982 still had not been recovered. Pension payments show a similar evolution. In addition, public spending for social programs has not compensated for this drop in wages, since it has also declined significantly.

% employed age 12 years and over (6)	Unemployment rate		Real salaries and wages[d] (1970 = 100) (9)	Average pension (1970 = 100) (10)	Per capita social spending (1970 = 100) (11)
	Without PEM and POJH (7)	With PEM and POJH (8)			
42.8	5.7	5.7	100.0	100.0	100.0
38.9	9.2	9.2	65.1	59.3	110.1
36.3	14.5	16.4	62.9	52.0	82.5
36.0	14.4	19.9	64.8	56.3	80.1
36.5	12.7	18.6	71.5	60.9	89.0
37.1	13.6	17.9	76.0	67.0	86.6
37.3	13.8	17.7	82.3	75.9	87.5
38.3	12.0	17.3	89.5	82.8	77.9
38.8	10.8	15.6	97.7	n.d.	72.9
34.7	19.5	26.1	97.2	n.d.	87.9

In a nutshell, the results of the Chilean monetarist experiment are negative in almost all aspects. Drops in production, investment, and employment have been accompanied by a strong deficit in the balance of payments and an overindebtedness with external sources by 1982. Unemployment has risen dramatically, and the income indicators show a sharp regression for wage earners.

In order to get a better understanding of how these results were achieved, we will examine in more detail in the next section the stabilization policies and the various phases that can be distinguished in the period 1943–82, signaling changes in policies or in the objectives of the stabilization program.

The Stabilization Program and Its Phases

The stabilization program in Chile can be separated into four different phases.[2] The first one I will call deregulation; the second consists of the so-called shock treatment; the third one centers in curbing expectations; and the fourth phase corresponds to the global monetarist approach. The main economic indicators for all four phases are given in Table 1.4 where trends for the various phases can be easily identified.

PHASE I: DEREGULATION, SEPTEMBER 1973–MARCH 1975

The main objective of phase I was to restore market mechanisms in an economy with extended controls and severe imbalances. Setting prices right was the first task, and this was done by devaluing domestic currency and by freeing up prices, except for thirty products whose prices were deregulated more gradually. The exchange rate was devalued by 230% between September and October 1973. A second objective of the policy was to reduce the public sector deficit by decreasing government expenditures and increasing taxes. The main tax changes consisted of the introduction of a 20% value-added tax and the simultaneous reduction or elimination of several direct taxes affecting capital: the tax on corporate profits was reduced, and the net wealth and capital gains taxes were eliminated. Additional contraction in demand was pursued by attempting to reduce the rate of expansion in money supply and by a contraction in real wages.

Other objectives consisted of preparing the ground for long-term structural changes. Policy measures in this area were varied. They consisted of returning to previous owners private property that had been taken over by workers or by the government. Previously expropriated American companies, mainly in the copper sector, were compensated for a presumed underpayment. New norms liberalizing imports and requirements for foreign investment, proposing across-the-board tariff reductions, setting the rules for a privatization of public enterprises, and stimulating the development of a private capital market were enforced. Collective bargaining was suppressed, and labor union activities were severely curtailed.

The course followed by the main macrovariables is shown in Table 1.4. The abrupt deregulation of prices led to a rate of inflation of 128.5% in the last quarter of 1973 (87.6% in October alone, where the average monthly rate between January and September had been 14.6%). But the dramatic upsurge in prices, reflecting previous repressed inflation and a price overshoot after deregulation, was not followed by similarly high rates in the next months. In fact, the price increases stabilized around 45% per quarter, or 14% a month (see column 1), during this phase, an average rate similar to that prevailing in the last year of the Allende government.

As a result of free prices, firms were stimulated into replenishing their low level of stocks, a result of strict price controls and high inflation throughout 1972 and 1973. Industrial production expanded in the last quarter of 1973, but stabilized at a lower level during 1974, as is readily observed in column 3. In early 1975, clear recessionary signs were present: industrial production in the first quarter was 15% below that of the last quarter of 1974. The recession was the consequence of a drastic reduction in real cash balances in the last quarter of 1973, as can be seen in Table 1.4 by comparing the expansion of nominal money supply and that of prices. The increase in prices almost tripled the increase in the quantity of money. Monetary contraction was reinforced by a fall in real wages, which reached around 40% (column 13) when compared with 1970 levels.

The unemployment rate was rapidly responsive to the new policies:

during the first three months it doubled, reaching 7% in the last qu
1973. It was to stay around 9.5% throughout 1974 and jump to 13.3%
first quarter of 1975 (column 4).

The recession was not more severe during 1974 mainly because
expansionary fiscal policy in spite of stated objectives to the contrary.
Public investment increased, particularly in the first quarter. It was hoped,
at this stage, that a reduction in public subsidies and employment would
bring the fiscal accounts in balance without having to resort to reductions
in public investment. A new finance minister in July 1974 did not share this
view and attempted to reverse the expansionary trend by curtailing budget
expenditures by 15% and public employment by 50,000 persons. At the
same time, subsidies to public enterprises were ended. It was this contractionary fiscal policy, sustained while the rate of inflation was accelerating
and other components of aggregate demand were falling, that generated
the more severe recession of early 1975.

One of the main concerns during this phase was the balance of payments, which was aggravated by the problems encountered by the government in rescheduling the external debt. The policies designed to reduce the
external sector deficit paid off in a rather brief period of time. During the
first quarter of 1974, there was already a net accumulation of reserves, a
result of rapid export expansion aided by unusually high prices for the main
Chilean export, copper, and by the large devaluation of late 1973 (column
2).

Exchange rate policy during this period followed the fluctuations in the
price of copper. The policy consisted of nonannounced minidevaluations
several times per month. When the price of copper was high, as in the first
semester of 1974, the exchange rate tended to lag behind domestic inflation. Real devaluations took place when copper prices fell, as was the case
in the last two quarters of 1974 (column 6).

Tariff reductions were announced at the beginning of 1974. They were
to take place over a period of three years with a maximum target of 60% for
nominal tariffs. This maximum target was reduced to 35% in 1975, with a
minimum of 10%. It was expected that the target would be achieved by
1978. The program was implemented gradually during 1974 and early 1975
(column 7).

Changes in the financial market allowed for the establishment of private financial companies that operated with no more restrictions than a
maximum monthly rate of interest of 25%. The interest rate for banks
(which at the time were part of the public sector) was controlled and fixed
at 9.6% per month. This discrimination in favor of private financial companies was deliberate in order to stimulate a transfer of funds away from the
government and toward the private sector.

By the end of 1974, the rate of inflation had stabilized around 45% per
quarter, production figures were showing a decline, and the price of copper

TABLE 1.4 Phases in the Stabilization Program, Chile 1973–1983

	CPI (1)	BP (2)	IIP (3)	Unem-ployment (4)	Copper price (5)	ER (6)
Phase I						
1973 II	51.9		106.3	3.1	73.9	
III	64.3		101.2		91.4	9.2
IV	128.5		122.5	7.0	99.3	30.1
1974 I	45.3	59.5	109.8	9.2	106.9	29.6
II	46.6	180.3	113.8	10.3	126.3	32.9
III	46.8	−3.9	111.0	9.4	78.4	33.3
IV	44.7	−375.6	109.7	9.7	62.0	37.1
1975 I	46.5	−189.3	93.1	13.3	57.8	45.0
Phase 2						
1975 I	46.5	−189.3	93.1	13.3	57.8	45.0
II	67.8	−82.5	88.8	16.1	57.1	46.7
III	41.4	44.1	73.5	16.6	56.1	45.2
IV	29.4	−47.0	85.2	18.7	53.1	44.9
1976 I	36.4	136.6	90.4	19.8	56.6	44.3
II	38.8	94.4	93.5	18.0	69.2	40.5
Phase 3						
1976 II	38.8	94.4	93.5	18.0	69.2	40.5
III	33.1	134.1	97.1	15.7	70.3	33.6
IV	20.0	103.7	100.3	13.6	58.2	34.2
1977 I	21.4	48.6	98.1	13.9	65.5	32.7
II	20.8	7.7	105.4	13.0	62.2	29.0
III	13.5	−59.3	107.9	12.8	54.5	29.5
IV	12.7	−3.6	104.9	13.2	56.5	31.7
1978 I	8.7	270.5	103.9	14.7	56.4	33.1
II	9.4	129.7	117.1	12.8	59.3	33.7
III	9.8	107.6	119.7	13.7	63.6	33.4
IV	6.6	109.5	117.5	14.8	68.2	33.4
1979 I	6.6	339.9	122.1	16.5	85.5	33.4
II	7.7	211.8	123.2	12.5	92.6	32.9
Phase 4						
1979 II	7.7	211.8	123.2	12.5	92.6	32.9
III	11.0	289.4	126.0	12.5	89.0	33.3
IV	9.0	206.8	125.2	12.7	96.4	31.0
1980 I	6.7	411.9	126.2	12.8	118.4	30.1
II	7.5	150.3	128.0	11.7	92.7	28.6
III	6.4	228.5	131.5	11.8	95.5	27.6
IV	7.7	−15.3	130.8	10.7	89.7	25.9

ANT (7)	ERM (8)	M_1 (9)	M_2 (10)	i_{non} (11)	i_r^y (12)	RWS (13)
		32.1	31.8			
		49.3	49.2			
94.0	58.4	45.4	45.7			
92.3	56.9	63.2	64.2			63.4
76.3	58.0	30.9	29.9			64.5
67.0	55.6	28.1	27.8			63.7
67.0	62.0	28.1	30.8	9.6	−24.4	68.5
54.7	69.6	44.8	51.9	9.6	−49.3	64.9
54.7	69.6	44.8	51.9	9.6	−49.3	64.9
52.0	71.0	25.0	38.7	16.5	−23.4	60.4
47.7	66.8	45.0	57.2	19.7	178.4	63.2
44.0	64.7	38.2	35.1	12.8	65.7	63.1
40.7	62.3	37.2	39.8	14.6	18.2	62.1
36.7	55.4	22.8	38.9	14.7	56.4	63.0
36.7	55.4	22.8	38.9	14.7	56.4	63.0
33.0	44.7	34.7	48.3	11.8	40.9	65.1
32.3	45.2	26.8	29.1	12.5	101.2	68.8
24.3	40.6	45.1	58.3	11.3	52.9	71.7
23.2	35.7	22.9	28.7	7.8	34.5	69.3
21.6	35.8	14.4	16.6	6.3	23.9	71.7
18.5	37.6	11.8	13.7	7.3	45.9	71.1
15.3	38.2	30.2	32.2	5.9	47.6	74.8
14.1	38.5	17.1	18.3	5.0	28.3	75.1
13.2	37.8	6.6	15.9	4.7	14.0	76.9
12.2	37.5	9.8	21.1	5.5	52.9	77.1
11.4	37.2	21.7	24.2	4.4	29.8	81.0
10.5	36.4	9.9	9.0	4.0	19.6	82.2
10.5	36.4	9.9	9.0	4.0	19.6	82.2
10.2	36.7	7.2	13.3	4.0	−1.2	83.2
10.2	34.2	11.3	11.2	4.0	23.9	82.8
10.2	33.2	16.6	13.9	4.1	23.9	86.7
10.2	31.5	13.9	9.8	3.1	10.0	89.1
10.2	30.4	7.2	12.5	2.9	9.9	88.4
10.2	28.5	13.7	14.3	3.0	6.2	93.1

TABLE 1.4   *(continued)*

		CPI *(1)*	BP *(2)*	IIP *(3)*	Unem- ployment *(4)*	Copper price *(5)*	ER *(6)*
1981	I	4.3	−192.3	129.7	11.3	83.0	24.9
	II	2.8	−207.7	132.9	9.0	79.6	23.7
	III	2.3	−3.9	134.5	10.5	78.3	22.8
	IV	1.6	−168.8	120.2	13.5	75.2	23.3
1982	I	0.7	−305.9	112.2	19.1	71.3	23.0
	II	−0.2	−353.8	108.1	23.0	65.8	23.8
	III	6.0	−465.3	108.2	24.8	65.3	30.5
	IV	11.7	−141.2	98.5	21.3	66.2	33.3
1983	I	4.4	−639.1	107.7	23.9	72.8	

ª Beginning in November, new tariffs were added for certain products.

ᵇ Beginning in March, the 10% across-the-board tariff was increased to 20% for all products.

Abbreviation key and sources:

(1) Consumer price index. INE, quarterly averages.

(2) Net accumulation of reserves, balance of payments. Banco Central.

(3) Index of industrial production, seasonally adjusted (1970 = 100). Sociedad de Fomento Fabril (SOFOFA).

(4) Unemployment rate for Greater Santiago. Departmento de Economía, Universidad de Chile.

(5) Price of copper in cents of U.S.$ per pound.

(6) Real exchange rate, in pesos per dollar, in December 1978 prices.

(7) Average Nominal tariffs. Banco Central.

(8) Real exchange rate for imports (real exchange rate corrected for changes in tariffs). R. Ffrench-Davis, "Políticas de comercio exterior in Chile, 1973–1978" (CIEPLAN mimeo, 1979).

(9) Rate of growth of the nominal money supply, defined as currency plus demand deposits. Banco Central.

(10) Rate of growth of the nominal money supply, defined as currency plus demand and time deposits. Banco Central.

(11) Thirty-day nominal interest rate. Banco Central.

(12) Yearly equivalent of thirty-day real interest rate. Banco Central.

(13) Real wages and salaries, based on CPI and official INE figures for nominal wages and salaries (1970 = 100).

ANT (7)	ERM (8)	M_1 (9)	M_2 (10)	i_{non} (11)	i_r^y (12)	RWS (13)
10.2	27.4	12.4	19.2	3.6	37.7	92.9
10.2	26.1	1.3	14.5	3.5	36.1	94.5
10.2	25.1	−4.2	13.3	3.5	36.1	99.7
10.2	25.7	5.6	4.0	3.7	49.4	102.2
		0.0	3.9	3.7	49.4	102.1
		−5.1	−0.7	3.3	45.9	103.1
		−6.2	−2.3	4.2	12.7	96.2
10–45[a]		−2.2	1.0	5.4	31.4	88.9
20.0[b]		34.8	−3.1	3.4	28.3	88.6

fell sharply, which was reflected in a loss of reserves of $375 million in the last quarter alone. The devaluations (30% in December 1974 and an additional 40% in March 1975) were responsible for an increase in the rate of inflation from 9% in December 1974 to 21.4% in April 1975. This bleak picture of recession, accelerated inflation, and balance of payments crisis led to a change in policies. Phase 1 was over. A shock treatment was in order if the negative trends were to be reversed.

PHASE 2: THE SHOCK TREATMENT, APRIL 1975–JUNE 1976

The new policies consisted of a contractionary shock on demand and a deepening of structural reforms. The demand shock was administered through various channels. Government expenditures were to be decreased by 15% in real terms in the domestic component and 25% in the import component during the year. In fact, total expenditures fell by 27% in real terms in 1975, with public investment reduced in half. Tax revenues were to be increased by imposing a surcharge on the income tax and eliminating exemptions in the value-added tax. Public enterprises rates were also sharply increased. Real wages were additionally reduced—as can be seen in column 13 of Table 1.4—by changing the benchmark against which compensation for cost-of-living increases was calculated. A make-work employment program was created (the Minimum Employment Program, or PEM), and a subsidy for firms hiring new workers was established in order to compensate for the negative effects of the recession.

The deepening of long-term structural changes was pursued by three simultaneous channels: more privatization of public enterprises, including the banks that were auctioned at the beginning of this phase; additional stimulus to the development of a private capital market by freeing interest rates charged by banks (once they had been transferred to private hands); and an acceleration in the speed and a lowering of the levels programed for reductions in external tariffs.

A study of the evolution of the main indicators shows mixed results. The rate of increase in the price level diminished from 68% during the second quarter of 1975 to 29% in the last quarter. At the same time, the loss of reserves was curbed during the second quarter, a consequence of a dramatic fall in imports and a continued expansion in nontraditional exports that at least partially compensated for the big loss in copper export revenues. By the end of 1975, the balance of payments was still in deficit, but the trend was encouraging in that the deficit during the second semester had reached only $5 million (compare figures for the third and fourth quarters in column 2, Table 1.4). The situation continued to improve in 1976 because the demand for imports was depressed by the recession and exports were still growing fast while the price of copper was slowly recuperating and inflows of short-term capital from abroad increased. The balance of payments showed a surplus of almost $500 million by the end of 1976, as was seen in Table 1.1.

On the negative side, the policies generated a huge recession. Industrial production fell by 35% in the third quarter of 1975 compared with the same period in 1974. Open unemployment went up to 19.8% in early 1976 (Table 1.4), in spite of public make-work employment programs that were fully effective at this time.

The exchange rate policy in this phase was discontinuous. After large real devaluations at the beginning of 1975, the exchange rate remained fairly constant except at the end of the period, when it lagged behind domestic inflation, perhaps owing to the trend to higher inflation rates in the first two quarters of 1976 (36.4% and 38.8%) as compared with the last quarter of 1975 (29.4%). A constant value for the exchange rate was accompanied by a continued tendency to lower tariffs (columns 6 and 7). As a result, the cost of imports was slowly reduced.

Financial policy and monetary policy offer interesting results. Financial deregulation led to an increase in real interest rates from −23.4% in the second quarter of 1975 to 178.4% in the third quarter (column 12). This abrupt increase generated a cost shock to firms that accentuated stagflationary effects originating in other policy measures, such as demand contraction and devaluation. Monetary policy, on the other hand, was complicated by the drastic reduction in the demand for imports that resulted in accumulation of reserves in the private sector, with an expansionary effect on the monetary base. This is the reason that the monetary shock was really sustained only during the second quarter of 1975.

Unhappiness with a recession that was deeper and longer than expected and the upsurge in inflation during the first quarter of 1976 led to a new change in policies. The strategy to contain inflation was modified, and it was expected that, as a result, inflation would fall and the economy would begin to recuperate in the level of economic activity. Phase 3 was inaugurated with the announcement in June 1976 of a "Program of Economic Recuperation."

PHASE 3: CURBING COST-PUSH FACTORS AND EXPECTATIONS,
JUNE 1976–JUNE 1979

The anti-inflation strategy in phase 3 changed in emphasis from demand contraction to curbing cost pressures and expectations. In June 1976 the peso was revalued 10%, and a thirty-day preannounced value for future exchange rates was established as a way of reducing costs and influencing inflationary expectations. The exchange rate was revalued again in March 1977. In February 1978 this policy was extended: the value of the exchange rate was announced for the next eleven months. This new approach was complemented by more drastic tariff reductions. Between December 1976 and December 1977 the maximum desired tariff went down gradually until an across-the-board maximum tariff of 10% was established as a target to be achieved in 1979, automobiles being the only exception. The movement toward free trade was reinforced by the withdrawal of the country from the Andean Pact and by a gradual but systematic deregulation of external capital flows that began in October 1977 and was completed in 1979.

Revaluation of domestic currency had a rapid impact on costs, expectations, and the rate of inflation, which decreased to 4.9% a month in August 1976 only to increase again to a monthly rate of 7%–8% in the following months. However, the medium-term trend was clear: quarterly rates decreased from around 40% for the second quarter of 1976 to about 13% in the third and fourth quarters of 1977 (accumulated rate for a three-month period). The downward trend continued in 1978, as can be seen in column 1. The quarterly rate of inflation stabilized between 7% and 9% until the end of phase 3 in June 1979.

The reduction in the rate of inflation encouraged an expansion in real wages, since nominal wages were indexed to previous inflation. Real wages increased by 5% in the second half of 1976 compared with the first half (column 13). This was a factor that helped industrial production, which showed an upward trend all through this phase. Unemployment went down from around 16% to around 13% and stayed at that level in 1978 and 1979 (column 4).[3]

The balance of payments was subject to contradictory forces during this phase. In 1976 it showed a surplus in spite of the negative effect of revaluation on the trade accounts: the depressed demand for imports predominated and was helped by an increasing inflow of foreign loans in such a way that a balance of payments surplus was generated. In the last two quarters of 1977, the situation was reversed because of the accumulated effect of two revaluations plus a higher demand for imports originating in the expansion of domestic production. A fall in copper prices of 13% with respect to the first two quarters of 1977 added to the forces that created a current account deficit of $500 million in 1977. To counteract the tendency, the exchange rate was devalued twice in 1977 (September and December), and again in 1978. Given the program of tariff reductions and the compensating effect of devaluations, the cost of imports did not change much in the period. External inflows of capital accelerated, facilitating the accumulation of reserves, as column 2 shows. The high level of reserves by mid-1979 made possible the transition to phase 4.

PHASE 4: MONETARISM FOR THE OPEN ECONOMY SINCE JUNE 1979

This phase corresponded to a stage when tariff reductions were completed. No import duties were above 10%, except for cars. Reserves were increasing, the fiscal deficit had all but disappeared, and the economy continued giving signs of recuperating from the recession. At this point, in June 1979, the exchange rate was first devalued 5.7% and then fixed. Given that the economy was now open to international trade, it was hoped that the rate of price increases in the world economy would automatically regulate domestic inflation. After a lag, the latter should approach the former. When this happened, there was no need for further adjustments in the exchange rate. Global monetarism provided full automaticity to adjustment mechanisms in the economy.

Results in this phase were illustrative of the way automatic adjustment operated in practice. A fixed exchange rate plus the elimination of the fiscal deficit worked in favor of a reduction in the rate of inflation to 1.6% in the last quarter of 1981. On the other hand, for two and a half years starting in June 1979 domestic inflation was consistently above world inflation. The practical consequence of this, given a fixed nominal exchange rate, was that the real exchange rate appreciated by almost 30% in the period from the second quarter in 1979 to the third quarter in 1981 (column 6). The loss of competitiveness implied by this figure resulted in rapidly expanding trade and current accounts deficits that were to be equivalent to 10.7% and 15.5% of GDP by the end of 1981. This deficit, which according to the monetarist perspective results from an excess of spending over income in the economy, set in motion the automatic adjustment mechanisms. These consisted of a sharp increase in the yearly interest rates, which went up in real terms to almost 50% in the last quarter of 1981 (column 12), and in a loss of international reserves (column 2).

High interest rates and loss of competitiveness were responsible for a deep recession that began in the fourth quarter of 1980. A year later, industrial production was falling at a rate of 8% for the year when quarterly figures were compared. At the same time, unemployment went up once again. It reached 13.5% of the labor force in Santiago and 12.4% nationally. But if those employed in the Minimum Employment Program are included (earning less than $30 a month), national unemployment reached 17% in September 1981 and deteriorated even more thereafter.

The recession, the high indebtedness of the enterprises, and a reduction in the flow of external credits led to a financial crisis. Its first symptoms were an increase in the nonperforming loans of financial institutions (see Table 1.5) and the temporary government takeover (or "intervention," to use the official term) of four banks and four financial institutions in November 1981. They represented 9.3% of the total capital and reserves of the financial system.

TABLE 1.5   Nonperforming Loans as a Percentage of the Capital and Reserves of Financial Institutions

Bank[a]	Dec. 80	Dec. 81	Dec. 82	Apr. 83
Banco del Estado	15.0	14.8	38.8	32.5
Banco de Chile[b]	11.3	40.0	68.6	224.5
Banco Español-Chile[c]	29.2	270.4[d]		
Banco de Talca[e]	10.5	81.6[d]		
Banco O'Higgins	5.7	20.9	43.0	85.9
Banco Osorno	8.3	29.4	64.3	111.1
Banco Sudamericano	9.6	24.5	29.4	49.0
Banco Crédito e Inversiones	11.1	31.5	31.2	60.8
Banco del Trabajo	12.1	48.0	16.0	28.4
Banco Nacional	2.4	27.0	30.7	49.8
Banco Concepción[b]	12.7	25.8	41.0	209.7
Banco Edwards	3.4	19.9	44.7	62.8
Banco de Santiago[b]	2.9	15.9	17.4	285.8
Morgan-Finansa		24.7	77.3	110.0
Banco Unido de Fomento[f]	11.4	27.6	90.0	
Banco Hipotecario y de Fomento Nacional	7.4	18.4	23.7	62.1
Banco BHC[f]	14.6	33.5	54.7	
Banco Colocadora Nacional de Valores[b]	0.4	4.9	31.0	92.4
Financial System	10.5	22.4[g]	39.1	107.3

[a] Banks with more than 1.5% of the financial system's banking, representing, altogether, 83% of all loans.

[b] Taken over in January 1983.

[c] Taken over in November 1981 and later closed.

[d] November 1981.

[e] Taken over in November 1981 and later sold to a foreign bank.

[f] Taken over and liquidated in January 1983.

[g] Does not include information regarding banks taken over in November 1981.

Source: Superintendencia de Bancos e Instituciones Financieras, *Información Financiera,* various issues.

During the first semester of 1982 the economic crisis became even more acute. The loss of international reserves from the Central Bank exceeded $600 million by June. However, the economic authorities continued to place their trust in the "automatic adjustment" mechanisms. As a result, industrial production during the second trimester of 1982 was 19% lower than the same period the previous year, the yearly real interest rate was over 45%, and unemployment in Santiago exceeded 20%. Under these circumstances, beginning with a 18% devaluation of the peso, the exchange rate policy was changed to one by which the national currency would be tied to a series of other currencies.[4] After this devaluation, the loss of international reserves continued at an accelerated pace, probably giving a widespread impression that the devaluation was insufficient and that it would be followed by others. In order to stop the continuing drain of reserves and to isolate monetary emissions from exchange rate fluctuations, in August the exchange rate was completely freed from controls. However, given the ensuing sharp rise of the dollar, the government began within a few days to intervene actively in the exchange markets. A week after the exchange rate was deregulated, the peso had been devalued by 36.2%.[5]

Meanwhile, the difficulties of the financial sector continued. To respond to its crisis the Central Bank created a mechanism through which it began to "buy" the nonperforming and risky loans from the banks. A few days before that, the authorities recognized the problem of related loans (those given to individuals and enterprises who had a proprietary interest in the financial institution granting the loan), and efforts began to force divestiture.[6] The same measures were extended to mutual funds and insurance companies. The "sale" of nonperforming loans could not resolve the fundamental problem, which was the incapacity of the debtors to pay; consequently, defaults continued to increase. Given the devaluation of the currency, debtors whose credits were drawn in dollars began to experience difficulties. At the end of August a preferential exchange rate was established for the repayment of these loans. Monetary emissions to subsidize the "preferential dollar" between September 1982 and May 1983 represented 4% of the 1982 GDP.

After the first devaluation the net inflow of foreign credits diminished, and after September it turned negative. At the end of that month a new exchange policy was set. It consisted of determining a "referent" exchange, whose value was given by the difference between the previous month's internal and external rates of inflation. This exchange rate could also vary within a certain margin. In addition, a free parallel exchange market was authorized; the official market was subjected to maximum sale quotas. The exchange policy was again altered in March of 1983: the practice of setting the rate daily was maintained, although this time only according to the previous month's internal rate of inflation. In nine months the official rate of exchange was devalued by almost 100%.

Beginning in November 1982 additional temporary tariffs were levied on certain import items, but in March of 1983 the across-the-board 10% rate was raised to 20% for all products for a period of three years.

During the second semester of 1982 and the beginning of 1983 the economic situation continued to deteriorate. The GDP dropped 14% in 1982, industrial production fell 18% in the last quarter of that year, and unemployment in Santiago reached 24% in March of 1983 (or 30% if the individuals in make-work public programs are included).[7] Although the real rate of interest dropped in the second quarter given the higher inflation, it returned to a 30% yearly level by the end of 1983. Beginning in December the Central Bank began to "suggest" gradually reduced interest rates for thirty-day deposits.

Inflation increased after the first devaluation, reaching monthly levels of more than 3% by the end of 1982 before declining in the next quarter. The retail and wholesale rates of inflation were nonetheless lower than the devaluations during this period, given the sharp depression of economic activity.

The high level of imports in 1981 was cut almost in half during 1982; the trade balance even tended to produce a surplus by the end of 1982.[8] This contributed to reduce by half the deficit in the current account (Table 1.3). However, the balance of payments for 1982 ended with a deficit of more than $800 million.

The financial system entered a new crisis in January 1983 with the "intervention" by the government of five banks, the closing of three others, and the direct supervision of another two. Two of the largest private banks were among the ones which were taken over; they were the centerpiece of the two largest private economic groups, to which the Central Bank had had to commit, by May of 1983, 73% of its yearly credits to the financial system.[9] The eight "intervened" and liquidated institutions represented 34% of the capital and reserves, 45% of internal credit, and 52% of foreign borrowings of the total financial system in the country. The total support given through various means by the Central Bank to the financial system between December 1982 and March 1983 represented 15% of the GDP of 1982.[10] Through the government takeover, the state by May 1983 controlled 50% of the credit in the financial system. It also acquired control of the main enterprises related to the economic groups, since they ceased payments on the loans which had been extended by the banks. Paradoxically, therefore, the state once again controls an important fraction of the productive activities in the country. The state has also assumed the external debt of the banks.

Despite the crisis, the basic postulates of the economic policy have not been abandoned. This is reflected in the very orthodox policy agreement signed with the International Monetary Fund, as well as in the reluctance of the authorities to initiate an economic reactivation program—since they trust that the latter will start "automatically." The various nonorthodox policies adopted since June 1982 (i.e., the rescheduling of debts not exceeding a certain level, the renegotiation of debts with state institutions, special tariffs for certain products, subsidies for mortgages, etc.) have stemmed not so much from a will to resolve the overall problems of the economy as from responses to pressures by affected groups.

Structural Changes

Having examined the course of short-term stabilization policies, let us evaluate the structural transformations which have occurred in the Chilean economy since 1973. I refer to the consequences of three long-range policy actions: the privatization of the economy, the opening to international trade, and changes in the composition of production and in the distribution of income.

PRIVATIZATION

One of the essential elements of the post-1973 policy has consisted in a drastic change in the role assigned to economic agents in Chile. The state was gradually reduced in importance by cutting public expenditures, by extensive deregulation, by fostering private initiative, and by limiting the number and size of productive enterprises in the public sector.

As Table 1.6 indicates, fiscal spending dropped from 28% to 19.3% of the GDP between 1974 and 1979. In subsequent years it rose once again,

TABLE 1.6   Fiscal Expenditures and Deficits (percentage of GDP)

Year	Total expenditures excluding the public debt	Fiscal deficit	Year	Total expenditures excluding the public debt	Fiscal deficit
1970	22.9	2.7	1977	20.9	1.8
1971	28.0	10.7	1978	20.2	0.8
1972	30.1	13.0	1979	19.3	−1.7
1973	43.6	24.7	1980	20.5	−3.1
1974	28.0	10.5	1981[a]	23.5	−1.6
1975	22.7	2.6	1982[a]	27.1	2.4
1976	20.1	2.3			

[a] Provisional figures.

Source: Banco Central, *Indicadores económicos y sociales, 1960–1982,* 1983.

especially given the large drop in the GDP during 1982. At the same time, the privatization of public enterprises meant that of 507 concerns in the state sector (affiliates of the Corporación de Fomento de la Producción, or CORFO), only 15 were projected to remain in it by 1980.[11] The state also diminished its developmental role, which had been an outstanding characteristic of its action since the creation of CORFO in 1939. Its developmental role had increased considerably during the Frei and Allende governments, as can be seen from the figures on public employment by sector in Table 1.7. The withdrawal of the state from developmental assistance affected mainly small producers in the agricultural, mining, and industrial sectors as well as the process of agrarian reform, which not only came to a stop but was in fact reversed by returning a significant share of expropriated land to its previous owners, as will be seen later. Where the state left the field, the private sector—either domestic or foreign—entered. Particularly important has been the growth of private financial institutions. Financial resources deposited in public institutions decreased from 49.3% in 1970 to 25.3% in 1980 (Table 1.8). Conversely the share of the private sector increased from 11.1% in 1970 to 73% in 1980. Finally, the state diminished its role as regulator of external flows. The tax treatment for foreign investment was liberalized. Restrictions on the remittances of profits abroad were eliminated, and the ceiling on external borrowing by the private sector was gradually lifted.[12]

This withdrawal of the state from economic activity was accompanied by a substantial decrease in public employment, which fell by a fifth

TABLE 1.7   Employment in the Public Sector

Year	Administrative services	Development institutions	Social services	Public enterprises	Total
	Thousands of persons employed				
1964	32.3	28.5	99.5	49.6	209.9
1970	46.1	44.3	133.8	55.8	280.0
1974	52.8	69.5	178.3	59.5	360.1
1978	46.2	34.4	176.9	35.9	293.4
1979	48.8	32.0	176.3	35.5	292.6
	Yearly growth rates (%)				
1964–70	6.1	7.6	5.0	2.0	4.9
1970–74	3.5	11.9	7.4	1.6	6.5
1974–78	−3.3	−16.1	−0.2	−11.9	−5.0

Sources: Finance Ministry, *Exposición sobre el Estado de la Hacienda Pública,* January 1978, except for 1979 figures, which were obtained from J. Marshall and P. Romaguera, "Empleo en el sector público" (CIEPLAN mimeo, 1981).

TABLE 1.8   Financial Savings in Public and Private Institutions
(percentage of total)

Year	Public sector	Mixed sector (savings and loans)	Private sector
1969	46.7	40.5	12.8
1970	49.3	39.5	11.1
1974	30.0	62.5	7.5
1975	29.7	56.2	14.1
1976	33.6	36.1	40.3
1977	31.4	17.8	50.9
1978	28.7	7.8	63.5
1979	31.8	3.5	64.7
1980	25.3	1.7	73.0

Source: Banco Central, *Boletín Mensual*, various issues.

between 1974 and 1978, as shown in Table 1.7. Thus, previously expansionary trends were drastically reversed.[13] The employment reductions were more important in developmental institutions (19% yearly reductions) and in public enterprises (10.5% yearly reductions). These figures represent the priorities in the new economic policy.

Organized labor is excluded from this picture. Not only were wages controlled and in fact drastically curtailed in real terms, but in addition no collective bargaining was allowed, strikes were forbidden, and no mechanism existed for the participation of labor in economic decisions. Only in 1979 was a "Labor Plan" implemented, which regulated, under conditions of subordination of workers to their employers, the functioning of labor unions and allowed for a very restricted form of collective bargaining.[14]

The changes in the role of economic agents which I have just described (less state participation, privatization of economic activities, modifications in labor legislation) were initially posed only as an efficiency requirement of the model. It was supposedly neutral as to its distributive effects. In practice this was not so. In fact, the economy's adjustment process to the desired conditions implied a massive transfer of resources toward the private sector, particularly toward financial firms and large industrial enterprises. This transfer of resources was made possible because of the particular form taken by the processes of privatization, market liberalization, and inflationary control.

Thus, privatization of state enterprises occurred in extremely advantageous conditions for the new owners. In Table 1.9 I have estimated the implicit subsidy for those who bought these public assets. The subsidy,

TABLE 1.9   Subsidy in the Sale of State Enterprises
(millions of dollars in 1978)

Discount rate		Sale value	Value of assets in 1978	Subsidy	Subsidy as % of asset value
1974–1978	1979–1983				
10	10	496.1	731.8	235.7	32.2
25	15	533.0	731.8	198.8	27.2

Note: The figures correspond to a sample of forty-one enterprises and banks, representing about 60% of the firms auctioned. The value of the sale updated to 1978 assumed a four-year payment period for the industrial firms and eight quarters for banks, with interest rates of 10% and 8%, respectively.

Sources: F. Dahse, *El mapa de la extrema riqueza: Los grupos económicos y el proceso de concentración de capitales* (Santiago: Editorial Aconcagua, 1979); and CORFO, *Gerencia de Normalización,* 1979.

calculated on the basis of the market value of assets, turned out to be equivalent to 30% of the firms' net worth and up to 40% and 50% of the purchase value.[15] The low sale price was influenced by the state's urgency to sell and its doing so in a moment of deep recession and high interest rates, a point at which short-term profitability of the enterprises decreased. Given these circumstances, only those firms which had liquid resources or access to cheap foreign credit were in a position to buy the auctioned enterprises.

Something similar occurred in the agricultural sector, in which the policy was to return a fraction of the lands expropriated during the agrarian reform to their original owners. Another part was subdivided into individual plots and handed over to peasants (see Table 1.10). In April 1979, 30% of the expropriated land had been returned to the former owners, and 35% had been assigned in individual plots to peasants and small farmers. Moreover nearly 40% of these lands had already been sold or leased by peasants to third parties in June 1978, as a consequence of the high cost of credit and reduced technical assistance.

The privatization of manufacturing firms, as well as that of the land reform sector, implied a transfer of assets, generally undervalued, either to former owners in the agricultural case or to business groups in the industrial and financial sectors. This tendency was reinforced by the particular form taken by the process of market liberalization, as was the case with the capital market and its opening to foreign sources, as we shall see later. Moreover, the process of market liberalization did not follow uniform patterns with respect to the relative prices of goods and salaries. Since prices were rapidly deregulated while salaries contracted, the result was a highly negative bias against the latter. As can be observed in Table 1.11, there

TABLE 1.10   The State of Agrarian Reform as of April 1979

Situation	Hectares	Percentage
Restored to former owners	2,965,640	29.8
Area assigned to beneficiaries[a]	3,521,141	35.3
Transferred to CORA[b]	1,639,772	16.5
In the hands of ODENA[c]	1,839,315	18.4
Total expropriated	9,965,868	100.0

[a] From the total of the area assigned to the beneficiaries of agrarian reform up to June 1978, almost 40% had been sold or leased for its exploitation to third parties.

[b] Land Reform Corporation; includes auction of lands and transfers to other public institutions (such as CONAF, National Forestry Corporation) or to private ones.

[c] Office of Agricultural Normalization.

Source: Presentation of the Government of Chile to the Conference on Agrarian Reform and Rural Development, 1979, in *Comentarios sobre la situación económica,* Department of Economics, University of Chile, 1st semester, 1979.

TABLE 1.11   Prices and Remunerations (Wages and Salaries) (1970 index = 100)

Year	Remunerations / wholesale prices (1)	Remunerations / export prices (2)	Industrial remunerations / industrial prices (3)
1970	100.0	100.0	100.0
1974	49.4	50.2	57.2
1975	38.8	35.1	47.9
1976	41.2	45.4	56.0
1977	52.5	59.4	69.0
1978	57.8	57.2	75.0
1979	56.5	63.6	74.9
1980	59.3	79.8	79.6
1981	70.2	103.1	92.2
1982	72.3	88.6	88.6

Sources: (1) Index of wages and salaries (IWS) and wholesale price index (WPI) for national products, Instituto Nacional de Estadísticas. (2) INE's IWS and yearly average nominal exchange rate as well as index of external prices in Ffrench-Davis, "Indice de precios externos," 1981, and later updates. (3) IWS of the industrial sector and WPI for industrial products.

was a drastic fall of the relative price of labor when compared to wholesale, export, and industrial prices. By this measure, wages were reduced between 50% and 65% in 1975, and have yet to recover 1970 levels.

These sets of relative prices are extremely favorable to productive enterprises, particularly those in export activities. Undoubtedly it allowed all of them to absorb a good part of the greater costs associated with the severe 1975–76 recession, and it provided them with a cushion that facilitated adjustment to the increased external competition resulting from lower tariffs. This effect was reinforced by the reduction in the employer's contribution to social security. The accumulated effect of both factors on the cost of labor in the industrial sector can be observed in column 2 of Table 1.12. Given labor productivity increases, the incidence of labor cost for the industrial producer dropped from 16.9% of the gross value of production in 1970 to 12.9% in 1980 (column 4).

Another important way in which resources were transferred to large business firms came about as a by-product of the policy of economic stabili-

TABLE 1.12 Productivity and Labor Costs in the Industrial Sector
(1970 index = 100)

Year	Wages (1)	Cost of labor (2)	Physical productivity (3)	Cost of labor over gross value of production (4)
1970	100.0	100.0	100.0	16.9%
1974	57.2	63.1	99.8	10.7%
1975	47.9	51.6	78.7	11.1%
1976	56.0	60.4	81.3	12.6%
1977	69.0	73.0	86.0	14.3%
1978	75.0	74.7	91.6	13.8%
1979	74.9	72.8	96.4	12.8%
1980	79.6	76.2	99.8	12.9%

Sources: (1) INE's IWS and WPI for industrial products. (2) Index constructed on the basis of (1) and of the employer contributions to social security. See Superintendencia de Seguridad Social, "Costo de la seguridad social chilena año 1979," 1981. (3) New national accounts and employment figures by Oficina de Planificación Nacional (ODEPLAN), Banco Central, Indicadores económicos y sociales, 1960–1982. (4) New national accounts. For 1970, I estimated wages and salaries and the gross value of industrial production on the basis of the changes in total wages and salaries and the value added by industry between 1970 and 1974. See Banco Central, Cuentas Nacionales de Chile, 1960–1980. For the following years I estimated on the basis of columns (2) and (3).

zation. This policy was characterized by a strict monetarist, closed economy approach, at least until mid-1979. The policy sought economic stabilization through partial use of the instruments at its disposal, principally the reduction of real wages, the fiscal deficit, and the money supply.

The approach was successful in producing a sharp drop in effective demand and in reducing real wages. Prices increased without relation to demand since the impact of expectations and costs was difficult to gauge in a situation which passed rapidly from "repressed" inflation to open inflation. Consequently, high inflation continued far longer than expected.[16] The economy entered a prolonged phase of recession with high inflation, a period characterized by generalized market disequilibrium. Market imbalances surfaced in the form of sharp and intermittent movements in relative prices.

Anyone with enough liquidity to react quickly to these fluctuations in relative prices benefited from those movements. So, obviously, did anyone with special access to economic information that allowed him or her correctly to predict those movements or to know ahead of time of any corrective measures planned by the government.

The economic groups which controlled the country's large firms and financial sector took full advantage of these opportunities for speculation. Market disequilibria and high inflation lasted over five years, long enough for those groups to corner for themselves the speculative gains available in different markets.

The 1981 social security system reform constituted another important area of privatization of the economy and gave the private sector a large amount of new resources.[17] The government must finance the pensions of those who remain in the state system through other means after ceasing to receive the contributions of the individuals who have transferred out of it. The new private pension schemes have reflected the concentration which exists in the capital markets. Four of the twelve enterprises which administer these funds are linked to the two greatest economic groups. In December 1982, 69% of all the contributors paid into these four enterprises, which had 71% of the total pension funds. Of the eight remaining enterprises, four additional ones were also linked to large economic groups. The banks of these economic groups administering pension funds controlled 54% of the credit in the financial system.

In short, beginning in 1973, the operation of the Chilean economy fundamentally changed not only because the economic roles assigned to different participants changed but also because the dynamic processes of adjustment to a new economic model made possible the real transfer of resources toward industrial-financial groups. These groups took advantage of this resource transfer, using it to acquire a dominant position in the country's productive apparatus, as will be shown below.

TRANSITION FROM A CLOSED TO AN OPEN ECONOMY

At the end of 1973, the average nominal tariff on imports to Chile was 94%. By June 1979, a gradual policy of tariff reductions brought nearly all tariffs down to a uniform 10% except for those on automotive vehicles. The tariff reductions, which took a little over five years, were part of a general liberalization of restrictions on foreign trade: elimination of nontariff barriers and a reduction on limits to foreign investment, foreign credit, and foreign exchange transactions. At the same time, however, the government attempted to maintain an exchange rate that would favor Chilean exports. The government also sought to encourage exports by exempting exported goods from the across-the-board value-added tax on all products sold in Chile and from export custom duties.

Policies designed to open the economy were resolutely put into effect from 1974 to 1978. By the end of six years, the Chilean economy was well on its way to becoming an "open" economy with few barriers to international trade.[18]

One of the objectives of liberalizing imports was to encourage the development of an export sector. Lower tariffs reduced the cost to the Chilean producer of intermediate goods. An increase in the volume of imports raised the equilibrium exchange rate for the dollar, creating an exchange rate more favorable to export growth.

The policy of export stimulation was helped by the low wage rates which prevailed during that period (see Tables 1.3 and 1.4) and by the special tax exemptions on exports mentioned above. The policy was also aided by excess capacity in the industrial sector, which resulted from the anti-inflation program.

The growth of exports in the period was undoubtedly significant. Normalizing for the price of copper, total exports rose from 15% of GDP in 1970 to 18% in 1977. Nevertheless, the greater success was obtained in the growth of nontraditional exports, as shown in Table 1.13. During the period 1974–79, nontraditional exports tripled. This expansion was accompanied by export diversification. If copper is excluded from total exports to avoid the effect of excessive price fluctuations, industrial exports rose from 59% of total exports in 1974 to 65% in 1978.

Imports grew rapidly after 1978, as seen in Table 1.13. The expansion is particularly significant for imports of nonfood consumption goods, which more than doubled between 1974 and 1979. On the other hand, imports of capital goods fell during the recession, and only in 1978 did they recover 1970 levels.

What impact did the opening up of the economy have on the structure of production, particularly in the industrial sector? The manufacturing sector suffered the simultaneous impact of recession and tariff reduction,

TABLE 1.13   Imports and Exports (in millions of 1977 US$)

	1970	1974	1978	1979	1980
Imports					
Food consumption goods	110.5	85.9	117.0	133.1	297.5
Nonfood consumption goods	189.8	237.9	415.3	540.7	752.5
Capital goods	566.0	337.9	573.2	683.9	857.2
Intermediate goods	1,085.5	1,778.3	1,594.0	1,969.8	2,186.0
Total	1,951.8	2,440.0	2,699.5	3,327.5	4,093.2
Exports					
Traditional	1,951.4	2,268.0	1,250.1	1,757.7	2,041.2
Semitraditional	95.9	175.4	230.0	300.0	360.8
Nontraditional	232.4	274.5	650.7	894.0	986.2
Total	2,279.7	2,717.9	2,130.8	2,951.7	3,388.2

Source: R. Ffrench-Davis, "Liberalización de importaciones: La experiencia chilena en 1973–1979," *Colección Estudios CIEPLAN,* no. 4 (1980).

which negatively affected production levels. The two effects are not easy to separate. Yet, using the study by Vergara, I have grouped in Table 1.14 sectoral data that will allow us to distinguish among sectors depending on how they had been affected by the opening up to trade and by recession, respectively. In group A in Table 1.14 I have classified those sectors that were simultaneously affected by falls in domestic demand and by tariff reduction. In these sectors production decreased and imports increased, giving way to a marked desubstitution of imports. This group includes textiles, shoes, and clothing, as well as some intermediate inputs for industry. Group B includes those activities in which, despite an increase in domestic demand, production fell. At the same time, imports increased significantly. These are sectors typically affected by the opening up to trade: the electronics industry, transport, and others. Group C consists of intermediate inputs for construction and rubber and plastics. These sectors are affected mainly by recession rather than by tariff reduction. This may be verified by observing that in the face of contractions in demand, both imports and production decreased, but the former fell even more sharply. Group D represents export-oriented activities that successfully adjusted to lower tariffs, like wood and paper. In group E, whose principal components are food, beverages, and tobacco, I have included sectors where both production and imports grew.

At the time this study was done, however, it was impossible to make a

TABLE I.14   Effects on the Industrial Sector of the Opening Up to World
Markets: Annual Variation Rates, 1969/70-1978 (percentages)

	Production	Imports	Exports	Domestic demand[a]	Import substitution[b]
A. Affected by opening and fall					
of internal demand	−2.6	3.4	19.2	−1.6	−9.7
Textiles, clothing, and foot-					
wear (321–324)[c]	−1.6	6.1	46.0	−1.2	−3.4
Industrial inputs (351, 354,					
361, 382)	−5.9	3.1	18.5	−2.3	18.9
Others (342, 385)	−1.7	2.2	6.3	−0.3	−15.6
B. Affected by opening up to					
trade	−1.1	8.7	23.3	2.0	−17.7
Electronic equipment (3832)	−1.1	14.0	−15.4	6.7	−27.2
Transportation material (384)	−1.2	6.9	46.5	1.2	−14.4
C. Affected by the fall in internal					
demand	−1.6	−7.4	4.6	−3.0	8.2
Intermediate for construction					
(369, 371, 381)	−1.5	−6.0	12.9	−2.9	6.7
Unvulcanized rubber and plas-					
tics (355–356)	−1.9	−16.4	−8.7	−3.6	13.2
Others (342)	−1.8	−12.5	−8.6	−2.9	10.0
D. Oriented to exports	2.9	−1.4	11.4	−0.2	0.4
Timber (331)	4.4	−6.4	15.4	3.0	0.6
Paper (341)	0.6	2.4	10.0	5.9	−2.0
E. Others (311–314, 352, 362,					
383, 390)	2.1	4.8	17.1	1.7	−1.4
Total industrial sector	0.4	1.8	14.1	0.1	−1.7

[a] Measured as a proxy by the difference between production plus imports minus exports.

[b] Variation in the import coefficient over total supply.

[c] Figures in parentheses identify branches according to the International Standard Classification of Industry by the United Nations. No figures with this sectoral breakdown are available after 1978.

Source: P. Vergara, "Apertura externa y desarrollo industrial en Chile, 1974-1978," Colección Estudios CIEPLAN, no. 4 (1980).

definitive evaluation of the impact of the new economic policies on the industrial sector.[19] The process of opening to foreign trade concluded in 1979, and in June of that year the nominal exchange rate was fixed until June of 1982. For a year and a half the internal rate of inflation was substantially higher than the external one. This produced a revaluation of the peso, thereby sharpening the drop of effective protection for the industrial sector.

The impact of the opening varied by size of enterprise and by line of production. Table 1.15 shows the decline in the number of industries and employment by industrial sector. The relative size of the enterprises also has dropped.[20] Since the goods they produce are more vulnerable to foreign competition, the larger enterprises are disproportionately affected; furthermore, since they rely more on credit, they are more sensitive to the sharp rise in real interest rates. Tables 1.16 and 1.17 show the evolution of industrial production and employment by branch of activity. The sectors which are most affected in terms of production are textiles, shoes and leather, and garments.

The loss of competitiveness produced by the revaluation of the peso and the high cost of interest for those enterprises that did not have access to external credit led to increasing difficulties for the industrial sector after 1981. This sector is one of the most affected by the crisis of 1982. While the GDP fell 14%, the production of manufacturing industries fell by 22%. Since part of the loss of production and of industrial employment results from the bankruptcy and closing of enterprises, it is very likely that the installed capacity of Chilean industry is undergoing a reduction which will affect the possibilities for a reactivation of activity in this sector. This negative effect will be compounded by the low levels of investment during the 1974–82 period.

TABLE 1.15   Evolution of the Number of Enterprises and of Employment in the Industrial Sector between 1967 and 1981 (1967 = 100)

Industry	No. of enterprises	Employment
Food, beverages, and tobacco	110	112
Textiles, clothing, and shoes	64	58
Wood and furniture	84	67
Paper and cellulose	103	92
Chemicals and plastics	110	110
Nonmetallic minerals	74	72
Basic metal	78	33
Machinery and equipment	81	66
Other industries	79	61
All industries	87	74

Source: Censo Manufacturero 1967 and unpublished information of the *Encuesta industrial de 1982.* Table drawn from V. Tokman, "Monetarismo global y destrucción industrial" (PREALC mimeo, 1983).

TABLE 1.16   Industrial Production (1970 = 100)

Industry	1974	1976	1978	1980	1982
Food	108.9	106.5	104.3	116.3	112.9
Beverages	101.2	110.3	146.5	167.8	159.7
Tobacco	142.7	134.4	149.6	159.5	116.4
Textiles	102.4	64.1	76.4	63.2	42.2
Shoes and clothing	100.3	71.0	81.3	80.5	42.1
Wood	82.5	73.5	69.0	92.2	65.7
Furniture	100.3	63.7	51.6	112.6	89.3
Cellulose and paper	130.1	123.7	136.1	160.5	139.8
Printing	59.0	52.8	51.9	60.2	70.8
Leather	71.7	63.3	61.7	44.1	28.8
Rubber products	112.3	69.5	70.5	77.6	50.5
Chemical products	106.8	72.7	90.7	117.3	97.5
Oil and coal derivatives	121.7	109.2	129.2	129.7	99.1
Nonmetallic minerals	132.3	76.9	93.6	118.8	58.1
Basic metals	121.9	109.4	133.8	148.6	131.2
Metallic products excluding machinery and transport equipment	112.6	64.7	99.0	101.3	64.0
Nonelectric machines	119.4	110.7	103.1	116.9	32.5
Electric machines	105.7	65.6	98.5	132.3	59.1
Transport equipment	101.7	29.0	78.3	108.9	72.0
Other industries	165.4	109.3	105.3	91.0	54.4
Industry Total, INE	108.6	81.9	96.9	110.6	84.2
Industry Total, SOFOFA	107.3	92.0	110.9	124.8	103.0

Sources: Sector indexes: INE, index of industrial production; SOFOFA, index of industrial production.

CHANGES IN THE PRODUCTIVE STRUCTURE

The economic policy changes imposed since 1973 obviously have repercussions on the overall productive structure. Since these changes take time to manifest themselves, here I will only point to the trends that are currently beginning to appear.

Table 1.18 shows the structure of production and employment in the main areas of economic activity. The primary sectors—agriculture and mining—have increased their relative importance in production from 16.7% in 1970 to 19.5% in 1982. However, their participation in employment has dropped from 25.8% to 19.3% between the same years. By contrast, the manufacturing sector's participation in the GDP dropped; between 1981 and 1982 alone it diminished by 4%.

TABLE 1.17   Industrial Employment (1970 = 100)

Industry	1974	1976	1978	1980	1981[a]
Food, beverages, and tobacco	107.0	103.4	99.1	102.3	104.1
Textiles, clothing, and leather	109.9	87.1	87.6	84.2	78.3
Wood	99.5	72.2	99.3	75.9	72.3
Paper	109.3	98.0	94.5	87.0	88.7
Chemicals and plastics	114.1	102.3	98.5	94.9	91.7
Nonmetallic minerals	117.4	91.6	86.0	87.0	87.2
Basic metals	112.6	101.3	88.9	82.3	77.6
Metallic products, machinery, and equipment	117.8	92.0	84.3	79.3	76.5
All industries	110.4	92.6	92.0	87.2	84.6

[a] January–May.
Source: SOFOFA, index of industrial employment.

Commerce and services were the most dynamic sectors of the whole period. They jointly increased their participation in production from 40.2% in 1970 to 46.5% in 1982. One of every two jobs in the economy was generated in these sectors toward 1978.[21] The importance acquired by the service sectors was such that their participation in generating the product and in employment was higher than that of all productive sectors jointly considered (agriculture, mining, and industry). On the other hand, infrastructure and construction activities decreased in importance. The latter reduced its participation in the product by a third.

In sum, the changes in the structure of production and employment were meaningful in spite of the short time that transpired. A part of these changes do not reflect modifications in the productive capacity but only in the degree of utilization of that capacity.[22] The direction of the changes is clear: the production of commerce and services grew at a significant rate, while industry and the sectors of infrastructure grew at a very slow pace. These imbalances in sectoral growth, if persistent, will probably end up modifying permanently not only the productive structure but also income distribution patterns.

CHANGES IN PATTERNS OF DISTRIBUTION

An economy which undergoes profound changes such as Chile experienced beginning in 1973 will probably, in the long run, sustain changes not only in its production and trade structure but also in its patterns of distribution. Some of the important factors related to changes in income distribution are changes in patterns of property ownership, in the relative power of differ-

TABLE 1.18   Distribution of Production and Employment by Sector
(percentages)

Sector	1970 Produc-tion	1970 Employ-ment	1974 Produc-tion	1974 Employ-ment	1978 Produc-tion	1978 Employ-ment	1982 Produc-tion	1982 Employ-ment[a]
Agriculture	9.4	22.6	9.3	18.3	9.6	17.9	9.9	16.6
Mining	7.3	3.2	8.5	3.7	8.3	3.2	9.6	2.7
Industry	27.4	17.8	27.4	18.5	24.1	17.6	20.2	17.5
Construction	8.3	6.9	7.2	5.7	4.5	4.0	5.4	4.5
Energy and transport	7.3	7.4	7.6	7.6	8.3	7.9	8.4	8.3
Commerce	18.3	12.1	15.9	12.7	19.0	13.9	18.9	15.8
Services[b]	21.9	30.0	24.1	33.5	26.2	35.3	27.6	34.6
Total	100.0	100.0	100.0	100.0	100.0	100.0	100.0	100.0

[a] Figures are for 1981, the last year for which there is information.
[b] Excludes home ownership.
Sources: The production columns correspond to the new national accounts in constant prices; the employment figures come from ODEPLAN. See Banco Central, *Indicadores económicos y sociales, 1960–1982,* 1983.

ent participants in the economy, and in the importance of different productive sectors.

What has happened to the first two of these factors in the period we are studying? We saw earlier how the roles of the economic participants changed as a result of the reduction of the role of the state and the rapid privatization of economic activities. This process and the government's general policy orientation favored privileged participation and access to resources by the business sector, particularly by large and medium-sized firms and by the financial sector. These were the sectors which most benefited from the massive transfer of resources that accompanied the transition from high inflation and a closed economy to more moderate prices and an "open" economy. This point will be developed in the next section, where I refer to the distributive effects of the new policies in the short term.

The changes in distribution are greatly influenced by the high rate of unemployment and the reduction of real salary levels. The expansion of employment, which during the 1960s had grown by an average yearly rate of 2.1%, was only of a 0.8% yearly average between 1974 and 1982 (Table 1.2). During these latter years, there has been a 14% increase in the potentially active population. This explains the fact that unemployment rates during this period have been twice as high as they were in the past. As can be seen in Table 1.3, the lowest yearly unemployment rate was recorded in 1981, at 10.8% (column 7), although adding the individuals in the government's make-work program to this rate gives a figure of 15.6% (column 8). Unemployment increased again in 1982 and reached 26.1% if we include the registrants in the by then two public make-work schemes (column 8). Real salaries have also declined during the military government, as we have noted (see, in particular, Table 1.3, column 9).[23]

The simultaneous reduction in employment and wages generated a regressive distribution of income, a proxy for which we consider household consumption expenditures by income brackets. The figures in Table 1.19 point to a concentration of consumption in the high-income brackets.[24]

Moreover, empirical evidence shows a marked stratification in consumption. The consumption of nonessential imported consumer goods, which grew about 300% between 1970 and 1978, was highly concentrated in the highest 20% of families. These families consumed 51% of the total.[25] Consumption by the lower 20% of the families was negligible.

While the high-income groups increased their luxury consumption, essential food consumption per family for the poorer groups showed a reduction of 20% in real terms between 1969 and 1978 (see Table 1.20). The consumption per family of the same basic food products for the high-income groups grew slightly. This marked dualism in consumption seems to be an essential characteristic of the model. It is in agreement with the patrimonial changes and with the income distribution patterns previously discussed.

CONCENTRATION AND FINANCIAL CRISIS

A concentration of assets (and, therefore, an increase in the size of some economic groups) has been produced by the manner in which the privatiza-

TABLE 1.19   Distribution of Household Consumption by Quintiles: Greater Santiago, Chile (percentages)

	Share of total consumption	
Quintiles	1969	1978
I	7.7	5.2
II	12.1	9.3
III	16.0	13.6
IV	21.0	20.9
V	43.2	51.0
Total	100.0	100.0

Sources: INE, *Encuesta de presupuestos familiares,* 1969; and INE, *Encuesta de presupuestos familiares,* 1978.

TABLE 1.20   Average Consumption of Basic Products by Household
(pesos in June 1978)

Product	Lowest 20% of households			Highest 20% of households		
	1969	1978	Variation (%)	1969	1978	Variation (%)
Flours and starches	387.6	406.8	5.0	778.6	719.6	−7.6
Meats	357.9	219.1	−38.8	1,534.5	1,627.2	6.0
Oils	105.4	71.2	−32.4	269.4	201.0	−25.4
Dairy and eggs	138.9	106.1	−23.6	618.3	641.5	3.8
Vegetables and legumes	144.0	97.5	−32.3	257.9	197.4	−23.5
Sugar	97.0	73.4	−24.3	191.8	154.2	−19.6
Energy and fuel	227.3	181.8	−20.0	501.6	641.1	27.8
Urban transport	129.8	102.9	−20.7	277.8	284.5	2.4
Total	1,587.9	1,258.8	−20.7	4,430.0	4,466.5	0.8
Percentage of total consumption		49.9			18.0	

Source: INE, Encuesta de presupuestos familiares, 1969 and 1978.

tion of productive activities was carried out as well as by the characteristics of the external opening of the financial system.

According to one study, at the end of 1978 six of the seven groups which are listed in Table 1.21 controlled 54% of the assets of the 250 largest private enterprises in the country.[26] An update of that study indicates that the assets of the enterprises owned by five of these groups doubled between 1978 and 1980 in real terms.[27] There are reasons to suspect that this process continued after 1980. As we have seen, the economic groups formed enterprises to capture pension funds.

Concentration was greatest in the financial system, which is precisely one of the reasons for the crisis which has affected it since 1981. In December 1982, the two major economic groups owned 30% of the capital and reserves of all financial institutions, and they controlled 42% of credit.[28] In addition, the proportion of credits to enterprises and individuals who are related by ownership to the banks extending the credits is high. As Table 1.21 shows, in the case of one bank, over 40% of all credits were related loans, while in the case of seven other banks such credits are close to or over 20% of the total.

In order to sustain these related loans, the banks maintained high interest rates, which led to the insolvency of the debtors and to the increas-

TABLE 1.21 Economic Conglomerates and the Financial System

	As % of the system in Dec. 1982			Related loans as % of institution's total lending	
Group and bank	Capital and reserves	Loans	External credits	June 82	April 83
BHC					
BHC[a]	2.1	3.3	3.6	28.2	27.4[c]
Chile[b]	12.5	20.0	28.1	16.1	17.8
Morgan-Finansa	1.0	1.6	1.4	7.2	7.1
Cruzat-Larrain					
Santiago[b]	11.8	11.8	12.1	44.1	47.8
BHIF	1.8	3.3	1.9	17.1	19.8
Colocadora[b]	1.4	2.0	1.5	23.4	24.2
Edwards					
de A. Edwards	2.0	3.1	3.3	15.9	14.4
Errázuriz					
Nacional	1.9	1.9	1.5	29.1	27.5
Luksic					
Sudamericano	3.1	4.6	6.4	13.0	18.1
O'Higgins	2.7	2.8	3.3	8.0	12.1
Matte					
BICE	1.0	1.2	1.4	4.0	4.2
Yarur					
Crédito e Inversiones	3.8	5.1	4.9	8.6	12.1
Other Banks					
Concepción[b]	3.5	4.1	4.4	17.0	12.0
Internacional	1.2	1.1	0.6	20.1	20.5
Trabajo	2.3	2.9	2.9	1.6	3.3
Osorno	2.3	2.1	1.0	3.4	9.4
BUF[a]	1.3	2.1	1.9	5.1	7.6[c]

[a] Closed for bankruptcy in January 1983.
[b] "Intervened" in January 1983.
[c] December 1982.
Source: Superintendencia de Bancos e Instituciones Financieras, *Información Financiera.*

ing difficulties of the banks. The strong increase in defaults after some banks were taken over in December 1982 (Table 1.5) is probably explained in part by the renewal of credit lines to the faltering enterprises related to the banks, which then ceased payments.

Access to external sources of credit also favored the economic groups. Thus, at the end of 1982, 48% of the external credits flowing into the financial system had been received by the biggest groups.[29] This occurred because of the manner in which access to external credit sources was deregulated: a limit was established to external indebtedness which was set as a certain proportion of the assets of each enterprise. Therefore, only the large companies, the banks, and well-established financial enterprises had access to external credit. And since domestic inflation levels were superior to external ones, the foreign credits, which were comparatively cheaper, became a source of large profits. Zahler has estimated that profits accruing from the differences between external and internal interest rates amounted to about $800 million for the period between 1976 and 1979.[30]

Conclusion

The monetarist, neoconservative experiment in Chile represents a combination of orthodox stabilization policies and revolutionary changes in the structure of the economy stemming from an ideological blueprint.

The macroeconomic policy applied between 1973 and 1982 ended in a resounding failure. The economy did not grow, the rate of investment dropped sharply, the external sector reached an acute crisis, unemployment more than tripled past levels, real salaries and pensions decreased, and government spending for social programs declined.

By mid-1983, the bankruptcies of productive enterprises continued. The financial sector as a whole became insolvent, since nonperforming loans amounted to over 100% of the capital and reserves of the banks. Most remaining productive enterprises were overindebted, and given the sharp 1982–83 recession, there is little expectation that they will be able to repay their loans since they cannot produce enough.

The external debt in 1983 is approximately equal to the value of the GDP, and debt services for the rest of the 1980s are expected to remain at levels over 70% of the value of exports.

These macroeconomic indicators are, nonetheless, only the more visible, perhaps dramatic, but certainly not the most important aspect of the revolutionary transformations which have occurred in the Chilean economy during this period. The economy has been substantially privatized, and a radical process of liberalization of external trade and financial resources has been carried out. There has also been a reorientation of the resources and capacities of entrepreneurs from productive activities toward financial speculation and import commerce.

As a result of these changes, internal productive activities, having lost their protectionism, decreased sharply. At the same time, the changes generated the conditions for the emergence of powerful financial conglomerates which acquired a preponderant influence in the management of the economy. It is they who channelled the great majority of the external credits, and it is they who bear the principal responsibility for the insolvency of numerous enterprises. The downfall, in turn, of the major economic groups towards the end of 1982, led to the collapse of a large part of the financial system, which had then to be taken over by the Central Bank. The failure of the experiment has left massive poverty. A third of the labor force was out of work by mid-1983, and wage levels continue to deteriorate. The paralysis of production and the external crisis insure a prolonged period of severe deterioration of living conditions for the majority of the population.

Notes

This chapter constitutes a revised and updated (as of mid-1983) version of material previously published as Chapter 3 of the author's *Latin American Experiments in Neo-Conservative Economics* (Berkeley and Los Angeles: University of California Press, 1983).

1. The latter figure includes among the unemployed the individuals working for the Minimum Employment Program (PEM).

2. For a good description of the policies and their interrelationship with social behavior and ideology, see T. Moulian and P. Vergara, "Estado, ideología y políticas económicas en Chile, 1973-1978," *Colección Estudios* CIEPLAN, no. 3 (June 1980), and T. Moulian and P. Vergara, "Coyuntura económica y reacciones sociales: Las fases de la política económica en Chile, 1973-78," *Apuntes* CIEPLAN, no. 22 (November 1979).

3. Notice that these unemployment figures correspond to Greater Santiago only. Also, they do not include the unemployed absorbed in the Minimum Employment Program (PEM). National unemployment figures including and excluding PEM are given in Table 1.3.

4. In order to recover competitiveness, the authorities planned as an alternative to the devaluation a reduction in nominal salaries, which did in fact occur in some enterprises. According to one estimate, if wages bore the brunt of the lowering of costs they would have had to drop about 36%; see J. P. Arellano and R. Cortázar, "Del milagro a la crisis: Algunas reflexiones sobre el momento económico," *Colección Estudios CIEPLAN,* no. 8 (July 1982).

5. This value represents an average calculated by the Central Bank.

6. In June 1982, related loans constituted 18% of all loans granted by banks and financial companies for which there is information. These institutions issued 75% of all loans.

7. These programs were expanded during the second semester of 1982 with the addition of the so-called Program for Heads of Households (POJH).

8. The trade balance for 1982 was positive if exports and imports are measured f.o.b.

9. The sum total of these credits is $1.2 billion—in other words, 3.6 times the capital and reserves of the two banks.

10. See J. P. Arellano, "De la liberalización a la intervención: El mercado de capitales en Chile, 1974-83" (CIEPLAN mimeo, May 1983). The means in

question are direct payments to financial institutions that were forced to close, urgency loans, and special overdrawing rights.

11. See CORFO, Gerencia de Normalización, and *El Mercurio,* 27 February 1980. The figures refer to CORFO-owned enterprises. [*Editors' note:* In fact, twenty-three enterprises remained as CORFO affiliates in 1980; a new goal lowers to thirteen the number of CORFO enterprises. See Table 3.2 in this volume.]

12. J. E. Herrera and J. Morales, "La inversión financiera externa: El caso de Chile, 1974–1978," *Colección Estudios CIEPLAN,* no. 1 (July 1979).

13. In 1973 public employment dropped 25%, representing a decrease of 100,000 persons.

14. The Labor Plan is discussed in Chapter 7, below.

15. The calculation was made on the basis of the figures of F. Dahse, *El Mapa de la extrema riqueza: Los grupos económicos y el proceso de concentración de capitales* (Santiago: Editorial Aconcagua, 1979), for a sample of forty-one enterprises, as explained in the note to Table 1.9.

16. See J. Ramos, "The Economics of Hyperstagflation," *Journal of Development Economics* 7, no. 4 (December 1980).

17. Until December 1982, the pension funds equalled 3.7% of the GDP of 1982. For a detailed analysis of the characteristics and consequences of the social security reforms see J. P. Arellano, "Elementos para un análisis de la reforma previsional chilena," *Colección Estudios CIEPLAN,* no. 6 (December 1981).

18. What follows is based on studies by R. Ffrench-Davis, "Políticas de comercio exterior en Chile, 1973–1978" (CIEPLAN mimeo, 1979), and P. Vergara, "Apertura externa y desarrollo industrial en Chile, 1974–1978," *Colección Estudios CIEPLAN,* no. 4 (November 1980).

19. For a more detailed discussion of the effects of the opening of the economy, see Chapter 2 of this volume.

20. For a more detailed analysis, see V. Tokman, "Monetarismo global y destrucción industrial" (PREALC mimeo, Santiago, 1982).

21. This occurred in spite of the fact that employment in education and health was reduced. Employment in other services increased by 21% between 1975 and 1977.

22. Of course, to the extent that idle capacity is maintained as such for an extended period in some sectors, it may become a signal for further expansions to be oriented toward other activities, those where the "new" demand is concentrated.

23. It should be added that the indicator for wages and salaries used in these calculations underestimates their levels for the economy as a whole. The indicator is adequate only for the average wages and salaries in industrial enterprises of more than twenty persons, and in the mining as well as service sectors. See Universidad de Chile, Departamento de Economía, *Comentarios sobre la situación económica,* second semester, 1978.

24. This information, which is in accord with wages and employment data, contradicted official statements that the income distribution in 1978 would not

be significantly different from that in 1970. According to a study by I. Heskia, the distribution improved even in the worst recession years. See I. Heskia, "Distribución del ingreso en el Gran Santiago, 1957–1978," *Documento de Investigación,* no. 41, Departamento de Economía, Universidad de Chile (Santiago, 1979). For a criticism of Heskia's results, see R. Cortázar, "Remuneraciones, empleo y distribución del ingreso en Chile, 1970–1978," *Colección Estudios CIEPLAN,* no. 3 (June 1980).

25. [*Editors' note:* The author cites an earlier version of the paper by Ricardo Ffrench-Davis that is included in this volume as Chap. 2. The data can be examined in Table 2.4.]

26. Dahse, *Mapa de la extrema riqueza.*

27. See F. Dahse, "El poder de los grandes grupos económicos nacionales" (Universidad Católica, Instituto de Sociología mimeo, June 1982).

28. These figures increase to 41% and 49%, respectively, when the Banco del Estado is excluded from the calculation.

29. This percentage increases to 54% if the external debt of the Banco del Estado is excluded.

30. R. Zahler, "Repercusiones monetarias y reales de la apertura financiera al exterior: El caso chileno, 1975–1978," in *Revista de la CEPAL,* no. 10 (April 1980).

Import Liberalization: The Chilean Experience, 1973–1982

2

Ricardo Ffrench-Davis

Chile's economic policy since 1973 has been among the most orthodox in the world. The official policy placed profound faith in the market's ability to function efficiently, dynamically, and competitively. The government expressed this confidence in the market system by refraining from direct intervention in productive activities and by adopting economic policies which it claims are "neutral."

The distinctive characteristic of the foreign trade policies that have been implemented is their unswerving movement towards freeing the exchange of goods from government regulations. Chile effectively liberalized imports to a degree unprecedented in modern economic history, either in Chile or in any other semi-industrialized economy. By establishing a uniform tariff of 10% for nearly all imports, this liberalization suppressed the use of selective criteria for allowing imports. The opening to foreign trade was accompanied by an opening, also unrestricted, to foreign investment and by a reduction of restrictions on foreign exchange dealings and on capital movements.

The implementation of a free trade policy raises four questions. First, has the policy allowed more efficient use of available resources, or has it produced important new divergences between market and social "efficiency"? Second, what degree of dynamism has characterized the process, compared with its historical behavior; and how has the intensity and the timing of the liberalization affected employment, investment, and consumption? Third, how much competition or economic concentration has the policy produced? Lastly, how effectively "neutral" are these "nondiscriminatory" economic policies? These policies, seemingly neutral, were applied to different spheres of the economy which coexisted in a framework marked by inequalities. This implies that these policies may produce assymmetrical and distinct effects among different productive and social groups. The result, then, could be a greater concentration of power and wealth, an increase in unemployment, inefficient adjustments in the productive structure, and a nondynamic economy.

Consequently, according to one's point of view, the results of this policy might be *a priori* mutually contradictory. Available evidence supports this hypothesis.

In previous publications, I have examined Chile's recent export and exchange rate policies in detail.[1] Here I concentrate on analyzing the import liberalization process which took place after the 1973 coup. Together, these studies represent an attempt to elucidate some of the questions which have been raised, focusing on those most related to the functioning of the foreign sector and its repercussions on the national economy.

The first section of this study shows the trajectory which the reduction of import restrictions has followed. This section centers on tariff liberalization and on the evolution of the real exchange rate to determine to what degree the exchange rate played the compensatory role which it was assigned by the government's policy. The second section analyzes the behavior of the principal categories of imports—in particular, consumption goods—and examines the distribution of imports by different income brackets. The third section studies the general impact of import liberalization on manufacturing and employment; the effects of liberalization are illustrated by examining available information on the behavior of some industrial sectors. The last section presents the main conclusions of this study.

The Import Liberalization Process

A remarkable reduction in the barriers which protected import substitutes at the beginning of the new regime constituted the central element of foreign trade policy. The rapid liberalization process, which began in 1973 and officially ended in June 1979, induced a drastic change in market comparative advantages by modifying both the profile of effective protection as well as its average.

During the period of liberalization, the target of the process underwent significant changes. What initially appeared to be headed for moderate reform, with maximum tariff rates of 60%, ended up as a drastic revamping of the tariff structure with a final uniform tariff of 10%.

The first steps in the process consisted of suppressing the main non-tariff barriers and in dropping to 200% all tariffs which were above that level. Most import prohibitions and import deposits were eliminated. These deposits, with a rate of 10,000%, which were charged on more than half of actual imports, constituted one of the most often used mechanisms to regulate imports in 1972-73. The deposits were waived on the condition that importers fix their import volumes within the quotas recommended by the government. Since this mechanism was applied along with an undervalued exchange rate to several thousand products, it generated innumerable supply bottlenecks and speculative windfall gains for importers.[2] The "normalization" of the foreign exchange market, which took place in October 1973, and a significant increase in the price of copper during the second half of that year facilitated the rapid removal of quantitative restrictions and the initial tariff reductions.

At the beginning of 1974, the government announced a tariff liberalization which would take place gradually over a three-year period and indicated that it would be accompanied by a parallel rise in the real exchange rate. The finance minister defended the policy in several declarations. He asserted that it would generate growth through exports and that even workers would benefit, "as it would create more jobs in expanding sectors than the number of jobs that could disappear in some highly inefficient sectors."[3] The government's original announcement gave no indication of the levels tariffs were projected to reach. The first such indication came in May 1974, when the government declared that "in 1977, no tariff will be higher than 60%. This clearly defines the tariff policy which will be followed in the future so that domestic industries can make whatever adjustments are necessary and prepare themselves so they are in good shape to meet foreign competition."[4]

Despite these announcements, the tariff policy still was not really defined, as the proponents of a fully orthodox policy and other important government officials with a more pragmatic bent differed in their policy criteria. Towards the end of 1974, it was informally hinted that the maximum tariff rate in the future would be only 30%. Internal government documents mentioned a range of 25% to 35% within which the majority of tariff rates would fall.[5] Later, in 1975, the government formally declared that tariff rates would fall between 10% and 35% and that this range would be reached, by gradual reductions every six months, during the first half of 1978.[6]

Although the apparently more pragmatic approach gave way step-by-step to the free trade orthodoxy, the policy as presented by 1975 contained two important heterodox elements. For one, it contemplated nonuniform nominal tariff rates (from 10% to 35%) according to the degree of elaboration of different categories of products. It also contemplated keeping the tariff obligations contracted under the Andean Pact, the economic integration agreement which then included Bolivia, Colombia, Chile, Ecuador, Peru, and Bolivia.[7]

The gradual tariff reductions were made approximately once every six months, as can be seen in Table 2.1. Nevertheless, the final reductions, scheduled for the first half of 1978, were made well ahead of the official timetable. The tariff reform process was completed in August 1977, when 99.6% of all tariffs reached the 10% to 35% range, with a 20% simple average.

It seemed from the repeated official statements that the reduction of

TABLE 2.1   Tariff Liberalization, 1973–1979 (RATES ON C.I.F. VALUE)

Date	Maximum tariff		Modal tariff		Average tariff[b,c]	No. of items
	Rate[a]	% of items	Rate[b]	% of items		
12/31/73	220%	8.0%	90%	12.4%	94.0%	5.125
3/01/74	200	8.2	80	12.4	90.0	5.125
3/27/74	160	17.2	70	13.0	80.0	5.125
6/05/74	140	14.4	60	13.0	67.0	5.125
1/16/75	120	8.2	55	13.0	52.0	5.125
8/13/75	90	1.6	40	20.3	44.0	4.958
2/09/76	80	0.5	35	24.0	38.0	4.952
6/07/76	65	0.5	30	21.2	33.0	4.956
12/23/76	65	0.5	20	26.2	27.0	4.959
1/08/77	55	0.5	20	24.7	24.0	4.981
5/02/77	45	0.6	20	25.8	22.4	4.984
8/29/77	35	1.6	20	26.3	19.8	4.985
12/03/77	25	22.9	15	37.0	15.7	4.993
6/78	20	21.6	10	51.6	13.9	4.301
6/79	10	99.5	10	99.5	10.1	4.301

Note: Dates refer to the official decrees on general changes of custom tariff rates between December 1973 and December 1977. On the latter date the government issued a decree of monthly adjustments lasting until June 1979. To illustrate this process I have chosen rates in force in June 1978 and June 1979.

[a] Does not include the few exceptional cases, involving mostly the automobile sector.

[b] Rates do not include tariff exemptions, the most significant of which applied to free zones (amounting to 6% of imports in 1979) and to imported inputs for exports production.

[c] Simple average of tariffs.

Source: Chile, Banco Central.

protection for import substituting firms had been completed in August 1977. Three months later, however, the finance minister announced another policy change. This change called for reducing tariffs still further, with a target rate of a uniform 10% to be reached in mid-1979. This additional tariff liberalization was carried out in monthly steps between December 1977 and June 1979. By the later date, a uniform tariff of 10% was charged on nearly all imports to Chile. This flat rate is unusually low for developing countries, and even in developed countries a uniform rate is exceptional. Some comparative information illustrates this. In a semi-industrialized country such as South Korea, which is usually presented as a prototype of the free trade model, even after a decade of following its present overall economic policies, tariffs still ranged between 0% and

150%, with many locally produced items enjoying nominal rates of protection between 30% and 60%.[8]

Developed countries, despite their position at the forefront of world industry, usually maintain discriminatory (nonuniform) rates of protection for different products, with levels notably higher than 10% for significant groups of products. A study recently published by the Economic Commission for Latin America shows that, first, effective tariff protection in the United States, Japan, and the European Economic Community was relatively high for categories of products such as textiles and clothing (wearing apparel), processed foods, and light manufactured goods.[9] For instance, textiles and clothes enjoyed effective tariff protection of about 40% in all these countries. In Japan, the effective tariff protection on processed foods was 68%.[10] Secondly, the ECLA study also shows that imports into these countries are restricted by many nontariff mechanisms which significantly affect a growing number of industrial exports from developing countries. Given the great heterogeneity which characterizes nontariff regulations, it is important to estimate their equivalent tariff value. Estimates for 1973, covering France, the United States, Japan, and Sweden, indicate that the average ad valorem rates of protection of nontariff regulations (such as health regulations, import quotas, the so-called "voluntary" export restrictions, and import licenses) can be as high as 40% to 90% for some product categories.[11]

In short, low and across-the-board uniform tariffs are proposed only in the most orthodox textbooks on international economics. Chile, in addition to liberalizing tariffs, has also revoked all nontariff regulations. Some of these were quite rightly eliminated, since they hinder economic development and/or generate windfall gains (such as the broad use of the 10,000% import deposit). However, it has also eliminated other mechanisms which undoubtedly should have remained (such as those which blocked the transmission of external price instability into the domestic economy).[12]

Since 1973, public officials have stated repeatedly that the evolution of the exchange rate and the reductions in tariffs would keep step with each other, the real exchange rate rising as effective tariff protection dropped.[13] The government declarations implied an extremely naive view of causal relationships in the economy, a view which is valid for a competitive model which has neither capital movements nor export incentives and which imports only finished products. In practice, however, the large capital movements in particular brought in significant deviations from this supposed univocal causal relationship.

During the period in which the most sizeable tariff reductions were made, the real exchange rate dropped in tandem. Table 2.2 shows the evolution of the import exchange rate (column 1), nominal rates of protection (columns 3 and 4), and the total cost per dollar of c.i.f. imports for items subject to the maximum and average tariffs (columns 5 and 6) on

TABLE 2.2   Cost of Imports (1977 pesos per 1977 US$)

Phase	Date	Exchange rate[a] (1)	Percentage change in each phase (2)	Nominal tariffs		Average total exchange rate[b] (5)
				Maximum (3)	Average (4)	
	10/73	20.36		220%	94%	39.50
I			67.5%			
	4/75	34.11		120	52	51.85
II			−39.2			
	7/77	20.74		45	22	25.30
III			12.7			
	6/79	23.37		10	10	25.71
IV			−32.9			
	6/82	15.68		10	10	17.25

[a] Nominal exchange rate deflated by the corrected CPI (see R. Cortázar and J. Marshall, "Indice de precios al consumidor en Chile, 1970-1978," *Colección Estudios CIEPLAN,* no. 4 [November 1980] and multiplied by the index of external prices (IPE).
[b] Obtained by multiplying column 1 by (1 + 4/100).
Sources: Chile, Banco Central, *Boletín mensual,* various issues; R. Ffrench-Davis, "Indice de precios externos para calcular el valor real del comercio internacional de Chile, 1952-1980," *Notas Técnicas CIEPLAN,* no. 32 (June 1981); and Table 2.1.

selected dates. In this paper I selected the dates according to the evolution of the cost of imports and the relation between the two components of the cost that I have considered here: the exchange rate and nominal tariffs.[14] Using this information, we can distinguish four phases in the liberalization process.

The tariff reductions made in Phase I, which lasted from the end of 1973 until April 1975, were made when exchange rates were very high. Moreover, a significant part of the tariffs were then redundant, which meant that the initial reductions did not have substantial effects, as they represented mostly unused levels of excessively high protection rates. Because of this, there were no significant increases in "nontraditional" imports during Phase I. Moreover, especially in the last months of 1974 and the first months of 1975, the real exchange rate rose at an accelerating pace which more than compensated for the liberalizing effects of the falling nominal tariffs.[15] At the end of Phase I, the average cost of the import dollar exceeded the cost when Phase I began. Hence, during Phase I the tariff reform process was principally one of "rationalization," in which the large dispersion in effective protection rates was diminished without causing a substantial impact on the manufacturing of import substitutes. The import liberalization and the rise in the exchange rate did have a positive effect on exports; given that exports previously enjoyed customs exemptions for imported components, it was the exchange rate policy that had stronger effects on increasing exports.[16]

The situation faced by importable goods changed appreciably during Phase II, which lasted from April 1975 until mid-1977. During this period, reductions in nominal protection were greater than in Phase I, dropping from an average of 52% to 22% in these years. The exchange rate fell 39%, strongly reinforcing the effects of reduced tariffs. Thus, for two years, as the tariff liberalization was carried out, the real exchange rate was parallelly revalued. Consequently, the 30-point reduction in the average nominal tariff meant a 50% fall in the average cost of the import dollar (column 5 of Table 2.2). There was little chance for the country's economy to gradually adjust to the strong impact of this rapid reduction, unexpected because it contradicted repeated official statements that the exchange rate would "indissolubly" compensate for the dismantling of tariffs.[17]

The net result of tariff reforms in Phase II was a rapid increase in "nontraditional" imports, particularly nonfood consumer goods. The resulting deficit in the 1977 balance of payments' current account was covered by an inflow of foreign loans.

In Phase III, which lasted until 1979, when the nominal domestic price of the U.S. dollar was frozen, the exchange rate was periodically adjusted to compensate for tariff reductions, as can be seen in column 5 of Table 2.2. During the first half of this phase the real exchange rate recovered strongly, although it dropped slightly in the second half. Consequently, there were important fluctuations in the average cost of the import dollar during Phase III stemming from adjustments in the exchange rate, even though the average cost at the end of Phase III was about the same as at its beginning. Naturally, products which were relatively more protected at the start of Phase III lost their privileged position as customs duties converged towards a uniform 10%. These changes occurred in an economy which was more sensitive to the evolution of the international economy than it had been during previous stages. The average tariff had dropped from 94% to 10% during these three phases, while the real exchange rate at the end of the process was only 15% above the rate established at the outset of the policy, which culminated in June 1979 with the quasi-unrestricted opening of the economy to foreign trade.

Finally, in Phase IV the real exchange rate was revalued steadily. This appreciation was a consequence of the fixed nominal rate (which was the outcome of the adoption of a monetary approach to the balance of payments) and of a domestic rate of inflation larger than the international rate during the three years in which the exchange rate remained frozen. In June 1982 this phase was ended by an abrupt devaluation.

In short, the tariff policy took shape gradually with successive government announcements, each one of which was presented as the final one.

Thus the policy evolved from one which sought a moderate opening to foreign trade, explicitly declared to be compatible with the process of Andean Pact integration, towards a policy of practically free imports. The "gradual" character of the announcements, whether it was deliberately planned or happened by chance, allowed the executors of the policy to slowly free themselves from the constraints of those within the government who held opposing views. As for the supposed compensatory role of the exchange rate, the facts show that, in general, the exchange rate did not fulfill this function as it should have according to the assumptions of the economic model.

Import Composition

The drastic changes in the structure and level of protection for import substitutes had a significant impact on the composition of imports. As could be predicted, consumer goods, which had previously been the most restricted category, were the most favored by the overall tariff liberalization. Within this category, imports of nonfood consumer goods were the items which showed the largest growth (see Table 2.3).

Many variables other than those of trade policy itself affected the behavior of imports during the transformation of the Chilean economy. Among the most important variables were the intense contraction in aggregate demand in 1975–76 (which caused a drop in imports for those years), the low rate of investment during the entire liberalization period (which produced a drop in annual equipment and machinery imports between 1974–80), and the rise in the cost of oil.[18] Similarly, some groups, such as wheat and corn, experienced variations from year to year owing to fluctuations in external prices or in domestic production.

It is important to examine the variables mentioned above not only to understand the behavior of trade, but also to analyze the repercussions which imports have on economic efficiency, employment, and domestic production. Before examining the interrelationship among these variables, we will look in this section at how the main categories of imports, classified according to their use, changed.

Selecting a base year for comparing data is difficult and, unavoidably, is to some degree arbitrary. As is well known, 1973 was hardly a normal year. Therefore, we shall use the figures for 1970, considered a relatively "normal" year, for comparison, and shall first compare those with the figures for 1980, before the 1981 disequilibria in the external sector became evident.

Between 1970 and 1980, total imports increased 95%. If purchases of fuels and lubricants are subtracted, the increase is 71%. If we consider what happened during the past decade and how radical the import liberalization program actually was, these increases appear relatively modest. We

TABLE 2.3   Main Imports of Consumer Goods and Total Imports, 1970, 1980, 1981 (millions of 1977 US$)

	1970	1980	1981	Percentage variation 1970–81
Main Consumer Imports				
Confectionery items	0.2	8.2	10.5	5,150.0
Leather and fur manufactures	1.3	9.0	17.5	1,246.2
Alcoholic beverages and cigarettes	1.1	22.8	27.5	2,400.0
Carpets, clothing, knitwear, textiles, and fabrics	24.8	171.9	271.6	995.0
Photographic and cinematographic products	8.0	17.4	25.2	215.0
Footwear, hats, umbrellas	2.1	24.0	43.3	1,961.9
Musical and optical instruments	4.4	18.1	28.7	552.3
Toys and recreational goods	3.5	32.0	42.4	1,111.4
Processed foods from cocoa, meat, shellfish, vegetables, and market produce	5.3	34.6	41.3	679.2
Perfumery and cosmetics	0.1	13.7	19.6	19,500.0
Television sets	0.7	49.0	66.2	9,357.1
Radios	4.7	46.0	45.8	874.5
Cars and motorcycles	19.5	144.4	263.0	1,248.7
Total	75.7	591.1	902.6	1,093.0
Total Imports				
I. Total main consumer imports	75.7	591.1	902.6	1,093.0
II. Wheat, maize, and sugar	43.6	309.9	262.1	757.3
III. Fuels and lubricants	118.0	666.9	689.5	484.3
IV. Other consumer and intermediate goods	1,155.5	1,561.2	1,714.3	48.4
V. Transport equipment	157.4	317.5	395.8	151.5
VI. Other capital goods	408.6	376.6	480.6	17.6
Total	1,958.8	3,823.2	4,444.9	127.0

Sources: National Customs Authority for 1970 and categories II, III, V, and VI; import registers of the Central Bank for the rest in 1980 and 1981.

must, nevertheless, keep three factors in mind. First, the increased petroleum price is, for Chile, a permanent feature which requires the country to generate additional resources to pay for the larger expense, either by reducing other imports or by expanding exports. Second, in 1980 imports of equipment and machinery, as a share of GDP, were significantly below 1970. Third, GDP per capita barely increased during the period under consideration. The result is that imports other than equipment and machinery, per unit of GDP, grew 70% between 1970 and 1980, and three-quarters of the rise was concentrated between 1977 and 1980.

In short, total imports measured in terms of constant purchasing power grew significantly compared to domestic economic activity. This was predictable, given the drastic liberalization of imports. Increased imports were not a response to an income effect, as per capita production was practically stagnant,[19] but rather were due predominantly to the liberalization program.

Different import categories behaved heterogeneously. The influence of the liberalization policy, at the aggregate level we are working with in this section, can be observed mainly in the nonfood consumer goods category, where the greatest number of "new" nontraditional imports are concentrated. Purchases of nonfood consumer goods increased 282% between 1970 and 1980. For the period in which the liberalization took place—that is, from 1973 through 1980—nonfood consumer good imports rose 273%.

The share of machinery and equipment in total imports dropped from 20% to 11%, and their participation in GDP fell by one-fifth. This decrease reflects the lack of investment which the economic policy brought with it during these past years. At the same time, patterns of investment were probably also related to the abrupt and extreme character of the opening to foreign trade, as I will suggest in the following section.

Although I am conscious of the limitations of the figures, in Table 2.3 I show the groups of consumer items (food and nonfood) which most increased between 1970, 1980, and 1981, the latter a year of record imports.[20] The thirteen groups disaggregated in this table cover 70% of all consumer good imports in 1981. During the eleven-year period they grew over 1,000%—that is, at a rate notoriously larger than even that of fuels (which increased 484%). As can be seen, most of these nontraditional imports are items which had traditionally been considered dispensable or luxury. In several cases the varieties of these new imported items were not locally produced, even though they did replace similar domestically produced items. There has, then, been a significant diversification in the composition of consumption.

Despite the great diversification of the types and models of imports, consumption of goods whose imports have grown most significantly is highly concentrated. Naturally, this phenomenon is related to the concentration of income and wealth, although this effect is magnified by the fact that consumption by income levels is more concentrated for importable goods than for total consumption (Table 2.4). Undoubtedly, the low-income sectors have been able to buy new varieties of consumer products, but these purchases have been limited by their scarce purchasing power. In the meantime, these consumer imports have negative economic implications, as I shall discuss in the last section of this chapter.

TABLE 2.4   Distribution by Income Brackets of Consumption of Imported
Goods, 1978: Main Nontraditional Import Items (percentage of total
consumption)

Item	Highest 20% of households	Middle 60% of households	Lowest 20% of households
Color television sets	100.0	0.0	0.0
Automobiles	98.6	1.4	0.0
Imported whiskey	94.0	6.0	0.0
Imported cigarettes	92.0	8.0	0.0
Cassettes	72.8	26.8	0.4
Tennis racquets	71.8	28.2	0.0
Electric blenders, mixers, and food processors	71.7	28.3	0.0
Motorcycles	65.3	34.7	0.0
Watches	59.7	34.7	5.6
Toys	56.1	41.4	2.5
Stereo equipment, record players, and tape recorders	51.3	48.5	0.2
Transistor radios	32.9	57.8	9.3
Black-and-white television sets	18.8	71.2	10.0
All items	51.0	43.8	5.2

Note: Unless otherwise specified, includes consumption of domestic and imported goods.
   Source: Instituto Nacional de Estadística, *III Encuesta de Presupuestos Familiares,* vol. 3
(Santiago, May 1979).

In the years since the coup, the distribution of income and wealth has
deteriorated significantly.[21] Between 1973 and 1975, wages and salaries
lost between 24% and 37% of the purchasing power that they had had in
1970. In 1981, average wages were still lower than at the beginning of the
seventies, according to the official index of wages and salaries deflated by
the corrected consumer price index.[22] This deterioration was reinforced by
a large increase in the unemployment rate: it went from 5% to an average
of 17% in 1974–81, and stood at 27% during 1982.

As for the distribution of consumption, according to family budget
surveys in Santiago done by the National Institute of Statistics (INE), families in the upper quintile increased their share of total consumption from
44.5% to 51% between 1969 and 1978, while families in the lowest quintile
decreased their share from 7.6% to 5.2%. According to this survey, the last
available, consumption by the poorest fifth of the population, properly
deflated, decreased 31% between 1969 and 1978. The 1978 survey also
reflects the concentration of the consumption of nontraditional imports that

year. As can be seen in Table 2.4, the richest quintile of the population consumed a high percentage of the main imported goods. In eleven of the thirteen groups of importables included in that table, the richer quintile spends a proportion of total Chilean expenditures in the given group that exceeds the bracket's average share in total consumption (51% in 1978). The two groups in which this income strata purchases less than its average include "inferior goods": for the higher-income levels, purchases of black-and-white television sets are replaced by color televisions, and transistor radios are passed over in favor of stereo sets and table radios.[23] This change in the composition of consumption takes place at relatively high income levels; in 1978 the middle-income brackets were intensive consumers of transistor radios and black-and-white televisions, as can be seen in column 2 of Table 2.4.

Overall Effects of the Liberalization on Industry

Evaluating the effects of the liberalization process is a complex task. First, the effects which occurred within each phase were quite different from the effects in the other phases. Second, there were many other important changes which took place simultaneously with the liberalization process. On the one hand, there was a drop in aggregate demand, wages, and investment, and a rise in unemployment; these factors influenced strongly the nature of the adjustment process. On the other hand, the export expansion, which began before the impact of the liberalization process was substantial, contributed in a certain degree to the recovery of economic activity and offered opportunities for investment in that sector.

In the first part of this section I will examine the global changes in the industrial sector. In the second part, I will try to examine more in depth the effects of import liberalization by studying the behavior of some product categories representative of the industrial sector.

MICROECONOMIC EFFECTS

This section will examine the overall changes in industrial production. The data appear in Table 2.5.

Industrial production was drastically affected by the economic recession of 1975. That year, industrial output dropped 25%, while the GDP fell 13%. As could be predicted, this meant that the subsequent recovery was more intensive in the industrial sector than in the others, producing high rates of "growth" from 1976 to 1979. Still, this recovery was not sufficient to recoup the industrial sector's share in GDP at the outset of the liberalization process. In 1981, more than eight years after the orthodox economic policy was first implemented, industrial value added per capita was still below its 1970 level and was 6% less than its 1973 value, as can be seen in

TABLE 2.5   Manufacturing Output: Chile and the World Economy
(1973 = 100)

Year	Value added per inhabitant of Chile	Total value added		
		Chile	Developing countries	Industrialized countries
1974	95.8	97.4	106.3	100.1
1975	70.2	72.6	108.1	91.8
1976	73.2	77.0	116.7	100.1
1977	78.1	83.5	125.3	103.7
1978	83.8	91.3	133.6	107.9
1979	89.0	98.5	139.7	113.3
1980	92.9	104.6	146.8	112.3
1981	93.7	107.3	147.0	112.8
1982	72.0	83.8	149.6	108.5

Sources: For Chile, calculations based on Banco Central, Cuentas nacionales de Chile, 1960-1980; for developing and industrialized countries, United Nations, Monthly Bulletin of Statistics, May 1983.

Table 2.5. The unsatisfactory behavior of industrial production resulted in a notorious drop in the share of manufacturing in the gross domestic product. Finally, this deterioration is also revealed in industrial employment: since 1976 it has remained at levels markedly lower than those of 1970. This was caused in part by the diminished importance of labor-intensive industrial activities such as the production of textiles and garments. But there was also a drop of employment in areas where production increased (2 digits of the International Standard Industrial Classification [ISIC] rev. 2) according to data for 1970 and 1979 released by the SOFOFA, one of the country's main industrial employer's associations.

Consequently, even the official figures reveal the lack of substance in statements which claimed that the industrial sector had been behaving dynamically. On the contrary, overall production and employment in the manufacturing sector was deficient from 1973 through 1981, and output in 1982 fell 22%.

It is revealing to compare the evolution of output in the manufacturing sector to its trend in the sixties. Column 2 of Table 2.6 presents a hypothetical alternative for the evolution of industrial value added for the years 1970-82. "Normal" production is estimated for the 1970-73 period using the historical growth rate for industrial value added during the 1960s (5.9% per year).[24] To compile estimates for the 1974-80 period, I applied the 1960s growth rate to the actual value of production in 1974. Finally, in order to take into account international recessionary effects, I used the rate

TABLE 2.6   Actual and "Normal" Manufacturing Output (millions of 1977 US$)

Year	Value added		Output losses	
	Actual (1)	Historical growth (2)	Annual (3)	Cumulative (4)
1970	3,225.2	3,371.0		
1971	3,666.6	3,569.9	96.7	96.7
1972	3,769.5	3,780.5	−11.0	85.7
1973	3,524.0	4,003.5	−479.5	−393.8
1974	3,492.6	3,492.6	0.0	0.0
1975	2,535.9	3,698.7	−1,162.8	−1,162.8
1976	2,708.7	3,916.9	−1,208.2	−2,371.0
1977	3,039.4	4,148.0	−1,108.6	−3,479.6
1978	3,276.7	4,392.7	−1,116.0	−4,595.6
1979	3,565.0	4,651.9	−1,086.9	−5,682.5
1980	3,785.8	4,926.4	−1,140.6	−6,823.1
1981	3,883.5	4,970.7	−1,087.2	−7,910.3
1982	3,033.0	5,015.4	−1.982.4	−9,892.7

Note: Manufacturing value added for 1977, expressed in 1977 pesos, was divided by the average exchange rate for that year. This value was used to construct the series in column 1, utilizing the annual real rates of change in the ODEPLAN series, which was expressed in 1965 pesos. The figures for 1980–82 are based on the rates of change provided by the new national accounts. Column 2 is based on the 1960–69 annual cumulative growth rate of industrial value added. This rate (5.9%), compounded annually, was applied to the actual value of 1969, to estimate 1970–73, and to that of 1974 to estimate 1975–80. For 1980–82 a rate of 0.9% was used equal to the average increase of manufacturing value added in LDCs in this period.

Source: Oficina de Planificación Nacional (ODEPLAN).

of growth of manufacturing in LDCs (0.9%) for 1980–82. This methodology assumes implicitly that the usable productive capacity at the beginning of the 1974–82 period was 5% less in 1974 than in 1971, judging from the output figures for those years. A low outcome is supported by two facts: investment was low in the 1971–73 period and the sector's organization was disrupted, with some of the deterioration probably being irrecoverable. Nevertheless, assertions by supporters of the military coup that the industry was "destroyed" in 1973 are belied by the resumption of production immediately after the September 1973 coup: there was no generalized destruction, although there definitely was a halt to growth, as can be seen in columns 3 and 4. Presumably, the methodology which takes the actual level of industrial production as representative of its "normalized" level does not overestimate, but rather clearly underestimates, the actual productive capacity in 1974, because the excessive contraction of aggregate demand had already begun in the second half of 1974 and was negatively affecting the annual level of output.[25] The effect can be partially seen by observing that between October 1973 and September 1974—that is, during the first twelve-month period of the new government—industrial production was 3.4% higher than during the 1974 calendar year.

The gaps between actual and trend production in the period 1975–82, which are evident from data in columns 3 and 4, were caused by a series of events. Output losses in 1975 were due primarily to the contraction of aggregate demand.[26] During the 1977–80 period, however, production presumably responded principally to the changes in demand patterns induced by the across-the-board liberalization of imports, by the concentration of income, and by the drop in domestic investment. For every one of those years, effective production was about 25% below "normal."[27] This loss of production, measured by the method described above, is remarkably large. Between 1975 and 1982 the cumulative production gap totaled US$10 billion in 1977 dollars (column 4).[28]

As I have repeatedly pointed out, the behavior of production responds to many variables, stemming from both internal and external factors. Nevertheless, even without distinguishing the separate effects of these factors, we can see from Tables 2.5 and 2.6 that there is no basis for claims that industry has grown at an accelerated rate.[29] All that happened was that by 1980 industry recovered output levels of six or eight years before, with a consequent loss in the country's relative position in the world, as can be seen by comparing row 2 of Table 2.5 with rows 3 and 4. Production losses, which in a significant part stemmed from domestic policies after 1973, should be calculated as part of the cost of the transformation imposed on the economy during these years.

It is undeniable that the import liberalization did not "destroy" national industry as a whole, just as it is all the more undeniable that it was not destroyed in 1972–73. The liberalization did, however, contribute strongly to the overall poor performance of the industrial sector and of the entire Chilean economy between 1973 and 1982. The productive capacity of the sector was seriously damaged, many firms were destroyed, and various areas of production practically disappeared. And the net balance is overwhelmingly negative. The information presented below provides additional support for these assertions.

EFFECTS ON THE STRUCTURE OF INDUSTRIAL PRODUCTION

The structure of industrial output changed significantly during the 1970s. To detect more precisely the impact of import liberalization on the industrial sector, we must examine the behavior of the different production branches.

The close relationship between the domestic industrial sector and foreign trade can be seen first in the global evolution of exports and imports of manufactured goods.[30] Industrial exports grew significantly from 1974 until they totaled 10% of the gross value of the sector's production in 1981, while imports equaled 21% of the sector's production value. The respective figures for 1969–70 were 3% and 18%. It is well known that the behavior of exports is not unequivocally tied to import policy; furthermore, export promotion can be fully compatible with a policy of selective import substitution.[31] Because of this, the effects of import and export policies on domestic production can be analyzed separately.

There are few studies available on the sectoral effects of import liberalization (and export expansion).[32] Here, I will discuss briefly the data available for the period 1969/70 to 1978, which covers most of the process of deep liberalization. It is clear, however, that all the effects of the policy had not yet been felt by 1978 and that the subsequent performance of the economy has provided a much more negative balance than could have been envisioned in that year.

Information broken down into twenty-nine groups (ISIC, rev. 2, 3 digits) shows that the composition of consumption, output, and trade changed substantially during the decade. First, foreign trade was dynamic in the period 1969/70 to 1978 in the sense that exports increased in sixteen groups while imports rose in eighteen;[33] moreover, both imports and exports grew in ten of these groups, implying that, at the level of three-digit information, there was intra-industrial specialization. There were drops in output and consumption in seventeen groups each, while in fourteen of these branches both output and consumption decreased. This suggests that domestic demand decisively influenced output in the period we are studying.

At the level of disaggregation we are working with, many of the groups include goods whose production processes and marketing channels are quite diverse among themselves. Notwithstanding this heterogeneity, the information allows advancing some conclusions.

First, only two groups show a growth in production which is associated with exports (wood and paper); in two groups exports play a significant role (food and industrial chemicals), even though this role is not as prominent as in the preceding groups.[34] When data is broken down still further, it can be shown that a large share of export expansion concentrated in only six "products": pulp and paper, wood, molybdenum oxide, fishmeal, and semi-wrought copper. After a sizeable diversification in the period 1974–76, the share of these products fell in 1976 to 58% of industrial exports, but in 1978 it rose to 64% and in 1981 to 66%.

For imports, diversification was greater, as shown in the second section of this chapter. This diversification is also reflected by the larger number of groups where imports are significant. Three groups were strongly affected by imports: electrical machinery, transport equipment, and professional equipment. In the first two groups, the rise in domestic demand ameliorated the negative impact of imports on production, while in the third group, a receding domestic demand exacerbated the negative impact. In six groups, the opening to foreign trade together with a significant impact from the reduction in domestic demand led to a decline in output (textiles, wearing apparel, leather, petroleum derivatives, pottery and china, and nonelectrical machinery). In four other groups (footwear, printing and publishing, nonmetallic minerals, and iron and steel), the determinant variable in declining output until 1978 seemed to have been the decrease in domestic demand. One group (other chemical products), showed remarkable increases in consumption and production, although foreign trade was small. Data on the other groups is more difficult to interpret as the results depend largely on which years are compared, the adjustments made in the data in order to homogenize it, and the methodology used to estimate the change of each variable.

As can be demonstrated, the behavior of domestic demand had a decisive effect on the level of production. To a certain degree, this effect makes it difficult to evaluate the impact of import liberalization, while changes in demand contributed to the increased export of items in oversupply on the local market. Naturally, to the extent that domestic demand has recovered (although with a persistant, deteriorated distributive pattern), the relative weight of different variables changed; thus, after 1978 the consequences of import liberalization gained weight vis-à-vis aggregate demand as an explanatory factor of the poor performance of manufacturing. It was clear that, by 1978, the effects of import liberalization were not fully realized. At that stage, the trends shown by the data indicated that export growth was loosing speed, while imports, particularly of consumer goods, were rising fast. This trend was manifest in 1978 and in 1979, before the nominal exchange rate was fixed. Subsequently, the freezing of this rate and the real appreciation of the peso that followed reinforced the lagged effects of import liberalization. Consequently, the opening to foreign trade had larger detrimental effects on industrial production than studies through 1980 had detected. The negative impact of nontraditional imports increased its weight as compared to the effects of exports and of changes in domestic demand. Aggregate demand became more intensive in imported components, the quantum of non-resource-based exports ceased growing in 1980, and imports (especially of consumer durables, as shown in Table 2.3) rose even faster than in the previous two years. The outcome was even worse in 1981.

To complete this section, let us touch briefly on two themes. First, we will look at some additional information on the textile sector. Then we will examine some of the adjustment mechanisms which industry used to face liberalized imports.

The textile sector, in addition to being one of the industrial sectors with the most available information, is important because of its weight in production and employment in manufacturing. The textile industry is also significant because it was one of the sectors most negatively affected by the current economic policy.

By the late sixties, the textile sector represented about 13% of the value added in manufacturing. In 1980, this figure dropped to 9%.[35] On the basis of information available for 1978, increased imports—which multiplied by four between 1970 and 1978—had by then captured an estimated, at the very least, one-sixth of the market that had formerly been supplied by domestic textile and clothing producers. Meanwhile, less than 1% of the sector's sales were exports.[36] Between 1978 and 1980 real imports grew 75%, and a further shock was suffered by the domestic textile industry in 1981, when imports accelerated even further while exports were disappearing. By the latter date, imports were capturing over half of the market that had previously been supplied by domestic producers. Thus, this relatively labor-intensive sector was seriously shocked by the implementation of the free trade policy.

At the time the new foreign trade policy was adopted, the textile sector was one of the most protected. The average nominal tariff for the sector was 100% (127% on final goods) in 1974. This figure dropped to 29% (33% on final goods) by 1977. Thus, in the course of three years, the textile sector faced a significant reduction in the protection which it enjoyed. The sector was also affected, however, by changes both in overall aggregate demand and in income distribution. The sequencing of phenomena—the opening to foreign trade and changes in demand—differs in time, a fact that must be kept in mind in order to understand what happened in the textile and clothing sector.[37]

From the beginning, the sector was strongly affected by the current economic model. Price liberalization caused a relative rise of prices in the sector. With the recession that began in 1974, textile and clothing demand, and later production, suffered a decline that was notably more rapid and stronger than that in the rest of the manufacturing sector. This decline caused a reduction of relative prices during 1974.[38] In broad terms, it was not until 1976 that the opening to foreign trade influenced the sector substantially. Nevertheless, in keeping with the overall behavior of the industry, while the recovery of aggregate demand took place, it had a positive effect on output larger than the negative effect of trade opening. Because of this, production in the textile sector recovered, though slowly. Even this recovery, however, was accompanied by a growing "desubstitution" of domestic inputs. In both textile and clothing production, the ratio between domestic and imported inputs dropped remarkably, most especially in clothing.[39]

Because of the chronological evolution of the relevant variables, until

1978 import liberalization, and the corresponding dramatic increase in the supply of foreign products, was not a force which reduced prices and/or production but rather a constraint on the recovery of relative prices in the sector and on the sector's level of activity. As a result, in 1978 gross production was 13% below 1970, and employment was similarly affected. The number of firms with more than fifty workers appears to have decreased 28%. After 1978, the negative impact on the sector was more drastic. Output fell, losing part of what had been recovered, and relative prices deteriorated somewhat more. By 1980, the domestic relative price for textiles and clothing had worsened by close to 30% as compared to 1970.[40]

The sector adjusted to foreign competition in three ways. One was simply to declare bankruptcy or close down plants.[41] In other cases, firms began to specialize within the industry in two ways: merging with other firms and, to a lesser extent, suspending lines of production within a firm. Finally, firms which survived often not only reduced the number of their production lines, but also began to import goods they marketed instead of those they previously produced. These adjustment mechanisms, which contributed to the survival of industrial activities, were reinforced by a fall in labor costs derived from an increase in average *gross* output per industrial worker and a large fall in real wages. As a whole, there has been no reoutfitting of textile firms through significant investments in machinery. About 1978, there was some recovery in machinery purchases, apparently influenced by revived sales. Nevertheless, investment lagged again after 1979, pari passu with the continued growth of imports and fall of output.

Marketing imported products enabled firms affected by import liberalization to capitalize on the relative advantage they had because of their knowledge of the demand and their sales outlets. This adjustment mechanism had several interesting effects. First, in this case production and importation were not independent functions but were directed by the same decision unit; thus, external competition would be operating in a more limited fashion than is assumed by orthodox theory. Second, a larger share of businesses leaned towards commercial and financial activities rather than performing as producers. The extent of this bias is shown by changes in the composition of gross domestic product recorded in the national accounts: the dynamic sectors are value added in financial activities and in the marketing of imported goods.[42] The resulting foreign exchange gap (growing current account deficit as seen in Table 2.7), which was created by the asymmetrical responses of producers in sectors hurt by new foreign trade policies and producers in sectors favored by them, has been financed by an increase in the foreign debt. Third, although some firms defended themselves by switching to some degree to imports, this switch negatively influenced employment; in fact, as is obvious in a situation like the one described, productive employment decreased per unit of sales and even per unit of output.[43] Many workers were fired outright, and in addition, in some sectors there was a decrease in subcontracting by large enterprises with self-employed workers and small firms. This can be observed, for example, in case studies in the plastics sector.[44]

Elements for an Evaluation

The analysis of foreign trade policies followed by Chile since 1973 is especially interesting for three reasons. First, these policies represent a drastic change from the policies followed by governments with very different orientations during the past forty years and have produced very profound modifications in the national economy.[45] Second, the unrestricted opening to trade has significantly altered the nature of Chile's participation in the international economy. Third, "free-exchange" thinking gained momentum during the last decade in Latin America, partially as a pendulum reaction to "inward-looking development" policies. Therefore, studying the first recent experience in which the model of unrestricted opening has been fully implemented can provide useful information for other developing nations. This study offers the possibility of testing to what degree the results of this policy are related to or differ from the hypothetical results which proponents of the model assume.

In the preceding section, some of the principal effects of the import liberalization policies have been analyzed. As was pointed out, it is difficult to evaluate the effects of the policies which have been followed since 1973. The import liberalization was carried out at the same time other important changes were occurring in the domestic economy.

In these concluding remarks, we will first look briefly at the macroeconomic effects of foreign trade policy on the balance of payments. Next, some points will be raised about the effects which those policies could have on the efficiency, the dynamism, and the competitiveness of the Chilean economy.

BALANCE OF PAYMENTS AND THE CURRENT ACCOUNT

The main foreign sector accounts have changed remarkably, as can be seen in Table 2.7. Practically all of the foreign trade components expanded during the period under study, especially the categories of nontraditional imports and exports. The expansion of imports was larger than that of exports, causing a growing trade deficit which increased markedly between 1976 and 1981. A similar phenomenon occurred in the current account.

Because of "abnormal" levels of important trade components, the content of trade flows must be examined more closely. The two components which deviate most from "normal" values are imports of equipment and machinery, and the price of copper.[46] To recover their relative share of real

TABLE 2.7   Balance of Payments, International Reserves, and Cost of Imports

	1974	1976	1978	1980	1981	1982
Balance of Payments (millions of 1977 US$)						
Balance on current account	−255.8	158.5	−964.5	−1,382.3	−3,347.7	−1,696.1
Trade balance	432.7	692.9	−377.7	−535.8	−1,806.7	155.2
(Exports f.o.b.)	(2,607.3)	(2,280.2)	(2,180.9)	(3,299.7)	(2,753.8)	(2,704.4)
(Imports f.o.b.)	(−2,174.5)	(−1,587.3)	(−2,558.5)	(−3,835.5)	(−4,560.5)	(−2,549.2)
Nonfinancial services	−477.6	−212.3	−215.4	−273.5	−617.5	−462.8
Financial services	−224.2	−351.3	−433.5	−652.2	−993.0	−1,549.7
Net autonomous capital	264.2	214.4	1,725.2	2,219.7	3,316.4	928.5
Direct foreign investment	−20.6	−1.1	156.9	119.2	261.5	259.9
Autonomous credits	284.8	215.5	1,568.3	2,100.5	3,054.9	668.6
Balance of payments	−66.7	446.1	631.2	872.4	48.7	−829.5
Gross international reserves	408.8	667.5	1,245.2	2,943.1	2,659.0	1,839.8
Cost of Imports						
Real exchange rate (1977 pesos per 1977 US$)	23.40	25.89	23.81	20.09	16.93	19.63
Average tariff (% over c.i.f. price)	75.5	35.7	13.7	10.0	10.0	10.1

Source: Calculations based on figures in current US$ of Banco Central, *Balanza de pagos* and *Boletin mensual*, no. 663 (May 1983). Current US$ were deflated by an index of external prices (Ffrench-Davis, "Indice de precios externos," 1981), which is a weighted sum, according to its incidence in Chilean trade, of the indexes of export prices and of the exchange-rate relations of the Federal Republic of Germany, France, Great Britain, Japan, and the United States.

aggregate demand, imports of equipment and machinery should have exceeded by one-quarter their actual 1979–80 level.[47] For its part, copper was priced at about one-seventh lower than the "normal" price.[48] Nevertheless, the net inflow of foreign exchange from copper exports increased as a result of two factors. On the one hand, investments made between 1967 and 1970 made it possible for copper production to increase 50%. On the other, the 1971 nationalization of the large mines permitted the government to capture a greater share of the economic rent (surplus) from the rich Chilean copper deposits.

The current account deficit by 1979–80, which equaled 33% of exports (26% with a "normalized" value), was covered by extraordinarily large capital inflows. Almost all inflows consisted of foreign bank loans; the limited foreign investment that took place was directed primarily to the purchase of already existing businesses. The huge size of foreign loans was a response to a phenomenon common in other developing countries that have had growing access to the international private capital market. In Chile's case, the new resources were captured primarily by the private sector.[49] The large inflow of autonomous capital not only covered the deficit in the current account, but also allowed the accumulation of international reserves, which in 1980 reached a gross level equal to nine months of that year's imports (Table 2.7, line IV).

In short, even after adjusting the value of exports by the normalized copper price, the Chilean foreign trade sector shows a significant deficit in the current account, equivalent to 8% of GDP in 1979–80, and 21% in 1981. Thanks to massive foreign loans, the economy was able to bear the deficit. The crucial question in this area was whether the presumably increasing foreign exchange gap could (*a*) continue to be financed, (*b*) remain stable, and (*c*) avoid pervasive political strings by international private financial institutions. If not, since the Chilean economy has become accustomed to a level of imports which it cannot sustain in the future without a growing inflow of foreign savings, the economy would then be subjected, once again, to a costly process of readjustment. This has actually already happened, and no one should have been surprised by it; the need for adjustment in Chile was a predictable fact, even without the international economic crisis.

EFFICIENCY, DYNAMISM, AND COMPETITION

The theoretical foundation of the current economic policy asserts that resources should be allocated according to "comparative advantages" and that the market, free from government interference, achieves that objective. This theory, which constitutes one of the extremes of the range of many existing economic approaches, implies a simplistic and idealized conception of "comparative advantage." In reality, market comparative advantage depends on the level and stability of the exchange rate, the degree of activity in the domestic and international economies, and many other factors. Market and social comparative advantages are not the same because of the disequilibria and distortions characteristic of developing economies. The differences between the two can be noteworthy in a country facing a radical change in economic policy, with high unemployment, and with a public sector that *abruptly* abandons its guiding and directing role in productive activity. The resulting disequilibria and distortions can be significantly more costly than the inefficient actions of an active public sector, as the recent Chilean experience suggests.

The Macroeconomic Framework and Efficiency

The efficiency of any economic measure depends on the context in which it is applied. The generally recessive domestic economic situation of the period we are studying has been relatively conducive to export promotion, but on the other hand has constituted one factor which has made inconvenient import liberalization policies.

The expansion of exports provided an outlet for excess production which otherwise would not have had a market. In effect, the excessive contraction of domestic demand—in particular, during the period from mid-1974 to mid-1976—left a significant share of the domestic industry with underutilized installed capacity. The rising exchange rate, access to the Andean market, and the efforts of Pro Chile, a government export promotion agency, supplied a market abroad for several firms with excess production. In general, that expansion of nontraditional exports promoted increased efficiency in the allocation of resources, principally through an increase in the rate of utilization of capital and labor.

For imports, the situation has been precisely the opposite. In fact, if a trade liberalization process is excessive, too rapid, or undertaken at the wrong moment, it will provoke premature and unnecessary plant shutdowns, cause the underutilization of capital and labor, and discourage investment. Therefore, to evaluate the effects of the policy on the Chilean economy, we must distinguish the different stages of the liberalization process and consider the macroeconomic context in which it was implemented.

In the first stage (Phase I), clearly excessive levels of protection were eliminated. Therefore, the first tariff reductions affected redundant effective protection and served to limit national producers' ability to set sales prices which would reap abnormally high profit margins.

The character of the second stage (Phases II and III) was distinctly different from that of the previous one. The additional tariff reductions, which lowered the maximum rate of nominal protection from 120% to 10%, had a much greater effect than earlier reductions from the higher previous levels. The impact was heightened as the tariff reduction process was carried out, while the real exchange rate was unstable and dropping (see Table 2.2). Consequently, the behavior of both tariffs and the exchange rate acted to reduce the effective net protection previously enjoyed by import substituting sectors of the economy.

The most painful part of import liberalization was carried out rapidly and its negative effects were reinforced by the exchange rate revaluations. This policy was implemented during a situation in which wages had deteriorated, internal demand was very depressed, investment was low, and open unemployment was remarkably high. These four factors must be closely examined to evaluate the effects of lifting tariffs.

First, wage repression acted as an artificial protection mechanism which, although obviously regressive, compensated for reduced tariffs on imports. In fact, in 1976, the ratio of wages to exchange rate was less than half that of 1970.[50] By 1980, the wage/exchange-rate ratio had recovered only four-fifths of its 1970 level. Because repressed wages lowered direct costs, producers of a wide range of import substitutes could defend themselves against foreign competition.

Second, the recession of economic activity helped make the effects of liberalization less evident, but it also made this process more inefficient. After the recession hit bottom, the economy would inevitably sooner or later begin a recovery towards previous levels of activity. Given the depth of the recession, recovery rates for demand and production should have been high. Since the tariff liberalization took place during this recovery, a superficial observation of data could lead to the conclusion that the liberalization process encouraged the increase of output. As was demonstrated in the preceding section, however, just the opposite occurred. The imposition of a free trade model helped maintain the recovery of domestic production at a level lower than that of the recovery of aggregate demand; the production process and aggregate demand became more and more intensive in imported inputs. The recession itself negatively affected the efficiency of the process. The initially reduced overall demand tended to raise the average cost of production to domestic producers, making it more difficult for them to face foreign competition. At the same time, the widespread underutilization of installed capacity discouraged domestic investment.

The low level of investment was also associated with high domestic interest rates, which were several times above "normal." Real interest rates on the order of 40% between 1975 and 1980 discouraged investment[51] and distorted relative prices and "comparative advantages" observed in the market. This subnormal investment level was clearly insufficient to facilitate a symmetrical or positive adjustment between the sectors which contracted and those which expanded in response to the suppression of tariff protection.

Finally, open unemployment widened the gap between the market and social comparative advantages. A high unemployment rate and an abnormally low level of investment implied that the possibilities of actually achieving an effective reallocation of resources was low. These factors also suggest that the opportunity cost of resources freed by the sectors negatively affected by the opening to foreign trade was lower than their market price. Consequently, the corresponding "desubstitution" of imports of goods whose domestic cost of production was overestimated by the market has been predictably inefficient in many cases.

Consequently, a drastic dismantling of tariff protection should not be undertaken in a situation such as that which existed in the Chilean economy in 1974–79. Some proponents of this policy argued that if the policy had not been implemented so rapidly, it would not have been possible to carry out the policy at all. The answer to this argument is threefold. First, it can be better not to undertake tariff reduction as drastic as those initiated in 1975 (covering Phases II and III) than to attempt them in the midst of a depression. The data discussed in the previous section on the loss of industrial production suggests that short-run costs in this case can be predicted to largely surpass hypothetical long-term benefits. Second, foreign exchange appreciation should not be superimposed on tariff liberalization. This action also flagrantly contradicted the government's repeated assertions that "tariff reductions will be indissolubly accompanied by exchange rate increases." Third, unemployment, low investment, and depressed demand generated a real framework which differed substantially from the theoretical framework on which arguments in favor of free trade were based. It is not superfluous to point out that even if there were full employment, the presence of indirect and dynamic effects and the nature of market information available in a developing country like Chile give theoretical and practical weight to policies which selectively protect national production and which actively regulate the market.[52] These types of policies allow the country to augment social efficiency and increase the amount of investment. Neither excessive protection nor extreme liberalization would be the appropriate solution.

To summarize, the designers of the current policy claimed that the unrestricted liberalization of markets would rapidly lead to an efficient reallocation of resources. They assumed that markets work in a fluid and efficient manner, except when distorted by government intervention. Nevertheless, even in the context of a static analysis, while the markets have shown that they resolve a gamut of problems, they have also demonstrated that they can aggravate certain problems and generate several others. One of the most significant instances of inefficiency caused by the current policy is the marked increase of unemployment. This situation was accentuated by the contraction of many labor-intensive import substitution activities. On the other hand, the expansion of exports enabled jobs to be created. As I pointed out in another study, however, this expansion would also have been essentially compatible with a tariff policy quite different from the one that was implemented.[53]

Dynamism and Efficiency

The conclusions of the preceding paragraph are reinforced when dynamic aspects are incorporated into the analysis. I will confine my discussion to three points, concerning the degree of symmetry of the adjustments, the investment rate, and the "dynamic comparative advantages."

I have already pointed out that the speed of adjustment in the sectors which were hurt and those which were favored by the change in foreign trade policy seems to have been asymmetrical. Presumably, the message to reallocate resources was clearer for sectors which were hurt by the liberalization. This phenomenon was reinforced by the widespread depression of aggregate demand and by high real interest rates which made it difficult for affected firms to continue to stay in business, whether or not they were efficient under "normal" or socially optimum conditions. All these factors made it hard for potential investors to identify those productive areas with a comparative advantage.

A remarkably low level of gross domestic investment contributed to the asymmetrical character of the adjustment. It is obvious that reallocation is easier in an economy with a high rate of growth. The stagnation exhibited by the national economy during the period made it necessary for many of the hurt sectors to reduce absolute output in order for the relative adjustment to take place. Limited sectoral and regional mobility of resources and the reduced rate of investment were obstacles to the effective reallocation of freed resources: it was predominantly the expansion achieved in the export sector, therefore, which compensated for the resulting lack of dynamism in the economy. As I have previously stated, a growing proportion of the scarce domestic investment was channeled to the export sector. This investment was concentrated mainly in activities intensive in natural resources. Investment was less significant in products which were intensive in value added to a natural resource base and in "acquirable" comparative advantage.[54] In fact, available background information supports the hypothesis that it was easier to identify comparative advantages which possessed a strong natural resource base. The many changes taking place in the Chilean economy, depressed internal demand, an unstable exchange rate, and the extreme passivity of the public sector made it difficult to identify the whereabouts of possible comparative advantages in the rest of the country's economic activities. The existence of *diffuse* comparative advantages has presumably been one of the factors explaining the low rate of investment.

Competition and Efficiency

One result the government's economists expected from the import liberalization was an increased "competitiveness" in the domestic market. This would be achieved by the effective or virtual presence of importable foreign products which would put an upper limit on the domestic price. It is undeniable that this did happen to a significant degree. What also happened, however, was that there were important deviations from the types of relationships that were supposed to characterize a "competitive" economy.

First, a significant proportion of the nontraditional imports were in categories in which product differentiation played a decisive role. Consequently, competition among suppliers of these products was based to a larger degree on product differentiation than on pricing. The segmentation of the capital market (one example of which is the persistent gap between domestic and foreign interest rates) also brought an element of competition based on the terms of suppliers of credit. These factors provoked effects quite distinct from those which "competition" should have generated according to orthodox theory. Secondly, marketing channels are not completely open to any competitor. Consequently, in a number of cases, the producer of import substitutes became an importer of "competitive" goods. Third, the opening to foreign trade promoted a greater concentration in the management and ownership of domestic productive activities. This phenomenon was reinforced by the depression in aggregate demand and by the manner in which the capital market operated. These factors gave an important advantage to economic groups linked to financial activities and having access to foreign credit.

Finally, two types of problems arose in some products in cases in which the domestic price was in line with the external price. One problem was that foreign suppliers would dump into Chile extras or leftovers from the previous season abroad; for instance, this happened with powdered milk and textiles. The other problem was linked to the sizeable fluctuations in international prices, as occurred, for example, in the cases of wheat and sugar. The elimination of redundant protection and the absence of stabilizing nontariff barriers expedited the transmission into the domestic economy of the instability of international markets for those products. The susceptibility of domestic output to occasional dumping and to the fluctuations of international prices induced a reallocation of resources which tended to be inefficient for the national economy, since it responded to misleading short-run marketing signals. Furthermore, instability itself tends to foster "speculative" activities at the expense of "productive" investment.

A crucial argument for free trade policy refers to the benefits which competition allegedly brings to consumers, with the availability of a wider variety of goods, lower prices, and greater efficiency.

Within the framework of orthodox consumer theory, the opening to foreign trade is seen as positive because it allows demanders to equalize their marginal utility to the marginal cost of importation (which is assumed to be the same as the international price because Chile is a "small country"). The diversification of consumption is seen as welfare-increasing, as it would raise the freedom of choice of the consumer. In the second section of this chapter, I referred to the direct incidence which the opening and diversification had for consumers at different income brackets. Here, it is appropriate to add two comments, one concerning the indirect effects which these have on consumers in their role as producers, and the other concerning the impact on efficiency and on the level of economic activity.

First, the "desubstitution" of imports contributed, at least during the adjustment process, to directly generate unemployment and to retard the recovery of the economy's aggregate level of activity. This latter factor indirectly discouraged investment, which in turn had a negative impact on the creation of new job opportunities. Therefore, low-income consumers (who suffered the highest levels of unemployment), in their roles as producers (workers), bore much higher costs than the contingent benefits derived from the diversification of the basket actually available in the market to those with the corresponding purchasing power. Second, the diversification of consumption enabled a small, high-income sector to rapidly assume the consumption patterns of the well-off in the world's richest economies. The notorious increase in the income and wealth inequality taking place during these years apparently manifested itself more in a noticeable differentiation of lifestyles than in higher savings rates destined for productive investment. The drop in the rate of national savings which occurred both in relation to 1970 and 1973 supports this hypothesis. Finally, from the point of view of economic activity, unrestricted imports contributed to a fragmentation of demand for those types of goods in which product differentiation plays an important role. Naturally, this made it difficult for domestic producers to take advantage of economies of scale and contributed to raise average production costs. In cases of imperfect substitutes, the opening to foreign trade could thus result in price rises instead of reductions.

The Chilean experience has definitely taught heterodox lessons. The national economy had excessive margins of protection for innumerable import categories; therefore, some degree of trade liberalization and a search for greater dynamic complementation between import substitution and export promotion was required.[55] However, trade liberalization was excessive and ill-timed. What was lacking, as in other fields of economic policy, was the adaptation of theoretical concepts to the specific nature of the Chilean economy. On the other hand, it appears that the overall economy and the industrial sector have a certain capacity to adjust to changes in relative prices, even under the unfavorable conditions which the domestic market suffered as a consequence of the nature of the model imposed in 1973. At the same time, it is clear that part of that capacity to respond, particularly in the export sector, was based on the industrial development previously achieved through import substitution. Finally, the conventional hypothesis that an unrestricted opening to foreign trade would promote the expansion of labor intensive activities and result in a contraction of capital-intensive activities appears at least partially contradicted by the characteristics of changes which occurred in the productive structure and in the rate of utilization of available resources. This development was directly linked to the framework in which trade was liberalized, to the excessive intensity and lack of selectivity of that liberalization, to the passive role which was imposed on the public sector, and to the absence of a national development strategy.

Notes

This chapter was written and published in Spanish in 1980 as "Liberalización de las importaciones: La experiencia chilena en 1973-79," *Colección Estudios CIEPLAN,* no. 4 (November 1980). Its contents have not been changed except for the revision and updating of tables and some slight adjustments to the text in order to include discussion of the period 1980-82.

1. R. Ffrench-Davis, "Exports and Industrialization in an Orthodox Model: Chile, 1973-78," *Revista de la CEPAL,* no. 9 (December 1979); "Las experiencias cambiarias en Chile; 1965-79," *Colección Estudios CIEPLAN,* no. 2 (December 1979); and "Exchange Rate Rules," in J. Williamson, ed., *The Crawling Peg: Past Performance and Prospects* (London: Macmillan, 1981).

2. An examination of the foreign trade policies followed in 1972 appears in H. Assael, "Cómo manejar una 'sequía' de divisas?" *Panorama Económico,* no. 269 (June 1972).

3. Statement of 7 June 1974, reprinted in Dirección de Presupuestos (Dipres), *Somos realmente independientes gracias al esfuerzo de todos los chilenos* (Santiago: Ministerio de Hacienda, 1978), p. 61. This source contains the minister's various declarations.

4. Finance Minister, October 1974, reprinted ibid. The minister reconfirmed this goal on 24 April 1975 (ibid., p. 172).

5. See S. De la Cuadra, "La protección efectiva en Chile," *Documento de Trabajo,* no. 22 (1974), sec. 5; and D. Hachette, "Estrategias de liberación del comercio exterior chileno," *Estudios Monetarios* 4 (1976):63.

6. Chile, Banco Central, *Memoria anual de 1975,* 1976, p. 93.

7. The Andean Pact tariff regulations were analyzed in A. Aninat, "El programa de liberación y el arancel externo común en el Acuerdo de Cartagena," in E. Tironi, ed., *El Pacto Andino: Carácter y perspectivas* (Lima: Instituto de Estudios Peruanos, 1978).

8. Information on the tariffs charged in South Korea in 1976 and the targets of a planned tariff reduction appears in B. Balassa, *Policy Reforms in Developing Countries* (New York: Pergamon, 1977), pp. 148-51; also see C. Frank, K. Kim, and L. Westphal, *Foreign Trade Regimes and Economic Development: South Korea* (New York: NBER, 1975), and F. Fajnzylber, *ECLA Review,* no. 15 (December 1981).

9. P. Mendive, "Proteccionismo y desarrollo: Nuevos obstáculos de los centros al comercio internacional," *Revista de la CEPAL,* no. 6 (second semester 1978).

10. Ibid. The data refer to averages for the goods included in the study, which takes in a broad range of exported goods or those which Latin American countries are interested in exporting. The dispersion of the effective rates of protection by items or "products" is very high; for example, cigarettes have a high rate of 405% in Japan, refined oil has a rate of 466% in the United States, and butter, 1300% in the European Economic Community. The background information refers to the pre-Tokyo round of negotiations.

11. The estimate is based on twenty-six chapters of the Brussels Trade

Nomenclature, which considers products heavily affected by nontariff regulations. See V. Roningen and A. Yeats, "Non-Tariff Distortions of International Trade," *Weltwirtschaftliches Archiv*, no. 112 (1976).

12. An analysis which provides theoretical support for selective tariffs as an effective development policy mechanism for semi-industrialized countries and which examines the implications of alternative nontariff regulations is presented in R. Ffrench-Davis, *Economía internacional: Teorías y políticas para el desarrollo* (Mexico City: Fondo de Cultura Económica, 1979), chaps. 7 and 9.

13. See, for example, speeches by the minister of economy and by the director of the National Planning Office (ODEPLAN), on 29 August 1976 and 27 September 1976, respectively, reprinted in Dipres, *Somos realmente independientes*, pp. 275 and 291.

14. The dates covered by each phase and the levels of the real exchange rate are somewhat arbitrary, as they are sensitive to the price indexes used to calculate them; the same problem occurs with respect to figures on the average tariff, which can be calculated in very different ways. For the average tariff figures, I present the same calculations that are used by different government and private sources. As for the real exchange rate, sizeable swings in the rate are not affected by which indexes are used to compute it, although absolute levels of the rate are. Compare, for example, cols. 1 and 2, Table 4, in R. Ffrench-Davis, "Las experiencias cambiarias en Chile, 1965–79," *Colección Estudios CIEPLAN*, no. 2 (December 1979). Here, I use new information on Chilean inflation as measured by a revised index of consumer prices (R. Cortázar and J. Marshall, "Indice de precios al consumidor en Chile, 1970–1978," *Colección Estudios CIEPLAN*, no. 4 [November 1980].

15. Obviously, the nominal tariff for some products, in particular for consumer goods, dropped notably more than the fall in the average tariff. The corresponding reduction in effective protection was even sharper. Therefore, for many of these categories, the rise in the real exchange rate did not compensate for the effects of tariff liberalization. Data on the effective and nominal tariffs before tariff liberalization appear in J. Behrman, *Foreign Trade Regimes and Economic Development: Chile* (New York: NBER, 1976), pp. 137–44, and in De la Cuadra, "La protección efectiva en Chile." Information on the situation in 1975 appears in Junta del Acuerdo de Cartagena, "Protecciones efectivas vigentes en los países miembros" (Junta del Acuerdo de Cartagena, División de Política Económica mimeo, June 1976).

16. Ffrench-Davis, "Exports and Industrialization."

17. A notable deterioration in real wages effectively acted as a protective factor, despite the obviously regressive effects. See the last section of this chapter.

18. Increased spending in crude oil imports—the principal component of this category—was a result not only of higher prices, but also of a 128% increase in volume. Fuel and lubricant purchases rose from 6% to 16% of total imports between 1970 and 1980.

19. According to statistics of the government's National Planning Office (ODEPLAN), the GDP per capita grew barely 12% between 1970 and 1980.

Imports other than those of equipment and machinery more than doubled per capita.

20. Primary and intermediate goods have not been totally eliminated from these figures. This exaggerates the absolute amount but underestimates the rate of increase. At the same time, the absolute amount is underestimated by two other factors: first, there is a lack of data on imports from the free zones; and second, the aggregation of the information processed by the Central Bank did not permit identification of several nontraditional imports.

21. At the end of 1978, two economic groups controlled companies which represented about 50% of the wealth of corporations registered on the Santiago and Valparaíso stock exchanges. This figure is notably higher than in 1970 (J. E. Herrera and J. Morales, "La inversión financiera externa: El caso de Chile, 1974–78," *Colección Estudios CIEPLAN*, no. 1 [July 1979], p. 148). Information about the 250 largest private companies in Chile, both domestic and foreign, indicates that these two groups control at least 37% of the stock of these firms. See F. Dahse, *El mapa de la extrema riqueza* (Santiago: Editorial Aconcagua, 1979), pp. 146–47.

22. R. Cortázar, "Distribución del ingreso, empleo y remuneraciones reales en Chile, 1970–78," *Colección Estudios CIEPLAN*, no. 3 (June 1980), Table 1; Cortázar and Marshall, "Indice de precios al consumidor en Chile, 1970–1978"; and R. Ffrench-Davis, "The Monetarist Experiment in Chile: A Critical Survey," *World Development*, November 1983.

23. J. Scherman, "Distribución del consumo de bienes importados no-tradicionales" (CIEPLAN mimeo, April 1980).

24. Since the 1970 output was lower than "normal," partly owing to the effects of that year's presidential election on production and on sales in the domestic economy, the rate of "normal" growth is also applied to the actual production of 1969 in order to provide a hypothetical estimate of 1970 production. It appears this method does not overestimate production, as the actual production of 1971 was 3% larger than the "normalized" figure for that year.

25. To this was added the large drop in real wages which resulted from the new economic policy; if the surveys taken in January, April, and July by the Instituto Nacional de Estadisticas (INE) are considered, the average decrease is 16% compared to those same months in 1973. The decrease strongly influenced sectors which produced goods intensively demanded by middle- and low-income consumer groups. An outstanding example is that of the textile and clothing branches, which I discuss at the end of the next subsection of the text; see also J. Scherman, "La industria textil y de prendas de vestir y la apertura al exterior: Chile 1974–78" (CIEPLAN mimeo, October 1980).

26. The contraction of aggregate demand was associated, in part, with the worsening in terms of trade and in the balance of payments beginning with the second half of 1974. However, the direct impact of the decrease in the terms of trade on GDP, which in 1975 was 6% with respect to 1974, is already discounted from national account figures which refer to real GDP (gasto del producto interno bruto real). On the other hand, one should not forget that the decrease in 1975 followed a strong rise of the price of copper during 1973–74. In fact,

during the first year in which the current economic policy was applied, the copper price was extremely high. Nevertheless, the 1975 external shock necessarily involved internal adjustment costs. The size of those costs depended on, among other things, access to foreign credit and the economic policy which was adopted.

27. Estimates based on the SOFOFA index, disaggregated by group (3 digits of the ISIC rev. 2) show that productive capacity would be 37% greater than actual output in 1978 using the "maximum historical" method with moving bimesters (J. Ramos, "Tienen sentido políticas de estímulo a la demanda en Chile" [mimeo, Departamento de Economía, Universidad de Chile, November 1979]). Also see SOFOFA, *Encuesta industrial trimestral,* October 1977, and *III Encuesta industrial trimestral,* August 1978, for estimates on unused installed capacity gathered in surveys of businessmen taken in October 1977 and August 1978. These estimates give utilization indexes of about 75%. The index of actual production for the period October 1973–September 1974 was 10% higher than that of 1978, according to data on rates of change in value added estimated by ODEPLAN.

28. Adoption of a free trade policy should reduce, presumably for several years, the pace of expansion of the manufacturing sector. This reduction should be compensated by growth in the remaining economic activities. This compensatory growth concentrated in value added by financial activities and by marketing of imported goods. See Ffrench-Davis, "The Monetarist Experiment."

29. Furthermore, the SOFOFA gross industrial production index after three years of high rates of recovery, started showing very moderate increases as of the second quarter of 1979.

30. The figures that follow are mostly derived from P. Vergara, "Apertura externa y desarrollo industrial en Chile, 1974-1978," *Colección Estudios CIEPLAN,* no. 4 (November 1980).

31. An account of different country experiences appears in J. Bhagwati, *Foreign Trade Regimes and Economic Development: Anatomy and Consequences of Exchange Control Regimes* (New York: NBER, 1978), chap. 8.

32. Among the few are the studies made by Durán, Instituto Textil, Pollack, Scherman, Vergara, and Wilson. They are discussed briefly in the Spanish version of this paper (*Colección Estudios CIEPLAN,* no. 4 [November 1980]). There are also industrial surveys done by SOFOFA which include evaluations by businessmen representing about 300 firms on the impact of import liberalization. See SOFOFA, *Encuesta industrial trimestral.* Finally, relevant information on the industrial sector and on foreign trade policy appears in works which focus on other topics. See, for example, A. Foxley, "Experimentos neoliberales en América Latina," *Colección Estudios CIEPLAN,* no. 7 (March 1982), and R. Zahler, "Repercusiones monetarias y reales de la apertura financiera al exterior: El caso chileno, 1975-78," *Revista de la CEPAL,* no. 10 (1980).

33. See Vergara, "Apertura externa y desarrollo industrial en Chile." The basic information on production (classified according to the ISIC, rev. 2) is from SOFOFA and ODEPLAN. Information on imports comes from the Customs Office

(Superintendencia de Aduanas), and information on exports comes from the Central Bank. This text refers only to changes between 1969–70 and 1978, which represent more than 1% of the gross value of production for each group in the base period.

34. The principal exported food products are fishmeal, fish oil, and frozen seafood. The most important exported chemical substance is molybdenum oxide.

35. Estimates based on SOFOFA output and employment indexes. They cover 321 and 322 of ISIC (rev. 2).

36. These figures probably underestimate the incidence of imports because the indicator used to measure domestic production is for gross value and includes duplication, particularly because it takes textiles and clothing separately. One estimate of the Textile Institute (Instituto Textil de Chile, "Estudios de la evolución económica del sector textil: Período 1974–77," 1978, p. 106) gives a coefficient of 20%.

37. Scherman, "La industria textil."

38. The rate of inflation of industrial prices was 525% in 1974; this high level facilitated drastic changes in relative prices, which would not be viable in a framework of price level stability.

39. Scherman, "La industria textil," Table 7.

40. At first glance, the decrease in relative prices in the sector could be interpreted as an effect of decreased production. Nevertheless, available information suggests that the relative international prices of textiles and clothing also decreased in the period under study. See ibid.

41. Between 1977 and 1978, bankruptcies for thirty-one textile firms were recorded. See P. Wilson, "Efectos de la política de comercio exterior sobre el empleo en algunas ramas industriales: Chile, 1974–77," Monografía no. 12, Programa para el Empleo, América Latina y el Caribe (PREALC), 1978, p. 56. The figures, which also include the shoe sector, indicate that there were forty-two bankruptcies in 1979 and twenty-four in the first five months of 1980 (Estrategia no. 81, 12–28 August 1980).

42. See Ffrench-Davis, "The Monetarist Experiment."

43. This phenomenon can be interpreted erroneously as an increase in "productivity." However, it has negative social and economic consequences (a) when it implies a greater reduction in employment than in production, instead of a greater increase in production than in employment, and (b) when it takes place in a situation of widespread unemployment and worsened income and wealth distribution, as was the case.

44. Wilson, "Efectos de la política de comercio exterior."

45. E. Tironi, "El comercio exterior en el desarrollo chileno: Una interpretación," Chile, 1940–75 (Santiago: Instituto Chileno de Estudios Humanísticos, 1978).

46. A third component that shows a notable change is the price of molybdenum, a copper by-product whose real price has multiplied by six during the decade. Real export proceeds of this by-product (including molybdenum oxide and ferromolybdenum) reached US$309 million in 1979, compared to US$47

million in 1970. The difficulty in identifying the "normal" price made it hard to "normalize" molybdenum-based exports. The higher value of these exports is equivalent to 46% of the increased expenditure for oil and lubricants in the same period. Finally, imports of transport equipment also rose substantially.

47. This figure holds constant the share of machinery and equipment imports in GDP for the two-year period 1969–70. The estimate is compatible with a gross domestic investment rate on the order of 20%, a share measured following the new national accounts.

48. Here, the estimated "normal" price for electrolytic copper, in 1977, is US$0.80 per pound. See discussion of the methodology in R. Ffrench-Davis, *Políticas económicas en Chile: 1952–70* (Santiago: Ediciones Nueva Universidad, *1973*), chap. 4.

49. This issue is discussed at length in R. Ffrench-Davis and J. P. Arellano, "Apertura financiera externa: La experiencia chilena en 1973–80," *Colección Estudios CIEPLAN*, no. 5 (July 1981), and in Ffrench-Davis, ed., *Relaciones financieras externas y desarrollo nacional* (Mexico City: Fondo de Cultura Económica, 1983).

50. Ffrench-Davis, "Las experiencias cambiarias," Table 4, col. 3.

51. Ffrench-Davis and Arellano, "Apertura financiera externa."

52. Ffrench-Davis, *Economía internacional,* chaps. 4, 7, and 8.

53. Ffrench-Davis, "Exports and Industrialization."

54. Ffrench-Davis, "Exports and Industrialization," and "Comparative Advantage, Equity, and Collective Self-Reliant Industrialization," in G. Helleiver, ed., *Economic Theory and North-South Negotiations* (Toronto: University of Toronto Press, 1982).

55. Ffrench-Davis, ibid., and *Economía internacional.*

3 Changes in the Economic Functions of the Chilean State under the Military Regime

Pilar Vergara

The relationship of the state to the economy has undergone significant transformations during the military regime. The role of the state as producer and as regulator has been markedly restricted, and the size of the state apparatus itself has been reduced. These changes are directly associated with the foundational character of the Chilean authoritarian regime, with, in other words, its attempt to restructure the economy and society in order to generate a new capitalist model of development.

To institute its program of transformations with a free hand, the regime either neutralized or dismantled all the organizations of civil society which would be affected by the changes, and concentrated power in the head of state. As a result, political institutions have been altered in an opposite direction from the economic ones since the military coup: while the concentration of power in the executive has allowed it to act without having to pay attention to the political pressures of the society, the state's capacity to direct the economy has been purposively reduced through a transfer to the private sector of a great many of its functions.

This essay focuses on the changes which have occurred in the state-economy relationship since the military coup. It examines the extent to which the state's role as producer of goods and services has been reduced, and the degree to which even state functions such as determining overall economic regulation and establishing distribution of income and welfare policies have been transfered to the private sector. A brief introduction on the previous economic role of the Chilean state is necessary, however, in order to highlight the fact that the current project represents a sharp break with the past.

The State in Chilean Society between 1940 and 1973

Beginning in the late 1930s, the state increased its participation in the Chilean economy through a development model based on import substituting industrialization. Making use of a complex package of direct and indirect political instruments designed to stimulate the formation of capital in that sector,[1] the state transferred to industrial development a considerable volume of public resources through the Corporación de Fomento de la Producción (CORFO), which was created in 1939 for that purpose. These investments were made directly through infusions of state capital for the purpose of forming mixed enterprises or through financial backing of private initiatives. Large state-owned or mixed companies were therefore created principally in the areas of heavy industry and of intermediate products (energy, steel, cellulose, petrochemicals, metal products, rubber), all of which are essential to support industrial development. No less important was CORFO's work in research and training in various areas. In addition, during the sixties CORFO laid the foundation for a new export infrastructure, especially in fishing, chemicals, paper, and cellulose.[2]

The state also played a significant role in generating demand for industrial products. It did so through public spending, especially through investment in public works, which were of great importance as stimulants to an economy with a small market and a precarious industrial base.

The government's intervention for redistributive purposes was no less important. From 1938 on, the nature of government alliances and the rising pressures of organized middle-class sectors and workers was reflected in the objectives set for public policies, which were to combine the industrialization drive with progressive welfare measures and political democratization. In particular, this resulted in a notable increase of social spending in areas like health, housing, education, and social security; in indirect subsidies to workers and to businesses subject to price control programs; and in an incomes policy, which, despite its defects, tried to protect the buying power of wage and salary earners from erosion by a persistent inflation.[3]

When the Christian Democratic party came to power in 1964, government intervention in the economic, political, and social life of the country became even more pronounced. Public spending as a percentage of the GDP increased from 35.7% in 1965 to 46.9% in 1970, public investment as a percentage of gross national investment rose from 61% to 77%, and state expenditures in social programs went from 8.2% to 9.4% of the GDP—leading to an increase in public employment in these sectors from 119,000 to 153,000 people.

The presence of the state in the financial sector also continued to expand. In 1970 the Banco del Estado handled 44% of all investments and accepted 48% of all deposits made in both domestic and foreign currency. Through CORFO and/or the Banco del Estado the public sector came to control almost all medium-and long-term credit.

At the same time the Chilean state became part-owner of the principal copper companies, giving it greater control over the country's foreign earnings. It also inaugurated an agrarian reform process which, at the end of the Christian Democratic government, had expropriated some 17% of the country's farmland.

The Christian Democrats also modified the tax system to bring greater resources into the state treasury, as well as to make it more progressive. Studies of this period show that the state's application of fiscal policy in this area resulted in a significant promotion of greater equality of opportunity. This was the case despite the serious limitations that resulted from the inadequacy of available resources to meet redistributive goals, the regressive impact of indirect taxes and of social security contributions, and the channeling of benefits of some programs to the more affluent groups.[4]

In spite of the increasing importance of direct state action in the production and encouragement of investment, until 1970 the state did not attempt in any way to take the place of the industrial bourgeoisie nor to become its competitor. The prevailing economic organization in Chile was capitalist, and the main characteristic of public intervention was its complementary nature to, and its encouragement of, private enterprise. CORFO played a supporting role for the private sector by supplying the basic infrastructure in the case of projects which this sector either could not or would not undertake and by transferring financial resources at a subsidized rate.[5]

By contrast, the Unidad Popular government which began in 1970 gave a new and decisive impulse to the strengthening of the state apparatus, producing a qualitative change in the character of public intervention in society. The U.P.'s plan for the radical transformation of the economy and society led to the nationalization of the principal industrial enterprises, of the most important distributors, and of almost the entire banking system. It also led to an intensification of the agrarian reform process and to the nationalization of all of the large copper industries. As such, the government tried to establish state control over all economic processes and to set in motion a new style of development that would lead gradually but inevitably to socialism.[6]

The U.P. also gave new emphasis to the redistributive objectives of the state. Resources increased for aid programs for city dwellers and small rural proprietors. Subsidies for essential consumer goods expanded, and the prices of the most popular consumer products were controlled. By September 1973, the state played the central role in the Chilean economy, leaving to private enterprise those areas it considered marginal. The accumulation of power at the level of the state had been translated into a progressive subordination to the state of all the important activities of society, even those beyond the purely economic sphere. The extent of these changes help to explain the velocity and determination with which the military government proceded to dismantle the intervention of the state in the economy.

Capitalist Reorganization and Redefinition
of the Role of the State in the Development Process

The development strategy promoted by the military regime represented an attempt to alter radically the prior system of economic organization which dated back to the 1930s. The plan for capitalist reorganization did not seek to extend import substitution nor to intensify industrialization by means of a selective and moderate opening of the economy to the outside. What was proposed was the abrupt redirection of the previous development model toward a plan in which markets, acting freely in an economy fully open to foreign trade, become the principal mechanism for allocating productive resources. By comparison with the development model in force until 1973, this meant that industry had to turn to those economic activities in which the country has a natural comparative advantage in order to compete in foreign markets. It also implied that private capital, guided by market signals, would replace the state as the driving force of the development process.

The assumption behind government policy was that the economy can be both stable and experiencing a high rate of expansion only if all obstacles to the play of market forces are eliminated and a private capital market is developed to maximize the savings potential of the economy. The state's protectionist and interventionist policies were blamed for most of the problems the Chilean economy faced during the last few decades: slow economic development, the persistence of high rates of inflation, productive inefficiency, high rates of unemployment, and balance of payments problems. This "perverse" role which the state is said to have played in the past through a "discretionary handling"[7] of economic policy produced the economic, political, and social crisis of 1970–73, which, although it surfaced only then, "had been gestating for half a century."[8] The new orthodoxy has even attributed an extreme inefficiency to regulative and redistributive state policies, the latter now blamed for having a regressive impact. Hence, the state should not only cease to actively promote economic development; it should, in addition, abandon its efforts to moderate social inequalities through state-directed programs (with the exception of those aimed at alleviating the conditions of the extremely poor). State intervention should restrict itself to guaranteeing order and providing public goods such as justice and defense, and it should limit its contribution to the private sector to the creation of a basic infrastructure which the private sector cannot generate.

At first the authorities of the military regime said that, in accordance with the principle of subsidiarity, the state should be involved only in productive activities having a social character and/or a strategic importance for the security and development of the country. Increasingly, however, authorities came to adopt more radical positions regarding the respective roles of the state and of the marketplace in economic activity. Even areas traditionally considered "strategic"—telecommunications, energy, ports, transportation in general, etc.—could be transferred to the private sector.[9] Ideally, then, the state should turn over to private hands all productive enterprises.[10] In the area of social services as well, the state should keep its own functions to a minimum and transfer all others to the private sector.

MODIFICATIONS IN THE SIZE OF THE STATE ECONOMIC APPARATUS

In line with the goal of reducing the size of the public sector, cuts have been made in investment, spending, and public employment, and most of the enterprises held by the state have been privatized. As Table 3.1 shows, this meant a drastic reduction in the size and sphere of action of the state during the first years of the military regime.[11]

The Privatization of Public Enterprises

The clearest sign of reduced state intervention in the process of accumulation is the progressive and almost total privatization of the enterprises under CORFO. The speed with which this task was undertaken was due in large measure to the chaotic situation of the state enterprises prior to the coup. During the U.P. period, the incorporation of private companies into the public sector—like the expropriation of the agricultural estates—had been carried out amid a severe economic crisis, sharpened by the effects of

TABLE 3.1   Public Spending and Public Employment as Indicators of the Size of the State

	1970	1974	1975	1976	1977	1978	1979
Public spending (% of the GDP)[a]	40.6	39.6	38.6	30.7	32.4	31.8	30.3
Public employment (% of the active population)[b]	9.3	11.3	10.3	10.0	9.3	8.9	8.8

[a] Excludes the service on the public debt.

[b] Excludes defense, research, the affiliates of CORFO, and data for the agricultural sector, since this information was not available.

Sources: Public spending: J. Marshall, "Gasto del sector público en Chile, 1969-1979: Metodología y resultados," *Notas Técnicas* CIEPLAN, no. 3 (1981), based on figures from the Ministerio de Hacienda, Dirección de Presupuesto. GDP: ODEPLAN, "Cuentas nacionales," in *Boletín Mensual,* various issues. Employment: O. Muñoz, J. Gatica, and P. Romaguera, "Crecimiento y estructura del empleo estatal en Chile, 1940-1970," *Notas Técnicas* CIEPLAN, no. 22 (1980); Ministerio de Hacienda, Dirección de Presupuesto. Active population: P. Meller, R. Cortázar, and J. Marshall, "La evolución del empleo en Chile, 1974-1978," in *Collección Estudios CIEPLAN,* no. 2 (1979).

a political crisis unleashed by the radicalization of the political process. Both factors contributed to the disorderly way in which the companies were brought under public control. There was no definite strategy, and the government even expropriated, intervened, or requisitioned (by making use of different legal loopholes) many economically insignificant companies.[12] At the same time, the management of the nationalized companies and estates proved to be extremely inefficient, all the more so in the wake of increased runaway spending with few budgetary restrictions. Many firms ran up huge deficits, placing further pressures on an already sharp fiscal deficit.

This crisis in the productive apparatus of the state can explain, at least in part, why the new economic authorities saw themselves forced from the beginning to opt for a drastic and speedy solution to the problem of reducing the size of the public sector. The transfer of businesses and banks to the private sector was made with great haste, with very low prices set for the firms despite the high inflation rates, given the sharp recession in the economy.[13] Even with the conservative assumptions used in the calculations done for this paper, the adjusted sale values of the twenty-five largest companies and banks auctioned off between 1974 and 1978 ranged, on the average, between 63% and 77% of their net worth, thereby giving buyers substantial bargains.[14]

As a result of the policy of privatization, CORFO firms decreased from 479 at the end of 1973 to 24 in 1980—many fewer than in 1970, where there were 46 (see Table 3.2). The authorities' goal is to retain, at most, 13

TABLE 3.2   Enterprises and Banks Controlled by CORFO

	1970	1973[a]	1980	Goal
Enterprises	46	460	23	13
Enterprises under government control	0	233[c]	0	0
CORFO affiliates[b]	46	277	23	13
Banks	0	19	1[d]	0
Total	46	479[c]	24	13

[a] At the time of the September collapse of the Unidad Popular regime.

[b] Includes both enterprises in which CORFO holds stock in the share capital and affiliates of CORFO affiliates.

[c] To avoid double entries, enterprises that figure in more than one category have been excluded. Specifically, 26 enterprises brought under government control or requisitioned, in which CORFO (or its affiliates) already held capital shares, are excluded.

[d] Because of financial and legal problems, this one bank still has not been restored to its owners.

Source: Gerencia de Normalización de Empresas, CORFO.

industries under CORFO, all in key areas related to national development and security. These include communications firms, some public utilities companies, and the most important industries in certain subsectors, such as those in petrochemicals and explosives.[15] However, it is likely that many of these firms will also be sold off as the economic team presses for even further privatization.[16] Whether the large copper mines will be turned over to the private sector remains controversial.

In the future CORFO is neither to have its own investments nor to create mixed companies; rather, it is to be limited to performing the functions of a development bank in competition with the country's other financial institutions.[17] Public enterprises which remain under state control—the affiliates of CORFO as well as other legally constituted state enterprises—will be treated like any other private business, so that as of 1981 they are no longer included in the national budget.[18]

Paralleling the privatization of business, agrarian reform ended with 28% of the expropriated lands being returned to their former owners. Another 55% was distributed in the form of individual plots to some 40,000 peasants.[19] The remainder was transferred to the Corporación Forestal or sold to the highest bidder.

Reductions in Investment, Spending, and Public Employment

The economic policy objective of reducing the state's intrusion into productive activities was also reflected in large cuts in spending, public investment, and government employment.

Public investment, which in 1974 represented 60% of the gross domestic income in fixed assets, dropped to less than half that by 1979.[20] During this time this investment was reduced to an annual rate of less than 30% (Table 3.3). Since a larger private investment was not forthcoming, the result was a drop in the gross rate of investment.

Public investment between 1974 and 1979 dropped overall by 13.9%. It was reduced during the period in virtually all sectors, with public administration experiencing the most noticeable drop. In the productive sectors, public investment suffered large cuts in almost every category except energy and mining, which increased 24.5% but whose importance within the whole is in any case minimal. The largest drop, of 15.1%, was in public works. Investment in agriculture and fishing and in industry and commerce also fell at substantial rates, a fact which illustrates once again the state's intention of reducing substantially its involvement in the process of capital formation. In the social categories, the decrease in investment by the public sector was even greater than in the productive area, showing an annual drop of 15% on the average. The subsectors of health, housing, and social security were the most affected.[21]

By contrast with the public investment figures, the drop in total public spending and employment was much more important in the productive

TABLE 3.3   Rate of Public Investment (percentages)

Year	In relation to the GDI in fixed assets	In relation to the GDP
1974	58.8	10.0
1975	59.0	6.9
1976	38.3	5.1
1977	36.8	4.9
1978	26.5	3.9
1979	25.0[a]	3.9

[a]Estimate.

Sources: Public investment: Marshall, "Gasto del sector público" (see Table 3.1). GDI in fixed assets: ODEPLAN, "Cuentas nacionales," in *Boletín Mensual,* no. 637 (1981).

sectors than in the area of social services. Government spending in the productive sectors decreased dramatically by an average annual rate of 15.2% between 1974 and 1979.[22] The same was true for public employment in the productive sectors: it registered a 13% average annual drop during the same years. Its relative weight within total public employment was 31.9% in 1970, but only 20.2% in 1979.[23] The only productive subsector to register increases was energy and mining.

The drop in employment and public spending in agriculture and fishing, one of the sharpest, can be almost totally explained by a reduction—or simply the elimination—of activities and personnel in public organizations concerned with the development of farming, agrarian reform, training and technical assistance, and credit for small agricultural producers.[24] Spending and employment trends in industry and commerce can be explained by two factors: (1) the weakening of government efforts in support of production, formerly undertaken by CORFO and SERCOTEC (the latter provided aid and training for owners of small businesses); and (2) the reduction in personnel of the Empresa de Comercio Agrícola (ECA). It should be noted that the figures for public employment do not include CORFO affiliates, the vast majority of which had already been auctioned off and transferred to the private sector. Thus, the decline in public employment in this sector is obviously underestimated.[25] The strong contraction in total spending and employment in public works after 1975 (employment dropped to an annual rate of 45%) resulted from efforts to reduce spending and the fiscal deficit.[26]

Public spending in the area of defense, on the other hand, increased significantly with respect to 1970, even though defense traditionally already represented a high percentage of total public spending. The same is true for spending and public employment in general administration.[27] If the increase in employment in defense and police is taken into account — which is not included in official tabulations but which rose from 76,960 to 110,180 employees between 1970 and 1978—it is clear that total employment in the public sector increased by 46,520 people.[28] This would suggest that public employment did not drop but, on the contrary, must have increased between these years by about 13%. Accordingly, labor force participation in public employment does not drop (as in Table 3.1) but remains constant between these dates.

How do we explain this apparent paradox? It seems clear that the economic objective of reducing the size of the public sector—in this case, of reducing government employment—had to be subordinated to the goal of strengthening the political power of the state by exercising a firm control over society. Another, no less telling example of the priority given to the strengthening of the central power is evidenced by the sharp increase in defense spending, even in the face of a restrictive fiscal policy designed to reduce spending significantly.

TRANSFER OF STATE ECONOMIC FUNCTIONS TO THE PRIVATE SECTOR

The gradual transfer of key elements in the economic system to the private sector has been as important as, or more important than, the reduction in the size of the state economic apparatus. Following free trade prescriptions, the state ceased not only to intervene directly in the process of accumulation, but also to use a great many of the economic policy instruments that had previously enabled it to regulate the course of the economy and to exert an influence on the rhythm and orientation of the global process of accumulation.

At the end of 1973, most prices, which up to then had been under the control of the economic authorities, were decontrolled.[29] The government's lifting of price controls, in combination with the controls which, at least until 1979, were kept on salaries, brought on an abrupt change in the relative prices favoring productive enterprises, especially in the export area. On the other hand, it resulted in a deterioration of industrial prices in relation to those in the agricultural sector.[30]

The timely and orderly way in which the state handled the liberalization of controls over the various financial intermediaries permitted it to transfer gradually to the private sector—and, in particular, to a small number of economically powerful groups,—the role it had traditionally played in attracting savings and allocating credit.[31]

In May 1974, private finance companies were given free rein to set interest rates at will, with no requirement to maintain minimum reserves and with highly liquid financial instruments.[32] The development of private financial markets in an economy with very high rates of inflation, pronounced imbalances, and restrictive monetary policies brought on a severe and prolonged contraction of credit. Interest rates rose to extraordinarily high levels, thus transforming the money market into an important mechanism for redistributing surpluses to the benefit of the financial community.

By contrast, the preexisting financial system—that is, the commercial banks (still government-controlled or semi–government controlled) and the savings and loans institutions (the Sistema Nacional de Ahorro y Prestamos, SINAP)—remained subject to a multitude of controls, such as high reserve rates and set rates of interest on deposits that were much lower than the expected rate of inflation. The logical result of these measures was an accelerated transfer of financial resources from the banks and SINAP to the private financial institutions, which were paying higher rates of interest for short deposits.

Once the privatization of commercial banking was underway, the restrictions which until then had discriminated against the commercial banks and SINAP were gradually lifted. However, new controls were put on the financial institutions in the public sector in June 1975, when the savings certificates tied to adjustable rate mortgages (Valores Hipotecarios Readjustables, VHRs), the principal financial instrument of SINAP, were frozen. The measure started a new and massive transfer of resources from SINAP to the banks and to private finance companies, the majority of which were by then already in the hands of the large private economic groups. In response to this massive transfer of funds, the holders of VHRs were finally given the opportunity to exchange their VHRs for less attractive real fixed rate bonds (Bonos Hipotecarios Reajustables, BHRs) in the National Savings Association (Caja Central de Ahorro y Préstamos). Since VHR investors lost money as a result of this process, the public's confidence in SINAP was further undermined.[33]

Once the position of the economic groups in commercial banking had been consolidated, new measures began to include increasing restrictions on private financial institutions—for example, increases in the amount of capital required, prohibitions against informal associations becoming involved in accepting and investing savings—with the result that the operating rules for these associations and for the commercial banks were put on equal footing. But at the same time, SINAP's ability to take action in the financial system was limited even more when it was prevented from operating in the short-term credit market. On the other hand, the higher capitalization requirements imposed on the private finance companies served to strengthen those which were most highly consolidated. These were the only ones able to survive the new conditions, leading to heavy concentration in the money market.

In terms of external economic relations, the economic authorities decided to drop radically almost all tariffs to a uniform 10% rate. The economic authorities therefore gave up one of the most efficient tools for selectively stimulating the development of certain economic activities and for channeling foreign resources towards an increase in the investment rate.[34]

The opening of the economy to international investment capital—less drastic and more gradual than the opening of the economy to foreign goods—transferred to the private sector control over the allocation of a significant proportion of foreign resources. In this way the ability of economic groups operating within the financial market to determine the allocation of credit was reinforced. This occurred at a time when the hands of economic authorities were tied as far as controlling monetary expansion was concerned.

From the end of 1977 on, restrictions limiting the ability of private financial institutions to acquire short-term loans from abroad began to be eased. However, this liberalization was gradual, with restrictions being imposed on the total amount and length of the debts incurred.[35] If there had been a greater opening in this area, one that was more in line with both the free trade orthodoxy guiding the economy and the radical nature of the opening made in the area of real goods, the expansion of international liquidity would have permitted the greater influx of foreign credit to foster the equalization of domestic and international real interest rates.[36] But with the establishment of quantitative limits on indebtedness, conditions were created which permitted the groups in the private sector who had preferential access to foreign resources to profit greatly from the enormous differences between the two rates.[37]

Estimates by Ffrench-Davis and Arellano of the differences between the real rate of interest paid by the users of short-term bank loans and the cost of international loans reveal that in 1976 the former rose to a level equal to 13.3 times the latter. Although the difference between the cost of domestic and foreign money gradually decreased, in 1980 domestic rates were still about 300% above the international ones.[38]

The bulk of the profits thus obtained derived from the private businesses which had no access to foreign credit. It also derived from the public enterprises, who, already subject to strict controls as far as foreign indebtedness was concerned, saw themselves limited in their fiscal support and in the credit available to them from the Banco Central and were consequently forced to turn to the local financial market. Therefore, the way in which the economy was opened up to foreign capital and the means used to control the influx of foreign resources became an additional mechanism for transfer of public resources—as well as less solvent companies—to the same economic groups controlling key positions in the money market.

The influx of significant amounts of foreign credit channeled through the private sector into a country with a monetary base as small as Chile's turned foreign indebtedness into the principal determinant of the increased flow of money within the country. As a result, the economic authorities lost control over the expansion of the money supply. The influx of foreign capital nullified the government's efforts (through the contraction of domestic credit and restraints imposed on the financial sector) to control the expansion of the means of payment. In effect, between 1978 and 1980, 100% of the fluctuations in issues originated in the influx of foreign credit.

Finally, the unrestricted opening of the economy to foreign investment has meant that the state has given up its responsibility for regulating and negotiating the flow of foreign capital on behalf of the national interest. A new law affecting foreign investment guaranteed the latter equal treatment with domestic capital.[39] And yet, by the end of 1980 no significant amount of foreign investment had been recorded outside the mining sector.

In concluding I should note that contrary to the liberal concepts guiding public action, the state has kept under its control some key economic decisions. This is the case with respect to the exchange rate.[40] It is also the case with respect to wages and labor, as will be noted in the next section.

CHANGES IN THE REDISTRIBUTIVE FUNCTIONS

During the government of the armed forces, the state has also abandoned a large part of the responsibilities it had traditionally assumed for achieving a more equal distribution of income and welfare, through policies dealing with labor and wages, public social spending, taxation, and social security.

Labor and Wage Policy

Wage policy has not followed the same criteria as those adopted in other areas of the economy. Although most markets were decontrolled, labor remained subject to heavy restrictions. Strong government intervention has been maintained in the regulation of salaries and wages, and until 1979, collective bargaining was forbidden. As a result, the content of public action in this area has changed radically. Formerly, it was one of the purposes of the state to intervene in order to protect the real earnings of workers and to serve as arbitrator in labor disputes, guaranteeing respect for the rights of the weakest party in the negotiating process. At present, a public action is directed toward maintaining a restrictive wage policy.

After the military coup, the readjustment of earnings which should have been granted in October 1973 postponed until January 1974, despite the prevailing hyperinflation. At that time, a system of automatic quarterly adjustments, based on inflation in the preceeding period, was established, and collective bargaining was suspended indefinitely. This policy remained unchanged until 1979 when the Labor Plan went into effect. At the same time, subsidies for all essential consumer goods were gradually eliminated.

All of this, together with the unfreezing of most prices, was translated into a great drop in real income, with income in 1975 representing barely 60% of the value it had in 1970. In 1980 income was still 10% below the levels reached at the beginning of the decade.[41]

Public Spending in the Social Sectors

Social policies have also undergone thorough reorganization, both with respect to the level and nature of spending and with respect to the content of the policies aimed at each of the sectors.

Despite their inadequacies, public spending programs in the social sectors during the 1960s constituted an important means of reducing social inequalities.[42] It is appropriate, then, to ask how much activity by the public sector in this area during these last years has compensated for the negative effects wage policy has had on the distribution of income.

During the 1960s, public spending for social programs accounted for roughly 60% of total public expenditures. This proportion decreased dramatically, to 48.7%, in 1974, the first full year of military government. It then increased to a level between 55% and 61% over the course of the subsequent years.[43]

Consequently, after the steep drop in 1974, there has been little apparent change in the levels of social spending when these are measured as a proportion of total public spending. Some years even register levels which are higher than those of the previous decade; this is the case in 1979, when the proportion spent by the state for social programs reached 61.7%. However, these figures (which supporters of the government often use to present it in a favorable light) are inadequate indicators of the actual levels of spending, for two reasons. First, state spending for social programs is affected by large increases in two new items, a makeshift employment program (Programa de Empleo Mínimo, PEM) and a subsidy for hiring new workers. The PEM is not technically a welfare payment, since it requires an obligatory contribution of services; and the subsidies for hiring additional workers are paid to prospective employers, not to workers. If these items are eliminated from the calculations, the proportion spent by the state in the social sector (including health, education, social security, and housing) was in 1979 practically equal to the same proportion in 1970, when it reached 58.6% of total expenditures.[44]

The second reason why the proportional figures are misleading is that they mask significant declines in overall state expenditures. Since state spending in the economic sector has diminished dramatically during the military government, the proportion of total public spending on social programs has remained high. In absolute terms, social spending was 4.3% lower in 1979 than it was in 1970 (still excluding the amounts spent in the two new programs). An even more telling indication of the decline in social expenditures is revealed by Table 3.4. As the figures in this table show, there were two areas in which spending increased: public assistance and employment (which contains the new items mentioned above), and other cultural services (which includes basically greater support for sports, principally soccer). In education, 1979 expenditures recovered their 1970 lev-

TABLE 3.4   Per Capita Social Spending (1970 = 100)

Social sector	1974	1975	1976	1977	1978	1979
Health	97.0	76.3	67.1	76.7	87.0	85.9
Education	113.4	87.4	87.2	93.1	97.9	99.9
Public assistance and employment	83.3	994.4	2,533.3	2,250.0	1,733.3	1,555.6
Social security	69.1	64.7	59.6	65.5	68.5	75.4
Housing and urban affairs	131.0	78.3	56.1	70.1	53.4	54.4
Other cultural services	61.9	65.1	131.7	203.2	171.4	230.2
All social sectors	91.7	74.9	71.2	78.7	79.0	82.8

Sources: Social spending: Marshall, "Gasto del sector público." Population: Instituto Nacional de Estadísticas (INE).

els; this was due to greater payments to preprimary and university education.[45] However, despite the figures for these items, overall spending for social programs in 1979 was 17.2% below its 1970 level. The most dramatic decline occurred in housing and urban affairs. State spending for this item in 1979 was about half of the 1970 level.

This last fact is especially serious if we consider that the state had traditionally been responsible for the construction of 52% of new housing and that this was one of the social programs having the greatest redistributive effect.[46] It is estimated that, given the increase in population, 50,000 dwellings must be built every year just to keep up with the present deficit, which, according to official figures, reached 700,000 homes—that is, almost a third of the country's families. As can be seen in Table 3.5, during the 1974–78 period the average number of homes built did not reach 40,000 per year, and the proportion of these built by the public sector has fallen to insignificant levels.[47]

In addition, the per capita outlay for social security in 1979 was considerably below (by 25%) the levels reached in 1970. The large reduction in per capita spending in this area corresponds basically to the sharp decline in the average amount paid by the social security system in its two main benefit categories—pensions and family allocations—which represent something in the area of 90% of the total outlay for social security.[48]

Per capita spending in health has shown less of a decrease because in that sector (as in the area of education as well) between 80% and 90% of the disbursements correspond to wages and salaries. For this reason any cutback involves not only eliminating functions but above all reducing personnel. Despite this, the per capita outlay in this category for 1979 was still quite a bit below the levels of 1970 and even of 1974; the result was a sharp

TABLE 3.5   Housing Built by the Public and Private Sectors (yearly averages)

Years	Public sector	Public and private sector	Public sector representation in total housing built (%)
1965–70	17,300	33,481	51.7
1971–73	28,198	41,342	68.2
1974–78	10,925	27,967	39.1
1979[a]	328	33,372	1.0
1980[a,b]	1,416	26,692	5.3

[a] The figures for 1979–80 do not accurately reflect the efforts of the public sector in the construction of housing, since some of the buildings started by the private sector are completed by a system that the Ministerio de Vivienda y Urbanismo has called "precalificado" or "obra vendida." These are the buildings built by the private sector and acquired by the Servicio de Vivienda y Urbanización (SERVIU) once they are completed.

[b] Figures for January through September only.

Source: INE, *Boletín de Edificación.*

reduction in available material resources and in the number of benefits per capita provided by the Servicio Nacional de Salud (SNS).[49]

In addition to changing funding levels, the government has made substantial modifications in the content of social programs. These modifications also point to a progressive reduction in the state's sphere of action and influence in this field. The current regime's policy makers claim that, in this area as well, government efforts proved inefficient and that, from a redistributive point of view, public programs in the past probably helped to increase, rather than reduce, social inequalities. In accordance with the principle of subsidiarity, the private sector must assume the main responsibility for meeting the most vital needs of the general population. The public sector would assume the responsibility only for concentrating its efforts on programs directed toward groups suffering from extreme poverty.

Thus, in accordance with the new educational policy announced at the beginning of 1979, the state will no longer increase its presence in this field.[50] Therefore, it will transfer educational functions and the responsibility for meeting unmet educational needs to the private sector. State intervention will be limited solely to guaranteeing a basic level of education to the entire school-age population. But in order for the attainment of this objective not to bring with it a necessary increase in spending, the contents—and probably the duration—of basic schooling will be reduced to a minimum consisting of a basic knowledge of Spanish, arithmetic, civic education, and the history and geography of Chile.

Along with limiting state activity to meet educational needs—though not with respect to the content of educational curricula, the orientation and control of which the government reserves to itself—the government has also promoted the privatization of basic education by handing over to the municipalities the educational establishments previously under national state control, and by allowing the municipalities, in turn, to hand them over to private institutions. The state agrees to continue providing subsidies to the municipalities. However, these subsidies will be used only in pursuit of the minimum educational goal mentioned earlier and will not be allowed to exceed the amount that the state used to spend in the institutions previously under its control. The technical-professional schools will also be handed over to the private sector, and an attempt will be made to hand over the polytechnic institutes to the municipalities.

It is evident that the small size of the subsidies will automatically mean the transfer of many schools to the private sector. Alternatively, it will result in their being abandoned by the best-qualified teachers or in the reduction of instruction hours and the dismissal of part of the personnel when the budget is not sufficient to support them. Consequently, there will be a deterioration in the quality of instruction given. Nevertheless, this new policy guarantees a distribution of technical and human resources in accordance with the laws of the marketplace and, therefore, one which is functionally in line with the requirements of the present economic model.[51]

Access to secondary education (which will constitute "an exceptional situation") will be more restricted and will have to be financed by means of current or deferred payments on the part of the students themselves.[52] For the neediest sectors, scholarships and subsidies are offered to help ease the problem.

With respect to university education, the state, beginning in 1981, put a ceiling on its direct aid, with a view to reducing it year by year until the aid equals only 50% of the amount provided in 1980. The remainder of the state contribution toward the financing of the universities will be provided through student loans and indirect contributions.

The Law for Universities creates the conditions for the privatization of higher education by authorizing the establishment of new private universities as well as nonuniversity institutes of higher education.[53] However, the law states that a limited number of professional degrees, the most prestigious ones included, are to be granted exclusively by the universities (either public or private), with private institutes empowered to grant titles in the remaining fields. The new law thus opens up a large field for the private sector in this area. These private centers of higher education, since they are subject to the standards of profitability, will presumably take pains to match the supply of professional careers to the demands of the market-place and, therefore, conform to the economic model.

In the health sector a profound restructuring and shrinking of the National Health Service (SNS) has been initiated. The service has been the unit principally responsible for promoting, protecting, and restoring the health of the great mass of the population. The thrust of current policy lies in the strengthening of private medicine, thereby ending the social conception of medicine which had held sway in Chile. Public intervention is now being restricted to dealing with the sectors unable to pay for their own health care.

The present health system, particularly the SNS, has been broken down into twenty-seven regional agencies which are autonomously administered as if they were private businesses and are made to compete with each other. It is thought that the competition generated among them will force them to increase their efficiency. The stimulus, it is thought, will be provided by economic incentives, since both state and private aid will be proportional to the number of cases treated.

Moreover, private medicine will receive strong support with the new social security system the government is setting in motion, which is based on private pension fund associations. Although the existing public institutions will be maintained, the contributors to the new social security system will be able to choose the organization to which they want to entrust their health. Apparently little thought has been given to the fact that a reduction in the already insufficient resources on which public medical care institutions depend will most certainly undermine their capacity to deliver health services efficiently.

The trend toward privatization in the field of health can also be seen in the efforts to restructure the financing of the public health system. It is hoped that by 1985 state allocations will amount to only 10% of the expenditures (whereas in 1980 they covered 65% of the total), the rest being covered by payments from health insurance programs and from individuals. The expectation is, in addition, that the administration of all child care programs will be transferred to the municipalities.

As with educational reform, at the same time that the new policy promotes the atomization of the present health system, it accentuates the executive's control over medical care. Administrative positions in each of the twenty-seven autonomous units will be considered political rather than professional posts, with administrators answerable exclusively to the president of the republic.[54] As representatives of the state, they will also have oversight over private health institutions and over medical practice.[55]

The new housing policy aims at handing over to the private sector the task of building public housing. Public institutions will limit themselves to granting direct subsidies to the poorest families to enable them to buy housing available on the open market. The new policy, which got underway in 1978, set for itself the goal of providing 10,000 housing subsidies per year. However, after two years of operation, the new system's principal deficiencies could already be seen in the low utilization rate of the subsidies provided: 60% in 1978 and only 40% in 1979.

The principal difficulties in making use of the housing subsidy had to do with the inability to pay on the part of those eligible for the subsidy and with the scarcity of low-cost housing on the market. The amount of the subsidy only partially covered the cost of housing, and it was not available unless one could count on prior savings equal to 25% of the value of the house. In order to pay the difference the recipient had to resort to private financing.[56] However, the conditions that the banks impose for obtaining a loan, such as a guaranteed minimum income, prevented more than half of the lower wage population from having access to minimum housing. To these difficulties was added an insufficient supply of low-cost housing, which made it impossible to satisfy the demand.

The criticism leveled against the subsidies policy led the authorities to establish a new program which created 15,000 new subsidies (the *subsidios habitacionales variables*). To apply for these, it was not necessary to have prior savings. However, the new program has not succeeded in resolving the main flaws in the previous one. On the one hand, the subsidy covers only 75% of the value of the house, with the result that the beneficiary has to resort to securing a loan. On the other hand, the new subsidy limits the maximum cost of the house to which it can be applied. This will probably limit even more the supply of low-cost housing.[57] This problem is inherent in any subsidies policy directed at the lower-wage sectors in a free market economy. In this type of economy there is little prospect that the private sector will be interested in building low-cost public housing, unless it is guaranteed adequate profits, which in turn would result in a considerable increase in the cost of the housing.

It is beyond the scope of this paper to analyze in depth the distributive implications of these modifications in the social functions of the state, but it does not seem out of line to conclude that public endeavor in this area will lose a large part of the role it played in the past as a redistributor and equalizer of social opportunities. A system of subsidies in a free market economy with a marked concentration of wealth is not likely to function effectively, since meeting the essential needs of the poor does not constitute a particularly profitable endeavor.

The Tax System

Tax policy has undergone substantial modifications which have led to a more regressive distribution of the tax burden. The principal changes are contained in the tax reform that went into effect in 1975. The distribution of tax revenues by source can be examined in Table 3.6.

In the category of direct taxes, the tax on business income (*impuesto de primera categoría*) went through successive reductions, with the result that the rate, which reached as high as 17% in 1973, was only 10% a couple of years later. Members of professional societies and directors of corporations also benefited from a tax cut, since their tax rates dropped from 12% and 30%, respectively, to a uniform rate of 7% in 1975. By contrast, the rate for small businessmen increased from 3.75% to 7%, and until 1978 the rate of the flat tax (*impuesto único*), which affects salaries, wages, and pensions, remained unchanged. In that same year the rates of the income tax (*impuesto global complementario*), which constitutes the most progressive tax of the system, were reduced. The impact these changes had on the disposable income of the different income levels was proportionally greater for the high-income groups, who were favored by them.[58]

In addition, the system for figuring business taxes was modified in order to avoid—so it was said—having taxes paid on nominal or "fictitious" profits resulting from high inflation. With that purpose in mind, real profit was defined as the increase in the value of a company's property from one year to the next (as measured in money of equivalent buying power) and not, as before, in terms of the balance figure. According to rather conservative estimates, the new system in application meant that business taxes in 1975 were 64% to 80% lower than they would have been under the previous system.[59]

Finally, direct taxes of considerable redistributive potential—including a property tax and the capital gains tax—were abolished.

Among the indirect taxes, the application of the value-added tax (*impuesto al valor agregado*, IVA)—which is considered to be one of the most regressive in its effect on the distribution of income—was progressively extended to all products, including essential consumer items, as well as to books.[60] As a result, the importance of this tax, currently set at 20%, within total tax revenues increased considerably (from 34.5% to 49.1% between 1970 and 1979). This more than compensated for the drop in income derived from another important indirect tax, that on foreign trade, a development resulting from the reduction in customs duties. Furthermore, the rates for real estate and motor vehicle transfer taxes were lowered (from 8% to 1% and from 8% to 4%, respectively), and the tax on bank interest was eliminated.

In sum, as can be appreciated in Table 3.6, there was a tendency until 1978 toward a modification of the tax structure in favor of indirect taxes, a phenomenon associated with a more regressive distribution of the tax burden. This tendency was reversed beginning with 1979 as a result, among other things, of an improvement of the tax control system and of the reduction of rates affecting an important indirect tax, that on foreign trade. However, the importance of the IVA in terms of total tax revenues continues to increase, with clearly regressive results. Moreover, the taxes with the

TABLE 3.6   Sources of Tax Revenues

Tax	1970	1973	1974	1975	1976
Direct taxes	*27.3%*	*29.2%*	*30.3%*	*32.6%*	*28.2%*
Income	22.5	26.7	25.1	28.7	24.4
Property	4.7	2.4	2.2	3.5	3.7
Others	0.1	0.1	3.0	0.4	0.1
Indirect taxes	*72.7*	*70.8*	*69.7*	*67.4*	*71.8*
IVA	34.5	39.3	33.3	32.0	37.2
On specific products	8.7	10.3	14.4	15.8	16.9
On foreign trade	20.2	12.5	18.0	13.9	11.3
Others	9.3	8.7	4.0	5.7	6.4
Total	*100.0*	*100.0*	*100.0*	*100.0*	*100.0*

Note: In order to have figures in money of equal buying power, I have used the corrected CPI *of R. Cortázar and J. Marshall, "Indice de precios al consumidor en Chile, 1970–1978," Colección Estudios CIEPLAN,* no. 4 (November 1980).

[a] Tax returns estimated at about 4.52% were subtracted from tax revenues.

[b] The average annual rate of change for 1974–78 is included so that it can be seen how much the new norms for collecting taxes have affected the volume of revenue collected.

Sources: National general revenue figures (1970); Tesorería General de la República, *Refundido Nacional de Abonos* (1971–79).

greatest redistributive impact within both the direct and the indirect categories have become less important.

The Social Security System

Since 1974 a series of changes aimed at reducing inequalities have gradually been made in the social security system. In 1974 family allowances (fixed amounts paid monthly per child dependent) for white-collar and blue-collar workers were equalized; a uniform system of unemployment and disability subsidies was established; and support payments for those over 65 who had no income and for invalids over 18 were equalized. The rates for payment into the social security system were progressively reduced as a means of stimulating employment.

However, the positive and equalizing character of these measures—which previous governments had also tried, unsuccessfully, to impose—contrasts with reductions occurring in the real value of the principal benefits. In 1979 family allowances were about 46% lower than in 1970 and the average pension payment about 34% less.[61] On the other hand, while in

			Ave. annual rate of change		
1977	1978	1979[a]	1970–73	1974–78[b]	1974–79
26.2%	25.4%	30.6%	−5.6%	−1.0%	5.2%
21.8	21.0	27.0	−2.1	−1.0	7.0
4.4	4.4	3.7	−26.6	−22.5	16.6
0.0	0.0	—	−21.5	−75.5	—
73.8	74.6	69.4	−8.3	5.4	4.9
39.9	43.1	49.1	−3.4	10.4	13.4
15.7	13.3	6.6	−2.0	1.8	−10.0
11.4	10.0	7.5	−21.2	10.6	−12.1
7.0	8.2	6.3	−9.7	16.0	8.8
100.0	100.0	100.0	−7.6	3.5	4.9

1970 the average old age pension represented around 73% of the average salary on which it was figured, in 1979 this percentage was barely 58%.[62]

Another important measure adopted during these past few years was the change in the requirements for retirement. The granting of seniority pensions, which basically benefited white-collar workers, was eliminated. The effect of this measure on the financing of the social security system is twofold: it lengthens the period during which a worker pays into the system; at the same time it reduces social security spending, since the system is correspondingly not paying pensions to these workers. Arellano figured that by this means alone, the costs of the social security system are reduced by an amount equal to 60% of the present-day value of each worker's pension.[63]

In 1980, the government announced a reform of the social security system which would restructure it and place its management in the hands of the private sector. The reform, which affects only the pension system, began to be implemented in May of 1981. The authorities hope it will eventually replace the shared system Chile has had for decades with one involving individual capitalization. The new system will be administered by government-authorized corporations—the Administradoras de Fondos Previsionales (AFP)—with each worker theoretically being given a choice between remaining with the publicly administered system or changing to the privately run one.[64]

There is no doubt that the older shared system had serious deficiencies. However, it had had a progressive impact on the distribution of wealth; in effect, low-income pensioners received quite a bit more than they contributed to the system. Under the new capitalization plan, low-income pensioners will receive only one-fifth to two-thirds of what they received under the old one.[65]

In the short run, the changes in the social security system can contribute to an increase in government deficit spending. This is because the state will have to continue to pay the pensions of retirees who draw from the old system, while not receiving the payments of those who elect to transfer their pension funds to the new private corporations.

From the point of view of the concentration of wealth and of economic power, the repercussions of the new system will be no less important. Its adoption has turned it into one more mechanism for transferring large resources, public as well as private, to the large financial conglomerates operating in the economy. The magnitude of the funds which will be committed can be appreciated if we take into account the fact that, according to some estimates, social security contributions during one year could equal half the funds attracted by the money market during its first five years of existence.[66]

In sum, it can be said that the new social security system does not seem to demonstrate great advantages from the point of view of the problems it was supposed to solve: it will not end the increase in public spending, nor is it reasonable to expect from it substantial improvements in the situation of those receiving benefits from it in relation to what they used to receive under the old system. However, the reform of the social security system has the important function of transferring large quantities of public and private funds to the private economic agents who are seen as having the responsibility for making the process of accumulation more dynamic. Their economic importance is thus further consolidated.

Finally, the social security reform will reinforce a tendency toward fragmentation of the labor force to the extent that each worker will have to confront individually problems that were formerly faced collectively.

Final Considerations

An analysis of the principal changes in the Chilean state since the military regime came to power shows that we are in the presence of a state which is totally different from the one in power until 1973. Its changes in size and functions have occurred in two different ways.

There has been a marked diminution of the economic functions and apparatus of the state, together with a corresponding transfer of real and financial resources—and many of the principal economic decision-making capabilities—to a small number of entrepreneurial groups who have thereby accumulated a degree of economic power unprecedented in Chilean history. Politically, by contrast, changes have been in the opposite direction: there has been a strengthening of the authorities' power together with a concentration of that power in the executive. This has the important purpose of guaranteeing the exclusion of all groups and opposition social forces, thus generating stable conditions for social demobilization, an indispensable precondition for rendering viable the economic changes.

Although it has not been studied in this paper, on the specifically ideological-cultural level a strengthening of government power has also occurred. This has not been achieved by the state's assuming explicitly a coherent ideology, to be diffused throughout the governmental institutions and the society through special organizations created for that end. The state has simply limited itself to exercising control over educational curricula and over the principal means of ideological diffusion, and to designing a legal-institutional framework which will guarantee monopolistic control over the diffusion of cultural messages by certain private groups with which the authorities share definite affinities. The "subsidiary" state of the economic sphere thus becomes a "mentor" state in the ideological-cultural realm, a state which reserves for itself only the tasks of guiding and controlling. However, a "caretaker" state in the political arena constitutes a precondition for the existence, within the new form of society which is being built, of a merely subsidiary state in the economic sphere and a simply "mentor" state in the ideological-cultural realm.

Furthermore, this double process of privatization of the economic sphere and statization in the political realm is also reproduced at the various levels of society. This is the result of the whole array of policies designed to restructure the way society is institutionalized. Among the principal policies are the Labor Plan, the privatization of the social sectors, and the social security reform. These reforms are intended to produce an atomization of social classes and groups along with a fragmentation of social organizations, in an attempt to instill social relations which will be ruled more and more by the laws of the marketplace and by individual interests, without "distorting" political interference. The common trait in this process of privatization-atomization is that it is accompanied by a strengthening of the government's—especially the executive's—ideological and political control over the new activities and institutions emerging in society.

For instance, the transfer of the responsibility for education to the private sector is intended to produce, on the one hand, a segmentation of the demand for education and, on the other, a dispersion of the teachers' union; the state will no longer be, therefore, the object of collective pressures from the public or the union in this area to the same extent as before. A much more variegated market for educational services and employment will develop. And yet, the oversight of the state over educational programs and instructional content is strengthened.

The Labor Plan constitutes perhaps the most characteristic example of this process of privatization coupled with an intensification of political control over society. Through it labor organizations are fragmented and weakened, and workers are dispersed and even made to compete with each other. At the same time, however, through the Dirección y la Inspección del Trabajo the political control of the state over the functioning of labor organizations is intensified.[67]

The privatization effects of the economic policy and of the social reforms, together with the strengthening of the mechanisms of political and ideological control over the majority of society's institutions—the economic ones excepted—will probably tend to generate an individual adaptation strategy based on withdrawal and depoliticization. To this must be added the demobilizing effects of unemployment, employment instability, and impoverishment.

Still, the extent to which this scheme of social and political atomization will actually succeed in creating isolated individuals who act exclusively in terms of individual interests is an open question. One can only wonder whether other forms of social activity and organization, as yet unknown, will emerge, capable of conquering certain "ideological spaces," limited though they may be. For certain groups at least, such forms could make it possible to overcome the particularism of individual interests and, by invoking more universal values, could lead to the shaping of individuals with a true democratic conscience.

Nevertheless, these and other problems must not let us lose sight of the central fact that the new state which has established itself and profoundly transformed Chilean society constitutes one of the central parameters which will define in the future the limits of political alternatives. It is for this reason that it becomes indispensable to pursue careful, in-depth studies of the fundamental impact this new state may have had on society and on the structuring of the social classes, their values, behavior, and ideologies, with the aim of determining the characteristics that any project to restore democracy to Chile should have in order to be successful.

Notes

1. Among the indirect measures used by the state to stimulate the substitution of imports were strong tariff protection and special tax treatment, together with subsidies to offset the costs of production (fixing a subvaluated rate of exchange for the importation of machinery, equipment and intermediate goods, and credits at subsidized rates of interest). On this subject see, among others, O. Munõz, "Estado e industrialización en el ciclo de expansión del salitre," *Colección Estudios CIEPLAN* no. 6 (January 1977), and CORFO, "Instrumentos de política económica aplicadas en el sector industrial" (División de planificación industrial, Publicación no. 48, 1970).

2. Of fifty main companies which exported only industrial products in 1978, fourteen continued to be affiliates of CORFO. See P. Vergara, "Apertura externa y desarrollo industrial en Chile: 1973–1978," *Colección Estudios CIEPLAN,* no. 4 (November 1980), table 12.

3. With this purpose in mind, moreover, the government established mandatory readjustments in salaries, minimum wages for white-collar workers and later for blue-collar workers, and price ceilings for a full range of goods and services.

4. A. Foxley, E. Aninat, and J. P. Arellano, *Las desigualdades económicas y la acción del estado* (Mexico City: Fondo de Cultura Económica, 1980).

5. The merely complementary character of public activity in this area is evident in the fact that even in the mixed companies that were created either through contributions of capital and credit to the private sector by CORFO or through the purchase of shares from private companies, CORFO's participation in the management of the companies was in general less important than its participation in the capital resources of the companies. See O. Muñoz and A. M. Arriagada, "Orígenes políticos y económicos del estado empresarial en Chile," *Colección Estudios CIEPLAN*, no. 16 (September 1979, and M. Cavarozzi, "The Government and the Industrial Bourgeoisie in Chile, 1938–1964" (Ph.D. diss., University of California at Berkeley, 1975).

6. On the expansion of the state-controlled area of the economy and its political and social objectives, see S. Bitar and A. MacKenna, "Impacto de las áreas de propiedad social y mixta en la industria chilena" (Documentos de Trabajo series, CEPLA, Departamento de Industrias, Universidad de Chile, 1973), and J. López, "Sobre la construcción de la nueva economía," *Cuadernos de la Realidad Nacional*, no. 13 (July 1972).

7. Interview with Minister of Economic Affairs S. de Castro, published in *El Mercurio*, 15 February 1976.

8. Account of the State of Public Finance, Ministry of Finance, 1978.

9. See, among others, statements by P. Baraona, ex-minister of economic affairs, in *Realidad* 1, no. 7 (December 1979); interview with A. Bardón, president of the Banco Central, in *El Mercurio,*"Informe Económico Mensual," April 1980; and statements by J. C. Méndez, director of the budget, in *El Mercurio*, 7 December 1980.

10. The present scheme prevents public enterprises from coexisting with private companies in a single sector because of the unfair competition that this would involve. Public enterprises must not enjoy any type of favoritism, whether in terms of taxes, tariffs, budgetary support, or anything else. They must generate their own resources to finance themselves.

11. Because it is not a simple matter of returning to the situation existing in 1970, before the beginning of the U.P. project, but of imposing a qualitatively different scheme of capitalist development, the statistical comparisons in this work will take 1970 as the preferred year, or 1969 when information for 1970 is not available.

12. This was so to such an extent that the number of businesses in the so-called social property sector of the economy reached 479 by September 1973, whereas it was only supposed to consist of 91 enterprises.

13. In 1974 alone, 202 out of the 259 businesses placed under state control or appropriated by the previous government were returned to their former owners.

14. The 25 largest companies transfered by CORFO during this period were obtained from a ranking of 500 businesses, made on the basis of 1978 sales figures published by *Gestión* (see "Ranking de empresas nacionales," *Gestión* 5, no. 57 [1980]). Net worth corresponds to capital reserves of the businesses or banks which appear in the balance for the year immediately preceding the sale. This figure is adjusted in such a way as to make it correspond to the percentage transferred by CORFO. The current value of the flows was figured using two alternative assumptions: *(a)* a discount rate of 10% for each year and *(b)* a discount rate of 25% for the income corresponding to the years 1974 and 1978, and one of 15% for the flow of income from 1979 on.

Data on these flows were expressed in dollar values obtained at the time of each sale; this meant that they had to be converted into thousands of pesos at the December 1974 rate. To do this, the rate of exchange in effect at each date was used. To convert the data into December 1974 pesos I used the corrected consumer price index of R. Cortázar and J. Marshall, "Indice de precios al consumidor en Chile, 1970–1978," *Colección Estudios CIEPLAN*, no. 4 (November 1980). Data for those businesses whose terms of payment went beyond 1980 were figured on the basis of an assumed constant rate of exchange of 39 pesos per dollar, with zero inflation for 1981 and after. These assumptions give us an estimate of the minimum value of the subsidies implicit in the sale of the assets of CORFO.

The subsidy implicit in the conditions of sale was greater for the banks, although the payment period terms agreed on at the time of sale were less advantageous (a two-year term in the case of the banks as compared with a ten-year term for most of the businesses). In part this probably has to do with the greater speed with which the privatization of the banking industry was carried out, or with the fact that the process was pushed forward in the period of greatest inflation combined, as it was, with an acute economic recession. [*Editors' note:* See also Table 1.9, above.]

15. The full list of those companies is the following: Compañía de Electricidad, CAP, Companía de Teléfonos de Chile, Compañía de Teléfonos de Coyhaique, Compañía de Teléfonos de Valdivia, ENACAR, ENDESA, ECOM, ENTEL, LANSA, ENAEX, and SOQUIMICH.

16. In any case, the constant conflict between statements made by representatives of the economic team, on the one hand, and those made by civilian and military personnel in charge of public enterprises or having other responsibilities in government units involved in economic planning, on the other, show that there is no agreement within the government regarding a definite goal for the process of privatization.

17. See the interview with Minister of Economic Affairs S. de Castro in *El Mercurio,* 15 February 1976.

18. In addition to the affiliates of CORFO, there exist *(a)* state enterprises created by law and governed by norms of public or private law: ECA, ENAMI, ENAP, EMPREMAR, EMOS, LAN, EMPORCHI, ETC, Correos y Telégrafos, FF.CC. del Estado; *(b)* firms set up as corporations, ruled by norms of private law: Chilectra, Laboratorios Chile, etc.; and *(c)* enterprises created by law but subject to

special legal and financial rules, as in the case of CODELCO. It has been suggested that these enterprises will probably become part of a government holding company, with the aim of achieving a coordinated control and more efficient management of them.

19. Nonetheless, the absence of adequate channels of commercialization, as well as of technical and credit assistance, has prevented many small farmers from making full use of their lands. For this reason, they have been forced to sell their property. One estimate indicates that about 50% of these plots had been sold by the end of 1979 (J. Crispi, "El agro chileno después de 1973: Expansión capitalista y campesinización pauperizante" [paper presented at the conference entitled "Six Years of Military Government in Chile," organized at the Woodrow Wilson International Center for Scholars, Washington, D.C., 15–17 May 1984]). Decree 3,516 of December 1980, which permits the legal subdivision of land into plots of any size, will surely reinforce this tendency.

20. Figures for the GDI as a percentage of the GDP are as follows: 1974, 17.1; 1975, 15.4; 1976, 12.7; 1977, 13.3; 1978, 14.4; 1979, 15.6 (ODEPLAN, "Cuentas Nacionales," in *Boletín Mensual,* various issues).

21. All figures in the preceding paragraph are derived from J. Marshall, "Gasto del sector público en Chile, 1969–1979: Metodología y resultados," *Notas técnicas CIEPLAN,* no. 3 (1981).

22. Ibid.

23. See J. Marshall and P. Romaguera, "La evolución del empleo público en Chile, 1973–1978," *Notas Técnicas CIEPLAN,* no. 26 (February 1981), and O. Muñoz, J. Gatica, and P. Romaguera, "Crecimiento y estructura del empleo estatal en Chile, 1940–1970," *Notas Técnicas CIEPLAN,* no. 22 (January 1980). Public employment in the social sectors retained and even increased its relative importance in total public employment. However, employment figures for the education sector may be strongly underestimating a drop that occured in 1974, since they do not include teaching personnel per class hour, a category in which reduction of personnel is most easily effected. It is possible to get an idea of the extent of this ommission if we consider that, in 1970, employment in the Direcciones del Ministerio de Educación amounted to 82,000 people and the number of people employed per class hour was 8,700 full-time-equivalent workers, a figure representing almost 15% of the total employment in the sector. The increase in employment in education beginning in 1976 was the result of an expansion in the administrative apparatus of the Ministry of Education and of the national system of kindergartens.

24. Of the total decrease in employment in this sector, 95% can be explained by the elimination or reduction of personnel in six institutions related to the agrarian reform, to the regulation of agricultural prices, and to the regulation and development of animal husbandry.

25. Looking at just the ten state enterprises created by law and the twelve CORFO affiliates considered to be strategic, we see that employment dropped by some 12.3% between 1970 and 1978 (J. C. Méndez, "Un intento de medición del tamaño del sector público/empresarial del estado en Chile" [mimeo, Centro de Estudios Públicos, 1981]). If to this we add the more than 400 enterprises

transferred to the private sector, it is possible to arrive at an idea of the extent to which the decline in public employment in the productive sectors is underestimated by official figures.

26. In order to understand the drastic nature of the reduction of personnel in public works, it is necessary to keep in mind that in this area the public sector takes direct responsibility, through the Dirección General of this ministry, for the greater part of all construction that is undertaken. Since the majority of the personnel in this ministry are laborers, they are automatically dismissed as activities are suspended. Thus, the entire reduction of personnel in this sector (15,300 persons) occurred in the Dirección General del Ministerio de Obras Públicas, a decrease only partially compensated for by the increase in workers hired for the construction of the subway in Santiago (1,900).

27. The increase in employment in Administración General can be explained by the increase in the number of people employed in Administración Política, Relaciones Exteriores, and Protección y Justicia, and by an increase in expenditures for the police.

28. The figures are the estimates of Marshall and Romaguera, "La evolución del empleo público," done on the basis of the number of contributors to the Cajas de Previsión de la Defensa y de Carabineros.

29. In October 1973 most price controls were lifted, leaving under control about thirty products, whose prices since then have been gradually decontrolled.

30. On this topic, see A. Foxley, "Hacia una economía de libre mercado: Chile, 1974–1979," *Colección Estudios CIEPLAN,* no. 4 (November 1980).

31. A detailed analysis of the development of this process can be found in T. Moulián and P. Vergara, "Políticas de estabilización y comportamientos sociales: La experiencia chilena, 1973–1978," *Apuntes CIEPLAN,* no. 22 (November 1979).

32. The minimum period of deposit required for funds to earn interest was a mere four days. In April of 1975 this period was extended to fifteen days and later to thirty days.

The extreme freedom with which private financial involvement was allowed to play an intermediary role during the period of highest inflation, using very liquid assets and thus creating near substitutes for money, contributed to the increase in the money supply. This seriously lessened the possibility for monetary control by the economic authorities, despite the fact that this control would constitute the basis for the stabilization program.

33. In December 1975 the Banco Central discontinued the exchange of VHRs for BHRs and authorized their exchange for real savings certificates (Certificados de Ahorro Reajustables) of the Banco Central, payable in fifteen years and nontransferable.

[*Editors' note:* For figures showing the drop in savings in public institutions in favor of private ones, see Table 1.8.]

34. It is not surprising, then, that a considerable fraction of domestic savings and foreign financial resources have been channeled into the importation of consumer goods in order to satisfy the demands of the high income

groups, or toward short-term financial speculation, with a resulting negative impact on the investment process. See R. Ffrench-Davis, "Liberalización de importaciones: La experiencia chilena en 1973–1979," *Colección Estudios CIE-PLAN,* no. 4 (November 1980, and P. Vergara, "Apertura externa y desarrollo industrial en Chile, 1973–1978," ibid.

35. Certain limitations were also imposed regarding the minimum period of repatriation and the ability to grant endorsements.

36. The need for monetary control, an issue the government always raises, could have been handled through qualitative controls on indebtedness, as (for example) by fixing deposits or taxes on income.

37. Out of the total amount of foreign credit entering the country between 1976 and 1978 under the new liberalized regulations, 90% corresponded to indebtedness in the private sector and only 8% in the public. Credit in turn was concentrated in some few businesses and commercial banks: during this period the six principal commercial banks used 72% of the credit obtained by commercial banking; see J. Morales, "Principales usuarios y rentabilidad potencial del endeudamiento" (unpublished essay, 1979, and also R. Zahler, "Repercusiones monetarias y reales de la apertura financiera al exterior: El caso chileno, 1975–1978," *Revista de la CEPAL,* no. 10 (April 1980). These figures refer to the credit entering the country under article 14 of the Ley de Cambios Internacionales, which was the channel through which the bulk of foreign credit entered.

38. R. Ffrench-Davis and J. P. Arellano, "La apertura financiera: La experiencia chilena en 1973–1980" (paper presented at the Seminario Internacional sobre Relaciones Financieras Externas y su Impacto en las Economías Latinoamericanas, CIEPLAN, Santiago, 19–21 March 1981).

39. D. L. 600 of May 1977, enacted once Chile had withdrawn from the Cartagena agreement and was no longer subject to the norms regulating the influx of foreign capital into the countries of the area. In practice, the law discriminates in favor of foreign investment by assuring it of a stable tax rate for ten years and by allowing the entire capital investment to be withdrawn from the country at the end of three years.

40. In addition, despite the speed with which the massive transfer of real and financial resources to the private sector was carried out, the military regime kept for a long time—and still keeps—a large part of the legal powers, inherited from previous governments, on which the state had relied in order to intervene in the economic process. Although economic legislation has become much more liberal, the powers of the state to intervene are still quite broad, even though no use is made of them. The new decrees issued under the present government (those concerning CORFO's power to intervene in and administer companies in which the state has an interest, the naming of government representatives in cases of bankruptcy and of collective layoffs or unauthorized work stoppages, etc.) have not significantly diminished the legal powers of the state. Indeed, still in force is D. L. 1,379 of 1966, which contains a revised text of decree 520 and reproduces its principal points. See *El Mercurio,* 7 September 1980, and *El Mercurio,* "Informe Económico Mensual," April 1980.

41. See Cortázar and Marshall, "Indice de precios al consumidor en Chile" and Instituto Nacional de Estadística, *Indice de sueldo y salarios.*

42. Foxley, Aninat, and Arellano, *Las desigualdades económicas.*

43. See Marshall, "Gasto del sector público."

44. Ibid.

45. The pronounced expansion of spending in the category labeled "Other cultural services" in Table 3.4 is explained by a notable increase in the activities of the Dirección General de Recreación y Deportes (DIGEDER), an institution that is presently under the Ministerio de Defensa (J. Marshall, "Gasto del sector público").

46. Foxley, Aninat, and Arellano, *Las desigualdades económicas.*

47. During 1980, about 38% of the square meters of housing constructed in Santiago were concentrated in the two wealthiest of the city's seventeen *comunas,* as compared to less than 10% in 1970. The average size of houses built in those *comunas* was 114 square meters, higher than the average for Greater Santiago, which was 70 square meters.

48. J. P. Arellano, "Sistemas alternativos de seguridad social: Un análisis de la experiencia chilena," *Colección Estudios CIEPLAN,* no. 4 (November 1980).

49. For an analysis of the development of financial and human resources in the health area between 1969 and 1978, see CPU, "El sector salud y sus recursos financieros: Análisis de una década," *Documento de trabajo,* no. 187 (October 1979).

50. The central elements of this new policy are contained in the "Directiva presidencial sobre educación nacional," March 1979; in a letter of the president of the republic to the Ministry of Education, appended to the "Directiva"; and in the 5 March 1979 speech of the president of the republic at the opening of the school year.

51. Under the new policy, mayors and not the principals of the schools, will choose teachers. Since mayors are appointed by the president, this will grant strong power to the executive in the management of educational institutions. It will also put an end to the national *carrera docente* system, on which promotions and transfers of teachers depended. The result will be a great deal of instability and uncertainty for teachers, since promotion and dismissal will be decided exclusively by the employer, in this case the mayor. This can become an additional factor encouraging the transfer of the most qualified personnel to the private area.

52. "Directiva" (see note 50 above).

53. *Diario Oficial,* 3 January 1981. In accordance with the text of the Nueva Ley de Universidades, in the future universities will enjoy academic, financial, and administrative autonomy. The law says nothing about the methods for generating the authorities. However, the faculty, administrative personnel, and students are denied voting participation in the organs charged with directing the universities as well as in the election of the authorities.

54. Until now, only the position of director of the National Health Service had been considered a political position, with the person holding it named by the president of the republic.

55. Through each regional administration, the Ministry of Health will maintain a professional register and will be responsible for controlling professional practice. It will also authorize and supervise the functioning of establishments in the private sector. Only professional honoraria and private institutions' charges to patients will be outside its jurisdiction.

56. The cheapest houses had a value of approximately $12,500, and the subsidies, an amount which varied between US $4,000 and US $5,000 per house.

57. The maximum value a house can have is 266.7 Unidades de Fomento (U.F.), which is approximately $8,000 in U.S. dollars, current value as of May 1981. In practice, however, the amount of the subsidies sought will be much less than in the past, since, under the new system, the possibility of obtaining this benefit is inversely proportional to the amount asked for, a situation which favors those who ask for lower subsidies.

58. See Departamento de Economía, "Comentarios sobre la situación económica," first semester, 1978.

59. E. Tironi, "Reflecciones sobre la política económica chilena: Estimación del impacto de la reforma a la tributación de las empresas" (CIEPLAN mimeo, 1975).

60. Beginning in 1975, the great majority of exemptions involving essential consumer items have been progressively eliminated. On the other hand, the raw materials destined for the production of export items have been exempted from the IVA.

61. Both figured as an average of the liquid salaries white-collar and blue-collar workers were achieving at that time (Arellano "Sistemas alternativos"; Cortázar and Marshall, "Indice de precios."

62. J. P. Arellano, "Elementos para un análisis de la reforma previsional," mimeo, CIEPLAN, June 1981.

63. Ibid.

64. However, the law grants a reduction in rates to those who change systems, which means an increase in the worker's liquid pay. This, together with the small probability that pensions under the old system would improve, acts as a stimulus to changing over.

65. See Arellano, "Elementos para un análisis," op. cit., section 5.

66. Arellano, "Sistemas alternativos," op. cit.

67. The regulations which attempt the dismantling of social organizations affect not only workers or low-income sectors. They also extend to the professional organizations, including owner's associations.

This is how the 1980 Constitution, in an effort also to "privatize" the professions, abolished the obligation to affiliate with professional societies and the dues requirement which the latter imposed. This will inevitably result in the weakening of these organizations.

In the same vein, a decree was issued introducing modifications in business organizations.

Finally, the freedom from mandatory dues for some organizations of the petit bourgeoisie will have similar results: it will weaken their organizations, and will even to put their former members in competition with each other.

Although it has been discussed in this work, it is important to mention the fragmentation and isolation that agricultural policies have produced for small landowners and farmers. Formerly farmworkers could articulate their demands and express them collectively through their unions, cooperatives, or other organizations in that sector, the role of which was to negotiate and represent to the state the complaints of their members. Now farmworkers are atomized and scattered, with no power to negotiate collectively.

[*Editors' note:* For a discussion of the Labor Plan and of the labor movement, see Chapter 7.]

The Legal and Institutional Framework of the Armed Forces in Chile

Genaro Arriagada Herrera

The current political situation in Chile is characterized by a dramatic contradiction. A government that has very weak national and international political support nevertheless has very strong military backing. We can also say that since the 1973 military coup there was an asymmetrical evolution: while General Pinochet progressively increased his control over the armed forces, his government significantly lost its political and social support.

This chapter focuses on certain key aspects of the military policies of the Chilean government. It seeks to redress a common shortcoming in studies about military governments, which often neglect to refer to the armed forces, to military policies, and to the characteristic ways of thinking of the officer corps. However, the scope of this article is limited almost exclusively to the army. Its main concern is to identify certain internal elements of that institution which have made it possible for the present chief of state to control it.

I recognize that this focus neglects fundamental means used by autocratic governments to gain the complete loyalty of armies. These include measures to increase the standard of living of the officers (by improving salaries, benefits, and so on) as well as measures that more directly affect their institutional interests (such as the purchase of armaments, improvement of living quarters, artillery practice ranges, casinos, etc.).

This paper will give some, but not thorough, attention to ideology—in other words to the beliefs, ideas, and values that are used to legitimate, justify, and determine a course of political action while ensuring the loyalty of the armed forces.[1] Briefly stated, a particular version of anti-Communism, expressed in a certain conception of counterinsurgency warfare, is a fundamental element used in legitimizing the repressive practices of the authoritarian regimes of Chile and the Southern Cone. Out of this conception flows not only a militant anti-Marxism but also a strong rejection of political liberalism.[2] At the same time, from geopolitical thought emerges an organicist conception of the state that is counterposed to both the liberal and Marxist-Leninist conceptions of the state.[3] To the extent that the Chilean authoritarian regime, with its anti-Communism and its rejection of liberalism, expounds fundamental aspects of the political ideology of the military, it finds an overwhelming acceptance within the armed forces.

This article concentrates on those mechanisms which are internal to the military institution and which relate to the way the Army High Command is structured, to the prerogatives and rights of officers, and to the powers of the head of state and the chief of staff.[4] We will analyze how, under the present government, the military power that runs the institution, and that determines the extent and character of the political participation of the military, has structured itself. Despite their great importance, these factors are seldom analyzed and are practically unknown to the civilian world. We will examine four principal mechanisms. The first is the fusion of the positions of head of state and of chief of staff of the army. The second is the repeal, for the chief of staff only, of the rules concerning retirement on account of old age. The third is the installation of a new hierarchy of command that goes, in the case of the chief of staff of the army, from the position of member of the military junta to that of president of the republic. And the fourth mechanism is the power that the army chief of staff has over the careers of the officers.

This kind of study is eminently formal, and certainly this is its limitation. Nevertheless, in evaluating the convenience of this type of focus for military topics, it is necessary not to forget that the army is essentially a formal institution—a bureaucracy—that maintains great autonomy from society as a whole, both in its social structure and in its ways of thinking and judgement. In this bureaucracy, formal elements—ideology, judicial order, hierarchical structure, career patterns—have an importance that is in most cases overwhelmingly superior to that which they would have in the civilian world.

A final observation. Because of the enormously controversial character of a study such as this one, I have used only official sources in the public record, such as laws, decrees, rulings, speeches, and official pronouncements.

The Government's Position on the Duration of
the Regime and the Role of the Armed Forces

The regime's position on its own duration and on the role of the armed forces within it has evolved through a series of partially self-contradictory stages throughout these years. At the very beginning, the authorities presented their actions as ones which would restore a lost democracy. They developed a discourse that drew its predominant ideological elements from Chile's political tradition of democracy and respect for the rule of law.

They also expressed a strong anti-Marxism and an economic liberalism more moderate than the one which would develop later.

The two texts that best express the ideology of the government during this first stage are Edict No. 5 and Decree No. 1, by which the military junta was constituted. They point out the reasons invoked by the military for assuming "the moral duty that the Fatherland had imposed on them to bring down the government that, although initially legitimate, had fallen into flagrant illegitimacy." This illegitimacy had been "shown by breaking the fundamental rights of freedom of speech, freedom of education, the right to property, and the right in general to a worthy and secure livelihood." Edict No. 5 also said that Allende's government "sundered national unity by not following nor making the people follow the law," by "being at the margin of the Constitution on multiple occasions," by not implementing the decisions of the National Congress and the Judiciary, and by trying "in a blatant and deliberate way" to concentrate in the executive branch "the greatest amount of political and economic power, to the detriment of vital national activities and putting in great danger all the rights and freedom of the inhabitants of the country."[5]

The military regime claimed that it was assuming "power only for the length of time that circumstances may require,"[6] and that it was doing it with "the patriotic objective of restoring Chilean pride and justice, as well as the institutional framework that had been broken."[7] The new authorities did not commit themselves to building a new political and socioeconomic order.

The role of the armed forces in the political regime was presented as a subsidiary one. They had intervened only at the last moment because they were the ultimate safeguard of the state, being "the organization that the state had given itself to shield and defend its physical and moral integrity and its historical-cultural identity."[8] Without question the relatively moderate tone of this ideological phase was prompted by a search for legitimacy within the context of the preceding historical period. At that point, the principles evoked by the opposition to the Popular Unity government were those of freedom, democracy, autonomy of mediating social organisms, respect for the law and the constitution, and defense of the political, economic, and social accomplishments of the population.

The second stage found its most complete expression in the "Declaration of Principles of the Government of Chile," released in March of 1974, six months after the military coup. This document had a very different tone, since it did not define the military regime's task as a merely restorative one. It stated straightforwardly that the "armed forces and the police [carabineros] do not set timetables for their management of the government, because the task of rebuilding the country morally, institutionally, and economically requires prolonged and profound action," for which it was "absolutely imperative to change the mentality of the Chileans." The government rejected categorically the idea of "limiting itself to being merely an administration inserted between two similar party-based governments." Nevertheless, the junta declared that "at the appropriate time it will turn over political power to those whom the citizens elect through universal, free, secret, and informed suffrage." But it noted that "the previous statement does not mean that the armed forces will wash their hands of the issue of governmental succession, observing the outcome like simple spectators. On the contrary . . . [the military junta] considers it as part of their mission to inspire a new and great civilian-military movement . . . whose aims will deeply and lastingly reflect the work of the present government."[9]

The armed forces viewed this unlimited commitment to governing as part of their professional duty. When the junta, "at the right moment," returns "political power to those whom the citizens elect . . . the armed forces then will assume the specific institutional role that the new constitution assigns them, and it will be one appropriate to those in charge of guarding national security, in the ample meaning that such a concept has today."[10] The statement did not specify how broad that concept might be.

The third stage in the evolution of the government's policies, beginning in late 1975, was characterized by the clear predominance of two central themes of military ideology: the doctrine of counterinsurgency warfare and a geopolitical definition of national security. In this stage, more than ever, the ideology of the governing regime and of the military grew closer together.

This preeminence of key elements of military ideology was not a coincidence. They had been part of the regime's outlook since the beginning. They had already played a significant role in the "Declaration of Principles." In a subsequent government document, called the "National Objective of the Government of Chile,"[11] national security and a moderating dose of economic liberalism were the basic elements. An ideological viewpoint developed along these lines and reached its peak in the Presidential Message of 1976 and the prefaces to Constitutional Acts Nos. 2, 3, and 4. Here, on the third anniversary of the coup d'etat, the doctrines of national security and counterinsurgency were subscribed to totally by the military government.

The duration of the military regime was therefore presented as subordinate to the problem of the anti-Communist war. In the presidential message, the enemy, Marxism, was defined ideologically as "an intrinsically perverse doctrine which means that everything that comes out of it, even if it looks healthy, is made rotten by the poison that runs from its roots." Its practical consequence was characterized as "permanent aggression, which today is at the service of Soviet imperialism. . . . This modern form of permanent aggression gives rise to an unconventional war, in which territorial invasion is replaced by the attempt to control the state from within. In the presence of a Marxism based on permanent aggression, it is imperative to give power to the armed forces, since they are the only ones that have the organization and means to confront Marxism."[12]

This formulation is reminiscent of Ludendorff's theories of war as total in many and varied ways: it has no end, and there is no distinction between periods of war and peace. The war against Marxism includes all countries, but has no borders or national enemies, since the enemy is internal as well as external. It is a total war in that there are a variety of weapons: economic, social, psychological, and only at the end military. The inevitable corollary of this apocalyptic vision is "to root power in the armed forces" in a permanent way, since the aggression that threatens to destroy the state is permanent too. There is, without a doubt, no place in this plan for the people nor any perspective for democracy.

This ideological posture was too extreme to survive for very long. Actually, it was phased out over time. Put forward in the months following the promulgation of the decree to dissolve the National Intelligence Agency (DINA) and to create the National Information Center (CNI), it was probably the ideological framework best suited to the harshest period of the regime. In any case, some of its central elements were already present in the previous stage and carry over into the following ones.

A typical characteristic of the political stance of the Chilean regime is the continuous succession of measures and countermeasures. Thus, in July of 1977, six months after the most antidemocratic assertions of the third phase, Pinochet gave his "Chacarillas speech," which contained a very lukewarm statement about democratization.

This speech clearly initiated a fourth stage, one whose characterization depends on the point of reference. When compared with the first stage, its language is definitely antidemocratic, a serious development considering the time that had elapsed since the coup. One would arrive at the same conclusion in comparison with the second stage, since, as we have seen, the 1974 "Declaration of Principles" stated that power would be returned to authorities elected by universal suffrage. By 1977, this had changed. It was then asserted that the president of the republic would be chosen by an assembly two-thirds of whose members would be elected and one-third appointed by the regime. It could be argued that in March of 1974 the government did not have timetables but goals, and that in 1977, by contrast, a date was set for the return to power of authorities to be at least partially elected by the people. This was certainly an improvement, but it does not seem so notable if one considers that the change was to take place in 1991, fourteen years after the announcement of the "democratization plan."

The political role of the military in 1977 was presented differently from the one assigned to it in 1976. It was an ambiguous and curious role: "As an integral part of an authoritarian democracy, it will be necessary to reserve to the institutions of national defense the juridical participation that belongs to them regarding future security needs. Above and beyond all political contingencies, these institutions should be structured to represent the most permanent part of the nation and to exercise the utmost caution which their character suggests."[13] This is a very cryptic allusion. Nevertheless, the precise sense of these security needs would be clarified later, in the new basic law presented by the governmental Commission on Constitutional Reform.

A fifth stage in the ideological stance of the regime can be identified more recently. Its most concrete expression is the message of General Pinochet, pronounced on the sixth anniversary of the military coup. The big difference between this stage and any of the previous ones is the role of the armed forces in the political regime. For the first time, the armed forces were excluded from any significant role in the political arena, and emphasis was placed on the historic conception of military professionalism. At first sight it seems surprising that the traditional principles of the Chilean armed forces, characteristic of the period of democratic rule, would appear to have reemerged: apoliticism, nondeliberation, subordination to the executive power, professionalism. "Our armed forces and police," Pinochet asserted, "are not politicized, because they have understood that the power of the state lies in their Chiefs of Staff and their Director Generals, respectively." "High commanders," he emphasized, "should inform their subordinates about government matters, an obligation that the President of the Republic has made his own . . . by informing general officers and complete garrisons about national affairs and the actions of the government. But all this should be done without falling into political rhetoric, a mistake that has caused a deterioration in the unity and prestige of these commanders, leading to the overthrow of certain military governments in other countries as well as in our own before. It is this lack of politicization [the principle of nondeliberation] which has allowed us to maintain the forces of our national defense in an optimal state of professionalism and preparation."[14]

The development I have presented here can be described like the movement through a parabolic curve. The movement began as the Chilean armed forces, by assuming power, broke with their doctrine of nondeliberation, professionalism, and subordination to civilian and democratic governments. It continued as they extended their rule without time limitations, abandoning their initially expressed aim of restoring the previous democratic order; this they justified by asserting that civil society did not have the proper conditions for democratic governance and that these conditions would have to be created. Then the top military command in control of the government began to revive the old doctrine of subordination to political power, nondeliberation, and professionalism, leading to a progressive removal of the institutional participation of the armed forces in policy-making decisions. The end point in the parabolic curve—the subordination of the armed forces to the established government—is therefore at the same level as the initial one, but the end point's distance from the original one is also great: we have gone from a democratic to an authoritarian regime. This parabolic movement figuratively illustrates the development of the armed forces' relationship to the government during these years and clarifies Pinochet's military policies in his strategy to obtain complete control of the army.

The Chilean army was, without question, the most professional in South America. No other had incorporated to such an extent the principles of subordination to civil power, obedience, hierarchy, and nondeliberation. Removed from political struggles for forty years, its internal structure in general had not been fragmented by political quarrels nor by the penetration of civilian parties into the barracks in search of military support for their political designs. This started to change with the "Tacnazo" military insurrection led by General Roberto Viaux in 1969, four years before the military coup. The decomposition of the Chilean military tradition, which was dramatically accelerated under the Popular Unity government, was a decisive factor—although neither the only nor the most important one—in the military coup of 1973. Nevertheless, what appears to be contradictory is that after the coup Pinochet began to deliberately recompose the military tradition. This recomposition was carried out in a framework that I will call "tarnished professionalism" (*profesionalismo desvirtuado*).

The apparent contradiction lies in the fact that the processes of decomposition and recomposition of the Chilean military tradition both moved to produce the same result: first facilitating the coup d'etat (decomposition) and then serving to consolidate the authoritarian regime (recomposition). But this contradiction is resolved if we remember that we are not talking about the same type of professionalism. The traditional professionalism of the Chilean army before 1973 was followed by the construction of a "tarnished" one: both supposedly rested upon the same principles, but actually these principles have been fundamentally altered in such a way that they now serve not only a different political end, but they also destroy the bases of traditional professionalism.

In a nutshell, tarnished professionalism is a form of domination over the army itself, that has as its basis the abusive use, the manipulation in a dictatorial political context of a highly developed professional military tradition and of the values that characterized it—i.e., subordination to political power, obedience, nondeliberation, hierarchy, and discipline. Also important as an essential requisite is the creation of instability and arbitrariness in the decisions about promotion and retirement of officers, through which the same professional values now tend to be upheld by force. The concept of tarnished professionalism could have great explanatory value for the analysis of situations like the Chilean one, where it is not possible to talk simply about the professional army,[15] nor of the praetorian army,[16] nor of the revolutionary army, nor of the "new professionalism."[17]

The Increasing Duties of the Chief of State and the Commander in Chief of the Army

In a mature political system, and of course in a democracy, civilian control of the military apparatus requires that the chief of state fulfill the function of highest authority of the armed forces. The armed forces are a creation of the state, and they should be subordinated to whomever exercizes the highest authority in it.

In short, in a mature political system the political and military roles are perfectly differentiated, hierarchized, and legitimated in distinct ways. The head of state is the highest state authority, and the chiefs of staff and the armed forces are subject to his orders. The latter, in terms of their technical function, are protected from undesirable political interference. The head of state defines the political objectives of the military apparatus, and the chiefs of staff define its technical-professional function. The source of the legitimacy of the head of state is political; that of the chiefs of staff is technical and bureaucratic.

A military dictatorship confuses these roles. The duties of the chief of state and of the chiefs of staff are fused in the same person. This confusion of duties, as historical experience shows, leads to the rupture of the basic parameters of military professionalism. In the first place, it thoroughly involves the army in political contingencies and in the quarrels between parties. Tied to its chief of staff, who is at the same time the political head of state, the army not only fulfills a technical function within the society but becomes an armed guardian of specific policies being promoted by the government. This has an inevitable repercussion on the careers of officers, since it affects promotions and retirements. An officer's political and personal loyalty to the chief of state and his policies acquires higher priority than professional merits, including seniority.

In order to avoid this confusion and its drawbacks, the armies of other Southern Cone countries have established military regimes where the political and the military duties have been differentiated once again. In this way the armed forces reach political and military objectives that would be impossible were both functions to be given to the same person. Among the political objectives is that of trying to prevent power from becoming personalized; limits are therefore set on the personal power and tenure of whoever is exercising momentarily the function of chief of state. The military objective in separating the duties is to try to prevent a possible dictatorship of the chief of staff from being used, once consolidated, against his own army, destroying all ranks and manipulating the careers of officers to serve extraprofessional considerations.

Thus, the Argentinian, Uruguayan, and Brazilian regimes clearly differentiated the duties of president of the republic and of chief of staff. In Argentina, the military junta was formed by the chiefs of staff of three branches of the national defense: army, navy, and air force. This junta, constituted as the highest organism of the political system, "nominates and removes the president of the republic, exercises ultimate political control and tacitly retains for itself constitutional power. Individually, the chiefs of staff continue in command of the armed forces and the police, as well as having the final decision in relation to promotions and appointments within each branch. The president of the nation holds all the powers that the constitution assigns to that position, with the exception of the military command. On the other hand, he has congressional powers, which he shares with an organism of control and consultation made up of officers of the three branches of the armed forces."[18]

The Uruguayan regime had a structure of power that also distinguished between the junta, the military commanders, and the president of the republic. The president of the republic was a civilian, named by the junta (such was the case with Aparicio Méndez) or removed by the junta (Bordaberry's case). This civilian president exercised executive power without its military attributes. The chiefs of staff retained power within their institutions, in a balanced setting that tried to protect the careers of officers from arbitrariness and manipulations.

The Brazilian case differed from that of Argentina and Uruguay in that the armed forces were the decisive power in the nomination of the presidential candidate, who was to be chosen by an electoral college. This nomination has fallen, to date, on retired generals. Nevertheless, once the nomination was made, the powers of the president of the republic were those characteristic of a mature political system. The president named and removed the chiefs of staff and was the supreme chief of the armed forces during the presidential period, which originally lasted four years and now lasts five years.

Nothing like what I have mentioned happens in the Chilean case, where General Pinochet has accumulated in his own hands the duties of head of state and chief of staff, thereby becoming the holder of the most power of any head of state throughout the long history of the Chilean republic, even exceeding the power that Colonel Carlos Ibáñez had during his dictatorship from 1927 to 1931.

Repeal of the Rules for Retirement by Seniority with Respect to the Chiefs of Staff

Chilean military legislation prior to 1973, like that of practically all professional armies of the world, established rules for retirement by seniority of generals and the chiefs of staff. These rules noted that all officers who "have served for 38 years in that capacity, or 40 effective years toward retirement, should retire fully. Nevertheless the President of the Republic can reject the applications of those officers who will be acting as Institutional Chiefs of Staff and as the Chief of Staff for National Defense, allowing them to remain active for three more years."[19]

Several important reasons justified these rules. Politically, it did not seem prudent that such a powerful position as that of chief of staff should be held by only one person for such a long time; the risk in this case would be that of establishing the predominance of the chief of staff over other high officials, including the president of the republic, thereby breaking the balance of power within the state. This risk is obviously greater in a democracy, but it is not exclusive to it. In the other military regimes of the Southern Code (Brazil, Argentina, and Uruguay) the chiefs of staff were subject to rules of retirement by seniority.

In terms of military power, exempting chiefs of staff from rules of retirement is even riskier. It ends up personalizing the head of the armed service, which becomes a threat for the military institution itself as well as for the careers of the officers. The powers and the formal and informal influence of the chief of staff over the retirement and promotion of his comrades in arms are so significant that the continuous exercise of those attributes by the same person introduces the threat of developing a corps of generals and superior officers elected less because of their military merits than because of their personal loyalties and friendships. This leads to the failure of the fundamental principle of military professionalism.

Moreover, the long tenure of a chief of staff heading a corps of generals which is undergoing continuous renovation inevitably creates great differences of age, experience, and influence between the chief and his generals. This tends to destroy the collaborative work which is part of the essence of the general staffs and which is needed for the management of a great bureaucracy like the army. Within the army, which is the most hierarchized institution in society, there is no possibility for a valid exchange of opinions between the chief of staff and a general who is twenty years younger, who actually owes part of his career to the chief of staff and who was a captain or recently promoted major when his superior was already a general.

These rules were repealed on the last working day of 1976. On this date two decrees (Nos. 1,639 and 1,640) of very disparate meaning were enacted.

The first one established an exception to the rule of full retirement by seniority in favor of all the generals—generals of the army, air force, and police (*carabineros*), vice-admirals and rear admirals in the navy—who "found themselves fulfilling . . . government functions to be classified by the president of the republic by supreme decree."[20] This ruling had the effect of strengthening the power of General Pinochet over the corps of generals of his own service as well as of the other branches of national defense, since generals obligated to retire fully on account of seniority could remain in their military positions as long as General Pinochet, as president of the republic, wished. Despite the fact that they hold the highest ranks in their services, the positions of these generals in government functions therefore became absolutely precarious. Moreover, the decree opened the way to an "inflation" of the corps of generals, since it clearly established that each time a general was exempted from full retirement via this decree, then "it will be understood that the positions for generals in their respective institutional sites will be temporarily increased."[21] Thus, the corps of army generals has risen from twenty-five positions in 1973, to thirty-eight in 1979, and to forty-two in 1980.

The second decree, No. 1,640, was even more significant than the first. While the first one created phantom posts of general or vice-admiral or rear admiral, lacking any stability, the latter one established the positions of chiefs of staff practically for life. The precarious condition of the general in government functions thus contrasts dramatically with the lifelong stability of the office of chief of staff.

In effect, the retirement by seniority rules that affected the chiefs of staff were incompatible with the Statute of the Governmental Junta, the proto-constitutional Decree No. 527 governing the composition and modus operandi of the military junta. This decree states in its article 18 that the chiefs of staff of the military and police institutions, who constitute the junta, can lose their positions in the junta only by "death, resignation, or by a total impairment of the person." Decree No. 1,640 was drafted to resolve the contradiction. It simply stated that junta members—and therefore the chiefs of staff—"are not bound by the conditions leading to temporary or full retirement established by the present legislation. The only rule that will apply to them is what is stipulated in Article 18 of Decree 527, of 1974."[22]

The result of this measure has been to radically increase the seniority gap between the chiefs of staff and the rest of the corps of generals. For instance, in 1966, a typical year of the previous democratic period, the distance between the chief of staff, then Bernardino Parada, and the general with the least seniority was only one of four *promociones* (a term referring to the cohorts of graduates from the military academies). General Parada obtained his first appointment in December of 1927, while the general with least seniority obtained his three years later, in December of 1930.

By contrast, in 1980 there was a difference of fifteen *promociones* between the chief of staff and the most junior of the generals in the present corps. While General Pinochet received his first appointment in January of 1937, General Badiola, who was then the one with the least seniority, obtained his in January of 1951. This seniority gap will inevitably continue to increase under the current conditions.[23] Moreover, the gap between General Pinochet and the general second in seniority in 1980, Lieutenant General Raúl Benavides, is the same—four *promociones*—as that which existed between General Parada and the newest of his generals.

From Member of the Military Junta to "Generalissimo" of the Armed Forces

The Chilean democratic regime was obviously structured around the principle of subordination of military power to political power. That was, in the judgement of both military personnel and civilians, the fundamental basis on which the professionalism of the armed forces was built. As part of this subordination, the highest military authority within the state was the president of the republic. As stated in the Constitution, it was the president's responsibility "to provide the civilian and military jobs that the laws allow according to administrative statute, and to confer, in accordance with the Senate, the ranks of colonel, navy captain, and other superior officers of the army and navy. In the battlefield the President himself can confer these high military positions."[24] The president of the republic was also able to "organize and distribute the army and the navy in whatever way he finds convenient" and to personally command them with the consent of the Senate. In this case, the president of the republic could establish residence any place occupied by the Chilean army.[25] The text of the Constitution also assigned the president with overall responsibility for "the preservation of public order within the republic as well as the external security of the republic, in accordance with the Constitution and the laws."[26] Among the presidential powers was that of appointing the chiefs of staff, as well as of calling them into retirement. He could not go below the ranks of division general or brigadier general to fill these positions, it being his duty automatically to retire all those with higher seniority than the generals he designated. Hence, given only these minor restrictions, the position of chief of staff in any of the branches was left to the sole discretion of the president.

The disciplinary norms of the army gave the greatest prerogatives to the president of the republic (eighth rank in disciplinary prerogatives), followed by the minister of defense (seventh rank) and the chief of staff (sixth rank). As stated in the "Disciplinary Regulations" of the army, "the president of the republic, functioning as generalissimo of the army, and the minister of national defense, as a member of the executive, have the highest disciplinary prerogatives over military personnel and army employees."[27]

Two processes occurred after the military coup of 1973. The first one, to be discussed briefly, was the concentration of enormous power in the military junta, exceeding that of the presidency it replaced; and second one was the development within the junta of a growing amount of power in the chief of staff of the army.

The first process is evident in the fact that the National Congress was dissolved, a state of siege was declared which suspended individual rights, and all municipal authorities—who had always been elected in Chile—were removed and replaced by mayors named by the military junta. During the same month of the military coup (as we will see later when refering to the careers of officers) all the decisions about qualifications, promotions, and the retirement of armed forces personnel were given to the members of the military junta, each one of them acting with complete freedom with regard to his institution. In October of 1973, the universities were taken over, political parties of Marxist inclination were dissolved and prohibited, and all other political organizations were declared in recess.

In November 1973, the electoral registries were closed, and the government was authorized to expel people from the country for political reasons. In the same month, the military junta formally assumed constitutional power, with no limitations, which technically did away with the very concept of a constitution. In December 1973, labor union elections were suspended, and the government was authorized to remove and designate the union leaders. Rules that would allow the cancellation of Chilean nationality of political opponents were established, and new emergency measures affecting the career stability of armed forces officers were dictated.

In January 1974, the measures pertaining to the recess of those political parties that did not take part in Allende's government became more stringent. These measures lasted until March 1977, at which time the parties were finally dissolved, their property confiscated. In March of 1974, the suspension of elections for intermediate organizations, thus far in effect only for the unions, was extended to all the other formally recognized organizations of the country, such as neighborhood associations, professional colleges, and centers for mothers. During this period, the rules on control and censorship of the press became progressively tighter, culminating in March 1977 in a total censorship over all printed matter and in the prohibition on forming any means of communication without the prior authorization of the government. Finally in June 1974 the National Intelligence Directorate (DINA) was created.

Parallel to this escalation of power in the military junta, the second process—the increasing concentration of power in the office of the chief of staff of the army—was underway within the junta itself. The position of the chief of staff of the army, General Pinochet, was relatively weak politically when compared with that of the chiefs of staff of the navy and the air force, since the latter two appear to have been originators of the military coup, while Pinochet made a commitment to the insurrection only forty-eight hours before the coup took place, on September 11.

The first formal announcement by the new authorities expressly noted that the military junta had assumed "supreme command of the nation" without indicating any form of differentiation within the junta itself. However, the members of the junta quickly decided that they would "designate Army General Don Augusto Pinochet Ugarte as president of the junta, who assumes on this date [11 September 1973] the said position."[28] Despite this decision the relative standings of the chiefs of staff was at that point so equal that they even thought of rotating the presidency of the junta among each other for short periods of time. Thus, when he was before the press, the General Pinochet pointed out that "the junta worked like a single entity. I was elected because I was the eldest. But I will not be the only president of the junta; afterwards Admiral Merino will be too, and then General Leigh and so on. I am a man without ambitions, I do not want to appear as the only holder of power."[29] Until then, all powers were assumed by the military junta. "The junta has assumed constituent, legislative, and executive powers."[30]

The first substantial change in the structure of power came in mid-1974 with the enactment of the Statute of the Governmental Junta. This document reiterated the principle that executive power lay with the military junta, but it assigned the exercise of that power to the president of the junta. Moreover, it did not recognize the right of the military junta to designate its own president. From then on, the presidency of the junta was to be given "to its titular member who takes precedence according to the rules stipulated by Title IV."[31] That order of precedence could be changed only if the chief of staff of the army were to cease being a member of the junta. This could occur only by "death, resignation, or an absolute impairment of the person" as stipulated in the statute.[32]

In fact, the statute tied the exercise of executive power to Army General Augusto Pinochet, with no time limit and without the possibility of his being recalled by the rest of the members of the junta. General Pinochet became the "supreme chief of the nation," a name that had been used only in the first constitutions following the Declaration of Independence to designate the titular holders of executive power.

By virtue of the statute, the members of the military junta did retain within the executive power certain prerogatives. They can "collaborate" with the supreme chief in "the exercise of his executive functions by assuming the directions of those activities, areas or duties which he [the supreme chief] requests of them." In addition, the naming of ministers, ambassadors, governors, and administrative officers should be made "with the agreement of the Junta, although these civil servants will keep their posts as long as they enjoy the President's trust."[33] According to this same statute, the chief of staff of the navy should oversee the workings of the economic ministries, such as Treasury, Economy, and the Central Bank (Admiral Merino handled these), while the chief of staff of the air force would oversee the social ministries, like Education, Housing, and Health

(General Gustavo Leigh was appointed for these areas). Their power, however, was more apparent than real, since General Pinochet was the one who really held it. By the middle of 1976, Merino and Leigh were hardly mentioned as being in charge of the economic and social sectors of the country.

DINA was created three days before the Statute of the Governmental Junta was issued. Since 11 September 1973, there had been a spectacular development in intelligence services in all branches of national defense. Such services had grown enormously in human and material resources and displayed a lot of activity. There was also a strong rivalry between them. As a consequence, the repressive power of the state emanated from a variety of organizations that were autonomous and difficult to control, leading to abuse and juridical and political irresponsibility by the state police. By the end of 1973 and during the first six months of 1974, it became almost impossible to discover the whereabouts of political prisoners and the cause of their detention. The Ministry of the Interior was in charge only of the civil police, and each branch of the Ministry of National Defense had its own police answerable only to their respective chiefs of staff. It was therefore common for a person to be detained, interrogated, and released by one police service, and immediately thereafter stopped again by another police service.

With the creation of DINA, this situation abruptly ended. All intelligence activity was given to a "military organization with a technical-professional character that took its orders directly from the junta."[34] DINA was formed by personnel from all branches of the National Defense Ministry, plus specially selected civilians.

Although DINA was created to concentrate police power in the hands of the military junta, it did not happen that way, since power was concentrated solely in the supreme chief of the nation. Years later General Leigh, retired from the junta, recounted his experience as follows: "I increasingly took my air force officers out of DINA, not because they were behaving improperly, but rather because of the absolute predominance of the army within DINA. They asked for people from all branches of military service, but the result was that none of my top officers was given executive responsibility; they were assigned only administrative tasks. The organization was in fact linked directly to the president even though, legally, it should have been responsible to the governmental junta. In other words, I took away my people when I realized that I had no power to control DINA."[35]

Until DINA was disbanded in August 1977, it was the backbone of the regime. No other organization during this period had so much influence nationally. And of course this influence in the hands of the president of the military junta destroyed any vestige of balance of power between him and those who, in the months right after the coup, had been his equals.

DINA was formally dissolved because of very strong national and international political pressure, but it was replaced by the National Information

Center (CNI). The CNI was described in the law which created it, like DINA, as "a specialized military organization with a technical-professional character." However, the CNI, which remains the most important police service of the state, was from the very beginning subordinated to the head of the executive power. While DINA, formally speaking at least, "depended on the junta," the law creating CNI stipulated that it "will be linked to the Supreme Government . . . through the Secretary of the Interior"[36]—i.e., through a ministry that enjoys the full confidence of the chief of state.

Another facet of General Pinochet's increasing affirmation of power vis-à-vis the junta was the evolution of his title as head of state. When he was appointed, in mid-1974, "supreme chief of the nation," no one expected this designation to be short-lived. And yet, exactly six months after the Statute of the Junta was approved, a new constitutional decree was introduced with a very significant modification: it changed this title to "president of the republic," the one used by democratically elected Chilean heads of state. The decree establishing this change read as follows: "Executive power is exercised by the President of the Governmental Junta who, under the title of President of the Republic of Chile, administers the State and is the Supreme Chief of the Nation."[37]

Formally it was a minor modification. Juridically, however, it meant that General Pinochet would be able to exercise all the functions that the laws and regulations, throughout many years, had given to the president of the republic. Politically it had great significance, since the title of president of the republic was used to try to strip the regime of its de facto origins, covering it instead—or at least attempting to cover it—with the solemnity and stability which always was part of the position of president of the republic. Besides, this distinguished new title given to the president of the military junta helped distance him even more in the power pyramid from other members of the junta. With this title, General Pinochet has concentrated more power in his hands than has any other Chilean leader in this century. Nevertheless, in one sense he has had less power than the former presidents of nation's democratic governments. Curiously, this relative lack of power has been in the military field and requires a brief explanation.

There is no question that in his own service, the army, the power of General Pinochet since 11 September 1973 has been enormous and has encountered no resistance. However, if we examine the other branches of national defense—the navy and the air force—and the police, the situation has been quite different, since the title of president of the republic did not give Pinochet the right to appoint or call into retirement the chiefs of staff of those institutions, which are powers that all the constitutional presidents of Chile had.

As policy differences between the chief of staff of the army (Pinochet) and the chief of staff of the air force (Leigh) developed to a breaking point, this limitation on the power of the new "president of the republic" became more apparent. The struggle between the two members of the junta was resolved by force, since it was impossible to resolve it by law. As we have seen, the chiefs of staff were to hold their posts as commanders and members of the junta until "death, resignation, or an absolute impairment of the person" removed them from office. General Leigh did not want to resign, and he was in good health. On 24 July 1978, however, he was dismissed by a simple supreme decree of the Ministry of the Interior, which declared his "absolute impairment" to continue as a member of the junta.

This resolution was totally out of line with the statute, because the "absolute impairment" that the law referred to could only be physical or mental and should have had nothing to do with political differences, however profound. As has occurred in many other instances during the last decade of Chilean political life, the "absolute impairment" clause was therefore transformed into a legal subterfuge to expel a member of the junta for political differences. This transformation relied on an article of the Statute of the Junta that pointed out that "when there is some doubt as to whether the impairment that prevents a member of the junta from exercising his duties is of such seriousness that he must be replaced . . . the titular members of the junta are entitled to resolve that doubt."[38] Therefore, on the morning of 24 July 1978, all members of the junta except General Leigh declared that Leigh was "totally unable to go on performing his duties." This declaration is stated in a secret document that no one outside the junta, including General Leigh, has seen. Once this precedent was set, the president of the republic and his minister of the interior dictated a decree dismissing the third-ranking member of the junta. The controller-general of the republic, responsible for reviewing the legality of executive decrees, dispatched this one with a surprising statement: "It is understood that this action is juridically a law decree and not an executive decree."

Nevertheless, the subject of legality is not the key concern here: power is. In this sense, the dismissal of General Leigh meant that a new and decisive step had been taken in the concentration of power in the hands of the chief of staff of the army, and in the process of self-destruction of the military junta's power. From that moment on, General Pinochet started acting, de facto if not de jure, as generalissimo of the armed forces. In September 1979, for the first time in a presidential message, Pinochet used this title to refer to himself: "The high commanders are responsible for informing their subordinates about matters of government, an obligation that the president of the republic has made his own in his capacity as generalissimo of the armed forces and the police force."[39]

The ceremonial protocol reflected clearly this new enhancement of General Pinochet's position. During 1979, in the most important official functions and celebrations, General Pinochet made arrangements to differentiate himself clearly from the other members of the junta. For example, for the centennial of the naval battle of Iquique on 21 May 1979, as well as for the celebration of the birthday of Bernardo O'Higgins and the transfer of his remains to the so-called "Altar of the Fatherland," five flower offerings were presented. The first one was given by General Pinochet and his minister of defense for the presidency of the republic, and the following four were presented for the army, navy, air force, and police by the vice chief of staff of the army and by the respective members of the military junta—all of the latter aided by their second-ranking officers. The ceremonies highlighted the existence of a presidential power above the chiefs of staff in all the branches of national defense and emphasized the status of the generalissimo of the armed forces. This was particularly significant in an institution such as the military where the symbolism of rank is so important.

The Power of the Commander in Chief over Officers' Careers

An essential prerequisite of military professionalism is the career stability of officers and promotions based upon merit and seniority. Therefore, it is essential that decisions affecting the nominations, appointments, and retirement of military officials be free of political interference. These criteria are systematically undermined in a military dictatorship. Since the army is the center of dictatorial political power, personal and political loyalty are more important than professional accomplishment. To have a different opinion—even on a minor issue—from the chief of state can destroy an officer's career. Therefore the army becomes politicized in the worst way, since it becomes institutionally committed to sustaining the policies of the executive power, and its officers, even as individuals, are obliged to support those policies in order to keep their appointments. Such characteristics are typical of a praetorian army.

The historical experience of Chile in this matter is conclusive. Under military dictator Colonel Carlos Ibáñez, who ruled between 1927 and 1931, military professionalism was almost destroyed by the disruption of the mechanisms that guaranteed the officers' careers. A very well-known retired general described the military policies of Carlos Ibáñez as follows: "Important acquisitions of ammunition and elements to produce them were made, barracks were improved, and salaries were increased. Nevertheless the morale of the army, especially that of the generals, was low. A new rule was issued which stated that everyone should present his retirement papers as soon as he reached the rank of colonel, since to reach the rank of general he should enjoy the confidence of the government. This measure went against not only the highest moral values of a general—his character, independence, and pride—but also in an indirect way brought politics into the army. This measure did not take into consideration that the military serves the interest of the Fatherland, regardless of the kind of government and people that constitute it."[40]

The powers dictator Ibáñez gave himself over the professional life of his comrades in arms were a far cry from the mechanisms Chilean democracy adopted to insure the promotions and career stability of officers. It is necessary to describe what these were like in 1973, before the military coup.

OFFICERS' CAREERS UNDER CHILE'S DEMOCRATIC REGIME

The Constitution of 1925 and the existing legislation on military affairs had established certain guidelines in favor of military careers, based upon tying promotions and retirements to an ingenious system of checks and balances in which different authorities, collegial bodies, military personnel, and politicians all participated.

The system in force until 11 September 1973 was the following:[41]

1. Unit commanders each year graded the performance of the officers under their control, according to the following merit categories: 1—very good; 2—good; 3—conditional; 4—deficient.

2. Each branch of military service then convened its so-called Assessment Board. These boards were composed of generals-at-arms, which meant divisional and brigadier generals in the case of the army, vice-admirals and rear admirals in the navy, and aviation and air brigade generals in the case of the air force. The meetings of these boards were attended by the chief of staff of each institution, or if he was unable to be there, by the general next in seniority. The Assessment Boards had to prepare classification listings and, related to these, a retirement list. The retirement list was formed in succession by (a) those in merit category 4; (b) those classified for the second consecutive time in category 3; (c) those classified in category 3; (d) those classified in category 2; and (e) those classified in category 1. The officers classified under (a) and (b) were obliged to retire. The number of officers that had to retire annually was determined by the president of the republic upon receiving the recommendations of the respective chiefs of staff, who in turn had to make their recommendations before the assessment boards held their first meeting.

3. If an officer was not in agreement with the classification given to him by the Assessment Board, he had the right to appeal to the Officers' Board of Appeals, which was made up of the following five members: the minister of national defense; the chiefs of staff of the army, navy, and air force; and the general-at-arms next in seniority to the chief of staff of the officer's branch of service.

Once retirements were established, thus eliminating from the ranks those who were to leave the military, the procedure for promotion was started as follows:

1. Officers were promoted by seniority, although no one classified in category 3 or who had committed military offenses could advance. In addition to seniority, officers had to have served sufficient time in their rank, passed required courses and exams, and fulfilled certain professional duties. All these conditions were obligatory, although the president of the republic could exempt "an officer, only once during his career, from fulfilling one or more requirements for promotion, except that of time served in a rank."[42]

2. The promotion of lower officers (lieutenant colonel, frigate captain, group commander, and below) was done by an executive decree signed by the president of the republic and his minister of defense.

3. In the case of superior officers (army and air force colonels and navy captains, as well as all generals) the appointments were conferred by the president of the republic with the approval of the Senate.

In addition to the foregoing normally applied procedures, the president of the republic had certain exclusive powers in relation to promotions and retirements, namely:

1. He appointed the chiefs of staff, who would remain in their position as long as they retained the president's confidence. If he named a general who did not have the highest seniority, the ones who had been passed over would go automatically into retirement.

2. He could call any officer into temporary retirement. Any officer who remained in temporary retirement for more than three years would be given full retirement.

3. He could decide not to issue an executive decree to promote a lower officer, or could avoid sending to the Senate the appropriate references for promotion of a superior officer or general.

Similarly, the chief of staff had the power to indirectly put an officer into temporary retirement. For this he needed only to leave an officer without assignment for a minimum of three consecutive months.

By this system of checks and balances the Chilean democratic system insured the professionalism of the armed forces, the stability of the military career, and promotions based on seniority and merit. The appeal procedure whereby authorities outside of an officer's own service participated in decisions about officers' careers helped protect against abuse and arbitrariness. It also protected officers from being at the mercy of only one man or a single source of power. This is no longer the case.

OFFICERS' CAREERS UNDER THE MILITARY REGIME

The destruction of the state of law and the inception of the military regime has meant for military officers, no less than for the rest of the citizenry, the loss of the institutional mechanisms that guaranteed the stability and development of their careers free from arbitrary decisions.

The system of checks and balances I have described disappeared with the military coup. The functions granted by the Statute for the Armed Forces Personnel to the president of the republic, to the chief of staff, and to the Senate have been concentrated in one individual, giving him what is in effect unbridled power over the military institution. With the military junta as a surrogate legislative power, the laws which the Congress and various governments had enacted over many years to guarantee the stability of officers' careers and the fairness of their promotions were left only to the majority will of the chiefs of staff.

The changes began right after the military coup. Since there were divisions within the armed forces, the new authorities felt they needed mechanisms to allow them to drop officers who were too close to the former government or who were considered dangerous to the new regime. Therefore, in what was considered a temporary situation, the rules regulating the promotions and retirements of all the armed services officers were suspended, with almost total power given to the chiefs of staff.[43] These changes were accepted as necessary by most of the officers, since they were seen as affecting only certain ones among them. Moreover, the changes were more readily accepted at the time since the position of the chief of staff, particularly of the army, was not as strong as it would become later. The corps of generals was a very important decision-making group in those days, such that the very legitimacy of the chief of staff required support from other key generals who enjoyed great prestige inside and outside of their institution.

Within a year after the military coup, the system of officer assessments and promotions had been fundamentally altered. It was replaced by another system which has had two fundamental characteristics: first, it has left the questions of promotions and retirements exclusively to boards set up for each service (whereas under the previous system the appeals boards always contained a minority representation from each branch), and second, it has greatly increased the power of the chiefs of staff over the whole process.

The basis for the new system was set forth in Decree Law 624 of August 1974, which was designed in particular to set up Selection Boards for Superior Officers, a new version of the previous Assessment Boards.[44] These boards were to be composed of brigadier generals-at-arms who were charged with dispatching the merit classifications, the complementary rank, and the retirement lists. As in the previous system, any officer given a grade 4 assessment or a grade 3 assessment for two consecutive years must retire. But the decree law introduced a completely new factor into Chilean military legislation whose consequences has been to produce an extraordinary degree of instability in the careers of superior officers. The new legislation stated that "upon completing thirty years of effective service or three years in the rank, army officers are to present their applications for retirement. These applications will be considered by the Selection and the Appeals Boards."[45]

This rule applies to all colonels. An officer must remain at this rank for a minimum of four years before ascending, which means that every colonel who wishes to continue in the army must inevitably go through a period of uncertainty over his career for at least one year before his promotion. In addition, the rule allows an enormous degree of arbitrariness to be built into the assessment process. During the democratic period, there was only one reason for removing an officer from active service: mediocre or poor professional performance. The new decree permits any colonel who has sufficient time in the military or at his rank, however outstanding or brilliant he may be, to be retired if his application is accepted. Finally, and most importantly, the decree states that if an application for retirement is not accepted, it will continue to remain on file as long as the officer is in active service. No applications for retirement are ever rejected; they just remain pending. Hence, the uncertainty over an officer's career is made permanent at the higher ranks.

As intimated by the above-quoted reference to Appeals Boards, the August 1974 decree law also established these over the Selection Boards for Superior Officers. The Appeals Boards were to be presided over, in the case of the army, by the chief of staff and to be composed of the division generals. The necessary quorum for the Appeals Board to function was set at only three of its seven members, although the decree also allows the board to meet with only two division generals by adding the highest-ranking brigadier general to their number. By contrast, the Selection Board, even though it decides less important issues, must meet with a minimum quorum of "two-thirds of the members with a right to vote."[46]

This system at least preserved one characteristic of the one in force before 1973, namely, the principle that the boards charged with the assessment procedure, on the one hand, and with the appeals process, on the other, were to be composed of different individuals. However, a year later this principle was abandoned: a September 1975 decree added the division generals to the Selection Boards for Superior Officers.[47] The previous Assessment Boards of the democratic period also included the division generals, but the system in force then was completely different in that these generals were not in charge of the appeals process. The September 1975 change in the procedures had the consequence of effectively displacing the brigadier generals from any power in the merit classification. Or is it not a mere fiction to participate as equals in adopting a decision that later only some of the participants—in this case, the division generals—can review on appeal?

The September 1975 decree also modified the Board of Selection. The purpose of this change was to strengthen the power of the chief of staff, since "he could name the officer that would act as official reporter at every meeting of the boards."[48] Therefore, the chief of staff would have first-hand knowledge of the content of meetings that were supposed to be secret by appointing an officer who enjoyed his confidence.

Nonetheless, the most remarkable increase in the power of the chief of staff over the promotion and retirement system has been embodied in the so-called Extraordinary Selection Board, which has become a key institution for these matters over the length of the military government. The Extraordinary Board was created by decree on 24 December 1973 (with the name of Extraordinary Assessment Board) as part of the authorities' attempts to deal with the exceptional situation created by the immediate post-coup situation, although it has since been made permanent by its incorporation into the Statute for Armed Forces Personnel.[49] The Extraordinary Board, whose meetings can be convened only by the chief of staff of the army and whose decisions cannot be appealed by affected officers, can be activated in two situations.

First, when one or more generals retire, the chief of staff can convene the Extraordinary Board to propose which colonels should be promoted and which colonels should be retired or transfered to a complementary rank "despite having fulfilled the necessary conditions for promotion." The deleterious significance of this irregular procedure can hardly be exaggerated. The broad terms with which the decree empowers the chief of staff to act in proposing promotions and retirements raises the possibility that the decisions of the Assessment Boards, and therefore of the Council of Generals, can become completely meaningless. Under normal procedure the assessment of the merits of the officers, and therefore their promotion or retirement, was a collective decision, but with the Extraordinary Boards the chief of staff acquires the exclusive right to suggest who will be promoted to the rank of general, a recommendation which the members of the Council of Generals can only accept or reject. The power of the chief of staff is especially significant when it comes to deciding who should retire, since it is merely sufficient for the chief of staff to fail to propose the promotion of a colonel, despite his recognized qualifications, for him to be forced out or forced into the complementary ranks. This is the case since even if the chief of staff's proposition were rejected by the rest of the board, those officers not on the chief's promotion list cannot advance and must, therefore, retire. The chief's decision not to promote is consequently paramount, to the degree that whatever else may be said about the Extraordinary Boards, it is perfectly clear that with them it is impossible for a colonel to become a general without the support of the chief of staff. This was not the case before.

A second reason for which the chief of staff may convene the Extraordinary Board is when "special circumstances, determined by the Chief of

Staff, make it necessary to include immediately one or more Superior Officers [colonels] or Offices [Lieutenant-colonels or majors] in extraordinary retirement or complementary rank lists."[50] The decree speaks for itself.

The decree which created the boards did not stipulate any requirements for their functioning (e.g., who would preside at the meetings, what protocol is to be followed to convene it, what the necessary quorum is, which majorities are needed in order to arrive at a decisions). Such stipulations were needed, since the decree made it perfectly possible for the Extraordinary Board to meet and adopt decisions with, say, a minority of the generals in attendance. This deficiency was at least partially amended with the issuance of a new decree stating that the boards would be "composed of all the generals-at-arms and would be presided over by the division general with the most seniority. In his absence, the division general of highest seniority among those present at the session should take his place."[51] Nevertheless, the decree did not resolve the other lacunae.

One final point. As mentioned earlier, before the coup the president of the republic could exempt an officer, once during his career, from one or more of the requirements to be promoted except that of time served in a rank.[52] In February 1974, this privilege was extended for sixteen months to the respective chiefs of staff of the institutions of national defense.[53] In practice, this meant that even though an officer had received such dispensation in the past from the president of the republic, he could receive this exemption again. Ten months later, this power of the chiefs of staff was renewed, this time permanently, by a new decree which did add, however, a new restriction to it. Instead of speaking only of the impossibility of foregoing the time an officer spends in a rank, the decree added that no officer could be exempted from "classification in the recommendation lists."[54] However, these new exemptions could be made even if an officer had already been granted them under the decree that had extended this power to the chiefs for sixteen months. As a result, a decision which could be made only once in an officer's career during the democratic period can now be made repeatedly, to the degree that military promotions have been placed under the pale of frequent exemptions in the immediate post-coup period.

Conclusion

This paper has analyzed three sorts of changes that have taken place in Chile since the inception of the military regime. The first has been the transformation in the definition of the regime's tasks given by the authorities. Conceptions of national security rapidly led them to abandon the first stated aim of restoring a lost democracy in favor of a more profound attempt to restructure Chilean politics. This greatly increased the amount of time the military felt it had to control the government, and led to a great concentration of power in the military junta.

The second change relates to the process by which General Pinochet succeeded in affirming his power over his peers in the junta. He did this by progressively transforming his position from that of being, by virtue of holding the office of army chief of staff, the junta's leading member, to becoming its uncontested president, and finally, to assuming the title of president of the republic and of supreme chief of the armed forces—without relinquishing his position as chief of staff of the army. No one in Chilean history had ever held such unlimited and uncontested power.

The third change has been that of the system by which officers' careers are determined. The military regime has introduced a great deal of arbitrariness in decisions over promotions and retirements of officers by increasing, again to an unprecedented extent, the power of the chiefs of staff (virtually life-long incumbents) over the process. The result is that the current system has led to a "tarnished professionalism," in which the traditional doctrines of nondeliberation, respect for hierarchy, and subordination to political power serve the ends of a military dictatorship led by its commanding officer.

Notes

1. See Genaro Arriagada Herrera, "Ideology and Politics in the South American Military" (Latin American Program Working Paper of the Woodrow Wilson International Center for Scholars, Washington, D.C., 1980).

2. See Genaro Arriagada Herrera, "Seguridad nacional y política," in Genaro Arriagada Herrera et al., *Seguridad nacional y bien común* (Santiago: Centro de Investigaciones Socioeconómicas del Centro Bellarmino, 1976), paragraph III on "La guerra contrasubversiva"; also Genaro Arriagada Herrera, "El ejército chileno," and "La prusianización y la primera oleada antisocialista (1900–1931)," and "La guerra contrasubversiva en los ejércitos de Argentina, Brasil, Chile y Uruguay (1960–1980)," in *Ideología política de los militares* (Santiago: ICHEH, 1981).

3. See Manuel Antonio Garretón and Genaro Arriagada Herrera, *América Latina a la hora de las doctrinas de la seguridad nacional* (Santiago: Centro de Investigaciones Socioeconómicas del Centro Bellarmino, 1978), reprinted in Genero Arriagada Herrera, *Ideología política de los militares.*

4. [*Editors' note:* In this translation we have rendered the Chilean military title of *comandante en jefe* to its proximate American equivalent, chief of staff, to avoid the confusion with the American president's military rank, commander in chief, which the literal translation would produce. However, there is an important difference between the two positions in that the Chilean chief of staff has always been in the line of command. Legislation pending in Congress would, if enacted, change the American chief's position from its purely advisory one and place him also in the line of command.]

5. Edict No. 5 of the Governmental Junta of Chile, 11 September 1973.

6. Ibid.

7. Decree Law 1, 11 September 1973, Constitutional Record of the Governmental Junta, published in the *Diario Oficial*, 18 September 1973.

8. Ibid.

9. Governmental Junta, "Declaration of Principles of the Government of Chile," 11 March 1974.

10. Ibid.

11. Governmental Junta, "National Objective of the Government of Chile," recognized in Resolution 3,102 on 23 December 1975. It states that all ministers must carry out the objectives the Junta has stipulated in its general document.

12. General Augusto Pinochet, "Presidential Message," 11 September 1976.

13. General Augusto Pinochet, speech given on 9 July 1977 in the meeting organized by the National Ministry of Youth at Chacarillas Mountain.

14. General Augusto Pinochet, "Presidential Message," 11 September 1979.

15. Samuel P. Huntington, *The Soldier and the State* (New York: Vintage Books, 1957).

16. Amos Perlmutter, *The Military in Politics in Modern Times* (New Haven: Yale University Press, 1977).

17. Alfred Stepan, "The New Professionalism of Internal Warfare in Military Expansion," in Abraham F. Lowenthal, *Armies and Politics in Latin America* (New York: Holmes and Meier, 1976).

18. Virgilio Rafael Beltrán, "The 'Junta' Level in Military Government: The Argentina Case" (paper presented at the Ninth World Congress of Sociology, Research Committee on Armed Forces and Society, Uppsala, Sweden, 14–19 August 1978), p. 3.

19. Decree with Force of Law No. 1, 1968, Art. 166e.

20. Decree Law 1,639, 29 December 1976, published in the *Diario Oficial*, 30 December 1976.

21. Ibid., 2.

22. Decree Law 1,640, 29 December 1976, published in the *Diario Oficial*, 30 December 1976.

23. [*Editors' note:* By 1984, the gap had increased to 26 *promociones.*]

24. Political Constitution of the State, art. 72, no. 7.

25. Ibid., art. 72, no. 13.

26. Ibid., art. 71.

27. Estado Mayor del Ejército, "Reglamento de Disciplina," art. 32.

28. Decree Law 1, 11 September 1973.

29. *Qué pasa?* no. 127, September 1973.

30. Decree Law 128, 12 November 1973.

31. Decree Law 527, 17 June 1974, art. 7.

32. Ibid., art. 18.

33. Ibid., art. 8 and art. 10, clause 3.

34. Decree Law 521, 14 June 1974.

35. Florencia Varas, *Gustavo Leigh: El general disidente* (Santiago: Editorial Aconcagua, 1979), p. 78.

36. Decree Law 1,878, 12 August 1977, art. 1.

37. Decree Law 806, 16 December 1974.

38. Decree Law 527, 1974, art. 19.

39. Presidential Message, 11 September 1979.

40. General Ernesto Medina Fraguera, *Nuestra defensa nacional frente a la opinion pública* (Santiago: Imprenta Benaprés y Fernández, 1941), pp. 37–38.

41. Decree with Force of Law No. 1, 1968, chap. V, arts. 74–98.

42. Ibid., art. 41.

43. Decree Law 33, 21 September 1973, published in the *Diario Oficial,* 3 October 1973.

44. Decree Law 624, 26 August 1974, published in the *Diario Oficial,* 2 September 1974.

45. Ibid.

46. Ibid., art. 2, which replaces art. 79 of Decree with Force of Law No. 1, 1968, last clause.

47. Decree Law 1,165, 2 September 1975, published in the *Diario Oficial,* 3 September 1975.

48. Ibid., letter *a,* next-to-last clause.

49. Decree No. 14 of the Subministry of War, 4 January 1977, which adapted, coordinated, and systematized the text of the Statute of Personnel in the Armed Forces. The Extraordinary Selection Board was incorporated as paragraph V of Chap. V on "Qualifications."

The original decree law establishing the Extraordinary Assessment Boards (No. 220) was dated 24 December 1973, but was not published in the *Diario Oficial* until 23 March 1974. Nevertheless, the decree stated that it would take effect as of the December date.

50. Decree Law 220, art. 1*b.*

51. Decree Law 1,052, 2 June 1975, published in the *Diario Oficial,* 7 June 1975.

52. Decree with Force of Law No. 1, 1968, art. 41.

53. Decree Law 310, 4 February 1974, published in the *Diario Oficial,* 9 February 1974.

54. Decree Law 1,240, 28 October 1975, art. 3, published in the *Diario Oficial,* 5 November 1975.

Political Processes in an Authoritarian Regime: The Dynamics of Institutionalization and Opposition in Chile, 1973-1980

Manuel Antonio Garretón

This chapter describes and analyzes the political processes and trends within the Chilean military regime from the date it took power in September 1973 through 1980. My goal is to establish a framework for analysis, to provide order for a set of facts and problems, and thus to discern the "problematique" of the Chilean military regime. As such, the chapter is a statement of broad hypotheses, of analytical trends or principles for understanding the regime, rather than a detailed study of events. This explains its relatively abstract tone.

This study forms part of a body of literature which attempts to analyze the processes of change in authoritarian or military regimes. The basic proposition is that those political processes which have become known as "openings," "transitions," or "redemocratizations" (and we will return to these terms in this work) cannot be easily applied to the Chilean military regime. It is possible that the processes initiated by the state contain seeds and contradictions which could lead to deep transformations. It is also possible that they could provoke changes in the society and in the regime's opposition which could eventually lead to redemocratization. Furthermore, in the next few years a retrospective analysis might find in these transformations the beginning of a transition from an authoritarian regime. Nonetheless, from our analytical vantage point today, it does not seem that we are in the presence of regime change, but rather that we are facing a movement unleashed by the bloc in power tending to further institutionalize the regime. Much of the dynamic of the political system stems from this attempt at institutionalization and/or the resulting reactions against it.

The first part of this chapter discusses the principal features of the new authoritarian regimes in Latin America and establishes the analytical perspective and categories for a study of the Chilean case. It is, by necessity, very synthetic and schematic, providing only the principal argument with which to structure the discussion. The reader is referred to other works for a more complete development of these themes.[1] The second part analyzes what I call the process of institutionalization of the Chilean regime in its various dimensions and characterizes certain features which make it distinct in the Latin American context. The third section then attempts to formulate the "problematique" of the opposition to the regime and describe some of its dynamics. Finally, the study draws some conclusions based on the situation as of 1980. I will not attempt a comprehensive analysis of the regime nor a sectoral analysis; I concentrate only on strictly political processes.

On Authoritarian Regimes: Dimensions and Processes

THE TWO DIMENSIONS

There is a certain consensus with regard to the features of the military regimes which have been defined as "the new authoritarianism" in Latin America. Whatever their designation, they emerge in countries with a certain level of development, following a relatively long period of broad popular mobilization, and are organized around the armed forces, which destroy the previous regime and play the predominant role in alliance with the dominant economic classes. They rule through technocratic sectors in state leadership positions and propose a program to restructure society in terms of new mechanisms of capitalist accumulation and distribution and of a political reordering which is authoritarian, repressive, and exclusionary.[2]

Although all the analytical and political consequences are not always spelled out, it is generally affirmed that these political regimes cannot be defined as simple historical parentheses or as temporary interruptions of democratic traditions (which in some cases never existed). Nor can they be thought of as "necessary" formulas for the resolution of certain social problems which, once solved, would return the country to "normality." In effect, even when these regimes emerge from a political crisis, they do not exhaust themselves merely by reacting and responding to it. They are an attempt to reorganize society "from above," to provide a vehicle for domestic capitalist reconstruction and reentry, in a dependent position, into the world capitalist system. As such, they seek to put an end to one model of development and political style and to inaugurate a new historical stage and thus reject a simple process of restoration of the status quo ante. They are as much an expression of a counterrevolutionary will as of a will to establish new foundations, even though the victorious bloc may not be fully conscious of this fact; and some regimes may later abdicate this foundational dimension in order to maintain a purely defensive role, or convert themselves into the caretakers of permanent crisis.

Both dimensions, the reactive and the foundational, are complementary and cannot be separated. And even though they are more or less important, depending on the situation through which the regime is passing (the former predominates in the initial or installation phase and the latter in the consolidation phase), elements of both are present in all phases and mutually condition each other.[3]

The defensive dimension, or that of reaction to crisis, is expressed, above all, in the installation phase of these regimes, in which the preponderant role in the leadership of the state is assumed by the armed forces. It is characterized by pure repression and makes use of the necessity of war and the need to restore order after a period of "chaos and anarchy" as a legitimizing principle. The definition of the country as one in a state of war as well as the depth of the previous political crisis, measured both by the degree of polarization and the intensity of a perceived threat to the reigning social order by dominant groups and vast sectors of the middle class and their respective social and political organizations, led to an acceptance on the part of these elements of repression against the popular classes. In this phase, the dominant ideology consists of the doctrine of national security, a centerpiece in the socialization experience of the armed forces during the last few decades.[4]

But the defensive or reactive role has long-run effects which spill over into the installation phase of these regimes. Thus, the level of organization, popular mobilization, and political polarization, as well as the extent of the crisis in the very operation of society which preceded the military coup, will provide certain margins for the stabilization process and the process of capitalist readjustment, in terms of both their timing and their precise content and direction.[5] At the same time, the scope, intensity, and nature of the repression, as well as the character of the "normalization and economic stabilization" measures, are going to condition the economic and political processes of the model which is attempted during the phase in which the foundation task becomes the primary objective.

It is important to understand this foundational role not only as a set of requirements to fit a capitalist economic model, even though this is the key element, but also as a comprehensive attempt to reorganize society. This implies resolving problems of hegemony within the dominant bloc among groups with different aspirations, values, and interests while at the same time implementing a program which encompasses the diverse spheres of society. It is an attempt by the state to recreate the bases of social relations in order to construct a type of capitalism which eliminates all traces of anything which justifies a populist dynamic. Without abandoning the references to certain elements of an "ever-present war," the principle of legitimacy becomes different for each sector composing the dominant bloc, emphasizing each sector's particular interests. The principle of legitimacy emphasizes as much the successes of "reconstruction" as (by contrast with the first phase) the promise of restoring democratic practices purged of their "former vices."[6]

Understanding these regimes as belated attempts at capitalist revolutions from the state encompassing the dimensions of war and violence provided by the armed forces, where the *ancien régime* is represented by some variant of populism or some process of more radical transformation and whose principal enemy is the relatively organized popular classes, has important analytical implications.[7]

In effect, if we were dealing only with a traditional program of the defensive or reactive type, a holding action, an analysis of military power would suffice to understand the problems of maintaining the regime. Since we are also dealing with a program to lay the groundwork for a new social order, we must direct our attention to the capacity of diverse sectors in the dominant power bloc to achieve hegemony within it. The attempt to restructure society along capitalist lines can take several directions depending on the capacity of particular sectors to generalize these interests or to impose their own ideology within the victorious coalition. In other words, there is a problem of hegemony within the dominant bloc of these regimes, one that is initially resolved by the legitimacy of the military hierarchy, but which reemerges when the government confronts tasks which go beyond sheer repression. This makes it necessary to refer to the specific characteristics of a particular bloc as well as to the mechanisms and processes of cooperation, co-optation, and exclusion through which these hegemonic nuclei are formed.

But the problem of hegemony is not found just in the dominant bloc. The relations of this bloc with the rest of society cannot be reduced exclusively to the use of force, however brutal and extensive that may be, especially during the installation phase. It goes without saying that we are not in the presence of a hegemonic relationship and that these regimes do not rest on consensus.[8] The continuous presence of repression, overt or threatened, and its resurgence even in the most advanced stages of "normalization" or consolidation of the regime demonstrate the extent to which repression constitutes a fundamental explanatory factor in the relative stability of a regime. Nevertheless other factors must also be considered. Some of them are directly related to the element of force or repression, such as the generalized and internalized fear which leads people to recognize those who hold power and to obey them without accepting those leaders as legitimate. Others relate to the effort to restructure society through the partial adoption of an historic program which has results in the sectoral and heterogeneous advent of an order with a mix of the old and the new, disarticulating existing social organizations and modes of political representation. If we analyze the different layers of the population, we can find partial allegiance and hegemony. Certain themes which are present in some sectors and latent in others tend to become generalized, penetrating all of society, and becoming part of conventional wisdom. Themes of order, efficiency, and security, even the distrust of politics, are examples of this phenomenon, even though the degree of penetration of these themes is not the same for all social sectors. Distinct from the European fascist systems which sought to mobilize partial or sectoral support and to foment widespread politicization, these new authoritarian regimes seek to maintain a state of passive support and general demobilization.[9] Since their starting point was a highly mobilized, politicized, and polarized society, they seek to disarticulate and atomize the social base. Rather than generating consensus and support, they expect that fragmentation will lead to a preoccupation with particular interests, rendering the situation acceptable to different groups and making the alternative of change risky or threatening. Rather than mobilizing support, they seek to maintain latent support. Rather than inculcating doctrine, they reinforce attitudes of conformity and passivity by controlling the means of communication and, to a degree, the mechanisms of socialization with the idea that "things are now this way" and it is necessary to adapt and conform to the new rules. This is especially clear in the processes of institutionalization to which I refer further on. Thus, there is an attempt to provoke a process which, while not directly identified with the regime itself, tends to be identified with certain values, norms, and basic structures of society. This is expressed in the ideological plane, where the monolithic and Messianic nature of a doctrine of war gives way to a nucleus critical of the old society with certain programmatic features around which are grouped a heterogeneous set of elements appealing to diverse sectoral interests.

But the partial success of a program to reorganize society through structural changes conflicts with the program's limited inclusionary capacity, as well as with the limitations of a dependent and repressive capitalism which exacerbates inequalities, marginalizes large sectors of society, and indefinitely postpones the aspirations of others. Even the moments of relative success and the "economic miracles" which these regimes cite to claim legitimacy reveal their limitations, imbalances, and contradictions with raised expectations which generate diverse movements of social opposition.

OPENINGS, INSTITUTIONALIZATION, AND TRANSITIONS

One obvious and common element in all these regimes is the role of timing. After being in power a certain period of time, they can no longer claim the right to govern solely on the arguments they used to gain power, especially if one of the parameters of their success is the elimination of the causes which made the regime possible in the first place. If the nation's security was at stake and this justified the "exceptional" seizure of political power, the government must show some success in attaining security, and this very success erodes the initial source of legitimacy. To this must be added a loss of initial support and the appearances at the core of the dominant bloc of a concern about succession and uncertainty about the future. There are also international pressures and pressures arising from the reemergences of society after the installation phase of the regime.

All of this makes it impossible to avoid a clearer definition of regime purpose. Different alternatives are possible. One is simply a postponement of a definition of the problem by citing additional and more urgent tasks of reconstruction. Another is an attempt to establish a permanent authoritarian or military regime, or, more frequently, a rhetorical or programmatic call for some form of democracy containing mechanisms to exclude and restrict political participation and, in some cases, to provide a "guardianship" role for the armed forces.

It is around these options that the well-known division arises between hard-liners and soft-liners within the dominant bloc. The former seek the permanent or indefinite institutionalization of the military regime. The latter desire some type of political "opening" which will preserve what is essential in the development model and the conservative political order emanating from the changes made in the bases of society. This division, which appears in all regimes of this type, varies widely in its degree of relevance and importance and does not appear to be an element allowing us to predict the evolution of a regime in one way or another. I will return to this point in the second part of this chapter.

In any case, this search for a political model can have a double meaning. On the one hand, it reveals the profound problems which these regimes face in their incapacity to transform the permanent use of force, the resort to waves of repression, manipulation of terror, passive support, and partial hegemonies, into a unifying, hegemonic process. But it is a mistake to judge this effort to resolve the political model simply as an expression of weakness of the dominant bloc. In fact, it may be an indication of a relatively successful attempt to implement in part the program of capitalist recomposition and reentry into the world economy at a time when there is no widespread crisis and as a way of avoiding forced departures from power later on.

Faced with the need to resolve immediate political problems and the problems of the future of the political regime, the so-called "political openings," or regulated spaces providing for some participation, are introduced, either in the sphere of civil society or in the political sphere itself. To clarify their historical significance, it is necessary to place this phenomenon of "openings" into the broader context in which it occurs. In this sense, it can be useful to distinguish processes of institutionalization and processes of transition, even when their respective internal dynamics can lead from one to the other. By institutionalization, I mean the processes by which a certain regime sets its own timetable, rules, and norms. This phase follows the period of rupture, the length of which varies from case to case. By transition, I mean the processes through which a particular authoritarian regime changes into a different political regime.[10] It is possible to distinguish at least two major types of institutionalization. The first type comprises processes which lead to a shift from a dictatorship without rules to one which establishes its own rules while maintaining the power traits that it had at the time of the military coup. The second involves processes which lead to a political regime with features which differ from the way power was distributed at the time of the break but which maintain the same model of authority. The difference between the two is that in the first case we are looking at a self-regulating extension of the "emergency period" which has now been converted into normality. In the second, we are witnessing an attempt to create a regime which will resolve its succession problems without abandoning its exclusivist and authoritarian features. Both processes of institutionalization differ from processes of transition. In the former, we see a form of consolidation of the regime, even though it may claim new principles of legitimacy; in the latter, we see the substitution of one authoritarian regime for another, more or less gradually, depending on the case. Because of this, not every "political opening" which is proclaimed is necessarily part of a process of transition; it can be part of a process of institutionalization. Doubtless, there are interconnections among all these processes. A process which began as one of institutionalization can lead to one of transition, and vice versa. In any case, it is important to make the analytical distinction.

In this analysis, we will concentrate on processes of institutionalization. If we return to the foundation-building role of these regimes, we find two distinct levels. The first level refers to the strictly political sphere, where problems of leadership and its relegitimation, and problems of decision making are resolved. The second level has as its objective not just state power but the sphere of civil society, and consists of the normative crystallization of the changes which have been instituted by the state in different sectors of society. This is the feature of the process of institutionalization most closely tied to the historical process of capitalist restructuring and reentry. It also enables the regime to measure its degree of achievement, not only in the economy, but also in labor relations, education, state administration, and the like. Given the resistance encountered by the implementation of an historical program aimed at excluding popular participation and the conflict between the changes it calls for and the values, interests, and aspirations of very diverse social sectors, it is easy to understand why the two levels of institutionalization must complement each other.

At the level of general society, processes of institutionalization are ambivalent. On the one hand, they express the weak features of the regime: the erosion of certain support and the need to regain it; the response to growing pressure from international circles, such as the church, or from sectors which become bolder and gain an audience within their criticism; and the need to respond to internal anxieties about the destiny of the future regime. In short, the basis of support narrows, and trends arise within the bloc which weaken it. But the processes of institutionalization also express a certain dimension of strength. These processes do not mark the successful advent of an entire new sector order, but they are indeed a sign of partial success in changing the old order. There are structural changes in some sectors which modify the entire society and restructure the composition of classes and social actors and which have the ability to fashion new rules of the game. These new rules of the game are by definition part of all processes of institutionalization. Thus, they are instruments of consolidation which provide the space for the imposition of a new social order. At the same time, they delineate the space in which new contradictions and social conflicts arise; the place and the instrument through which social movements, with difficulty, reconstitute themselves; the gap through which the immobility of the first phase is broken. Because of this, the relationship is also ambivalent. The dominated sectors reject it entirely as a masquerade in which the rules of the game are fixed to favor those who hold power and those who support them. They also denounce the integrative or corporative character of the new rules of the game for their inadequacies and their intent to dismantle the social movement. However, these sectors also take advantage of any breathing space which is offered them by the new rules of the game, not only to seek satisfaction for their long-repressed demands but also to regroup and reorganize as a movement.

THE OPPOSITION TO THE REGIME

It seems natural to analyze the opposition to these regimes in terms of the opposition's capacity to provoke or accelerate the regime's fall, that is to say, to eliminate or replace it. Historical experience seems to show, however, that authoritarian regimes do not always fall because of the action of the opposition, though the existence of an opposition is very important.[11] Just as the success of these regimes can be judged by re-implementation of diverse objects of partial dimensions of the program and not the adoption of the entire historical project, so the value and success of opposition forces are not measured simply by the collapse of a regime or the complete failure of its programatic objectives, but also in terms of achieving smaller goals. These include the creation of relatively free breathing spaces; the preparation of new actions, such as the defense of certain rights, persons, and organizations; the maintenance of hope in an alternative; the creation of gradual inroads into the regime itself; the socialization of new sectors in a renewed tradition, thereby blocking progress of the regime's historical project; and the organization and encouragement of resistance in the different sectors of society. The opposition, at the risk of being totally immobilized, cannot escape a historical action which denies, denounces, and defies, while at the same time failing to block consolidation and legitimation of the regime. At times, mythical visions of "the resistance" obscure these points, as does the continuous affirmation that the prolongation of the authoritarian regime is due to the lack of an "alternative" provided by the opposition. Perhaps history will show us that regime change is due less to the existence of an alternative, "programmatic" formula bestowed from above than to a capacity to fully articulate demands arising from the new social movements.

During the first years of an authoritarian regime, the opposition cannot be anything but eminently defensive, ensuring the physical survival of people and organizations. This is true as much for the strictly political structures like parties as for the societal organizations, all of which the regime seeks to repress, eliminate, disperse, or dismantle. It is during the evolution of this phase that two other important phenomena for the formation of the opposition begin to emerge. In the first place, arenas develop to replace the political arena, such as those created beneath the umbrella of indisputably legitimate organizations, principally the church. In the second place, sectors which explicitly or tacitly supported the coup but do not totally identify with the regime move into the opposition. This gives the opposition a heterogeneous character which leads some observers to speak more of "oppositions." The time which this process takes favors the consolidation of the installed power and of the hegemonic nucleus within the regime.

But it is not only the political diversity of the opposition which makes it possible to speak of "oppositions" and which places on the table the themes of opposition "unity" and "alternative." There is something more to the opposition than political structures. As we shall see further on, the importance of political organizations varies to a significant degree depending on the experience which preceded the authoritarian regime and, more particularly, on the extent of articulation of political organizations with the social movement, and on the strength and autonomy of civil society. What is interesting is that the diversity of the social movement is recreated and reconstituted in those arenas which replace the political arena, in the very spaces created by the process of social institutionalization of the regime's historical program. Whether we are dealing with political organizations which have survived from the previous regime or with those that arose from the process of institutionalization or on the fringe of this process, the inherent characteristics of an authoritarian regime generate tension between the tendency to formulate policies at the top and the relative proliferation, dispersion, and search for autonomy of social organizations. In some way, the spaces which are created in these regimes bring about the formation of a social movement from below, just as the more or less traditional action of political parties tends to bring about the formation of a social movement from above. Between both processes there is a problematic relation of convergence.

Thus, the political diversity of the opposition as well as this problematic process of conflict between the political parties and the social movement reduce the ability of the opposition to perform as a true political actor and convert it into a space for partial agreements. This explains the opposition's behavior, which is rather adaptive and reactive to the dynamics generated by the dominant bloc.

Institutionalization of the Chilean Military Regime, 1973–1980

FROM THE ORIGINAL CRISIS TO THE STRUCTURAL DIMENSION

In the Chilean case, we seem to have a regime which takes to the limit the two dimensions, the reactive and the foundational, which characterize regimes of this type. The principal objective of the reactive or defensive dimension was to contain radicalized popular mobilization of the period of the Popular Unity government by dismantling its organizational bases and establishing "order." The juridical-institutional formula for accomplishing this was to proclaim a state of emergency in any of its varied forms.[12]

Without going into a detailed analysis here, we must recall that at the end of the Popular Unity government Chilean society lived through a crisis which can be described as a decomposition of the capitalist system without the emergence of an alternative system to effectively replace it. This was expressed as much in diverse spheres of everyday social life as in the breakdown of the state apparatus and of its capacity to lead. The crisis was also expressed in terms of a heightened political polarization through which the level of organization and radicalization of the popular sectors was counterbalanced by a high degree of mobilization of the middle classes, leading the political system to lose its legitimacy. Finally, there was the disinstitutionalization of political action on the part of key sectors of the Chilean right.[13]

The high degree of popular organization and mobilization, the terror felt by the bourgeoisie and its fear of losing all its power, and the tacit or explicit aid of middle classes and the political center, principally sectors of the Christian Democratic party, in the breakdown of the political regime, even when this endangered democratic values, together with the disarticulation of the capitalist system have at least three implications.

The first is the depth, extent, and duration of the repression, which reached unprecedented levels. The repressive and destructive military aspects of the current regime are sufficiently well-known, as much for the violation of individual and social rights as for the destruction of the system of mediation between the state and civil society, that is to say, of the political system in its broadest sense.[14] The second is the pressing and radical nature which the tasks of "normalization" and "stabilization" of the economy required. This resulted in an obscuring of the specific nature of the reconstruction and reintegration program and of the possibilities of the different directions which it might take. The third is that the political sectors of the center, polarized in favor of the overthrow of Allende either actively or passively, had to go through a long process of reconversion which progressively brought them to the field of opposition to the regime. The time which this "road to Damascus," as it has been called, took was the time necessary to consolidate the armed forces' leadership and to resolve the problems of internal hegemony of the dominant bloc.

It was with the economic crisis of March and April 1975 and the initiation of an economic Shock Plan that the precise direction of the program for capitalist reorganization and reentry began to be defined at the pinnacle of power.[15] In my opinion, this was also the moment in which the alliance between the leadership of the state and its hegemonic nucleus was consolidated.

I insist that the foundational dimension was not limited sheerly to economic aspects, but attempted with state power an overall reorganization of society, involving the creation of a new political order and a new form of interpreting society, its history, and its destiny—i.e., a new cultural model. This is not merely a restoration program, even though, as is obvious, old classes or sectors regained privileges lost not only during the years of the Popular Unity government, but also during those of the Christian Democratic government. Rather the program seeks to establish new bases of support for the development of capitalism. By the mid-1960s, many intellectual, business, and political sectors identified with the right had already begun to criticize the developmental style and political system of the last decades, objecting to the growing state intervention, the cyclical character of the economy, the excessive political participation and intervention (which was termed demagoguery and anarchy). They declared themselves in favor of a system of authoritarian government and a drastic reorientation of the model of development. In these sectors, there was a certain consciousness of the need for radical change in the society, but the ideology of structural reform and the democratizing trend of the preceding few years impeded the frank expression of this conception. An inchoate vision of this reconstruction program is found in the New Republic platform on which Alessandri ran as a candidate for president in 1970. The point is that the idea of an extensive renovation of the capitalist system and a political transformation along authoritarian lines which would make that possible was present long before the military coup of September 1973 and was only reinforced and catalyzed during the period of the Popular Unity government, acquiring a certain ideological coherence as a capitalist revolution opposed to all forms of reformist or revolutionary populism.[16]

What are the basic features of this program of capitalist reorganization and reentry?

As a model of development, this program called for a transition away from the industrial program of import substitution and a growing state participation in economic life, to reliance on the private sector and to an open economy model or "development toward the outside," reorienting the productive apparatus towards the primary sector and natural resources exports. Socially, the program called for a reversal of the process of democratization and the termination of the state role of creating opportunities with new patterns of distribution relying on the market. In all spheres of society, the principle of the market was to be the criterion which would determine the lines of development.[17]

The removal of the state role from both the economy and the creation of social opportunities and benefits leads to an atomization and segmentation of revindications and demands. That is, the restructuring of the state implies in turn a recreation of the mechanisms of mediation between the state and civil society. The central element here is the breakdown and fragmentation of social demands which is equivalent to an attempt at depoliticization. On the political plane, then, the reduction of public "breathing" space and the dismantling of a system of mediation through broad-based social and political organizations—that is, the liquidation of mechanisms of "general" representation and the limitation of these mechanisms to those of a sectoral or corporatist type—are not just reactive elements but essential parts of the reorganization program. But the absence of an alternative system of mediation—for example, one of a corporatist nature—in some way leaves the problem of the political regime unresolved and gives rise to diverse attempts to resolve it, all of which converge on an authoritarian formula.[18]

HEGEMONY IN STATE LEADERSHIP

To this point we have been dealing with an historical hegemonic program expressed by certain leaders of the state apparatus. Not all sectors which help or support the regime share all of its elements. On the contrary, there are differences and contradictions between the nucleus of leaders of the social apparatus and other sectors which also constitute the dominant bloc. We will see the manner in which these contradictions are expressed. What I am interested in emphasizing is that beginning in 1975, this has been the hegemonic variation of the structural program of the regime which took power in 1973.

As such, it has its expression in a certain and specific configuration of state leadership. This is captured by an image of a "traditional-style dictatorship with features of a modernizing revolution." The first part of this image refers not to the heritage of such dictatorships, but to a type of highly personalized leadership.

It is necessary to unwind the rational nucleus of such an image, point-ing out that the hegemonic leadership of the state resides in the alliance between the personalized leadership of the armed forces which secures the management of the mechanisms of political power, and the technocratic sector responsible for the leadership of the economy which expresses the interests of the dominant capitalist nuclei and which assures the "content" of state leadership over the society. That is to say, the hegemonic leader-ship lies in the alliance between Pinochet and the so-called "economic team."[19] How can this alliance be explained?

On the one hand, the relative cloistering of the armed forces for a number of decades, due to the ability of the political regime to establish a set of legitimate mechanisms to resolve conflicts, hindered them from developing an internally consistent political program at variance with the notion of civil supremacy. Their intervention during the 1970–73 period did not bring them to formulate a political program which was other than a "crisis consensus" once the constitutionalist sectors were purged or subju-gated.[20] The geopolitics of counterinsurgency doctrine and the ideology of national security were able to provide the armed forces with a self-image which was useful at a time of crisis and with the appearance of a program, but not a fully articulated program of government. Such a program had to be provided by certain social classes or factions and their representatives. Without a consensus on a basic program, the internal cohesion of the armed forces stemmed basically from the formal hierarchical structure, in which the legitimacy of the formal leadership is crucial. Since governing is a task which demands daily decisions and since in Chile the offices of the commanding general of the army and head of state were combined, this formal leadership became progressively more personalistic. This structural factor, and not psychological phenomena, accounts for personalization of leadership. And while there is a growing personalization of leadership, there is also a formal or hierarchical legitimacy to that leadership. This has an important consequence. The cloudiness of the political tendencies within the military, noted earlier, means that the internal alternatives also tend to hinge on personalities. But any new leadership options are at a relative disadvantage in the face of the already established leadership of Pinochet. This partly explains the failure of all alternative personalities which have tried to compete with Pinochet and the way Pinochet has exercised his management prerogatives in the exclusion and promotion of officers.

The personalization of leadership has been accompanied by a process of juridical institutionalization, leading from a situation of relative equality in the governing junta to one which calls for the appointment of a chief of state and culminates in the appointment of Pinochet as "president" with the governing junta relegated to a legislative or constituent role.[21] This convergence of the highest military authority and the highest state authority led to a problem of succession that was not resolved until the middle of 1980 and only through a formula which maintained Pinochet in power for a long time.[22]

The content of the historical-social program was set up by a group which has been called the "economic team," that is to say, by a homogeneous group of technocrats socialized in the economic doctrines of Milton Friedman and the Chicago School. This group seeks to extend its leadership not only over economic activities but also the entire range of state decision making. Initially linked to technocratic groups and to national academic and international financial circles, the members of the economic team progressively established solid ties with groups holding economic power. These ties are reflected in the frequent exchange movement back and forth from the public to the private sector of important members of the team, many of whom have become bank presidents.

The process by which this group increased its hegemony over state leadership was not accomplished without opposition from other sectors of the dominant bloc, particularly from nationalist groups and productive sectors opposed to the dismantling of the economic apparatus of the state and the lowering of protectionist barriers. These sectors have widespread support in military circles. The success of the economic team can be explained by Pinochet's decisive support of the economic model beginning in 1975. This is something of a paradox, as both the policies themselves and the ideology which inspires them appear to contradict the views of military officers, who generally favor strengthening the state and distrust the excessive power of the economic right. The paradox can be explained by various factors. Without a doubt, the economic model expresses the interests of certain capitalist factions, especially the financial groups. But in 1975, the mediation of the technocratic group appeared to be the only possible solution for the entire bourgeoisie, which had earlier feared loss of all power. The possibility of recovery stimulated by, among other things, the return of state companies, induced even the least privileged capitalist groups to accept the model. Likewise, the internal coherence of the model, its scientific appearance and universal rationale, meant that it could be presented to the military as a model capable of arbitrating sectoral interests. The antistatist debate over the model touched one of the sensitive spots of different segments of the dominant bloc, as state intervention was so closely tied to the politicization and the economic experience of the Popular Unity period. Furthermore, the technocratic group could provide a key element for the continuation of the regime, that is, the growing flow of foreign private capital necessary to revitalize the economy in a situation of international political isolation. In turn, this flow gave the armed forces funding for an extremely high military budget which sectoral factions of the bourgeoisie consider unproductive or competitive in its demands on state resources.[23] Finally, the demands for a political and social order which could not be legitimatized solely on the basis of a state of emergency and which is congruent with maintaining political domination, for example the labor legislation, seemed to flow naturally from the proposed economic model. No other sector in the dominant bloc could offer all these conditions in a single package to a leadership which held the resources of power but lacked a substantive program for the transformation of society.

Thus, an alliance in running the state between a hierarchical military leadership which became progressively personalistic and a technocratic leadership which offered a program of capitalist restructuring and reintegration became a crucial element in maintaining the stability of the regime.

One of the consequences of the personalization of leadership is that the perpetuation of that leadership is tied to the existence of the regime itself. Because of this, it appears to be a hopeful sign that certain clear-thinking sectors within the dominant bloc who are worried about the long-run stability of the capitalist restructuring and reintegration program are insisting on a separation between the regime and government.[24]

THE NEED FOR INSTITUTIONALIZATION

The problem of institutionalization is a permanent one for such regimes. During the early years it was resolved at the juridical-institutional level by concentrating all state power in the governing junta and by eliminating other demands for balancing the power of the executive.[25] At the level of relations between the state and civil society, that is to say, of the political regime, the system of mediation and representation was eliminated and was not replaced by a new order; the vacuum was filled by mechanisms of repression and social control. In this phase, the dictatorship exercised power by ignoring all juridical limits and basing its claim to legitimacy on the state of war and the permanent danger of subversion.

We have already noted the temporary nature of this source of legitimacy and the generic factors which create pressures for the institutionalization and relegitimation of the authoritarian regime. We will examine a few more specific ones.

The application of the economic model affected many sectors which initially supported the military government but which gradually became discontented because of the permanent blocking of all demands from social groups. Such sectors see the threat which created the regime as something from the past and feel that their expectations are frustrated both by lack of access to decision making and by the content of the economic and juridical measures. Protests come not only from certain business groups affected by economic policy, but also, and principally, from the trade organizations which were so important in the overthrow of President Allende. This phenomenon has more than just an economic root. Once the first stage of unanimity on the need for open and generalized repression passed, a debate arose on the future of the regime, its stability and permanence. Initially it was internal, but slowly it filtered to the public arena. The need to capture political support from groups for whom the initial principle of legitimacy has lost some of its value has created uneasiness and a potential for dispersion.

At the same time, it has become necessary to reply to the growing opposition, in which the Catholic Church and international pressures play an important role.

Finally, it is possible to discern certain challenges to the regime stemming from the very same societal transformations the regime has been responsible for. Many of them require clear rules of the game and institutions which are more or less stable and not subject to absolute unpredictability, as, for example, in the educational sphere or in labor relations.

Neither the erosion of support from sympathetic sectors, nor the demands of the growing opposition, nor the functional needs of certain social transformations, can be resolved solely by the use of the elements which characterize the political regime during its first phase. Repression and political control cannot continue to be the only visible elements of the relations between the state and civil society.

How is the problem to be resolved? How can new bases of institutional legitimacy be achieved, without abandoning repression?

First, there was an attempt to establish and legitimize a stable, military regime. This was principally expressed in Pinochet's message of 11 September 1976, which coincided with the promulgation of the Constitutional Acts incorporating into the constitution the decree which formed the military junta. The entire ideological statement of this message leads to the justification of military power: "In the face of Marxism, which has become a permanent aggression, there is an urgent need to place power in the hands of the armed forces, as they are the only ones with the organization and the means to combat it. This is the profound truth about what is happening in a great part of our continent, even though some refuse publicly to recognize it."[26]

But this attempt to establish a permanent military regime ran into serious difficulties, as we have already noted. It thus remained a permanent ideological reserve of the hard-line factions and returned to blossom in debates about the institutional future at the end of 1979 and 1980; in addition, some of its fundamental elements were incorporated into the institutional definition of 1980. However, in the so-called Speech of Chacarillas of 9 July 1977, Pinochet argued for both the institutionalization of the military regime and the promise of a long-run return to democracy.

This attempt to meet both objectives responded to the need to relegitimate the regime with sympathetic sectors as well as with the rest of society. This meant moving from a dictatorship without rules to one which

ɔlishes its own rules, that is to say, to one that is institutionalized. But
y analysis of the peculiarities of both the historical program as well as
ɔɪ ʌhe regime which promotes it is correct, the precise meaning of this
institutionalization is twofold in terms of the categories discussed in the
first part of this work.

POLITICAL INSTITUTIONALIZATION

There are three dimensions to institutionalization, which is quite different
in its goals and mechanism from the process of "transition" or redemocratization. The key to institutionalization has been the attempt to legitimate personalized leadership.

The first of these dimensions is a change in the methods of repression.
We noted that the first phase was characterized by the intensity and the
breadth of repression, exercised beyond all legal bounds, and with death—
real or threatened—as a fundamental feature of the repressive acts. A
notorious trait was the growing concentration and centralization of repressive operations, expressed in the predominance of the DINA (the National
Intelligence Directorate). The second phase, the beginning of which can be
traced to the dissolution of the DINA and its replacement by the CNI
(National Information Center) in August 1977, maintained the use of
repressive force but within a legal framework set by the government itself.
Most repressive acts were no longer justified in terms of the general neces-
sities of a war, but in terms of the legal regulations which had been established. The legislation on the state of emergency was revamped to serve
that end.[27] This was not, however, a lineal process of "the progressive
betterment of a repressive situation," as some consider it. There was not
only a recurrence of temporary repressive waves, bringing back the memory of the first phase, but also the continued presence of elements identified with the first phase who saw their imminent liquidation in any
"opening" and thus sought to preserve the features of the first phase,
either by segmenting or obtaining autonomy for the apparatus of central
security or by ensconcing themselves in it. The political allies of these
sectors tended, naturally, to be the civilian groups most adamantly opposed
to all forms of political opening. This process unleashed a dynamic of
internal confrontations between the security apparatus and terrorist acts,
in turn leading to a new hardening of the legislation on the state of emergency under the pretext of the reappearance of extremism. This naturally
would affect further political decisions about institutionalization.

The second dimension of political institutionalization consists of a set
of measures promulgated before or at the same time as the official
announcement of the "new institutionality" which attempt to crystallize
normatively political control and the idea of political exclusion. Among
them were the Constitutional Acts of September 1976, in which, among
other things, the norms of the state of emergency were rendered perma-

nent; the dissolution of the Christian Democratic Party in March 1977, completing what is referred to as the "political recess"; the establishment of norms which block those suspected of political affiliation or activities from participating in labor and interest organizations; and most especially, the regulations establishing stringent control over the news media.[28]

The third dimension refers specifically to the consolidation of political leadership. At the level of state power, the principal milestones were the Chacarillas speech of July 1977 with its program of a "new institutionality," the debate about the draft of a new constitution, and the culmination of this debate with the call for a plebiscite on 11 September 1980 to ratify the constitutional project of the military junta. At the level of the military, this consolidation was characterized by a process of internal discipline undertaken by Pinochet. Each of these points will be examined in turn.

As noted, by July 1977 it had become increasingly difficult to sustain the principle of a permanent military regime. The combination of a Carter Administration policy orientation sympathetic towards the establishment of democratic systems in Latin America, the actions of the Roman Catholic church, and the criticisms of sectors which managed to circumvent press censorship had repercussions in the dominant bloc and forced some type of formulation about the future political institutional arrangements of the country.[29] The Chacarillas speech responded to these pressures by proposing a series of steps leading from initial "recovery" to the formation of a new political order preceded by a transition phase in which the legislature is appointed by the military junta and the military maintains a dominant role. The goal of this was to establish a "protected" or "authoritarian" democracy. The timing of the transition was to be a function of the degree of maturity displayed by society.[30]

Diverse interpretations arose within the dominant bloc on the timetable and shape of the new institutionality after the Chacarillas speech. The internal debate became sharper when the Draft Constitution prepared by a government-appointed commission was made public. The draft created an authoritarian and restricted political system with the armed forces acquiring a guardianship role independent of civilian power. It also preserved constitutionally the basic elements of the economic model.[31]

In short, for some sectors, which will be called "soft" or "pro-opening," among which are elements tied to the economic leadership, the "new institutionality" implied a certain limited opening which resolved the succession problem, permitted the normalization of relations with the United States, and provided an image of political stability without changing the economic model. In the long run, the result would be a protected, restricted, or limited democracy.

Other sectors, the so-called hard-liners, disagreed sharply with this scheme, arguing that it would again result in political crisis without making any political concessions. They considered any constitutional attempt premature and were in favor of maintaining indefinitely the current leadership and strict political authoritarianism. They strongly criticized the economic leadership, favoring a certain redistributivist populism.[32]

But the different tendencies within the dominant bloc converged finally on one point: the maintenance of Pinochet's leadership. In effect, even though both sectors disagreed on the long-term political model and on the appropriateness of fixing timetables and stages, they agreed on the need for a "maturation period." The so-called pro-opening sectors were also involved in the restructuring dimension of the regime, which some call "modernization." This requires a "maturation" period, an expression of the hope that the structural transformations would produce a political order immune to radical excesses and transformations.[33] There appeared to be no other guarantee for this than the maintenance of rule by the armed forces, even if for only a limited time. This position was reinforced by the particular configuration of political forces in Chile. The political center, principally represented by the Christian Democrats, had been forced into opposition and did not constitute, as in other cases, the reserve ally which the pro-opening sectors could seek out as an alternative. The conditions which made possible a hegemonic bloc of the political center in which a defensive right took shelter in 1964 had changed radically. The privileged position of this group, whatever tensions may exist between it and other sectors of the dominant bloc, made unacceptable the price to be paid for a center which questioned not only the political scheme, but also certain substantive elements of the project of capitalist restructuring and reintegration.

Thus, the debate between the so-called hard-line sectors and the pro-opening or soft-line sectors has taken place within a framework of domination and does not involve any alternative to it, even though their long-run political models and respective paths to it may differ. The program which the regime uses as a vehicle and which is expressed in a certain configuration of forces and their respective perceptions, fixes limits on political options. The different internal tendencies await a decision by the already constituted military and political leadership, that is to say, by Pinochet. They limit their actions to a search for influence in making that decision. Perhaps the real importance of this debate is rooted in the fact that it constitutes the beginning of a process of autonomous restructuring and rearticulation of the Chilean right, which had renounced its own political expression in identifying itself with and allying with the military regime in 1973. The diverse organizations formed to communicate its positions on the institutional future are instruments of the political regrouping of sectors which have been dispersed since the military coup and of a younger generation. They may constitute the seeds for one or more new political parties of the right.

There was, then, a minimum common denominator in the debate within the dominant bloc: Pinochet must remain in power and his rule must be legitimated. It is understandable, then, that Pinochet and the military junta, with the proposed constitution announced in August 1980, sought a measure to consolidate the already constituted leadership for a relatively long period of time.[34] The constitutional document calls for the maintenance of military power for almost two decades under the combined political and military authority of Pinochet, until at least 1989, with the option of prolonging this for a period of eight more years. The goal is the establishment during this period of a limited "democratic" regime, authoritarian-style.

But the process of political institutionalization is not only a constitutional matter. It has been complemented by a process of internal alignment of the armed forces around the leadership of Pinochet through the promotion policy that has led to the replacement of the generation which accompanied Pinochet in the September 1973 military coup.[35] The president is thus no longer surrounded by his companions in arms, but by his subordinates. In armed forces such as the Chilean one, this implies unrestricted loyalty. The internal opposition and disagreements in the other branches of the armed forces—such as those in the air force on 4 January 1978, which culminated in the expulsion of its chief of staff, General Gustavo Leigh, from the junta—were never coherent enough to constitute a threat. All claimed the same principle of legitimacy, the "spirit of September 11," but none appeared to offer greater efficacy. The horror of a vacuum in the face of intermediate alternatives and the risk of breaking the internal cohesion and unity of the armed forces favored the perpetuation of the status quo. This process of consolidation and discipline enforcement within the army and the other branches of the armed forces was as important as that of consolidating the leadership at the state level. Even though a growing one-man leadership clashes with some of the bureaucratic traits of a military organization and generates dependent relations which affect the military's traditional modus operandi, the significant elevation of the military's economic, social, and political status has outweighed any organizational resistance to the process of personalization.

THE INSTITUTIONALIZATION OF SOCIETY

If the political institutionalization of the regime is necessary to guarantee the social and economic transformations of the program of capitalist reconstruction and reintegration, it must be accompanied by a second institutionalization process affecting civil society. This process seeks to crystallize normatively the transformations initiated by the state to create new societal institutions and is directly tied to the attempt at capitalist revolution. A systematic effort to frame new social relations emerging from reforms and innovations in different societal spheres (not only the economic one) began only in 1978.[36] The essence of this effort is to give free reign to private enterprises, contributing to social fragmentation and hierarchicalization and to the predominance of the principles and relationships of the market. In accord with these objectives, the government has adopted a new Labor Plan, a program for reorganizing the health sector, a new Educational Directive, and a new set of norms for the agrarian sector.[37] In terms of their content, all of these measures have some common elements: they overturn the democratization process of the past decade, they drastically reduce the intervening and redistributive role of the state, they broadly favor the mechanisms of the market (that is to say, the game of the most powerful economic groups), and they significantly limit or eliminate all interference or participation by representative grassroots organizations. The ideology which dominates these measures emphasizes their antistatist elements, the scientific-technical character of the norms, and values of efficiency and universalism in the face of the particular interests created.

This institutionalization of society—differentiating it from the strictly political sphere—has been resisted by various sectors and has undermined the loyalties of some elements which supported the military coup and declared themselves in favor of the military regime.[38] Many of these measures have been consciously taken, in the name of liberal principles and of a market economy, to undermine the political influence of middle-class organizations such as professional colleges and trade groups, whose organizational bases have been seriously weakened. If one adds the opposition which these measures have met in popular-sector organizations critical of the regime as well as the time required to assure the effect of social changes, it is easier to understand the government's insistence on dovetailing social institutionalization to political institutionalization as described above. But the process is not a smooth one. The problems of political institutionalization frequently tend to obstruct social institutionalization, diminishing and, at times, voiding innovative changes in the face of dominant-sector impatience with what is viewed as a regime immersed in the traditional task of administration.

It is difficult to evaluate the degree of irreversibility of these societal transformations and whether they will survive the regime which put them in place. In any case, they signify not only the "consolidation" of the historical program of the regime and the relative deepening of the social bases which facilitate an authoritarian political regime, but also the site of new social contradictions and conflicts and, therefore, of new forms of social movement. The Labor Plan and the norms which regulate the student movement are examples of new methods of social struggle, despite the evident switch in the rules of the game.[39] We will return to this point.

In short, the needs and pressures which lead to the institutionalization and relegitimation of the regime give rise to two processes which are shown to be interdependent both because of the opposition they generate and because of the need for a period of maturation. One is a process of political institutionalization defined as the relegitimation and the consolidation of the current leadership which directs the state. The other is a social process defined as the normative crystallization of the transformations introduced in the heart of society by the dominant structural program. The long-run political resolution of the model rests, in one way or another, on the hope that the transformation of society will give rise to a functional model of relations between state and society in a political game which will exclude the possibility of significant change. This twin process is not carried out without conflicts and contradictions which can be catalyzed at particular moments and which make necessary, given the characteristics of the regime, a permanent recourse to force.

Opposition to the Chilean Regime: Problems and Dynamics

An analysis such as this one runs the risk of limiting itself to the dominant agents, not leaving enough room for the phenomena of opposition and resistance. If I have concentrated on this theme, it is because the most significant political events have been generated by those in power. In analyzing the opposition, I will follow a different approach. More than merely showing the phases or development of a process, I will try to concentrate on what, in my judgement, is the problematique of the opposition in a regime such as the Chilean one. Using this as a base, I will then refer to the tendencies and principal dynamics of the opposition.

CHANGES IN POLITICAL BREATHING ROOM: PARTIES AND SOCIAL MOVEMENTS

The crucial element in describing the opposition is the problem of the elimination of the political arena. This appears to be an obvious statement when an authoritarian, repressive regime is being analyzed. However, the elimination or restriction of space for public participation and the intent to erradicate politics do not have the same effect on all authoritarian cases. In Chile, the political party was historically the principal instrument for the constitution and self-recognition of a class, group, or social category. Through the political arena these interests competed in an effort to fulfill themselves and attain universal appeal. Whatever the sociohistorical reasons which gave this role to the political party system, it is clear that in the Chilean case its elimination is more than a simple defeat; it is the destruction of the main axis of the popular movement and its most important nuclei.[40] It is much more than simply a reactive or defensive-repressive measure; it is a social structuring and reorganizing measure. Because of this redefinition of political space, the social movement must be reshaped or recycled. This is a long-term proposition. On the political party side, the party structure is necessarily frozen, as it is outside the political regime at the center of which the principal relations with the social movement are established. The party organizations do manage to perpetuate themselves and survive, despite the repression and imprisonment of their leaders and activists. But even to the extent that public spaces are opened, the party organizations tend to remain behind the social movement and experience great difficulties penetrating the fabric of society and, in turn, being influenced by it because they must operate clandestinely.

This phenomenon tends to be aggravated when the other characteristic of the Chilean regime which I have analyzed is recalled. This characteristic is the attempt at an overall reorganization of society directed from above. As I have said, the ultimate logic of this is to eliminate the structural bases which would permit the development of some form of populism. In this sense, the orientation of development "towards the outside," the progressive elimination of the redistributive intervention of the state, the atomization of productive forms, the unrestricted operation of market mechanisms (not only in the market but in all spheres of social life), and the elimination of "participationist" interference by social organization, all constitute formative measures which go beyond the mere attempt to eliminate and repress the opposition. This "active" dimension of the regime introduces a series of structural transformations and processes of institutionalization. Not all have been as successful as their promoters hoped. But, if we consider the Labor Plan, the transformation of the educational apparatus, the many cases in which public property was sold to the private sector, and the drastic changes in the agrarian sector, we clearly see that social stratification, class composition, behavior, and consequently, values, appear to have been profoundly altered. The structural bases on which the labor movement, the student movement, and the peasant movement rest, as well as the relations between the state and the middle class, have changed significantly. The society of Chilean parties as we knew them is on its way out. It is not only that the conditions and the political space have changed, but the entire society and the structural conditions on which social movements and their political expressions are generated have also been transformed.

Thus, the situation of the political party system in Chile is ambivalent.

On the one hand, the survival of political parties is an undeniable fact. Moreover, if political space is opened in Chile, perhaps the very parties which the state has been trying to eliminate might summon the electorate and be converted into valid and legitimate interlocutors. This is partly explained by historical and structural reasons, such as the firm implantation of a party spectrum with roots in society not limited only to a small political class and constituting the main mediation channel between society and the state. These parties have their own culture which can perpetuate itself at the national level and can establish symbols with which people can identify.[41] It is also partly explained by the very features of a regime which, in order to erradicate political parties, would have to resort to genocide or to totalitarian control through intense mobilization and fanatical control of a great many people favoring the military regime. The attempt to depoliticize society is a two-edged sword, as it freezes and solidifies structures which already exist. The elimination of the political arena converts new social organizations into the natural field of party activity. The need to work in secret reinforces existing party organization, making it difficult to create new apparati and new systems. The lack of political space impedes the renewal of leadership and strengthens the symbolic value of the old leaders, as they are the only reference point for the wider public. Thus, with the exception of the right—which renounced its own political expression by joining the leadership of the military regime and which only in recent times, as I have said, appears to be attempting the difficult process of rearticulating its political autonomy—the center and the left of the political spectrum keep their symbolic and organic identity.

On the other hand, both the elimination of the political arena and the introduction of changes in diverse spheres of society generate problems for a profound readjustment of party structures, which beyond the problem of visibility, find themselves challenged in their ability to rearticulate themselves through the social movement and become significant actors. During the entire first phase of the regime, the primary effort of political parties was necessarily devoted to maintaining the apparatus and concentrating on the tasks of preserving and developing internal organization. This had two important consequences: on the one hand, it led to an insistence on problems of self-affirmation and continuity, making it difficult to see the new things that were happening in society; on the other, the process of theoretical rethinking became rigid as the political language froze in the old formulas and categories. If the internal and interparty debates and public declarations of parties are examined during the period which I have called the first phase of the military regime, it is easy to observe that the old ways prevailed in the themes, theoretical references, and language. It was not until later, with a partial political opening and changes in the method of oppression, that new themes began to blossom. Only gradually have the new social realities begun to appear in the political parties, but in an imprecise manner, often dressed in old clothes and within organizational structures, which continue to be basically the same. Those spheres not controlled by the regime, those generated at the social level by the processes of institutionalization, and those which arise under an umbrella providing legitimacy and relative immunity such as that provided by the Roman Catholic church, all act as substitutes for the political structure as far as the constitution of the social movement is concerned. The political parties move with difficulty in these new spaces: the codes of social action have substantially changed.

Despite this fact, it is noteworthy that in other historical experiences, the funeral odes of political parties were also prematurely chanted. Despite years of authoritarianism, political loyalties were largely maintained, and old symbols not buried were once again capable of summoning social sectors which were supposed to have been radically altered by profound structural changes. However, this does not deny that, whatever the future result, what I have called the problematic process of convergence between political structures and the social movement occurs under the authoritarian regime.

Thus, two apparently contradictory phenomena, which are in fact complementary, appear to coexist. On the one hand, there is the crucial importance of the emergence in civil society of autonomous organizations affecting all spheres of social life. These organizations appear in spaces free of government control, where "substitute" actors (such as the church) emerge. The relationship between the social organizations and these substitute actors is analogous to, and exhibits a similar problematic to, the earlier relationship between the state and the political system—one of dialectical dependence and autonomy. They thrive through the progressive utilization of the instruments of social institutionalization which are created in a dialectic of negation and accusation on the one hand, and resignation, redefinition, and utilization on the other.[42] Yet, it is clear that even though what happens on the level of civil society is going to acquire a crucial role in the shaping of the opposition to the regime and even though up to now political organizations have only reacted to the processes unleashed by those who hold power, the existence of opposition can play crucial or defining roles in certain situations. In the political institutionalization process taking place today, there are moments in which there is an opening of the field to political will and options together with the crystallization of more or less structural tendencies. In such situations, many of the problems which I have noted to this point are resolved by the political parties' ability to summon and mobilize, and their actions could define the course of a process which appears strong and irreversible.

THE LEFT AND THE CENTER

Even though the problematique outlined here affects the entire political opposition, it takes different forms as one moves across the political spectrum.[43]

It is well known that the leftist parties and organizations suffered the brunt of the repression. Therefore, the first task faced by party structures was to ensure survival and to recover from internal disarray and the loss of contact with the social movement. The response varied depending on the party.[44]

The left constituted the most radical opposition to the regime but probably had little realization of the regime's staying power. During the entire first phase, even though the language and catchwords were adapted to new realities, these parties concentrated on self-justification and continuity together with the tasks of survival. Then came self-criticism about the past, even when it referred overwhelmingly to procedural errors and only tangentially to substantive elements and the formulation of party programs.[45] For a long time, the first calls for a "formation of broad anti-fascist fronts," for "democratic recovery," or for "resistance," depending on which party made the call, did not vary and did not directly refer to changes in the party projects. In recent years, the theme of an alliance with the political center and the reconnection with the spheres and movements of civil society which parallel the regime's process of consolidation has become the principal and predominant point of a new debate in the heart of the left. This debate appears to mark the end of expectations during the first phase that the intrinsic weaknesses of the regime would lead rapidly to its downfall.

Beyond an analysis of the situation or the specific trajectory of each of the political parties of the left, there appear to be two dimensions of what can be called the problematique of the Chilean left. Both point, not to a problem of organizational viability, but to the capacity of the left to structure itself as a significant actor, to overcome its adaptive dimension, and to shape the new reality. The first dimension refers to the organic problem and deals both with the question of the relevance of the current organizational spectrum of the left and its coordinating structures, and with the definition of party types which can reflect the extreme diversity of the populace. It also refers to the redefinition of relations with society, in which thinking and action which previously centered on the problem of state power and the system now must rediscover the autonomous spheres of civil society.[46] The second dimension refers to the ideological question; here, the principal problems to be overcome are related to the relative rigidity of the left's theoretical tradition, its schematic vision of society, and a language which contributes to its isolation from social forces which are not directly involved in its political program.

The problem of the political center, that is to say, the Christian Democrats, can be formulated in a different way. It should not be forgotten that both the leaders of the Christian Democratic Party (and of other sectors of the center) and many of its members explicitly or tacitly supported the 11 September 1973 military coup. However, the restrictive measures which the military government has imposed on the party for an indefinite period, the effects of repression, which have now touched the party's top leaders, activists, and sympathizers, and the growing perception of the real nature of the regime have pushed it clearly into opposition. In this process, the party has had to confront a classic historical problem: political isolation and difficulty in establishing solid alliances.[47] Its growing opposition to the regime, not only to the political model, but also to the economic one, its high degree of organic and ideological structure, and its autonomous and alternative political program did not convert the Christian Democratic party into a natural field of attraction for the soft-liners or pro-opening sectors disillusioned by the regime, a group towards which the party has yet to develop a coherent strategy. On the other hand, the party's old distrust of the left, which is reciprocated by the latter, has prevented a stable agreement with the left; many Christian Democrats regard such a move as potentially alienating to other supporters, especially because it would involve some sort of rapprochement with the Communist party. This tendency towards isolation is accompanied by a revindication of the democratic regime as a postauthoritarian alternative without a coherent strategy for eliminating the current regime. Doubtless, at the strictly political level the relations of the Christian Democrat party with other domestic and foreign centers of influence, as well as its greater possibilities for public action, give it advantages within the field of opposition because of its unity and its ability to exercise ideological hegemony. But as a result of its problems, the party's political behavior has been, up to now, fundamentally reactive.

SUBSTITUTE SPACES AND ACTORS

The dismantling of the political arena and the relative neutralization of the political party structure occurred at the same time that the church was becoming more relevant as an important political-social space and actor, becoming to a degree a substitute political force, at least during certain phases.[48] At first, the church acted to protect and defend sectors affected by physical persecution and repression. It acted as the only organization with sufficient legitimacy to speak to the military in defense of human rights. The reduction of the public arena occasioned by the military regime was accompanied by the expansion of the church and its growing, at times monopolistic, presence in that arena. In this there is an organizational dimension: in the face of a vacuum of social organizations and the atomization which the authoritarian regime has introduced, the church provided an organizational space to represent "general" interests and demands analogous to those provided by the political system before the "authoritarian break." But there is also an ideological-cultural dimension: the most organized and ideological expressions of the Chilean popular and social movements consisted of a development scheme and political system profoundly challenged by the regime. The vacuum could not be filled by the dominant bloc's ideology, with its weak degree of legitimacy. The church provided an ideological space in which its connotatively general categories could integrate interests, aspirations, and demands of the popular sectors and make them universal.

It should be made clear, in considering its dynamics, that the church has a dual character, as a space and as an actor. First, there is the relationship between the ecclesiastical hierarchy and the government, marked by a progressive distancing. The church's initial criticism of the regime's excesses, without, however, denying the government's "original legitimacy," became increasingly comprehensive and directed at the very bases of the regime. But this distance did not mean an open break or defiance as in the case of some Central American dictatorships. The relationship is more complex: the church's direct intervention to protect individuals and organizations led it both to negotiate with the government and to recognize publicly some of the government's minor achievements. Many times such negotiations guaranteed the independence and legitimacy of church intervention, affirming its validity as an interlocutor, while at the same time the government gained tactical advantage and the resource of time. In the long run, this increased the distance between them. At another level are the internal relations between the different sectors of the eccesiastical hierarchy, where the central problem is to maintain a certain image of unity. This necessitates an ongoing game of concessions. In turn, these intrahierarchical relations are affected by pressures from members of the clergy who have direct contact with the popular sectors and have urged a greater radicalization of hierarchical positions towards the government. There is also the dynamic itself of new forms of organizations in the ecclesiastical structure incorporating and making connections with different social sectors, many of which had no close relations with the church. Such organic forms—which also include relatively autonomous church groups at the highest levels of the hierarchy—tend to perpetuate within them the intragroup conflicts and competition which earlier took place in the political arena. Finally, there is the dynamic of the relations between the church and the political movement itself. Here it is possible to perceive a game of succession and substitution in taking initiative to the degree that the church tries not to appear identified with these movements, particularly with the Christian Democratic party, with which it has the greatest ideological affinity.

This entire complex of factors allows us to understand why the church, even while providing an ongoing political space and becoming a substitute political actor, can never take on a role equivalent to that of the political parties. The church's own historical dimension and dynamics give it a rationale and character that cannot easily conform fully to the new political role it has acquired.

On the other hand, there are other spaces in society where opposition groups and processes act on the fringes of the church's umbrella. These spaces arise in sectors of society not controlled either by political power or by the process of institutionalization. The church's almost exclusive role as a breathing space for action by different social groups during the first years of the regime has been reduced as a growing plurality of autonomous organizations in civil society develops. This is not a unilinear process, however, and is subject to the regime's ups and downs. Nor does it imply that the church has lost its central role.

THE OPPOSITION IN PERSPECTIVE

The problems of the opposition cannot be considered in static form; there has been considerable evolution.

On the one hand, to the tasks of survival and of occupying the public space opened by the church's criticism is added the task of reconstructing the social movement, both through new organizational forms and through adaptation and regrouping of old structures, as in the case of the unions. The challenge facing these social organizations is to conquer even the smallest space for the expression of demands when confronted by persecution and repressive threats while trying to avoid letting the corporatist dimension of their demands make them lose their ties to a social base fatigued by the dramatic problems of everyday life. In the face of the partial social institutionalization of the regime, these organizations, particularly the unions and the student groups, discovered new ways to relate to a fragmented social base. At the different planes of social life, they formed new circles or organizations and activities which took advantage of the spaces which the government cannot control. This is especially visible in the field of cultural activities. In certain situations, there have been times when public mobilization surpassed official prohibitions.[49]

There are other efforts to expand the opposition in an ambivalent relationship with party organizations, insofar as they are party statements, as well as efforts that could lead to the formation of new political groupings. One example, at the level of confrontation to the political institutionalization of the regime, is the so-called Group of 24. The importance of this group rests in its ability to attract ideologically diverse sectors to draw up a post-authoritarian institutional alternative.[50]

On the other hand, there is an evolution at the strictly political level, where the illusion of the government's early or imminent fall has given way gradually to the recognition of long-run tasks, to the difficult process of reconstruction, and, even when there is no national edict, to the search for bridges between the diverse, and sometimes antagonistic, sectors.[51]

Even when these processes mean something in themselves, especially those which occur in the autonomous sphere of civil society, their substitution role during the current regime cannot yet be evaluated with any certainty.

Conclusion: The Situation in 1980 and Its Projection into the Future

In the central political dynamics of the Chilean military regime there has been, on the one hand, an institutionalization of the regime which signifies, in the political sphere, the legitimation of an increasingly personalistic military hierarchical leadership and the freezing of political exclusion. In the social sphere, this process has led to a normative crystallization of the structural changes which are part of a delayed attempt at a socially regressive capitalist experiment. On the other hand, new expressions of opposition confront this institutionalization in its social dimension. However, the opposition's attempts to unify in the political sphere have clashed with problems stemming from the inheritence of "old" party divisions as well as the difficult apprenticeship in what is "new" during these years.

During the course of 1980, culminating in the plebiscite on 11 September of that year, various trends and processes noted above became further crystallized. The decision leading to that plebiscite is characteristic of a leadership style which takes the same sectors that are locked in battle within the dominant bloc by surprise. Despite all their previous disagreements, these sectors were forced to go along with the decision, as each sector saw some of its aspirations realized and none had a coherent and visible alternative.[52]

The new constitution ratifies the power situation which existed for the first eight years, while strengthening the concentration of personal power, excluding all political participation and activity, and institutionally ensconcing a state of unprotected social and individual rights. All of this was officially named the "transition period." Secondly, the plebiscite ratified those in power for another eight years, with the additional provision that Pinochet could be designated for a second term by the military junta. The constitution consecrated all the principles of a "protected democracy," with political representation properly restricted and limited and with the armed forces exercising the powers of a "guardianship" role.[53]

The plebiscite had all the characteristics of a political act of this type of regime:[54] the issuance of overwhelming government propaganda and significant restrictions on the opposition while at the same time instilling fear in the population, especially the middle sectors and the urban poor. The plebiscite was a unilateral presentation of the government's position. The government had absolute control over the entire election process and provided no guarantees to the opposition. There was no electoral registration system, no provision for write-in votes, and no effective way of monitoring for fraud during the voting process. Against this background, the government announced results of 67.96% in its favor and 30.17% against, with 2.27% of the votes annulled and participation by 93.1% of the eligible voter population.[55]

This is not the place for a detailed analysis of the results, especially since it is impossible to calculate the amount of fraud. For the purposes of this work, two observations of a theoretical nature, which run the risk of being premature and provisional, are in order.[56]

Despite the fact that the plebiscite was illegitimate, it was a political event of undeniable importance and a turning point in the development of the regime and in the evolution of the opposition. From the point of view of the regime and the dominant bloc, it was the culmination of political institutionalization around a personalized and hierarchicalized leadership of the armed forces. For the moment, it put an end to a process of erosion and clearly excluded alternatives which would have implied important modifications in the regime. Within the dominant bloc, despite all the differences which arose about the plebiscite, there is now a clear definition, considered legitimate and able to manage contradictions, and convince and obligate everyone.

In relation to the society as a whole, along with a degree of regime penetration which is relatively important in sectors not part of the dominant bloc, the process of institutionalization has de facto legitimacy, even though it is unstable. With the political process frozen for a long time, the regime now can turn to further work on its historical program of capitalist reconstruction at the level of society. It is likely that during this process, differences of orientation, control, and influence within the dominant bloc will arise once again and be expressed in the political sphere, meeting resistance from broad and diverse social sectors.

From the opposition's point of view, the plebiscite marked the high point of its capacity for political and social mobilization and for agreement on an alternative proposal structured as a response to a concrete situation. The opposition's action could only be a reaction and was limited by the rules of the game and context which it had not selected. This accounts for the "in-group" character of the opposition's action, even though this time it filtered much beyond the opposition's previously consolidated "cultural circuit." The opposition's message about the illegitimacy of the plebiscite, in some ways also the church's message,[57] was accompanied by a political proposal which could only have been intended to present publicly a possible alternative and to reach some military ears, without any hope that it was a feasible alternative. As often happens, the "hot" moments can catalyze processes which scrape along with difficulty for long periods of time. The passing of those moments does not mean they were in vain, as they leave new processes cemented in place, even though they have not resolved all the problems which reappear in the "cold" moments of the political process. This appears to have happened with the problem of unifying the political opposition. The opposition's call to reject the regime's proposal, making the plebiscite illegitimate, should be measured more in terms of a capacity for relatively unified mobilization than in terms of the results themselves.

I have said that the plebiscite and the constitutional definition of September 1980 catalyzed and crystallized the principal trends of the political process which developed in the Chilean regime during the past years.

The resolution of tensions within the dominant bloc by the relegitimation of its leadership, the fixation of time periods which freeze the current political regime, the future predominance of the tasks of structural transformation and social institutionalization, and finally, the new polarization which resulted from it between the dominant bloc and the opposition with advances and new problems in the latter's process of mobilization and unification, all justify the thought that we are faced with a new political scenario. If the basic trends are the same, the crystallization and relative culmination of them nevertheless define a relatively new political context.

In this situation, what are the possibilities of altering and accelerating the time periods set by the authoritarian regime? There are at least two factors which must be considered, excluding for the purposes of our analysis the hypothesis that the regime could collapse because of international phenomena or change because of accidental elements. On one hand, there are problems within the dominant bloc. Recapitulating what I have previously said, the argument can be summarized in the following way:

(a) The stability of the regime depends significantly on the formation of a hegemonic nucleus within the dominant bloc which is capable of securing the leadership and the substance of a capitalist reconstruction program. One of the problems which this nucleus faced was the possible negative results of the growing personalization of military leadership, whose replacement could mean a rapid breakdown in the regime to the extent that the regime appeared to be identified with that leadership. It is obvious that one of the clear possibilities at the beginning of the new scenario is a sharpening of the personalistic trend and its interference in the broader rationale of the program of capitalist reconstruction. It is not clear whether this trend would significantly contradict the more organizational and bureaucratic demands of the armed forces because the armed forces have benefited greatly from the regime, obtaining real advantages both as an organization and as individuals. But if this is the case, the same process of institutionalization and its new scenario have created a framework which allows something which appeared impossible before 11 September 1980: the eventual separation of the regime's stability from Pinochet's leadership in such a way that Pinochet's exit through internal processes in the dominant bloc would not necessarily mean an acceleration of the end of the regime.

(b) A second problem which this hegemonic nucleus faces is the possible change in the leadership of the capitalist reconstruction project. This could lead to the exacerbation of internal struggles over the issue of opening political spaces or over the structural transformations and the reconstruction and reintegration policies, thereby delaying the process of social institutionalization. All of this could unleash dynamics leading to a more or less rapid breakdown. I have already pointed out the limits to splits within the dominant bloc, especially the difficulties of some sectors in establishing significant alliances with the political center, given the structure of the Chilean political spectrum. The plebiscite demonstrated this; unless something extraordinary happens, it does not appear possible that an alternative to the regime will arise within it, or, should it arise, that it would attract outsiders. It is even possible in this new scenario that partial changes in the orientation of the capitalist reconstruction program and social reorganization, accompanied by the internal redistribution of power and influence, will not affect the regime's stability.

(c) In relation to the entire society, the regime does not depend, as I have said, on its ideological force nor on its ability to create loyalty, mobilize support, or socialize the population in the substance of a new culture. Nor does it rely on an active majority consensus. The attempts to systematize an ideology for these purposes have failed.[58] This, without a doubt, is one of the regime's weakest aspects. Nevertheless, there are certain substitutes for ideology. The regime can renew its artificial legitimacy through structural transformations and normative crystallizations which deepen society's stratification and fragmentation, break down society, and create stronger elites, at the same time that the regime exacerbates consumption-oriented behavior. This contributes to partial obligations, passive support, indifference, and conformism, producing in the medium run a cynical generation. The paradox of this process is that it also erodes the bases of support of certain sectors of an in-group political opposition, even though it does not strengthen the regime's active base of support, which can be turned around in periods of remobilization. It is worthwhile to recall that even when there is erosion of the regime, there is no guarantee that it will be replaced by a viable democratic regime.

From the opposition's point of view, the possibility of accelerating the end of the authoritarian regime and replacing it with a democratic regime faces another set of problems. I have noted the major tasks of the political opposition during the first phase of the regime and subsequent dynamic, as well as the opposition's problems of unity and diversity, and the efforts it displayed during the plebiscite. During all these phases, the opposition's task was either to maintain itself or to react to the regime's actions. The advances in achieving unity always concerned either temporary sectoral or global actions, or agreements on post-authoritarian alternatives, but the problem of the downfall of the regime was not posed. The resolution of this problem was fed by certain myths, such as the contradictions and internal erosion of the regime, isolation and international pressure, the "failure" of the economic model, and the confrontation with the church. At best, the opposition or sectors of it posed certain scenarios but left it to someone else, usually someone in the armed forces, to enact them, while taking no action to influence the outcome.[59] Perhaps the plebiscite's greatest consequence was not the electoral result, but its indirect contribution to a new consensus on the part of the opposition that it simply cannot wait for others to define the transition conditions. It was not only a matter of the absence of an alternative, but also the absence of a strategy which paralyzed the opposition. It is not enough to repeat that this type of regime cannot end by the opposition's action. Even if historical evidence and generalization show this to be the case, political options and actions must be designed.

The perception that the regime is now in a new phase and that opposition tasks should be redefined implies, in turn, a redefinition of the unity between center and left which was so painfully developed. There undoubtedly will be new fragmentations and realignments. There are sectors in the center, particularly in the Christian Democratic party, who may try to reach segments of the dominant bloc, but at the cost of party unity. The Christian Democratic party's feeling and fear of being surpassed in a growing process of social mobilization, of which the plebiscite situation can be an illustration; the fragmentation of the socialist sector, which has hindered its conversion into a stable interlocutor; the center's distrust of the secretiveness of the Communist party and its almost unlimited adherence to its proposals—all pose great difficulties for the opposition when it tries to go from defensive, reactive, declarative, or temporary opposition action, however great a value that may have, to the coherently active and offensive dimension required by the new strategy. The problem is compounded by internal divisions in the left and center groups.[60]

Perhaps the opposition's main problem is not merely to structure agreements at the top, but to reconstruct its ties to civil society. In this sense, there undoubtedly will be a shift from dealing with "superstructural" questions such as the formation of "fronts" or organic agreements, to strengthening all of society's autonomous organizations to conform to the new strategy. Even if the opposition cannot present a coherent strategy for accelerating the end of the authoritarian regime, or if it does not have the resources to implement it, it does have an immense field of action in the task of reconstructing and redemocratizing civil society, while the political system remains frozen. But this also assumes an act of political perception and will and a restatement of the way of doing politics—that is to say, an understanding that one world has disappeared and that it is necessary to discover new parameters for action in a type of society which already displays the symptoms of profound changes and in which people act very differently from the way in which an entire generation perceived them as acting. This will require a profound renovation of the elite and political class, accustomed to old ways.

In short, the dominant nucleus' inability to establish a political order based on consensus has led it to freeze in place the authoritarian and exclusivist model and to try to block all prospects of redemocratization in the short run. This demands a redefinition of strategy by the opposition.

Notes

1. Many of the ideas contained in this section have been developed in my "Discussion of the New Authoritarian Regimes in Latin America" (December 1979, prepared for the seminar "Latin America and Its Place in the International System," FLACSO-CLACSO, Santiago, and published in the series of Working Papers of the Latin American Program of the Woodrow Wilson International Center for Scholars, Washington, D.C.). The use of the expression "authoritarianism" or "authoritarian" regime is purely nominal and refers to the type of military regime in the Southern Cone of Latin America. The use of these expressions does not in itself imply any connotation, interpretation, or theoretical affiliation.

2. See Guillermo O'Donnell, "Reflections on the Patterns of Change in the Bureaucratic Authoritarian State,"*Latin American Research Review* 13, no 1 (1978), and David Collier, ed., *The New Authoritarianism in Latin America* (Princeton: Princeton University Press, 1979).

3. This twofold dimension helps differentiate the new military regimes in Latin America from traditional-style regimes. But not all of these regimes give equal emphasis to these dimensions.

4. Genaro Arriagada and Manuel Antonio Garretón, "Doctrina de seguridad nacional y regímenes militares," *Estudios Sociales Centroamericanos,* nos. 20 and 21 (1978).

5. There are many forms and many directions which this program can take. National historical characteristics, the level of previous development, and peculiar features such as population, the current and potential market size, the quantity, quality, and diversity of resources, etc., play determinant roles. In some cases this involves a new phase of industrialization; in others, a process of reorienting the economy toward the primary sector. See the works of Serra and Hirschman in Collier, *The New Authoritarianism,* for discussions of the direction and possible content of the historical program with which these regimes are linked.

6. Manuel Antonio Garretón, "De la seguridad nacional a la nueva institucionalidad: Notas sobre la evolución ideológica del nuevo estado autoritario," *Foro Internacional,* no. 73 (1978). In this work, legitimacy and the process of legitimatization refer to the principle invoked by the dominant group to justify its position and by which it expects obedience.

7. For these concepts, see the bibliography in my article cited in note 1.

8. The concept of hegemony is used in the Gramscian sense as a system's capacity to establish domination beyond mere coercion through cultural leadership and a relative consensus.

9. Although I do not completely share his conceptualization, I have borrowed some of Juan Linz's ideas. See "An Authoritarian Regime: Spain," in Erik Allardt and Stein Rokkan, eds., *Mass Politics: Studies in Political Sociology* (New York: Free Press, 1970), and "Totalitarian and Authoritarian Regimes," in Fred Greenstein and Nelson Polsby, eds., *Handbook of Political Science,* vol. 3 Reading, Mass.: Addison Wesley, 1975).

10. On the theme of transition, see the works presented by Bolivar Lamounier, Guillermo O'Donnell, Adam Przeworski, and Phillipe Schmitter at the conference "Prospects for Democracy: Transitions from Authoritarian Rule in Latin America and Latin Europe," organized by the Latin American Program of the Wilson Center, Washington, D.C. See also Kevin J. Middlebrook, "Prospects for Democracy: Regime Transformation and Transitions from Authoritarian Rule, A Rapporteur's Report" (Working Paper no. 62, Latin American Program, Wilson Center, Washington, D.C.).

11. I have borrowed some ideas from the article mentioned in note 1. Commentaries made by Juan Linz and Philippe Schmitter on this theme at the workshop "Six Years of Military Government in Chile," (Wilson Center, May 1980) have been very helpful to me.

12. For a synthesis of the formulations on juridical institutions, see Felipe Adelmar, "Estado de derecho en Chile," *Mensaje* (Santiago), November 1979. Also see the items cited in note 14.

13. On these themes see M. A. Garretón, "Continuidad y ruptura y vacío teórico ideológico: Dos hipótesis sobre el proceso político chileno, 1970–1973," *Revista Mexicana de Sociología,* no. 4 (1977), and "Sentido y derrota de un proyecto popular," *Mensaje,* January–February 1978. Also see M. A. Garretón and T. Moulian, "Procesos y bloques políticos en la crisis chilena, 1970–1973," *Revista Mexicana de Sociología,* no. 1 (1979).

14. Among the many reports concerning this, see the Inter-American Commission on Human Rights, Organization of American States, Document 21, October 1974; Document 15, June 1976; Document 10, February 1977; and the *Annual Reports* of the Commission for 1977 and 1978.

15. See Tomás Moulian and Pilar Vergara, "Estado, ideología, y políticas económicas en Chile," *Colección Estudios CIEPLAN,* no. 3 (1980).

16. On this see Augusto Varas, "La dinámica política de la oposición durante el gobierno de la Unidad Popular" (FLACSO, Working Document, Santiago, 1977), and Moulian and Vergara, "Estado, ideología, y políticas económicas."

17. There is an extensive bibliography on the economic model. Among the most recent works are the article by Tomás Moulian and Pilar Vergara mentioned above, and the studies by Foxley, Ffrench-Davis, and Vergara in this volume. For a pro-government perspective, see J. Cauas and A. Saieh, "Política económica, 1973–1979," *Realidad* (Santiago), September 1979.

18. M. A. Garretón, "Modelo político chileno y proceso de democratización," *Mensaje,* January–February 1979. for a pro-government perspective, see J. Guzmán, "El camino político," *Realidad,* December 1977. In relation to this, the "national security" ideology is relatively important during the reactive or defensive phase, and hardly important at all in relation to the structuring dimension. Concerning this image of society, the statement which appears especially relevant to me is the speech on the inauguration of the academic year at the University of Chile given by Pinochet in April 1979. On the regime's cultural model, see J. J. Brunner, "La concepción autoritaria del mundo" (FLACSO Working Document, Santiago, 1979).

19. I repeat here an idea in M. A. Garretón, "Modelo político chileno y proceso de democratización."

20. See G. O'Donnell, "Modernización y golpes militares," *Desarrollo Económico,* no. 47 (1972), and Garretón and Moulian "Procesos y bloques políticos."

21. See Chapter 4 in this volume.

22. The mechanism for internal succession in the junta is established by Decree Law 527 of 26 June 1974. Concerning the formula submitted to the plebiscite, see F. Adelmar, "Ratificación plebiscitaria," *Mensaje,* September 1980, and Hernán Montealegre, "Constitución y plebiscito" (Academia de Humanismo Cristiano, Santiago, August 1980), reproduced in part in "Una Constitución Encerrada en el Pasado," *Mensaje,* October 1980.

23. On foreign financing, see J. E. Herrera and J. Morales, "La inversión financiera externa: el caso de Chile, 1974–1978," *Colección* Estudios CIEPLAN, no. 1 (1979), and Chapter 2 in this volume. A more or less accurate figure on military expenditures is impossible to come by; the official figures in the budget do not reflect the amounts actually spent.

24. This was a persistent theme of the most coherent expression of the Chilean economic right, found in the newspaper *El Mercurio* from 1977 on.

25. That very 11 September 1973 Congress was closed. Maintaining the operation of judicial institutions gave them an appearance of independence, but, with very few exceptions, the judges have unconditionally followed the standards of the executive. See P. Méndez, "Crisis de confianza en la justicia chilena," *Mensaje,* November 1979.

26. Presidential Message of 11 September 1976. This attempt to legitimate the regime—partially repeated in one way in the draft constitution of the Ortúzar Commission, more moderately in the draft constitution of the Council of State, and renewed in the constitution submitted in a plebiscite (this time with a time schedule)—was explicitly defined as a path for all the countries of the Southern Cone by ex-president Bordaberry of Uruguay.

27. Decree Law 1,877, published in the *Diario Oficial,* 13 August 1977, adapts the regulations on state security to meet this need. This is also done by the Constitutional Acts of September 1976.

28. See Adelmar, "Estado de derecho." The news media is restricted by provisions of Decree Law 1,281, published in December 1975, and Edict 122 of November 1978, which modified Edict 107 of March 1977. The decree law concerns sanctions which can be used against publications and the edict concerns controls on new publications.

29. See Episcopal Council, "Nuestra convivencia nacional," March 1977. Also see J. Somavía and J. G. Valdés, "Las relaciones entre los gobiernos de EE.UU. y Chile en el marco de la política de derechos humanos," *Cuadernos Semestrales* CIDE, no. 6 (second semester, 1979), and Chapter 9 in this volume.

30. Chacarillas was the site of the pro-government youth rally of 9 July 1977, during which Pinochet announced for the first time a plan for the "new institutional organization." For an analysis of this speech, see Garretón, "De la seguridad nacional."

31. The commission, known as the Ortúzar Commission, was created in 1973; later, important members left the commission to join the Group of 24, an opposition group. The commission's work was done secretly and carried no weight for several years. For a good dossier on the commission, including a text of the draft constitution, see *Chile América* (Rome), January–February 1979.

32. To place the so-called economic team in one or another of the sectors of the dispute is a mistake. In general, one must be on one's guard against the assumption that the different groups involved in the debate have monolithic positions. See the debates published by *Hoy* during the first months of 1980.

33. See the article by Jaime Guzmán, one of the ideologues of the regime, "El Camino Político," *Realidad* (Santiago), December 1979. This view is reflected in the editorial commentaries entitled "La Semana Política" in *El Mercurio*.

34. The text of the draft constitution was published in the *Diario Oficial* on 11 August 1980. On this, see the items cited in note 22.

35. See Chapter 4 in this volume.

36. This is explicitly pointed out in Pinochet's message of 11 September 1978, and especially in his 11 September 1979 message.

37. See Chapter 7 in this collection. See also, on health policy, CESPO, "Informe preliminar sobre política de salud en Chile" (mimeo, Santiago, August 1979), and, on educational policy, the Interdisciplinary Educational Research Program (PIIE), "Debate sobre la política educacional del gobierno" (mimeo, Santiago, 1979).

38. For example, the Medical College and the transport unions, which criticized the drastic reduction of the state role in their area, privatization measures, self-financing policies, and the introduction of market principles which dismantled the bases of their organizations.

39. The spaces defined by the process of institutionalization are not the only ones. There are some which escaped the regime's control. The importance of the first type is that they are located in the center of the historical program which the regime promotes.

40. On the role of the Chilean political system, see Aníbal Pinto, "Desarrollo económico y relaciones sociales en Chile," in A. Pinto, ed., *Tres ensayos sobre Chile y América Latina* (Buenos Aires: Ediciones Solar, 1971). I have further developed this theme in "Democratización y otro desarrollo: El caso chileno" (Santiago: VECTOR 1979).

41. See Chapter 6 of this volume for this argument.

42. The importance which political party activists sometimes have in the creation and promotion of this type of organization cannot be ignored.

43. I will not try here to present a detailed analysis of the different political groups. *Chile América* gives an interesting report on their evolution. For information on the Christian Democratic party, see especially A. Zaldívar and T. Reyes, "Proposiciones al Plenario DC de Marzo 1977," *El Mercurio*, 12 March 1977 and "Una Patria para Todos," *Chile América,* nos. 35–36 (1977). On the Socialist party, see "Resoluciones del Pleno del Comité Central, Abril 1979,"

Foreign Secretariat, Central Committee of the Socialist Party, and "La Crisis en el Socialismo Chileno," *Chile América*, nos. 54–55 (1979). On the position of the Communist party, see Luis Corvalán, "Nuestro proyecto democrático," *Foreign Bulletin of the Communist Party of Chile*, no. 37 (September–October 1979). The position of these and other parties can also be found in their foreign bulletins.

44. The Communist party and the Socialist party were the most affected, along with the Movement of the Revolutionary Left (MIR). Nevertheless, the Communist party's ability to reorganize was greater, owing to its previous history. The rest of the leftist parties were affected to a much lesser extent.

45. A complete bibliography of works about the 1970–73 period, including documents of self-criticism, can be found in M. A. Garretón and E. Hola, "Bibliografía del proceso chileno, 1970–73." (FLACSO Working Document, 1978). A good selection of texts on the subject can be found in *Chile América* (Rome).

46. These aspects have been developed at greater length in M. A. Garretón, "Vigencia, crisis y renovación de los partidos de izquierda," *Análisis* (Santiago), no. 23 (1980).

47. See Garretón and Moulián, "Procesos y bloques políticos."

48. See Chapter 8 in this volume.

49. The public demonstrations on workers' day, 1 May, over the last few years, are one example of this. As for the corporatist-type organizations in the middle sectors (professional colleges, merchants' groups, etc.), during the last few years they have made some attempts to oppose the regime's efforts at social institutionalization in their own circles, but without any contact with the political opposition or with processes of globalization. Some of their leaders joined the rejection of the government's proposal in the plebiscite.

50. Originally pushed by the Christian Democratic party, the Group of 24 brought together sectors of the center and the left, although center groups dominated. Their task of drafting an alternative constitution is stated in different documents. Among these sources are the "Report of the Group of 24," published in *Hoy*, no. 117 (October 1979), and, on the fundamental bases of the constitutional reform, Bulletin No. 1 (October 1978), No. 2 (December 1978), No. 3 (June 1979), No. 4 (October 1979), and No. 5 (July 1980). Concerning the situation in which the plebiscite took place, see the "Compromiso con la democracia" by the same group (mimeo, 9 September 1980), and "Una alternativa válida: Transición de dos años," *Hoy*, no. 164 (September 1980). Because of its very nature, this group cannot provide the impulse for a coherent strategy to eliminate the regime.

51. Here, it is a question of comparing the polarization between the center and the left in 1973 with the positions taken at the time of the plebiscite, precisely seven years later, in order to evaluate the long road traveled in spite of the obstacles and difficulties which remained.

52. Fixing time periods and future political processes which appeared to be democratic, and thus creating the institutional framework to assure the development of structural changes, satisfied the aspirations of the soft-line

groups. Maintaining military power for a long time and freezing the political system satisfied the demands of the hard-liners.

53. On the characteristics of the draft submitted to the plebiscite—that is to say, the constitution which took effect in March 1980—see the texts cited in note 22.

54. One analysis of these characteristics is Jaime Ruiz Tagle's "Hacia una nueva democracia?" *Mensaje,* October 1980. A detailed description of the irregularities is given in Patricio Aylwin and others, "Presentación ante el Colegio Escrutador," *El Mercurio* (Santiago), 3 October 1980.

55. Although comparison makes little sense in this type of election, the percentages of the 4 January 1978 referendum were 75.04% in favor of the government (yes votes) and 20.32% against (no votes). From the referendum to the plebiscite, the government's votes would have increased by 26,551 and the opposition's by 760,217.

56. It is evident that the meaning of a yes vote is not unequivocal and that it does not necessarily imply support for the regime. On electoral processes in authoritarian regimes, see G. Hermet, A. Rouquié, and J. Linz, "Des elections pas comme les autres," *Presses de la Fondation Nationale des Sciences Politiques* (Paris, 1978).

57. This is the meaning of the conditions raised by the church in order for it to consider the plebiscite legitimate, conditions which obviously were not met. See the declaration on the plebiscite of the Bishops' Conference of Chile, 23 August 1980, *Mensaje,* September 1980.

58. The weakness of the "national security" ideology or the ideology which is expressed in the military government's "Declaration of Principles" are examples. Arriagada and Garretón, "Doctrina de seguridad nacional." As for the civilian-military movement announced the night of 11 September 1980, it was one of repeated, sporadic, vague calls without any serious attempt to organize it. The only thing which lasts is the regime's ability to mobilize student leaders, women, and others in certain circumstances for organization tasks directly connected to the government apparatus.

59. Examples of such scenarios are the early calls for a transition government, constitutional assemblies, and the like. Two important illustrations are the set of propositions suggested by ex-president Frei in the so-called Viña del Mar speech, "Opinión sobre el momento actual," *Chile América,* nos. 14–15 (February 1975), and the proposal of the Group of 24 at the time of the plebiscite.

60. The attempts of social democratic groups to reunite, or the attempts of the various socialist sectors to reach agreement, on the one hand, and the fragmentation of the Socialist party or of the Popular Unity front and its constituent parties, on the other, are examples of the contradictory nature of these processes. Along with this, there is a debate about the way to confront the regime which began with the Communist party's proposition to use forms of "acute violence"; this debate is reordering and reassembling the different components of the left.

Party Oppositions under the Chilean Authoritarian Regime

Arturo Valenzuela and
J. Samuel Valenzuela

During the 1970s the best writings on Latin American politics and society shifted away from a preoccupation with political development, the prospects for revolution, or the transition to socialism, to an emphasis on the origins and nature of authoritarian regimes.[1] The demise of the Popular Unity government in Chile in 1973 helped to strengthen this trend as it brought Chile, the longest-lasting democracy on the continent, into line with military governments in a majority of South American countries. The "rectification" of the status of this deviant case made it simpler for various schools to draw either on cultural, historical, or economic determinants (or a combination of these) to explain the emergence of corporatist military or bureaucratic-authoritarian regimes.[2]

The new literature has been rich and sophisticated. Preoccupation with the nature of the state and with the relationship between dependent capitalism and the advent of military regimes has brought us a long way from an excessive concern with ethnocentrically biased themes such as the functions of underdeveloped interest groups and parties, or with simplistic formulations about class consciousness. The focus has been on the attempt to uncover the socioeconomic etiology of authoritarianism or on regime characterization based on an examination of the formal outlines of the state and of official policy pronouncements and goals. The general emphasis has been on the more readily apparent elements of the authoritarian regime or "situation," those which flow directly from the overt economic, social, and political blueprints, objectives, and conceptions imposed by the ruling circles on themselves.[3]

There is a danger, however, that in stressing some of the commonalities of authoritarianism and the broad determinants of the authoritarian phenomena, the literature runs the risk of losing sight of the fact that a political regime is not defined simply by the structures and actions of the state: it is also, and primarily, defined by the interplay between the state and civil society. Much of the thrust of military dictatorships, in particular, relates to their effort to stamp out opposition forces. Through direct repression and a destruction of the political institutions and procedures for popular participation, they seek to create conditions for an emergence of alternative political forces at the end of the period of exceptional rule which would guarantee that those elements anathema to the regime cannot reemerge. Though these "bureaucratic authoritarian regimes" have specifically refused to set time-frames for a return to civilian rule and have deliberately argued that they are not merely regimes of transition, but of transformation, the fundamental objective is to make possible a political and social order in the future with a different type of political organization of society. The strategies followed to ensure the new outcome have varied widely. The Brazilian model preserved limited institutions of representation in an attempt to restructure the party system, even resorting to a grand (and ultimately unsuccessful) strategy of cooptation by creating an "official" opposition while manipulating electoral procedures. The Chilean military, by contrast, has closed the Congress, banned elected local governments, and disallowed party activity in the hope that repression, combined with fundamental transformations in the political and social order and in the functions of the state, will "sanitize" the political process, destroying party organizations and partisan affiliations within society. It is thus crucial to analyze what happens to opposition groups and forces during the authoritarian period in order to make judgements on the regime's success or failure in establishing its transformation project.

The fate of opposition elements, in turn, cannot be scrutinized by reference only to the authoritarian context: it is dependent on the historical importance of opposition forces in the period prior to the advent of authoritarianism. It is inconceivable in the Chilean case, given the importance of strong parties, to imagine the military authorities attempting to create, as in Brazil, two federated parties out of the remnants of historical party organizations, one favoring and one "opposing" the government. It is also hard to imagine the Chilean ruler, General Augusto Pinochet, approaching trade union leaders and party officials of the deposed regime in the same way that, in Argentina, Onganía attempted to recruit Peronistas, or that Galtieri sought a dialogue with party leaders before the conflict with Britain over the Malvinas.

The purpose of this chapter is to analyze the state of oppositions in the Chilean authoritarian "situation" by focusing on those opposition elements, namely political parties, which were at the center stage of the political system prior to the 11 September 1973 military coup. Of all opposition forces, they constitute viable regime alternatives and are thus primary candidates for government obliteration. Our aim is to describe the internal problems of parties forced to shift their functions from essentially electoral and policy-making organizations to semi or fully clandestine organizations attempting to maintain organizational vitality. We will also focus on the relationships which exist between the various parties as they seek to work out common strategies to replace the military dictatorship, as well as on the varying and complex ties and relationships between party organizations and other elements of civil society.

The creation of an authoritarian state is an obvious defeat for democratic political parties and opposition forces, including, ironically, those that supported a military solution to the Chilean political crisis of 1973. The prohibition of meetings, the banning of demonstrations, and the intimidation of leaders through killings, exile, or imprisonment directly threaten organizational survival. At the same time, the destruction of institutions and procedures such as the Congress, municipal government democracy, elections, the freedom of the press, and so on, through which political parties functioned and thrived, deprives parties of their most basic means of and justification for existence.

Our central thesis, however, is that the long-dominant Chilean party system will not be obliterated as easily as the military government sympathizers hope or as government detractors fear. The continuity of the party system in the body politic is assured by the existence of distinct political tendencies in the electorate, a "political landscape" which has evolved over several generations, reenforced by Chile's long tradition of electoral politics. Despite profound transformations in the role of the state and the privatization of the economy, this "landscape" will endure, and parties will continue to play important roles in a radically different political context. To be sure, these roles have changed. No longer do parties concentrate their energies on electoral appeals, the structuring of political coalitions, or the formulation of policy options. Instead, they must focus on the imperatives of organizational and ideological survival and on the structuring of opposition in other spheres of society.

In many instances parties appear to be taking a back seat to other elements of civil society which are thrust into the limelight as parties are repressed—elements such as the church, labor unions, and a host of informal community-based groups and associations structured to promote grassroots survival. The political vacuum occasioned by the stripping away of traditional institutions and mediating structures exposes in a stark fashion the very rudiments of civil society. The actual role of parties will vary depending on the nature of generalized repression, the range of political spaces available for party action, the level of support for the regime among other social sectors, and the degree of tolerance for the party in question on the part of the regime. In periods of significant repression, when few organizational spaces are available, party militants may become inactive and party members will turn to private pursuits.

But, it is crucial to emphasize that *demobilization* of society based on the repressive actions of the regime should not be taken to mean that the society has been *depoliticized*. The parties, by virtue of their prior insertion into the fabric of national life and their continuing and critical function as catalysts for the maintenance and expansion of organized dissent—in party and nonparty arenas—will continue to spearhead opposition to the regime. And perhaps more ominously for the authorities, they will succeed, as they did under even more adverse conditions in Spain, in maintaining an organizational presence and societal support such that they will once again become the principal mediating and defining forces of the political process once the authoritarian regime leaves power. The Chilean military will fail to create alternative structural arrangements and the necessary fundamental changes in allegiance patterns in civil society to ensure the perpetuation of the authoritarian coalition once and if democracy is restored.

Before turning to a discussion of parties as opposition groups under the Pinochet government, it is necessary to describe very briefly the range of opposition to the regime and the place of party politics within that opposition. It is also necessary to describe in more detail the nature of the pre-existing party system stressing those aspects which contribute to our understanding of their place within the new authoritarian context.

A General Note on Oppositions to the Chilean Military Regime

The stage for post-Chilean politics was set by the fact that the leaders of the 11 September *pronunciamiento* defined the nation's crisis as one of regime rather than one of government.[4] In their view, the crisis was simply a symptom of fundamental inadequacies in Chile's democracy and party system, characterized by forces pushing for the construction of an increasingly dominant and centralized state which exacerbated underdevelopment and by a rampant and divisive politicization which favored the rise of a Marxist left. Accordingly, their aim was not merely a reactive attempt to curb the perceived excesses of a mobilized society by providing a short interregnum that would allow a reversion to the status quo ante; they also saw their task as a regenerative one, intent on both destroying and rebuilding the fundamental features of Chile's economy, democracy, and party system.[5] The formulation of this renovationist project set the scene for post-coup politics, as it produced a fundamental distinction within the kaleidoscope of oppositions. Thus, it is possible to distinguish, on the one hand, an oppositionist but pro-military regime sector, one whose pro-regime stance stems from its acceptance of the need for and legitimacy of the regenerative task. It is also possible to identify an opposition characterized by its rejection of the renovationist project.

The pro-regime opposition corresponds to the groups or individuals that Juan Linz identifies as the "semi-opposition" to the authoritarian regimes, that is, those who "are not dominant or represented in the governing group but that are willing to participate in power without fundamentally challenging the regime. This attitude involves partial criticism and some visibility and identity outside the inner circle of participants in the political struggle."[6] The pro-regime opposition groups are not, however, nearly as numerous in Chile as they were under the Francoist regime which serves as the basis for Linz's analysis of oppositions to authoritarian regimes. One reason for that is that, unlike Spain, Chile did not have a large array of right-wing organizations—from Carlists to Falangists—each with its specific institutional blueprints for the future. Of three extreme right-wing organizations in Chile—Fatherland and Liberty; the Society for the Defense of Tradition, Family, and Property; and Opus Dei—only the first was well known, because of the visibility of its militants in street demonstrations, and only it can be said to have become representative of a semi-opposition.[7] Though Fatherland and Liberty has been formally in self-declared dissolution since 1973, its main leader, Pablo Rodríguez Grez, has insisted over the years since the military coup on the necessity of generating a "national civic movement" in support of the government; and at least until the approval of the 1980 Constitution, he argued in favor of a corporative institutional arrangement.[8] While it is true that many other individuals and groups that supported the government at the beginning, many associated with the rightist National party, have criticized the regime, particularly its economic policies, they do so on an ad hoc basis, with little organizational cohesion, and with no articulated alternative policy in mind.

A second reason for this relative paucity of semi-opposition groups in Chile, as compared with Spain, lies in the fact that the Pinochet government is a good deal less institutionalized and more rigid, principled, and narrowly based than Francisco Franco's ever was. The Franco regime contained representatives of virtually all the groups that opposed the losing side in the civil war, including the church and many moderate Catholics, as well as right-wing organizations. It developed a host of institutions at all societal levels for representation and control.[9]

By contrast, the Chilean dictatorship is a military regime, in which Pinochet has succeeded in gaining enormous personal power by virtue of his manipulation of the promotion system in the armed forces, the pillar of support for the government. Pinochet relies on a small circle of advisers who design policies by deriving them from a doctrinal free-market vision of society without even consulting the views of affected interests. Since any persistent criticism by groups outside the governing team will inevitably cause these groups to be suspected of harboring ulterior political motives, there is little space or incentive in Chile to create groups which will be visible opponents to specific policies but supporters of the overall regime. There is simply little chance that such groups will have any influence in the policy-making process, given the inflexibility of the government and its monolithic character, or that their visible leaders will be called upon to form part of the governing team, given the narrowness of recruitment to policy-making positions. Criticisms by individuals favoring the government therefore are generally expressed in private. The fact that the only vocal group of semi-opponents to the regime is an extreme rightist one only confirms this analysis: the extreme right was completely isolated under the previous democratic regime, and it therefore cannot be suspect of wishing to return to the past. It represents a "holier-than-thou" semi-opposition.

The lack of incentive to create groups of visible pro-regime opponents should not be taken to mean, however, that there are not appreciable differences of opinion among supporters of the authoritarian project to transform Chilean society. These differences do appear openly on the rare occasions when the government encourages public comment on a pending policy matter or, as is more often the case, when it unwittingly does so as it stalls on determining a clear course of action on a particular issue it has set out to resolve. Characteristically, however, these differences among various personalities, groups, or circles within the regime disappear rapidly under a veil of consensus once the chief of state charts a clear course of action. The debates preceding the unveiling of the new constitution of 1980 provide an example of differences of opinion among regime supporters regarding a pending and highly important question, since they led to a distinction between the so-called hard- and soft-liners. Both groups were clearly motivated by the attempt to generate a political framework which would pre-empt the reemergence of the Marxist parties. And yet, the hard-liners argued in favor of an indefinite continuation of military rule, or in terms of designing a corporative charter that would break Chile's constitutional tradition. The soft-liners argued in favor of a return to a constitutional system approximating the previous liberal-democratic one, with parties and elections based on territorial rather than corporative units, noting that the Marxist parties would be prevented from reemerging by the profound changes that the government's policies would produce in the Chilean economy and society—all of which would in the long run create a consensual political and social order.[10] However, in a characteristic way, these apparently profound differences were put aside by the regime's supporters when Pinochet announced a definitive course of action. Thus, at least for the moment, these internal debates have produced factions within the regime but not clear-cut semi-oppositions. For this to occur, the regime would have to become less narrow and inflexible, allowing institutionalized and legitimate spaces for the expression of disagreements within the broader framework of the authoritarian polity and project.

We will now turn to the antiregime oppositions which will concern the bulk of these pages. They can be classified along two dimensions as summarized in Table 6.1. The first dimension refers to the character and objectives of opposition groups—that is, whether they can provide power alternatives or whether they are constituted for some other purpose. Political parties and clandestine military organizations are the only opposition groups with the will and capability of providing an alternative to the mili-

TABLE 6.1   Anti-Regime Opposition According to Level of Toleration and Character as Regime Alternative

	Tolerated	*Not tolerated*
Regime alternative	Christian Democrats	Popular Unity parties Clandestine military groups
Nonregime alternative	Church Unions Research groups	Clandestine political networks in the labor and student movements

tary government. Other organizations have neither the objective nor the organizational and leadership capabilities to constitute a new regime, though they can raise the costs of ruling, help maintain political space for regime alternative oppositions, and contribute to delegitimizing the authorities.

Nonregime alternatives include overtly political groups, such as labor federations and some intellectual and university student groups, and latently political mediating groups or institutions, such as social service organizations at the grass roots of civil society. The latter include soccer clubs, soup kitchens, local unions, mothers' clubs, mutual aid associations, and informal networks of solidarity and support for the unemployed and impoverished. These groups are best characterized as latently political since many of their leaders have ties to parties or become linked to party activists as they gain prominence within their organizations, and because the groups are vehicles to a significant oppositionist culture that expresses itself multifariously through music, art, formal discussions, jokes, and so on. In periods of significant repression they mute their politicism to become overtly apolitical. In periods of liberalization they become important channels for partisan organization and expression and constitute an important link between the parties and civil society in a nonelectoral context.

Anti-regime opposition groups also vary significantly according to the degree of governmental toleration for the group or institution's activities. This second dimension is a continuum rather than a clear-cut duality and is not immutable. The level of toleration may change for all groups or for particular groups depending on circumstances. Some anti-regime groups in Chile have enjoyed a high level of toleration. After the initial years of repression, independent intellectual groups, supported in large measure by international foundations, have achieved a precarious acceptance as participants in the restricted national debate. Other groups, such as labor unions, the press, and professional associations (once purged of leadership directly identified with the Popular Unity parties), have been generally tolerated because they are functional, as opposed to primarily political, organizations, and their complete destruction would contravene efforts to encourage privatization in economic and social spheres. Still others, such as the Christian Democratic party, have been tolerated because the domestic as well as the international costs to the government of repressing a party which was so closely identified with the democratic opposition to the Allende government generally outweighed the benefits. Nevertheless, the government has increasingly moved against the party as it has continued to assert itself as a major threat to Pinochet's rule.

On the other end of the continuum are the parties and labor organizations closely identified with the Popular Unity government, which have suffered the brunt of official repression and continue to be closely monitored by the security apparatus.

The most important "nonalternative" opposition institution under the Chilean military regime is without a doubt the church. It has been able to operate relatively freely because of its strong institutional legitimacy.[11] As we will note in more detail below, it has played a key role in providing a political umbrella for much of the activity of opposition organizations—and has thus provided the parties with organizational spaces which have helped to keep them alive.

The identification of the church with opposition elements is another key difference from the Spanish case; there, the church vigorously aligned itself with the Nationalist cause and lent the Franco regime its institutional and spiritual legitimacy. The position of the Chilean church, which has strongly endorsed liberal and democratic institutions and criticized the government's human rights record, has deprived Pinochet of a crucial legitimizing factor.

The Historicity of the Party System: Misconceptions and Realities

The cardinal objective of the regenerative project of the Chilean military junta is to do away with the traditional party system. There is a consensus in government circles that this can be accomplished directly through repressive measures and the creation of new intermediary organizations purged of party influence, and indirectly through significant transformations in the economy and society. These transformations would presumably lead to greater modernization, a greater stake in the system by the majority of citizens, and hence a more consensual political process in which the politics of outbidding and Marxist groups become a thing of the past. The official line is that Chilean parties have already become obsolete, and that all that is left are a few unemployed former leaders clinging to the past.

This political project is based on certain assumptions about the Chilean party system which have only recently been elaborated by government spokesmen. The best statement is an article written by government ideologue Jaime Guzmán, a member of the committee which drafted the new constitution and a close adviser and speech writer for General Pinochet. The article, "El camino político," was reprinted prominently in *El Mercurio*, the country's leading newspaper.[12] Guzmán, in an argument which closely parallels some of the major speeches of the chief executive,[13] maintains that Chilean parties were an abnormal expression of the politics of an underdeveloped society with the formal trappings of democratic procedures. Though Chilean democracy functioned well in the nineteenth century, when popular sectors were excluded from the political system, it deteriorated significantly with the expansion of the electorate and particularly with the 1960 electoral reforms, which contributed to a dramatic increase in the number of voters. The advent of mass democracy in an underdeveloped country which lacked the requisite economic wealth to ensure the loyalty of the population to the prevailing socioeconomic order explains, Guzmán argues, the electoral fortunes of Marxist parties, who fueled the politics of outbidding in their successful effort to overwhelm the other parties and gain control of the state.

This analysis assumes that the growth of the left is a recent phenomena, one closely tied to the extension of suffrage. Leftist voting is a product of underdevelopment, the natural result of a mobilized but impoverished population which is easy prey to demagogic appeals and radical solutions.

While opposition leaders and intellectuals strongly disagree with the government on most issues, including its claim that the economic model will succeed, many are concerned that government economic and social policies will seriously undermine the major Chilean parties. They view with trepidation free-market policies which have flooded the country with imported goods available even to low-income sectors, fearing that a consumerist bonanza will erode the appeal of traditional political forces. They also worry that the privatization of health care and social security will have the effect of tying too closely the fate of working-class elements with those of the private sector, reducing political militancy. And, more fundamentally, they are alarmed by the implications of an open economy model that has seriously weakened the industrial infrastructure which provided a base for the parties of the left.[14]

Both government supporters and critics base their analysis on the assumption that political loyalties in Chile were relatively ephemeral, that the parties did not have strong roots in society. According to the former, the parties depended on opportunistic or ideological leaders and militants with no real following in the body politic. According to the latter, they were the product of particular underlying economic forces which if changed, would change the pattern of loyalties. It follows that either an elimination of party militants and leaders or a gradual "modernization" of society would contribute to a substantially different political and party system.

It is our contention that the major parties have not disappeared nor are the fundamental political loyalties within the society likely to erode in the foreseeable future. The assumptions behind the "party decline" thesis are based on a series of misconceptions about Chilean party politics. An examination of these misconceptions will help not only to point out the limitations of government policies, but also to provide the necessary background to understand the continuity of the party system under the Chilean authoritarian situation. It should be underscored that these "misconceptions" are closely interrelated and are separated only here for analytical purposes.

MISCONCEPTION NO. 1: *The rise of the left is closely associated with the incorporation into the Chilean political system of large numbers of previously unmobilized sectors of the population.*

By comparison with other countries, Chile did have a lower level of electoral participation until the 1960s. However, as Figure 6.1 indicates, there is no clear-cut correlation between the levels of electoral participation since 1920 and support for the Communist and Socialist parties. Levels of partici-

FIGURE 6.1   Electoral Participation and Votes for the Left, 1925–1973 (Congressional Elections)

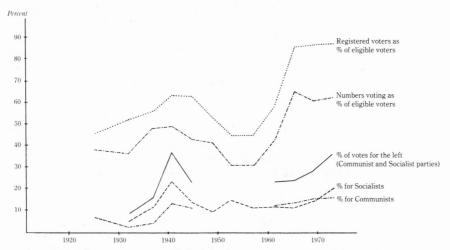

Sources: Atilio Borón, "La evolución del régimen electoral y sus efectos en la representación de los intereses populares: el caso de Chile," *Revista latinoamericana de Ciencia Política* 11, no. 3 (December 1971): 436; and Dirección del Registro Electoral, Santiago, Chile.

pation increased dramatically during the 1960s, especially after a 1962 law which made electoral registration compulsory, and yet the left at its peak voting strength in 1973 only recovered the support it had thirty years before, when the percentage of participants in the electoral process was approximately a fifth to a quarter lower. In addition, while the Socialist vote fluctuates more (and therefore largely accounts for the peaks in the total leftist voting strength), the overall trend in both the Communist and Socialist lines is relatively flat after surpassing the 10% level; by contrast, the participation lines show much sharper changes.

Figure 6.1 may be further analyzed by dividing it into the three periods suggested by the discontinuity in the Communist and in the total leftist vote lines. In the first period, until the mid-1940s, there does appear to be some relationship between voter participation and the vote variables. However, at the beginning of the thirties the left was in a process of reorganization after the Ibáñez dictatorship (1927–31), and the Socialist Party of Chile was not even founded, through the merger of several socialist groups, until 1933. Therefore, the left's rise between the 1932 and the 1937 elections can be explained by the fact that the parties were merely reaching their "normal" levels of support. The peak vote for the left, in 1941, came when both parties were part of the Popular Front government coalition, and it resulted without a corresponding increase in the numbers of voters over the total eligible to vote. In absolute terms the Communist and Socialist parties gained 76,607 votes, while there were only 38,018 more voters in 1941 than in 1939. The drop by the 1945 election does appear to correspond with a drop in the percentage of voters as compared to the total eligible; again, however, in absolute terms there were only 318 fewer actual voters in 1945 than in 1941.[15] The parties of the left simply lost their peak level of support.

The interruption of the Communist and total leftist vote lines during the second period is caused by the outlawing of the Communist party between 1948 and 1958.[16] The drop in electoral registration and participation levels was caused partly by the elimination of Communist party members and known sympathizers from the electoral registries and partly by the 1949 extension of the franchise to women—which greatly increased the total numbers of eligible voters without generating immediately a proportionate rise in registrations. During this period the participation variables can therefore be compared only to the Socialist party vote, and it is clear that no relationship exists between the two. In fact, the Socialist vote increased slightly between the 1949 and the 1953 elections, while the participation levels fell off sharply.

Finally, during the last period it is, once again, difficult to see any relationship between the variables. The vote for the left increases significantly after the 1970 election of the Allende government, as voters gave greater support to the president's party, while the great gains in electoral participation occurred in the immediately preceding years.

Correlational analysis between electoral participation and party voting also confirms the general observations derived from Figure 6.1. Table 6.2 reports the correlation coefficients between the percentage of the eligible population registered to vote in 1969 (after the significant expansion of the electorate), and voting for each major party, showing virtually no relationship between the two variables. It therefore cannot be said that communes of greater electoral registration favor any particular party. The only very slight positive association (.13) is not with the parties of the left, as the misconception we discuss here would have us believe, but with the rightist National party.

Both Figure 6.1 and Table 6.2 relate the party votes with electoral participation variables which express relative, not absolute, values. It could be argued that the proposition should be tested only by relating the leftist vote to increases in the absolute numbers of voters per commune, regardless of the total number who are eligible to vote. To test this particular way of defining the problem we calculated the correlations between party votes and increases in the size of voter turnout per commune in the period 1958–73. This was a period of great expansion of the electorate, given the return of the Communist party to electoral politics, the 1962 law that established penalties for not registering to vote, and the 1970 electoral reforms extending the suffrage to illiterates and reducing the voting age from 21 to 18. The total vote rose from 880,000 in the congressional election of 1957 to 1.4 million in 1961. By 1969 the electoral population was close to 2.5 million; by 1973 it had risen to 3.5 million. Registered voters had doubled from about 15% to 30% of the total population.

Table 6.3 presents the results of these correlations between selected years. The years were chosen on the basis of the significant changes they could potentially capture. Column 1 reflects the impact of the relegalization of the Communist party; columns 2, 3, and 4 examine the successive

TABLE 6.2 Correlations between the Vote for Major Chilean Parties and the Percentage of the Eligible Population Registered to Vote by Commune, 1969 Congressional Election

Party	Level of participation
Communist	.04
Socialist	−.04
Radical	−.03
Christian Democrat	−.05
National	.13

Source: Calculated from electoral data on 287 communes available in the Dirección Nacional del Registro Electoral, Santiago.

TABLE 6.3　Correlations between the Vote for Chilean Parties by Commune and the Increase in Electoral Turnout, Selected Years

Party	Electoral increase				
	1957–61 (1)	1961–65 (2)	1961–69 (3)	1961–73 (4)	1969–73 (5)
Communist	.40	.08	.04	−.10	−.01
Socialist	.11	.04	.12	.13	.09
Radical	.08	−.13	−.17		
Christian Democrat	−.11	.25	−.12	.06	−.09
Conservative	−.15	−.08			
Liberal	−.08	−.16			
National			.05	1.2	−.07

Note: The National party was formed by the fusion of the Conservative and Liberal parties. Results for the Radical party are not reported after 1969 because the party split. Correlations are simple Pearson correlation coefficients.

Source: See Table 6.2.

impact of the 1962 decision to force people to register; and column 5 reflects the latest extension of the suffrage. The only correlation of any significance is the expected correlation between the vote for the Communist party and the electoral expansion occurring in 1957–61 after the party was legalized. At no other time is there a strong correlation between leftist vote and increased electoral turnout. The only other correlation which stands out is the weak one of .25 for the Christian Democrats during their years of dramatic expansion from 1961 to 1965. That that correlation is as low as it is underscores the fact that increases in participation did not benefit any particular party to the detriment of others. The dramatic increase in voter participation in Chile was accompanied by a commensurate increase in the ability of all of the major parties to capture the voters added to the rolls. This meant that the fundamental political tendencies in Chilean society shifted only gradually over time, with the major shift involving the gradual decline of the right and the rise of the Christian Democrats as a new center force, replacing the Radicals. The political shifts which took place were the results of coalition shifts, such as the support of the right for the Christian Democrats in 1964 (with spillover into the 1965 election) and the instability of the center in a polarized party system.[17]

　　The most telling evidence of the misconception that there was a direct relationship between suffrage expansion and a vote for the Marxist left is the fact that Allende received at most 13% of the new voters that were added to the rolls from 1964 to 1970, with the bulk going to the candidate of the right.[18] This explains why Allende received a smaller percentage of the total vote in 1970 than he did in 1964 when he lost to Frei.

MISCONCEPTION NO. 2: *The fortunes of the left are closely tied to its appeal to impoverished sectors of society. The availability of cheap imported consumer goods will severely tax the loyalty of these sectors to leftist parties.*

The important research findings of Alejandro Portes have effectively put to rest deprivationist and relative deprivationist hypotheses about leftist voting in Chile.[19] Portes has shown that the lower the income and occupational status of respondents among the working poor, the less likely they are to support the left. Nor is status inconsistency and social frustration associated with voting for Marxist parties. The most humble and frustrated citizens have levels of leftist voting "quite similar to those exhibited by the highest and least frustrated category—intermediate services and white collar."[20]

Though the left in Chile drew more on working-class sectors, and the parties of the center and right had strong support among middle- and upper-class elements, all Chilean parties had heterogeneous bases of support and drew the bulk of their voters from the poorer sectors of society. In Portes' sample the Christian Democratic party received as much support from low-income elements as did the Communists and Socialists. The National party always relied on the rural poor for much of its voting support. Conversely, other surveys have noted that certain categories of professionals and middle-level managers were more likely to support the left than the right. Aggregate data analysis yields similar results. An examination of the socioeconomic correlates of the vote for Chile's parties reveals that with the exception of the Communist party, with strong roots in mining areas, only a small percentage of the variance in party voting was explained by economic or occupational variables.[21]

Nor does it follow that voting for the left is a feature of underdevelopment which will disappear with access to a higher standard of living. Leftist voting in France increased as the country became more industrialized and as its standard of living rose to one of the highest in the world. As Richard Hamilton's work has shown, the availability of a wealth of new consumer products for French workers did not translate into lower militancy.[22] The French experience contradicts the simplistic notion that economic development or a consumerist bonanza will create the ground rules for consensual as opposed to ideological politics. It should be recalled that in Chile, the Popular Unity government was able to maintain a higher percentage of the vote in the 1973 election than it obtained in the 1970 presidential election at a time of enormous economic hardship. Had the electorate been motivated mainly by short-term economic benefits, it would have turned against the government at a time of massive shortages and triple-digit inflation.

MISCONCEPTION NO. 3: *Government economic policies, by dramatically changing the economy, will erode the bases of support for political parties.*

The military junta has instituted far-reaching changes in the Chilean economy, unprecedented in the nation's history. Reversing policies begun over fifty years ago, it has sought to reduce the role of the state as regulator, catalyst, and owner of the nation's productive resources. By reducing tariff barriers it has encouraged domestic industry to compete with international firms, with the net effect that many of Chile's overprotected industries have failed. What are the likely political effects of these changes? Will the destruction of many enterprises, the high level of unemployment, the return to primary products for export, and so on, lead to the erosion of the natural constituencies of political parties?

As noted above, all Chilean parties, including the parties of the left, have a heterogeneous base of support. Though it is true that the left relied on the industrial working class for core support, industrial workers also voted for other parties, and the left drew substantial support from nonindustrial workers and middle-class elements. In the absence of further research, it is difficult to judge the level of industrial decline required to bring about significant political changes. Nor is it merely a matter of examining overall decline in industrial employment: we need to know more about particular industries and how they have fared. The evidence to date suggests that the opening of the Chilean economy to foreign competition has led to an increase of the tertiary sector, while employment in construction and industry has declined, the latter to 74% by 1981 of what it was in 1967.[23] However, employment in mining, where the parties of the left have had strong support, has not declined, and in fact, it may increase if new investments are realized.

Still, it is doubtful whether an even steeper decline in industrial employment would cripple the parties of the left to the advantage of center and right parties. As noted earlier, the percentage of the vote garnered by the left in 1970 was comparable to that of 1943, before much of the expansion of Chilean industry based on the import substitution strategy of the Radical governments. Furthermore, most of the industries that have failed have been small or medium-sized industries not noted for strong unions and with a greater heterogeneity of partisan attachments. Nor does it follow that in those industries where the work force was reduced, political militancy will be reduced accordingly. Indeed, layoffs and plant closings might have the opposite effect. Alejandro Portes found that while leftist voting and radical political orientations are explained primarily by "social context and interaction"—organizational efforts taking place in working-class settings—a pattern of unemployment or threats of unemployment was one of the few "objective" variables promoting higher levels of "political militance."[24] Rather than weakening the left, the current economic difficulties might in fact contribute to a strengthening of the left. Smaller craft industries, where the left was weaker, have been decimated, while larger enterprises, where the left was strong, have been hurt enough to encourage organizational efforts of militants. Finally, it is not at all certain that unemployed workers will lose their militancy. In moving to other spheres of employment, they may in fact become catalysts for further organizational efforts in their new areas of activity, as most research efforts indicate that organization, and not the nature of work, contributes to militancy. As Hamilton noted for France, radicalization in certain industrial areas in that country was due in part to the fact that radical peasants from rural areas brought their militancy with them.[25] What is important is not the aggregate shifts in employment, but the continuation of organizational capabilities and political militancy, a subject we will turn to below.

MISCONCEPTION NO. 4: *The Chilean party system consists of cadres and militants who developed in and benefited from the previous political system, but who have a few roots in society.*

To characterize the Chilean party system as ephemeral is to deny the development over several generations of a party system deeply rooted in society. Political leaders and militants not only structured political alternatives, but drew on and responded to more basic and historically defined tendencies in the electorate, a complex and dialectical relationship to be described in more detail below. At this point some observations will be provided on the historicity of party alternatives in Chile and their importance in creating what we call a "political landscape," or pattern of partisan identification in the electorate.

THE CREATION OF A POLITICAL LANDSCAPE

The basis for party formation lies in the presence of a series of historical, social, and ideological cleavages in a national society which develop issue polarities around which segments of the political elite and groups of militants cluster.[26] Two fundamental generative cleavages have acted to create the Chilean parties: state versus church and worker versus employer. Regional cleavages ceased to be important in the early years of the republic as Santiago-based elites succeeded in imposing their authority through defeat of regional challenges.[27]

The three centenarian Chilean parties—Conservative, Liberal, and Radical—trace their roots to differences in elite opinion in a Catholic country, which crystallized in the second government of Manuel Montt (1856–61). The Conservative party, dominated originally by extreme ultramontanist sentiments, defended the authority and interests of the church, while the Radical party became an ardent proponent of anticlericalism. The Liberals were also committed to a secular society and to the authority of the state, but distinguished themselves from their Radical colleagues through a more moderate anticlericalism. They played the center game in nineteenth-century politics, forging alliances of convenience with both Conservatives and Radicals. The presence of the Radicals in the political game, decades before their counterparts in Argentina had access to power, helped to cement the allegiance of all politically relevant sectors to the developing democratic system.[28]

These traditional parties were, in Duverger's terms, of "parliamentary origin." They emerged from controversies and debates over the role of the church in society centered in congressional and intellectual circles. By contrast, the parties of the left, as elsewhere, were parties of "external origin."[29] Their development was associated with the difficult process of building the labor movement.

The history of working-class parties shows that leaders and militants who succeeded in organizing unions were also those with the best chance of creating parties that would become expressions of working-class constituencies. In time, these parties diversified their base of support considerably, especially in situations of regular electoral contests. Chile, unlike other Latin American nations, developed Communist and Socialist parties in conjunction with the labor movement. This resulted from a complex chain of events that was partly accidental and partly conditioned by a political opportunity context which favored radical militants in the labor movement.

This context included a highly repressive response to workers whenever they organized to present concrete demands. Under such circumstances modern union leaders did not succeed in garnering worker support. They could not show tangible results for their leadership efforts and had no clear ideological explanations for their lack of success. The first and most important victims of this repressive environment were the labor leaders tied to the ideologically centrist Partido Democrático. The extensive wave of anti-union repression which followed in the wake of the 1907 Iquique massacre limited them to relatively ineffective mutual aid organizations with no relationship to workplace bargaining with employers.

The political opportunity context also involved considerable freedom for workers to organize outside the workplace, a freedom associated with the existence of competitive electoral politics. This meant that the early labor leaders could publish newspapers, call rallies, present candidates for regional and local elections, and debate publicly the issues of the day.

Ironically, while radical leaders were repressed for organizing at the industrial level, they had ample opportunity to communicate their revolutionary message at the political level, articulating political and social organizations into an embryonic labor movement with a strong political content. By the end of the 1930s, with the advent of the Popular Front government, both Socialists and Communists had gained important footholds in the labor movement and had become the principal political expressions of Chile's organized urban working class.[30]

The religious and class cleavages were, in turn, woven into a complex of "interconnected dimensions," to use Sartori's term.[31] The emergence of a class dimension did not lead to unambiguous polarization, even though the traditional parties became the defenders of the dominant sectors. The sharp divisions within the elite over clerical matters encouraged the establishment parties to seek alliances with the new actors in order to maximize their own electoral fortunes vis-à-vis traditional adversaries. When the half-hearted efforts of the Conservatives to capitalize on the emergence of a politically aware working class fizzled, the Radicals were able to structure a pattern of alliances with the new working-class leaders which would become a principal and, at times, dominant feature of Chilean politics until the 1973 coup. Both the Popular Front (1938–46) and the Popular Unity (1970–73) governments were forged with Radical support, an alliance safe in its secularism and even anticlericalism, but threatened by differing positions on class issues, leading over the years to shifts in the Radical family.

And, in what can be labeled for convenience the "Christian bloc," a group split from the Conservative party in the 1930s as a result of the development within Catholicism of forces that took a much more progressive stance on the worker-employer cleavage. This group became the Christian Democratic party in the 1950s and gradually replaced the Radicals as the country's premier center party as it sought to advance a progressive position on class matters, while attracting the support of many voters, particularly women, who retained an attachment to the church.

Lipset and Rokkan have noted that, once formed, a party system becomes "frozen" in place.[32] The freezing image is somewhat overdrawn, however. Important changes do occur over time. The most important change in recent decades is the decline of the salience of the state versus church dimension. This has been accompanied by an increased emphasis on the worker-employer cleavage as the principal criterion for evaluating the ideological basis of the various parties. Indeed, the Conservative and Liberal parties found themselves virtually indistinguishable on the class dimension and joined together to form the National party after their poor showing in the 1965 congressional elections. This fusion was aided by the fact that the Chilean Catholic church, which mirrored the international church, severed its close ties to the Conservatives, openly favoring the

Christian Democrats. This relationship is very different from the one which existed between ultramontanist bishops and tradition-bound conservative elites. There is a wide consensus today in Chile on the basic outlines of the separation of church and state.

Even if the freezing image is too strong, it does capture the outlines of an important reality: once formed, party systems have remarkable endurance. The decline of the religious issue after the adoption of the 1925 constitution has left the Chilean party system with two center parties—one "Christian" and one "anti-clerical." Christian Democrats and Radicals continue to exist as separate parties, stressing the symbols which separate them, competing for control of white-collar organizations that provide an important base for the centrist vote, and jockeying for alliances with the less volatile extremes of the system on both right and left.[33] In a polarized party system, both parties are vulnerable to shifts in electoral fortunes, even if the center vote is a relative constant; and both suffer from actual and potential splits, either to the left or right, which only intensify competition.

The continuity of a party system is the result of organizational efforts of militants and leaders in each party under challenging circumstances. It is also a product of what we have labeled a "political landscape," the development of which requires a history of regular electoral contests over several generations in order to become firmly entrenched in the minds of the citizenry. This landscape consists, in the first place, of the voter's awareness of the issue polarities which generated party alternatives together with a self-identification at some point along a political continuum separating the extremes of each polarity. In Chile this means identification along the left-right dimension, a manifestation of the salience of the worker versus employer cleavage, and to a lesser extent, a degree of identification along the clerical-anticlerical dimensions, a throwback to the church versus state cleavage. It also involves an understanding of a set of party alternatives located along the various points of the most salient polarities, and a certain identification with particular parties and labels. Finally, it entails a familiarity with a set of political leaders associated with various parties, a name recognition factor which results from the exposure these leaders receive through electoral campaigns of national importance or through holding highly visible government posts.

The stability of electoral cleavages between left, center, and right over several decades, alluded to earlier and summarized in Table 6.4, is evidence of the continuity of the Chilean political landscape. Not even the catastrophic political upheaval of the Allende years was able to shift the basic parameters of Chilean voting patterns, as the 1973 congressional elections practically duplicated the results of the 1969 election.[34] This continuity is also evidenced in analyses of surveys of Chilean voters, such as

TABLE 6.4 Percentage of the Total Vote Received by Parties of the Right, Center, and Left in Chilean Lower House Congressional Elections, 1937–1973

	1937	1941	1945	1949	1953	1957	1961	1965	1969	1973	Mean
Right[a]	42.0	31.2	43.7	42.0	25.3	33.0	30.4	12.5	20.0	21.3	30.1
Center[b]	28.1	32.1	27.9	46.7	43.0	44.3	43.7	55.6	42.8	32.8	39.7
Left[c]	15.4	33.9	23.1	9.4	14.2	10.7	22.1	22.7	28.1	34.9	21.5
Other	14.5	2.8	5.3	1.9	17.5	12.0	3.8	9.2	9.1	11.0	8.7

[a] Conservative, Liberal, National after 1965.
[b] Radical, Falangist, Christian Dem., Agrarian Laborist.
[c] Socialist, Communist.
Source: Dirección Nacional del Registro Electoral, Santiago.

the one done by James Prothro and Patricio Chaparro, which reflects remarkably little change in the ideological splits in the electorate between 1958 and 1970.[35]

Further evidence is provided by the analysis of electoral data presented in Table 6.5. The table records the simple correlation coefficients, by commune, between the vote for Chilean parties in the municipal election of 1963, held during the conservative Alessandri administration at the outset of the expansion of suffrage, with the vote for the same parties in the highly visible 1971 municipal elections held during the Allende administration. Between these two years the voting population increased from 2 million to 2.8 million, an increase of voters to total population from 20% to 28%; and the country underwent significant political changes with an increase in political mobilization, unionization of the rural sector, and heightened political competition between Christian Democrats and the parties of the right and left.

The table shows that the stability of the vote for the two parties at the extremes of the political spectrum was very high, with a correlation of .84 for the Communist party and .72 for the National party. The coefficients were also high for the Socialists and Radicals, while the Christian Democrats, the new surge party which benefited most by electoral changes in the 1960s, had the lowest correlation (.27). However, the correlation for the Christian Democrats in 1963 and 1971 was .69 and .93 in regions V and VIII, respectively.

THE DIALECTICAL RELATIONS BETWEEN MILITANTS AND FOLLOWERS

To say that there is an endurance in the political landscape should not be taken to mean that there is a strict or mechanical relationship between

TABLE 6.5   Correlations between the Vote for Major Chilean Parties in the 1963 and 1971 Municipal Elections by Commune

	Communist	Socialist	Radical	Christian Democrat	National
Nation	.84	.53	.45	.27	.72
Major Urban Centers	.85	.39	.82	.49	.71
Region I					
Tarapacá-Coquimbo	.83	.60	.43	.47	.65
Region II					
Aconcagua-Valparaíso	.80	.60	.67	.27	.73
Region III					
Santiago	.83	.22	.55	.23	.64
Region IV					
O'Higgins-Ñuble	.74	.60	.42	.12	.73
Region V					
Concepción-Arauco	.72	.59	.47	.69	.70
Region VI					
Bío-Bío-Cautín	.86	.28	.33	.03	.35
Region VII					
Valdivia-Chiloé	.57	.43	.05	.12	.60
Region VIII					
Aysén-Magallanes	.67	.60	.24	.93	.93

Note: The vote for the Conservative and Liberal parties was added for the 1963 election. Major urban centers are those with a population of over 50,000, a total of 40 communes.
Source: See Table 6.2.

electoral constituencies and party leadership. In all societies there is often considerable difference between the orientations of party leaders, party militants, and party electorates. The party leaderships, and to a lesser extent the militants, articulate, formulate, and organize programmatic alternatives laid before the electorate and tie these to more or less coherent ideological visions. The dramatic change in Communist party strategy in 1935, from a rejection of coalitions with other groups to an acceptance of the Popular Front, was clearly a leadership decision that had little to do with sentiments in the party's electorate. Nor is the socialist electorate a factor in the frequent splits and divisions in the Socialist party, or with the shifts in programmatic orientations, as witnessed most recently in the 1967 Chillán Congress. Party elites structure the issues which will be discussed publicly and have a major effect on the greater or lesser polarization of opinion in the mass public. The relationship is dialectical, however; the leadership cannot be completely out of tune with the sentiments of the electorate without losing its support in the end. The orientations of the electorate constrain the choices and positions of party elites and cadres, as the party leaders searching for compromise during the Allende years became painfully aware.

Given this dialectical relationship between electorate and party leadership, a "consensual" citizenship (such as that which exists in the United States) provides no effective room for Marxist party leaders. The constraint of having to build electoral support stifles the development of party options that deviate substantially from the basic orientation held by the majority.[36]

Despite the expectations of officials of Chile's military government, the development of a consensual citizenship is out of the question within the foreseeable future. The Spanish case provides a sobering reminder of the stability of a political landscape and an indication of what Chileans might expect in a transition back to democratic politics. Juan Linz notes that after nearly four decades of Franco rule, the self-identification of the Spanish electorate is still shaped by the left-right ideological continuum. Party leaders at various points along the continuum are able to find a segment of the electorate willing to respond to their programmatic options and symbolic appeals. The importance and relative independence of party leadership formulations can be appreciated from the fact that the polarization of public self-identification in Spain increased significantly once the political system freely permitted the formation of party organizations and the dissemination of ideological and programmatic messages.[37] This experience would be repeated in the Chilean case.

AUTHORITARIAN RULE AND THE ENDURANCE OF THE POLITICAL LANDSCAPE

The political landscape is more or less impermeable to change once it has been firmly established. Periods of authoritarian rule, however long, do little to undermine it. The notion that an authoritarian government can somehow start anew and produce a "new generation of citizens" may be attractive to the rulers, but runs against the stubborn resistance of the very past they seek to eliminate.

A characteristic of most authoritarian situations, regardless of the clarity of the cleavages in the political landscape, is that it freezes name recognition for prominent leaders of periods of democratic opening. This is an unexpected consequence of the elimination of electoral contests, and helps to explain the ubiquity of the same "old" political leaders in Latin America. As democratic politics returns, the preexisting leadership is thrust into center stage because new leadership lacks the name recognition to take its place. It is for this reason that Víctor Raúl Haya de la Torre, Fernando Belaúnde Terry, José María Velasco Ibarra, Juan Domingo Perón, Ricardo Balbín, Hernán Siles Suazo, or Víctor Paz Estensoro (in countries with interrupted electoral politics the list is long) retain their positions as central figures in any democratic opening.[38] It goes without saying that the longevity of individual leaders is a necessary condition for this leadership resurgence to occur. It is not one of the minor ironies of authoritarian regimes that the effort to displace all politicians by banning political activities results, in the end, in permitting the retention of the very set of political leaders the authoritarian rulers moved against in the first place.

In countries where the party system was not well developed, political parties tend to be identified closely with the surviving leaders, often taking their names (Peronista, Velasquista). In countries where the party system had more time to develop before the advent of authoritarianism, and thus where it reflects more closely a clearly delimited political landscape, party labels will remain household names even if the dictatorship outlasts party leaders. The party organization itself is the conduit for the generation of new leadership, provided, of course, that the organization is sustained by the militants and that new leaders are able to survive the internal dissension which is so typical of clandestine organizations. The emergence of Felipe González, capitalizing on the historic Partido Socialista Obrero Español label, furnishes an excellent example of the retention of a party identity which predated the authoritarian regime.[39] The lack of continuity of party labels of the center and right in Spain reflects, to a large degree, the dissolution of those party organizations through the Franco years.

It must be underscored, once again, that the survival potential of particular organizations is ultimately the product of the retention within the mass public of a sense of self-identification with a political tendency in the overall landscape. In turn, the political landscape is reinforced under authoritarianism through political socialization, which is most effective if there are strong memories of civil war or repression. It is also reinforced by the survival of clandestine organizational efforts and by occasional contacts with civil organizations through which partisan political messages are diffused. The inevitable process of evaluating all public declarations by government, military, religious, and civil authorities in light of preexisting political categories also provides continuity. After four decades of Franco rule, the correlations between the 1936 and 1977 votes were as follows: PSOE/PSOE, .60; Left / Communist, .68; Confederación Española de Derechas Autónomas / Unión de Centro Democrático, .46; Right / Acción Popular, .38. By contrast, the party most explicitly tied to the Francoist legacy (Fuerza Nueva) gained only one deputy in Parliament in 1977, and the centrist UCD electorate identified itself more closely with the Communist party than with the antidemocratic right.[40] The Chilean military authorities would do well to recall that Franco's attempt to reduce all political differences to the "legítimo contraste de pareceres," in a society in which the party system was far less developed than in Chile, met with resounding failure despite the fact that authoritarianism survived the generation of the civil war.

The Repercussions of the Authoritarian Situation
on the Internal Structure of Chilean Parties

The imposition of authoritarian rule has profound consequences on parties as organizations. Leaders have great difficulty maintaining ties with the rank and file. Party decisions are often made without consulting party members and followers, leading to serious difficulties in legitimizing leaders' decisions and authority. Party congresses cannot be held openly, and in order to escape detection, party meetings involve few individuals. Militants suffer from a lack of information regarding party activities in other areas of the country, engendering isolation, rebellion, or simply apathy. Limitations on party activities increases the importance of study groups for ideological and programmatic purposes among core militants. Ironically, the effort to depoliticize society by imposing a political recess encourages a greater stress on ideological debates among leaders and militants seeking to retain a sense of distinct identity.[41]

However, authoritarianism affects party autonomy differentially, depending on the position of the government with respect to individual parties, the degree of rejection of the authorities by party leaders and followers, and the preexisting structure and relative cohesiveness of parties prior to authoritarianism.

THE RIGHT

The National Party and the much smaller Radical Democrats (Democracia Radical, a conservative offshoot of the Radical party), as well as the electorally insignificant fascist mini-groups of which the most prominent was Fatherland and Liberty (Patria y Libertad), were declared in "recess" by government decree.[42] This meant, officially at least, that the parties could not accept new members, renew their leadership, or hold meetings without notifying the authorities. The rightist parties responded favorably to government action because, with few exceptions, they identified closely with the regime and accepted its definition of the Chilean crisis.[43] As a result of this identification, the rightist parties have largely ceased to exist as organizations, though individuals associated with the parties have occupied important positions in the judiciary, the Council of State, the constitutional drafting committee, the diplomatic corps, universities, and most local governments.[44]

Even so, the identification of conservatives with the government has not been total. Some individuals, such as Hernán Correa Letelier and Julio Subercaseaux, moved to the opposition by forming part of the so-called "Group of 24," the highly visible constitutional and legal studies committee set up with representation from all parties to propose an alternative constitution to the one being drafted by the government. Others, as noted earlier, constitute a semi-opposition, disagreeing with specific government policies but willing to enter government service if conditions are right. This is the case with former Senator Francisco Bulnes, who has acted in the diplomatic service but whose public declarations have emphasized preference for a democratic model different from that envisioned by the military. By contrast, Pedro Ibáñez, Sergio Onofre Jarpa, and Mario Arnello, representatives of the less "traditional" wing of the National party, have given steadfast support to the government.[45]

Though the right-wing parties have not maintained their organic unity, many of their programs and policies have been implemented, to their satisfaction, by the military. But many leaders of the right worry that the disbanding of political organizations is a serious matter, reducing the right's ability to present a coherent and unified electoral appeal when a democratic opening takes place. With the serious economic difficulties the country faced in late 1981 and 1982, sectors of the business community (who would normally have turned to an organized rightist opposition option) approached Christian Democrats to express their dissatisfaction with policy and their concern with the future. By identifying so closely with a government that eschews politics and condemns parties, they have provided no space for a rightist democratic option to the regime. This in Chile presents a serious problem for a democratic future. Without a rightist electoral organization, the Chilean party system runs the risk of becoming "argentinized,"with an organizationally weak right (which has substantial support in Chile) turning to nonelectoral means and military alliance in order to advance its interests.

THE CHRISTIAN DEMOCRATS

The top leaders of the Christian Democratic party never accepted the military's definition of the Chilean crisis as being one of regime and society. From the outset they criticized the legitimacy and validity of the renovationist themes in the government's long-range project.

And yet, the Christian Democrats were at the forefront of the coalition which opposed the Popular Unity government, and the party's national directorate welcomed the 1973 military coup as the inevitable outcome of what it saw as the Popular Unity government's errors, ambiguities, and creeping totalitarianism.[46] The Christian Democrats thus proved to be a serious thorn in the side of the military government. They had the "legitimacy" of having opposed "Marxism," and yet their rejection of the military's effort to blame the Allende years on Chilean democracy, rather than on the Popular Unity government itself, inevitably led the party into growing confrontation with the government and closer ties with the leftist parties. The Christian Democrats did not accept the political "recess"as the parties of the right did, and sought to retain and expand their organizational coherence and vitality. This inevitably meant that they were suspect of "doing politics,"leading the authorities to repress the party in various ways, from a curtailment of its broadcasting outlets, to censorship of its publications, to removal of party leaders and members from the civil service, municipalities, public enterprises, and universities.[47] A few leaders were imprisoned and others, including two presidents of the party, were sent into external exile.[48] Continued "violations" of the "recess" on the part of the Christian Democrats finally led the government, in March of 1977, to issue a new decree declaring the dissolution of the party under the guise of dissolving all parties.[49]

As an opposition force, the Christian Democratic party enjoys clear advantages over the parties of the left. Its principal leaders and public figures remain in Chile and are often quoted in the press. Its labor and student leaders are public figures. The party retains certain media channels, including the country's largest weekly news magazine, a radio station, and publishing houses, though these remain in business by exercising a carefully balanced strategy of self-censorship which at times makes them appear timid and ineffectual. Its close ties with the church, and the church's increased opposition to the regime, which paralleled the falling out between the party and the government, provides the party with an umbrella of support, an umbrella which also benefits the parties of the left, as we will note below.

The relative ease with which the party has been able to act within Chile has allowed it to renew its top leadership, to hold frequent meetings with current and past middle and even local leaders, and to hold some consultation for informative purposes with a significant portion of the rank and file. These meetings are necessarily low-key and take place during periods of decreased repression. The objective of the meetings is primarily to maintain party presence, and to study and reflect on various policy problems with party experts and leaders, rather than to plan strategies for immediate political action. The Christian Democrats worry that their middle-class supporters, perhaps more than the core supporters of the other parties, will lose commitment in a time of middle-class prosperity. The meetings help ensure party loyalty and identity, and reflect the leadership's attempt to counteract the possible influence of government propaganda campaigns on the rank and file.

The death of former president Frei in early 1982 deprived the party of its most visible leader and the nation of a leader with great popular appeal. His opposition to the military government, though measured at first, was a continuous problem for Pinochet, and Frei would have played the leading role in any transition attempt. Yet, his death may not be as devastating for the party and the opposition as many observers thought. Frei was a constant reminder of the past. Not only was he a controversial figure on the left, but also a much resented figure in rightist circles. Within the party, he often served as a mediator, but at the same time his presence had something of a stifling effect on efforts to create a dynamic response to authoritarian rule. His death means that it will be easier for party leaders, provided they avoid a bitter internecine succession squabble, to ensure continuity of the party image per se, without having that image inexorably intertwined with Frei's.

THE PARTIES OF THE LEFT

The Popular Unity parties bore the brunt of governmental repression and have been severely hurt by the dispersion of their most prominent leaders throughout the world. They also lost many experienced middle-level leaders who were highly visible in neighborhoods, small towns, and the labor movement. As a result, the parties have faced enormous difficulties in the complex task of recreating a leadership and organizational structure capable of surviving the authoritarian experience. The most significant problem is that the rebuilding of internal leadership under authoritarian rule leads to the questioning of the legitimacy of the new leaders by militants and followers. It also contributes to differences between internal leaders, working in a clandestine environment, and the highly visible external leaders who command the attention of the international press and continue to play key roles in delineating broad party positions on significant issues and long-term programs. These problems affect some parties more than others, depending on the degree of prior cohesiveness of the party in question.

The Socialist party has been most affected by authoritarianism because it lacked a cohesive leadership prior to the events of 1973 and did not have a developed sense of internal party discipline.[50] The party has always been plagued by competing factions and considerable internal dissent, which at times has led to the creation of new splinter parties. The current problems within the party stem from the 1967 Chillán Congress, which adopted a revolutionary line not shared by many party leaders. The militant sector of the party backed Senator Carlos Altamirano as secretary general in January 1971, a choice which Allende concurred with for complex reasons relating in part to his personal rivalries with other moderate party leaders and in part to his frequently used strategy of attempting to co-opt opponents by giving them responsibility. During the Popular Unity years, the Altamirano leadership became a source of continual difficulties for Allende, who could not count on the undivided loyalty of his own party when party militants felt he was not pushing fast enough in the implementation of a revolutionary program. While Allende never broke openly with Altamirano, he continually attempted to shore up the position of his foreign minister, Clodomiro Almeyda, in the top party leadership as a moderating, countervailing force. After the coup, the party divided into several fractions, the most important of which are followers of Almeyda and Altamirano, with Almeyda holding a decisive edge of support within the country after the Altamirano faction had temporarily produced a semblance of coordinated party activity. The split has consumed much of the energy of leaders and followers. A breach has also developed between the more visible and less vulnerable leaders, such as intellectuals, and the new leadership in the union movement, content for the time being in tending to strictly organizational tasks in their own spheres.

The Socialists face the intractable problem of a basically democratic party attempting to legitimize its leadership under conditions of political repression. Under democratic politics, leadership disputes could be brought out and settled, at least temporarily, in party congresses attended by delegates elected by local party organizations. A more or less open electoral process had for decades helped to define the relative importance of various party factions. Furthermore, under democratic conditions, the electoral calculus—the need to coalesce in order to ensure a respectable showing at the polls—was always a powerful incentive to party unity.

While the absence of effective internal mechanisms aimed at legitimizing leadership and resolving balances within the party is time-consuming and has contributed to exacerbating ideological and factional disputes and to a degree of paralysis in party activities, these difficulties are not as serious as may appear at first glance. Party fragmentation, a process aided by the authoritarian context, does not mean party disintegration. Indeed, given the Socialist party's lack of organizational experience with clandestine action, there is some advantage in terms of its survival for the party to be divided into disparate and uncoordinated nucleii. If these fragments are capable of sustaining themselves as carriers of a Socialist political subculture if not organization, the changing context of a democratic opening will place pressures on them to resolve the problem of unity and central authority. The work being conducted by intellectuals (known as the "Swiss," for their neutrality) to bridge gaps between various factions in what has come to be known as the "convergencia socialista" is not likely to produce dramatic results in the near future. Nevertheless, it plays a crucial role in preparing the road for more serious unification efforts when and if electoral alternatives once again become the order of the day.

The Communist party, though severely affected by government repression, has managed to weather authoritarianism more successfully than the Socialists. Its experience with clandestine organizing during the 1950s, when it was outlawed, and its much greater internal party discipline and cohesion have enabled the party to maintain a segmented party organization without a serious loss of unity and direction. Of particular value has been the cellular organization of the party, the practice of appointing an alternative and clandestine central committee as soon as the incumbent one assumes leadership, and the longevity of the current leadership. The Communists have also benefited significantly from access to highly powerful short-wave radio broadcasts from Moscow to Chile which have kept the regular party leadership before militants and followers while providing them with information on the internal situation and party activities.

The split between an external and internal leadership, however, is not without serious problems for the party. While the internal group is in charge of immediate political strategy and the external leadership provides broader, long-range policy directions, it is at times difficult to separate the two. The most serious crisis resulted from the declaration of party leaders in Moscow, perhaps with Soviet pressure, that the party would turn to an insurrectionary strategy to overthrow the junta after the adoption of the 1980 Constitution. So far, however, the party has not implemented this strategy, as local leaders have objected to its advisability. The party is also under substantial pressure in Chile from some elements within the party, as well as from other political circles in the opposition, for its open support of the Soviet Union's invasion of Afghanistan and of the Polish military's crackdown on Solidarity.

The smaller parties of the left face some of the same difficulties that the Socialists do, but their fragmentary nature and the fact that they have no clear place in the traditional Chilean party spectrum mean that they are not likely to have much of a presence in a democratic opening, regardless of the energy of their organizational efforts. Their activities tend to be reduced to the small-scale operations of embryonic networks attempting to maintain a sense of identity. As will be noted below, they do play an important role in providing for links between various political groups and for maintaining a presence in intellectual and journalistic circles.

The Articulation of Party Networks in Civil Society

Chilean parties penetrated most organizations of civil society. Party militants were present in neighborhood committees, student associations, mothers' clubs, soccer clubs, and evangelical churches. They also structured the debate in labor unions, trade groups, and professional associations. The military authorities have interpreted this interpenetration of party networks with civil organizations as a manifestation of an unhealthy politicization. For them, the elimination of parties and the creation of a consensual order implies the extirpation of partisan influence from the nation's secondary associations.

Because political parties played such a central role in mediating between institutions of civil society and the state by organizing interests and articulating demands, their abrupt removal from center stage has given Chile a vulnerability that is not apparent in other authoritarian contexts where elements of civil society were more independent of party networks and have been able to survive with more autonomy and vitality in expressing opposition to the regime. The "cordobazo" of May 1969, in which mostly locally led Peronist unions flexed their muscles against General Onganía's military government in Argentina, is not conceivable in the Chilean case. Furthermore, the lack of experience of Chilean parties with survival under military rule makes them less capable than some of their neighbors in maintaining a visible presence.

However, as noted in the introduction, political demobilization does not imply a depoliticization of society. In fact, the elimination of institutions of representation and mediation displaces political conflict from the state and public level to the institutions of civil society, which become a surrogate political arena as party activities are maintained by an identification with sectoral interests.

Politicization is, however, qualitatively different. In the absence of outright party activities and elections, the political arena is significantly reduced, with many followers turning to nonpolitical and private activities. Those activities which are undertaken are often undertaken in an "apolitical" fashion, with leaders and militants maintaining some distance from more prominent party leaders in order to ensure the effectiveness of organizational efforts and the primary short-term goal of creating associations outside of the control of the state. This contributes to the impression of quiet "normality" so typical of authoritarian regimes, as soccer clubs or Bible study groups go about their daily business.

Some organizations, including mutual aid groups, cultural clubs, and sports clubs, are specifically created by political militants as part of their organizational strategy. In most cases, however, political parties seek to retain a presence or enhance their influence in established organizations such as professional associations, student organizations, or labor unions. Even in cases where party-identified leaders have been purged and mechanisms are created to select new leaders in an "apolitical" fashion, such as through the new labor code or through class representation in the universities, rank-and-file members soon become aware of the partisan attachments of various potential new leaders. Independents who emerge as "natural" leaders are quickly recruited by party militants, who compete with each other to capture the allegiance of the ablest figures. Partisan allegiance furnishes them not only with organizational support and resources, but also with a common identity which helps them draw on supporters with established or potential affinities. The distinction between party militants and independent figures is one which is consciously blurred, however, as the activists present themselves first and foremost as members of the constituent group in question. The process in Chile is very similar to the one which took place in Spain under even more difficult circumstances, during the repression of the immediate postwar period. As José Maravall notes, "The emergence of the working-class and the student movements was dependent on the underground survival of the parties of the left. Those parties provided the strategies and the leaders, and it was the capacity of these parties to survive that kept the workers and the students' resistance alive in the long and difficult period of the 1940s and 1950s, and that later rekindled the struggle."[51]

The parties vary in the degree to which they are able to shift partisan activities to the sphere of civil organizations. Those most favored are those that had higher organizational presence in the various organizations in question prior to the advent of authoritarianism and those best able to take advantage of the "organizational spaces" afforded by the new context. These spaces include the church and a whole series of organizations that have emerged under its auspices, the trade unions and professional associations, and cultural and social institutions.

THE CHURCH AND ITS "UMBRELLA"

During the first years of military government, a restrictive lid was placed on the activities of most of the organizations of Chile's civil society. Elections to renew officers in all organizations in the country were suspended, freezing in place leaders who were not removed by order of the authorities, and no meetings of any kind were permitted to take place without official permission. This latter stipulation was enforced so strictly that one of its violators a few months after the coup, the women's society of the Methodist church in the provincial city of Angol, meeting in a private home, was surrounded by armed soldiers, and the leaders were forced to explain that their activities were not political.

The Roman Catholic church and its organizations escaped the restrictions placed on unions, student and neighborhood associations, and other private organizations identified as "political." As Brian Smith notes, most of Chile's bishops welcomed the coup as an inevitable outcome of the chaos of the Allende years. However, as the human rights situation deteriorated, the church quickly parted company with the junta, and it became an open adversary of the military government when prominent Catholic laymen and the Christian Democratic party came under attack.[52]

In the early years, the church occasionally lent its prestige to the authorities in ceremonies such as the dedication of the Maipú memorial to the nation in the spring of 1974. On occasion it has acceded to government demands when these have been uncompromising, as it did when the authorities appointed an admiral as president of the Catholic University and removed the institution from church control. However, the church has refused to allow the regime to use Catholicism as a legitimating formula, and it has strongly rebuked the government for its disregard of human rights and for the social costs of the economic model. It has also rejected the "regenerative" formula of the regime, preferring a return to Chilean constitutional practices.

In opposing the regime, the church, and particularly the cardinal as archbishop of Santiago, has created a host of institutions to support its activities. The Vicariate of Solidarity (originally the Committee for Peace) has served as the principal organization assisting in legal defense and has produced extensive documentation on human rights violations. Organizations of the Workers' Pastoral Vicariate, as well as countless organizations in church parishes, have helped in the creation of neighborhood organizations, soup kitchens, committees for families of the disappeared, mothers' clubs, and the like.

The church has also supported the creation of institutions to provide technical aid and credit to peasant cooperatives and worker self-managed enterprises. And when faculty members were dismissed from the Catholic University, the cardinal set up the Academy of Christian Humanism, a loose organization which houses several important research groups of various political tendencies.[53] Since the church is not subject to prior censorship, it provides an outlet for publications, both directly and through the Academia. The magazine *Mensaje*, published by the Jesuits, has become a most hard-hitting mass circulation publication, publishing popularized versions of serious research on national issues. *Análisis*, under the auspices of the Academia, has also been an important organ for the dissemination of dissent opinions. *Solidaridad*, published by the Vicariate, is the basic organ for human rights.

There is little doubt that the Christian Democrats, whose leaders are close to the hierarchy, benefit most from the position assumed by the church. The church provides the party with an institutional base to retain ties with nucleii of support in shantytowns, in rural areas, and even in the labor movement. Some of the church-sponsored support organizations are staffed by prominent leaders of the Christian Democratic party. Party militants thus remain active through church conduits, helping to ensure the survival of the Christian Democratic party option in a democratic opening. The contrast with Spain on this score is instructive. The anticlerical excesses of the Republican forces in Spain thrust the church into the anti-Republican camp and a close identification with the Franco regime. This identification made it difficult to retain the organizational viability of a Catholic option when the democratic opening took place.[54]

However, the close tie between the church and the Christian Democrats should not be interpreted as having a negative effect on the other parties. Quite to the contrary: by providing for the existence of base communities, by sheltering workers and intellectuals, and by encouraging the publication of dissenting views, the church has created an "umbrella" for the parties of the left. Indeed, and sometimes to the chagrin of the Christian Democrats, many of the organizations that survive under church sponsorship are dominated by leftist parties able to make new organizational inroads, or simply to maintain traditional strengths through new organizational channels. Thus, some of the committees associated with the Vicariate of Solidarity are primarily Communist, the Academia includes many researchers from two leftist splinter parties that broke away from the

Christian Democrats in the late 1960s (the MAPU and the Christian Left), and neighborhood and parish organizations have a broad representation of political groups.

THE TRADE UNIONS AND PROFESSIONAL ASSOCIATIONS

The trade union movement provides one of the best organizational contexts for party organization when electoral contests are suspended. Unions allow the parties to place their militants in important positions of working-class leadership and to retain active contact and presence among the rank and file. They also provide an important arena of organized activity, especially when some form of collective bargaining is allowed. And since they can claim to speak for thousands of workers, top union leaders can become key political actors at a time when party leaders are denied the limelight.

In the first few years after the coup, the labor movement was quiescent. The leadership ranks had been extensively purged, and all meetings and elections banned. Plant-level leaders were selected by appointing workers with the greatest seniority to fill vacancies. Labor movement activities were reduced to an occasional public declaration issued by top confederation leaders, primarily Christian Democrats. The severity of the economic recession further dampened the activities of militants, who expressed themselves through small May Day rallies or occasional job actions in the large copper mines.

Pressured by the AFL-CIO, which threatened to establish a boycott of all shipping to and from Chile unless the government allowed union elections and collective bargaining, the junta finally called elections and promulgated a new labor law. The elections, called with a forty-eight-hour notice, were held on 31 October 1978. Workers with a recognized history of partisan activities or those who held union leadership posts were barred from becoming candidates. Since there were no ballots with printed names of candidates, voters could vote for anyone by filling out a blank ballot and handing it to the government labor inspectors.

Despite the extraordinary restrictions on the electoral process, labor leaders and informed observers estimated that the results did not alter the pre-1973 division of political allegiances: labor leaders overall continue to be split into roughly equal thirds favoring the Communist, Christian Democratic, and Socialist parties (although the Socialist party's presence in the organized activities of the labor movement has been less felt than before 1973).[55] The results illustrate the fact that a formal suspension of union activities does not eliminate the development of informal ties and associations among workers. New workers rely on the aid and guidance of more experienced ones and turn to individuals with leadership qualities for leadership roles. Party militants can fit those roles much better than others. Not only are they generally more articulate and knowledgeable, and willing to take risks in a repressive environment (as the founding figures of the labor movement did in the early years), but they also have access to outside resources (such as legal advice, political contacts, financial aid, and solidarity) that workers can appeal to in time of need.[56] Furthermore, in an election which makes use of write-in procedures resulting in a broad dispersion of the vote, the results will favor individuals who are more visible and have organizational ties, no matter how small.

The government's new labor legislation places limits on the power and effectiveness of unions, and as such has received the condemnation of all labor leaders, including that of a small group forming part of a government-inspired labor federation. The legislation prescribes a highly atomized and controlled bargaining process. At the same time, however, it made possible the holding of union assemblies for the first time since 1973, providing the workers with a renewed forum for the expression of grievances and union leaders with a new platform. Because of the complexity of the law, unions are forced to turn to outside legal advice, once again making relevant the party ties of the leadership.

Because of the high degree of party competition in the unions, the Socialist party, with its current divisions, is at a distinct disadvantage as compared with the Christian Democrats and the Communists. What is important, however, is not the extent of support for a given party in raw numbers but the continued survival of its organizational capacity, no matter how fragmented. As Maravall notes, the Communist party in Spain clearly gained the upper hand in the organizational struggle in the "comisiones obreras" under Franco, particularly in the period of the most significant repression. But despite this advantage, once democracy was restored, the Socialist party, by virtue of the survival of its organizational effort, was able to make significant headway in capturing that segment of the labor movement with Socialist proclivities.[57]

The professional and trade associations did not suffer as much from government repression as the unions did. In fact, most trade associations were controlled by elements who opposed the Allende government, and those leftist leaders that did exist were removed after the overthrow of the Allende government. For some time after the coup, the associations gave general support to the government while seeking to advance their interests. However, many associations soon became disenchanted with the free-market and laissez faire policies of the government, which directly affected their interests. Truckers, taxicab drivers, small businessmen, and civil servants all rejected a policy that deprived their members of government benefits and threatened their economic interests. As a result, in each of these associations, leadership identified with opposition parties, particularly the Christian Democrats, came to the fore.

A similar phenomenon occurred with professional associations, which in 1981, through Supreme Decree 3,621, lost many of their privileges, including the right to screen and limit members and to police standards.

Elections in the *colegios profesionales* led to the structuring of slates based on political understandings among opposition parties opposed to the "official" slates. In several colegios, including medicine, pharmacy, journalism, social work, and civil engineering, the opposition slates won a majority of leadership positions. In agronomy, physical therapy, dentistry, and law, pro-government slates prevailed. However, even in the Bar Association, characterized by its strong support of the government after the coup and the conservative predispositions of many of its members, the opposition slate obtained several seats, with over 48% of the vote.[58]

In these professional and middle-class associations, the activities of members and sympathizers of parties do not proceed in a clandestine or semiclandestine manner, as in the labor movement or in community associations; they continue in a more or less open fashion, and with more or less informal procedures to structure opposition alternatives. It is at this level that the right has succeeded in maintaining some organizational presence, either as a majority or as a significant minority, for the most part defending government policies and positions.

SOCIAL AND CULTURAL INSTITUTIONS AND THE STUDENT MOVEMENT

Before 1973, party activists and sympathizers were often instrumental in creating a whole series of social organizations and cultural events which revolved around the life of the party. Small towns in many areas, for example, were noted for their Radical clubs, social centers where people could pass the time of day playing parlor games or gather for a meal. Volunteer fire departments were often organized and manned by individuals of the same political coloration. Sports clubs and social clubs were favorite devices to bring youth into a party network. The party headquarters themselves often served a multitude of functions, from job-seeking assistance, to mediation of petty disputes, to marriage counseling. The phenomenology of small-town and neighborhood Chile abounds in such examples. These aspects of Chilean society continue in evidence today, although the party labels have disappeared. Since 1973, party militants have devoted considerable effort to creating innocuous organizations such as sports clubs.

Theatrical productions and folklore festivals, never devoid of political messages in the past, carry these messages in a more charged atmosphere, though in more veiled fashion. The double entendre with political meaning is developed into a fine art, so that a poem about, say, a dog written by Pablo Neruda is capable of bringing the house down as audiences cling to lines that suggest an inner meaning for the current predicament. Occasionally, audiences will respond spontaneously to cues in public places, by booing government spokesmen at soccer matches, or refusing to sing the stanza of the national anthem added after 1973 which glorifies the armed forces, forcing the authorities to bring choirs to athletic events to try to camouflage dissent. Obviously, artistic productions reach a limited public. However, their effect is to keep alive an oppositionist culture which reinforces the broad tendencies not represented in government circles.

The universities constitute one of the most important centers for the maintenance of an oppositionist culture. The student movement channels a good deal of effort into cultural and folkloric events which emphasize elements of Chilean tradition related to an oppositionist posture. Pablo Neruda plays a particularly important role in this regard. Since he is a Nobel-winning poet of international renown, the government cannot censor his work or erase his memory.

The student movement has been largely reduced to such activities because the military government has continued to keep a close watch over higher education. In 1982, universities were still run by officers appointed by the president. Student leaders have been appointed directly by the authorities, or elected under restricted circumstances. In April 1979, elections were unexpectedly called at the University of Chile to elect class presidents. Most observers, including those writing for the conservative *El Mercurio,* described even that election as a victory of the opposition student movement. This occurred despite the renovation of the student body, its reduction in size, and the purging over the years of faculty and students associated not only with the left but also with the Christian Democrats. Students, following the political allegiance of their families and influenced by the presence of party-affiliated leaders who emerge in a manner similar to the one described for the union movement, provide an important base for continued party organizational efforts. As in Spain, the continued organizational viability of the political parties provides a base for the continuation not only of the labor movement but also of the student movement.[59]

Finally, opposition parties do not confine their influence simply to cultural institutions or civil organizations created by the parties to maintain their strength. As does the labor movement, they attempt to establish a base in some of the organizational spaces created by the regime itself. Though it is difficult to judge the extent to which parties actually operate within government-sponsored organizations, there is evidence that some parties, particularly the Communists, have made efforts to participate even in organizations such as the welcoming committees that greet the head of state when he travels to the provinces, or the charitable associations set up by the wives of the junta leaders with substantial government funding.

Summary and Conclusion

While this paper has stressed the importance of political parties in the Chilean political landscape and their ability to maintain a presence in the organizational space provided by other institutions and by the regime itself, it is important to conclude by noting that Chilean parties are not absent from a public debate with the military authorities. Significant efforts have been made to reach across party lines in an effort to define the postauthoritarian regime and the party system of the future.

Public opposition to the regime has been carried out primarily by the Christian Democrats. Its position as a semilegal organization close to the church, whose principal leaders, including the late former president Eduardo Frei, were immune from repression, has given the party considerable ground for maneuver. Its various media outlets, as noted earlier, have given it the ability to maintain critical scrutiny of government policies.

One of the most important activities to date was the work of the counterconstitutional committee, the "Group of 24," so named because of the number of members in the principal working group. The committee provided a forum for broad consultation across party lines in the period prior to the adoption of the government constitution. Representation on the committee came from all parties, including the Communists and the Conservatives.

The committee was an extraordinary achievement because it succeeded in breaking down the barriers which had been erected between rival political groups during the Allende period and in the immediate aftermath of the coup. Its work included the structuring of countless subcommittees that have included approximately one thousand scholars, experts, and community leaders throughout the country. Its mandate was broad, ranging from highly theoretical discussions of "nationality," to considerations about the future of the judicial system, to examination of the controversial and complicated issue of social property and state enterprises (which proved to be a severe stumbling block to compromise under Allende), to the volatile issue of party organization and conduct. In its public pronouncements, the committee stressed the importance of electoral democracy as the only viable system for the nation, stressing that any constitutional innovations had to accord with the basic outlines of Chile's fundamental constitution, the Constitution of 1833, as modified in 1925. Juan Linz has noted that a similar unified and broad-based organizational effort to define a future regime never took place in the forty years of Franco Spain, and has been rare in other cases of authoritarian rule.[60]

While the referendum approving the constitution drafted by the government brought to an end the momentum of the Group of 24, efforts continue to arrive at broad understandings across parties. Such efforts have been aided by the progress being made in the Socialist party toward Socialist unity. However, they have also been set back by the pro-Soviet line of the Communists in the aftermath of the Afghanistan invasion. It is certainly not our intention to belittle the enormous obstacles which still remain. The heightened importance of ideology under authoritarian regimes devoid of elections is a clear stumbling block to finding common ground, as is the uncertainty of the timing of a political opening, which discourages common efforts and favors short-term survival strategies. Indeed, it is unlikely that Chilean parties will be able to structure a united alternative to the regime, or be a decisive factor in overthrowing the regime.

However, as this paper has suggested, the parties will succeed in maintaining their autonomy and identity, denying the regime the possibility of creating a significant constituency of its own, while maintaining continuous pressure on the authorities. Furthermore, the parties remain posed to rapidly mobilize followers should the regime falter, either through a severe economic crisis or an open split in military ranks. And they also stand ready to provide for the reorganization of mass politics and electoral contests when a democratic opening occurs.

The experience of other countries such as Spain, with a much longer trajectory of authoritarianism following a more ambiguous period of democratic rule, points to the durability of the political landscape and the continuity of partisan options when organizational efforts are maintained. The limitation placed on organizational and electoral activities, rather than undermining politics, contributes to freezing the positions of recognized leaders and shifting party organizational activities to available spaces in civil society. Such a task has been facilitated by the dissolution of the right's organizational presence and the unwillingness of the military authorities to risk the consequences of launching a political movement of their own to absorb the traditional right and mobilize middle-class elements. This unwillingness is not only the product of a reluctance to engage in "politics," but also the result of their perception that they would face a severe challenge from enduring partisan allegiances.

It is possible to describe the Chilean regime as one which fits the general pattern of reactive Latin American military dictatorship which came to power to curb excessive mobilization and/or implement a more dynamic model of development in accord with the pressures of local and international interests. Such a description, however, runs the risk of overlooking the broader and, in the long run, significant differences between these regimes. These differences stem from the prior political experience of the nations in question and the interplay of these historical political forces with those created by the new political context.

The key is that a characterization of regime must go beyond a mere characterization of government. The latter is preoccupied with the intentions of the rulers, their advisers and allies, and the short-run impact of repressive policies on target and nontarget groups. Regime characterization is broader in focus: it transcends government actions and intentions and analyzes the nature of opposition elements and their interaction with one another and with the authorities. Oppositions can be understood, in turn, only by understanding the historicity of groups, and particularly political parties, prior to the advent of the dictatorship.

We are not arguing for a form of cultural relativism—i.e., that each country will face different conditions even in the face of what appear to be striking parallels in the nature of authoritarian regimes. Nor are we arguing against the importance of the effort to come to a generalized understanding of the authoritarian phenomena. What we are suggesting is that a taxonomy of authoritarian regimes cannot rely exclusively on the outward characteristics of those regimes, but must take into consideration the contexts within which those regimes are imposed. The important differences between the Chilean and the Argentine cases are due less to differences in the level of repression or of governmental policy than to the different characteristics of the political and party system which succumbed to military rule. This insight is important not only for characterizing regimes but also for understanding their future prospects and the prospects for an eventual democratic opening. Thus, the autonomy of the institutions of civil society in Argentina, and particularly of the labor movement, gives the appearance that Argentines are better able to resist repressive policies than their Chilean counterparts, whose parties were so pervasive and controlling, and yet more easily repressed. While this observation is correct, it does not follow that the future outcome in Chile is more likely to favor the project of the authorities. The Chilean party system, though more quiescent, is more deeply rooted in the country's political landscape and has a clearer set of partisan alternatives associated with it, making the prospects for a restructuring of the same or a very similar party system much more likely in the future.

Notes

This chapter is a joint effort in the fullest sense of the word. Our names appear in alphabetical order. Research for this article was conducted in Chile in July 1979, January 1980, March 1981, and November 1981. Additional interviews were conducted with observers and party leaders in the United States and Europe. For obvious reasons, interviewees must remain anonymous. We are grateful to them for sharing their experiences so freely with us. Arturo Valenzuela wishes to acknowledge the partial support of the SAREC project at the University of Sussex in the preparation of this paper, and Samuel Valenzuela, the support of the Ford Foundation for his research trip to Chile.

1. For an excellent review and evaluation of work in this area, see David Collier, ed., *The New Authoritarianism in Latin America* (Princeton: Princeton University Press, 1979). This book reflects on the pioneering effort of Guillermo O'Donnell, *Modernization and Bureaucratic Authoritarianism: Studies in South American Politics* (Berkeley: Institute of International Studies, University of California, 1973). Other works on authoritarianism include James Malloy, ed., *Authoritarianism and Corporatism in Latin America* (Pittsburgh: Pittsburgh University Press, 1976); Alfred Stepan, ed., *Authoritarian Brazil:*

Origins, Policies, and Future Prospects (Princeton: Princeton University Press, 1973); Fernando Henrique Cardoso, *Autoritarismo e democratização* (Rio de Janeiro: Paz e Terra, 1975); Norbert Lechner, *La crisis del estado en América Latina* (Caracas: El Cid Editor, 1977). For broader conceptual analysis of authoritarianism see Juan J. Linz, "Totalitarian and Authoritarian Regimes," in Fred Greenstein and Nelson Polsby, eds., *Handbook of Political Science*, vol. 3 (Reading, Mass.: Addison Wesley, 1975).

2. For cultural explanations of authoritarianism see Howard Wiarda, "Toward a Framework of the Study of Political Change in the Iberic-Latin Tradition: The Corporative Model," *World Politics* 25, no. 2 (January 1973): 206–35. For an influential essay on corporatism see Philippe Schmitter, "Still the Century of Corporatism," *Review of Politics* 36, no. 1 (January 1974): 124–49. An early attempt to evaluate the Chilean experience in light of this literature is Robert Kaufman, *Transitions to Stable Authoritarian Corporate Regimes: The Chilean Case?* Sage Professional Papers, Comparative Politics Series 1, no. 01-060, 1976.

Guillermo O'Donnell provides the political-economic set of explanations to the rise of authoritarianism. For a recent article which discusses the Chilean case within the same framework of other Southern Cone cases, see his "Reflections on the Patterns of Change in the Bureaucratic-Authoritarian State," *Latin American Research Review* 13, no. 1 (1978).

3. Juan Linz uses the term "authoritarian situation" to refer to those authoritarian cases which have little political institutionalization; he explicitly contrasts this notion with that of "authoritarian regime." See his "The Future of an Authoritarian Situation", in Stepan, *Authoritarian Brazil*, p. 235.

4. This assessment by government officials is apparent in all their important declarations on the past and visions for the future. For the most significant of the early statements in this regard see the "Declaración de principios de la Junta de Gobierno de Chile" contained, among other sources, in *El Mercurio, International Edition*, 10–17 March 1974, p. 4.

5. Again, all important policy pronouncements by the government refer to the necessity of pursuing this regenerative task, a theme which was already contained in the government's "Declaración de principios." However, the regenerative task received its most explicit formulation in General Pinochet's "seven modernizations" speech; see *El Mercurio*, 12 September 1979, pp. C-6 to C-8, for its text. This speech complements an earlier, vaguer formulation of the regenerative task which is contained in Pinochet's address to the government's youth movement at Chacarillas hill in Santiago. Known as the Chacarillas Plan, the text of this speech appeared in *El Mercurio*, 10 July 1977, pp. 33 and 37.

6. Juan Linz, "Opposition to and under an Authoritarian Regime," in Robert Dahl, ed., *Regimes and Oppositions* (New Haven: Yale University Press, 1973), pp. 191–92. We have eliminated the emphasis which appears in the original.

7. For a brief analysis of these groups see Armand Mattelard, "Un fascisme créole en quête d'idéologues," *Le Monde Diplomatique*, July 1974, p. 7.

8. Rodríguez's line of thought obviously did not prevail over others, since the 1980 Constitution contemplates mechanisms of corporate representation only for the municipal level. However, Rodríguez declared himself satisfied with the 1980 document when interviewed by *El Mercurio*. See this paper's edition of 17 August 1980, p. D-1, where he argues that a corporatist political framework in fact requires a greater "political maturity" than that which Chile has.

9. For a discussion of the wide variety of groups that took part in the Franco regime over the years, see Amando de Miguel, *Sociología del Franquismo* (Barcelona: Editorial Ergos, 1975).

10. This is particularly the line of thought of the Grupo Nueva Democracia, which publishes the magazine *Realidad*. It is close to that of the "Chicago boys" who articulate and implement the government's economic policy.

11. On the position of the church under the current military government, see Brian Smith's *The Church and Politics in Chile: Challenges to Modern Catholicism* (Princeton: Princeton University Press, 1982), and his contribution to this volume (Chap. 8).

12. See *El Mercurio*, 26 December 1981, pp. C-4 and C-5.

13. See General Pinochet's "seven modernizations" speech, *El Mercurio*, 12 September 1979.

14. In his thought-provoking paper in this volume (Chap. 5), Manuel Antonio Garretón notes that there are "sectoral structural changes which modify the whole society and reconstitute the structure of classes and social actors and are capable of redefining the rules of the game."

15. These figures are taken from the Dirección de Registro Electoral's electoral compilations. The 1941 leftist vote includes that for Socialist splinter groups, namely, the Vanguardia Popular Socialista and the Socialista del Trabajo.

16. The Ley Permanenta de Defensa de la Democracia was adopted in 1948 in the wake of the onset of the Cold War by the administration of Gabriel González Videla, who had, ironically, been elected in 1946 with Communist party support and had included members of this party in his cabinet. The turnabout resulted primarily from a concern over the increasing electoral fortunes of the Communist party and from considerable pressures applied on Chile by the United States. The law led to the arrest of numerous prominent Communist party militants, including a good number of union leaders, and proscribed the party from participating in electoral contests. The law became an issue in the presidential campaign of 1952. The winning candidate, former president Ibáñez, promised in the course of the campaign to abrogate the law, but he did not do so until 1958, months before the presidential elections of that year.

17. For a discussion of the Chilean party system see Arturo Valenzuela, *The Breakdown of Democratic Regimes: Chile* (Baltimore: John Hopkins University Press, 1978) chap. 1.

18. See ibid., p. 39.

19. See Alejandro Portes, "Political Primitivism, Differential Socialization, and Lower-Class Leftist Radicalism," *American Sociological Review* 6, no. 5 (October 1971): no. 820–35; "Status Inconsistency and Lower-Class Radicalism," *Sociological Quarterly* 13 (Summer 1972): 361–82; and "Occupation and Lower-Class Political Orientations in Chile," in Arturo Valenzuela and J. Samuel Valenzuela, eds., *Chile: Politics and Society* (New Brunswick, N.J.: Transaction Books, 1976).

20. Portes, "Occupation and Lower-Class Political Orientations in Chile," p. 217.

21. A. Valenzuela, *The Breakdown of Democratic Regimes: Chile,* pp. 11, 13, 86–87.

22. Richard Hamilton, *Affluence and the French Worker in the Fourth Republic* (Princeton: Princeton University Press, 1967).

23. See Table 1.15 in Chapter 1, above.

24. Portes, "Occupation and Lower-Class Political Orientations in Chile."

25. Hamilton, *Affluence and the French Worker in the Fourth Republic.*

26. We take the notion of party-generative cleavages from Seymour Martin Lipset and Stein Rokkan, "Cleavage Structures, Party Systems, and Voter Alignments," in Lipset and Rokkan, eds., *Party Systems and Voter Alignments: Cross National Perspectives* (New York: The Free Press, 1967).

27. For a discussion of center-local cleavages in Chile, see Arturo Valenzuela, *Political Brokers in Chile: Local Government in a Centralized Polity* (Durham, N.C.: Duke University Press, 1977), chap. 8.

28. For an analysis of nineteenth-century Chilean politics and of the origins of these parties see J. Samuel Valenzuela, *Democratización vía reforma: La expansión del sufragio en Chile* (Buenos Aires: IDES, 1985), chap. 2.

29. See Maurice Duverger, *Les partis politiques* (Paris: Armand Colin, 1951), pp. 2–15.

30. For a study of the historical process that led to the formation of the Chilean labor movement in connection with Communist and Socialist parties, see J. Samuel Valenzuela, "Labor Movement Formation and Politics: The Chilean and French Cases in Comparative Perspective, 1850–1950" (Ph.D. diss., Columbia University, 1979). See also his "The Chilean Labor Movement: The Institutionalization of Conflict," in A. Valenzuela and J. S. Valenzuela, *Chile: Politics and Society,* for a brief overview of the legal framework of Chilean labor relations as well as a succinct account of the manner through which the Communist unionists accepted it.

For an account of the Popular Front government, see John R. Stevenson, *The Chilean Popular Front* (Philadelphia: University of Pennsylvania Press, 1942).

31. Giovanni Sartori, *Parties and Party Systems: A Framework for Analysis* (New York: Cambridge University Press, 1976).

32. Lipset and Rokkan, "Cleavage Structures," pp. 50–54.

33. It is unlikely that the electoral constituencies of both the Christian

Democrats and the Radicals would balk at a fusion of the centrist parties by bolting massively either to the right or the left. Such a fusion is bound, however, to meet great resistance among the party leaderships—and is therefore improbable. And yet, if the Christian Democrats were to drop the religious reference from their label, the Radicals would have some difficulty in the context of a possible future democratic Chile to retain their electoral constituencies by stressing their secularism, given the fact that the Christian Democrats have already taken over the center. The current attempt by the Radical party leadership to develop a "Socialist-Democratic" program is an expression of the effort to stave off just such an eventuality by locating the party visibly to the left of the Christian Democrats—in other words, to differentiate the two parties clearly on the left to right rather than the anticlerical to clerical dimensions. Paradoxically, the Christian Democratic leadership may welcome such an attempt as a means of developing a non-Marxist interlocutor to its left.

34. See A. Valenzuela, *The Breakdown of Democratic Regimes,* table 27, for a full breakdown of the votes received by the various parties in the 1969 and the 1973 congressional elections. The Communists, the Christian Democrats, and the Nationals received virtually identical proportions of the total vote; these parties were supported by two-thirds of the electorate. The Socialists gained 4.2% (the result, primarily, of the fact that a Socialist was president), and the Radicals lost votes proportionately (the result of the fact that the party split into three groups, all of which gained 5.7% fewer votes than the 13% the united party garnered in the 1969 contest).

35. James W. Prothro and Patricio E. Chaparro, "Public Opinion and the Movement of Chilean Government of the Left," in A. Valenzuela and J. S. Valenzuela, *Chile: Politics and Society.* These authors argue that the shift to the left in government coalitions resulted from changes in party alignments rather than from a shift of public opinion to the left.

36. On the consensus of U.S. citizenry, see Robert Dahl, *Pluralist Democracy in the United States: Conflict and Consensus* (Chicago: Rand McNally, 1967) esp. pp. 329–37. Naturally, in addition to this majority consensus over fundamentals, institutional and administrative procedures and divisions in the United States militate against the success of political leaders with deviant views.

37. See Juan Linz, "The New Spanish Party System," in Richard Rose, ed., *Electoral Participation: A Comparative Analysis* (Beverly Hills: Sage Publications, 1980), table 7. The data are difficult to interpret, however, since it is likely that the early surveys after Franco's death and before the legalization of the Communist party underestimate the size of the electorate that places itself on the left. And yet, the spread is a sizeable one: from July 1976 to July 1979 the percentage of respondents in a national sample who placed themselves on the left increased from 18% to 38%, while those placing themselves in the center decreased from 38% to 37%, and those on the right from 22% to 13%.

38. A significant exception to this observation can be found in the Brazilian case, because the post-1964 Brazilian situation generated new civilian political leadership. And yet, this is an exception which proves the rule because the

military government did not do away completely with all political space for civilian leadership. The mere facts of forcing the organization of two parties, of holding elections, and of having a parliament grant such a space. Still, figures such as Lionel Brizola and Miguel Arraes have been able to return as political leaders in present-day Brazil because of their previously established name recognition.

39. Gil Robles is the only major figure to have survived the nearly four decades of authoritarian rule. Josep Taradellas' return to Catalonia had a symbolic legitimating importance, but Taradellas was too old and too frail to become a factor in the leadership constellation. Santiago Carrillo and, of course, Dolores Ibarruri date back to the Second Republic, but they were not major political figures, particularly before the onset of the Civil War.

40. Linz, "The New Spanish Party System," p. 134 and table 1. All correlations are at the provincial level.

41. These observations are based on our interviews with both party leaders and militants as well as with knowledgeable observers.

42. The recess was imposed by Decree No. 77 of September 1973.

43. For a telling interview with the principal leader of the National party during the Popular Unity government, Sergio Onofre Jarpa, see *Qué Pasa?* no. 144 (25 January 1974). In it, Onofre Jarpa stated clearly that the military government had adopted the policy line of the National party, and that the party willingly accepted the political recess. He also stated that it is necessary to go beyond simple reforms to create a "new state."

44. After the military coup, the government appointed many Christian Democrats to the nation's mayoralties. However, they were soon forced out of office in favor of rightists and military personnel.

45. Ibáñez has argued that democracy is "congenitally" bad. See his interview in *Hoy,* 5–11 December 1979, p. 13.

46. There was by no means unanimity in the party in the initial reactions to the 1973 events. See in particular a document dated 7 November 1973 written by Radomiro Tomic, in which he analyzes the divisions in the party. Though meant for internal party debate, the document achieved wide circulation through multiple photocopying. See also the declaration signed by Bernardo Leighton, Ignacio Palma, Renán Fuentealba, Fernando Sanhueza, Sergio Saavedra, Claudio Huepe, Andrés Aylwin, Mariano Ruiz Esquide, Jorge Cash, Jorge Donoso, Belisario Velasco, Ignacio Balbontín, Florencio Ceballos, Radomiro Tomic, Waldemar Carrasco, and Marino Penn—all prominent Christian Democrats who energetically condemned the military coup and disagreed with the bland statement virtually accepting the military's action issued by the party's National Directorate. These declarations are contained in *Chile-América,* no. 4 (January 1975): 43–44. *Chile-América* published a very useful chronology of the relations between the Christian Democratic party and the military government during the latter's first year and a half, which details the growing opposition and confrontation between the two; see nos. 4 and 5 (January 1975), and nos. 6 and 7 (April 1975).

47. All this following the same Decree Law No. 77. Christian Democrats

refer colloquially to their removal from office as *salameo*, i.e., the cutting of the party's positions of power slice by slice as a salami cutter would.

In fact, the deterioration of the relations between the military government and the Christian Democratic party began the very moment that Eduardo Frei, the Christian Democratic former president, refused to go along with the two other former presidents, Gabriel González Videla and Jorge Alessandri, in greeting the four members of the governing junta after the traditional independence day Te Deum mass on 18 September 1973. General Pinochet mentions the incident in his account of the manner in which the military coup was planned and executed, and attributes Frei's attitude to the latter's annoyance at not having been informed prior to the fact of the closing of Congress and of the retrieval of his official car (Frei was at that point president of the Senate). See Augusto Pinochet, *El día decisivo: 11 de septiembre de 1973* (Santiago: Editorial Andrés Bello, 1979), p. 153.

48. An account of the first detentions of Christian Democrats and of the party leadership's reactions appears in *Chile-América*'s chronology of the relations between the party and the military government, cited in n. 46, above.

49. See the text of the Decree Law (no. 1,697) in *La Tercera de la Hora*, 13 March 1977, p. 2. The commentary in the newspaper clearly notes that though the dissolution is a measure taken against all parties in "recess," it is directed exclusively at the Christian Democrats, since "the National party dissolved itself *motu propio* after the armed forces took power and the Radical Democratic party practically does not exist."

The same 13 March 1977 issue of the newspaper reprints internal Christian Democratic documents, the existence of which provided the military government with evidence that the party was violating the political "recess." It is probably correct to say that some of the party leaders wished to give publicity to the papers as a means of making their position on current events widely known.

50. For a comprehensive treatment of the crisis in the Socialist party see *Chile-América*'s dossier entitled "La crisis en el Socialismo chileno," nos. 54–55 (June 1979): 81–137.

51. See José Maravall, *Dictatorship and Political Dissent* (London: Tavistock, 1978), p. 166.

52. See Chapter 8 in this volume.

53. See "The Academia de Humanismo Cristiano," a report to the Inter-American Foundation, prepared by Arturo Valenzuela, coordinator, and William Glade, Henry Landsberger, Pablo Latapi, and Larissa Lomnitz, for details on the Academia and its role in Chilean intellectual life.

54. For a good account on Spain, stressing the anticlerical excesses of some of the Republican forces, see Gabriel Jackson, *The Spanish Republic and the Civil War, 1931–1939* (Princeton: Princeton University Press, 1965).

55. This is based on interviews conducted in Santiago by the authors. See also Chapter 7 in this volume.

56. For a description of this process in the formative years of the labor movement, see J. Samuel Valenzuela, "Uno schema teorico per l'analisi della formazione del movimento operaio," *Stato e mercato* 1, no. 3 (December 1981).

57. Maravall, *Dictatorship and Political Dissent*, pp. 168–69.

58. See the article in *Hoy*, 11–17 November 1981, pp. 9–10.

59. Maravall, *Dictatorship and Political Dissent*, p. 164.

60. Private communication.

The Development of Labor Movement Opposition to the Military Regime

Manuel Barrera and
J. Samuel Valenzuela

The 1973 military coup that put an end to Chile's long-standing democracy signified a sharp break in the position which the labor movement had in national life. From being a respected and important actor in economic, social, and political affairs, the labor movement suddenly found itself persecuted and repressed. The new authorities tried from the very beginning to justify their seizure of power by asserting that they had acted in order to restore fundamental national values which, in their estimation, had been undermined by the nefarious influence of Marxism. Since the labor movement was one of the areas of society where the Marxist parties had considerable influence, the unions became a battleground in the war which was declared against them following the new national security doctrines. Moreover, with the elimination of all political institutions (including elections, the Congress, and the freedom of the press) through which the parties exerted their influence, the labor unions lost important sources of support for obtaining favorable legislation and other state actions on behalf of their interests.

However, no authoritarian regime, even one that sees the labor movement as a political enemy, can adopt a totally repressive posture towards workers for long. In the short term, repression may succeed in generating obedience and discipline within the labor force, but this quiescence will not necessarily insure a long-term increase in productivity or even in production. Given current technologies, patterns of industrial organization, and international markets and contacts, workers have many opportunities to express their discontent in ways that threaten the productive process or market shares. From a strictly economic point of view, it is therefore more efficient to provide some channel for the expression of worker grievances than to try to stifle them. Hence, even the most rigid authoritarian regimes end up generating some space for labor organization.

While the authorities hope that this space will be used by workers and labor leaders to voice very specific demands over wages and working conditions, it can also be used to express disagreement with economic and labor policies. Therefore, labor movements can become one of the most important sources of opposition to authoritarian regimes; after all, the capacity to disrupt production constitutes an important power resource, especially in a political context that greatly limits oppositional power capabilities. Consequently, it is not surprising that decisions over labor policies are among the most difficult for authoritarian regimes. Such policies must, on the one hand, try to secure the commitment of workers to production by allowing the necessary space for them to formulate their grievances, but, on the other, they must limit the opening for labor organizations to such a degree that it cannot be used as a platform to launch a political challenge to the regime. It is ultimately not possible to conciliate these two objectives, which explains in part why authoritarian governments typically go through cycles of repression and of opening in their relations with labor.

The Chilean case is no exception to these generalizations, although its particular scenario is a dramatic and complex one. The labor movement had important nonleftist (mainly Christian Democratic) leadership groups, which created within it ideological and partisan fissures that at the time of the military coup ran deeper than ever. The three years of the Popular Unity government had been ones of an increasingly bitter polarization of forces, which was felt with particular virulence in the labor movement, given its significance for the politics of mobilization both for and against the government. As a result of this backdrop of conflict and division, there was an initial affinity between the military authorities and the most outspokenly antileftist labor leaders. This affinity not only immunized these labor leaders personally from the fierce repression that decimated union leadership ranks, but also made them willing to become the new authorities' labor movement interlocutors.

The dialogue between the government and the nonleftist labor leaders did not, however, remain cordial for very long. Soon after the military coup the authorities placed severe restrictions on all union activities, thereby preventing unions from serving as an effective channel for worker grievances. Although the authorities presented these measures as temporary while they devised new labor relations, the years went by without any lifting of the restrictions even though there were lengthy discussions in official circles over the best way to reform the field. In the absence of a capacity to mobilize workers to press for their demands, the nonleftist labor leaders realized that their dialogue with the authorities did not give them the ability to pressure the government into changing any of its policies. As a result, they ran the risk of being perceived by the rank and file as pawns in the regime's labor containment strategy at a time of drastic policy-induced reductions in the workers' standards of living. The nonleftist union leaders therefore began to voice an increasingly bitter opposition, which in the end led to a convergence of the different ideological and political strands in the labor movement against the authoritarian regime.

The unusually lengthy suppression of union activities was a result of a combination of factors, such as the outright repression of worker militants, a very lax labor market, and the deep divisions among labor leaders that weakened the labor movement as a whole. By 1977–78, the situation had changed considerably. The repression of worker militants had decreased, the economy was showing signs of an upturn, and the divisions among labor leaders had given way to a shared rejection of the military regime. The conditions were therefore laid for workers to press for a lifting of the strictures confining unions to inactivity. A resurgence of labor conflict in 1977 (especially in the copper industry) and the threat of a boycott on Chilean foreign trade in 1978 by inter-American labor organizations sympathetic to Chilean workers forced the government's hand. The authorities lifted the restrictions on union activities, replacing them with a new set of regulations, and developed collective bargaining procedures. The new legislation, known as the Labor Plan, carefully attempted to restrict unions to bargaining over a limited range of issues at the enterprise level, but it led to the reactivation of local unions, and opposition to its provisions became an additional rallying cry for the different strands of the labor movement. By 1983, the labor movement had become a leading segment of the overall opposition to the military regime, and a central catalyst for the mobilization of people against the government in a series of monthly national protests.[1]

In the pages that follow we discuss the evolution of the labor movement under the military regime in detail, following mostly a chronological order, and we conclude with some general observations on the Chilean case as an example of a certain type of relationship between an authoritarian regime and the labor movement. However, it is necessary to begin this discussion with a brief analysis of the characteristics of the Chilean labor movement before the 1973 coup in order to better situate the subsequent developments. To this we now turn.

Chilean Unionism before 1973

The Chilean labor movement has a long history, although its organizational characteristics and modus operandi at the eve of the 1973 military coup dated back to the 1930s. During the first half of that decade many of the preexisting unions reorganized following the legal strictures laid down in the then recently enacted Labor Code, and towards the end of that same decade there was a sustained increase of industrial employment as well as of state-aided unionization. From then on the labor movement began to acquire an important place in the nation's economic and political life, even if its strength and influence oscillated between clearly distinguishable periods of ascent and decline.[2]

Chilean unionism presented a complex picture of organizations at all levels. The most important distinguishing feature between them resulted from their legal or alegal status. The legal unions were those explicitly recognized by the state, which meant that they enjoyed certain advantages but that they were subjected to a series of clearly defined administrative controls by the officials of the Labor Ministry's *Dirección del Trabajo*.[3] The great majority of the local unions in the private sector and in the industrial and mining enterprises owned by the state were of this type.

The legal unions included industrial, craft or professional, and agricultural unions. The industrial unions could be formed only in plants with more than twenty-five blue-collar workers; since affiliation with them was mandatory once a majority had voted through a secret ballot to create the union, and inasmuch as they were financed largely by a legally established participation in the profits of the enterprise, these unions were the most characteristic and important ones for urban blue-collar workers. The craft or professional unions had voluntary membership, and comprised workers of a specific occupational category or line of work—or white-collar employees—who could either be working in the same or in different enterprises. The agricultural unions, whose legal status dated back only to 1967, also were voluntary but were created by affiliating into locals the workers who were employed in the same district—following the lines of the state's administrative subdivisions of the national territory. A scaffolding of union federations following industrial or occupational lines was built over these various types of unions. Since federations did not formally enter into collective bargaining except in the case of the agricultural sector and the leather and shoe industry, collective bargaining was highly decentralized in Chile. The principal interlocutors of the union federations were usually the state and the political parties.

The alegal unions had no formal state recognition, but their existence was consistently tolerated by the governments. They grouped mainly the employees of the central and decentralized state administration, of the municipalities, and of the autonomous state enterprises. There were over two thousand of these organizations with various denominations such as "councils" or "associations," since the use of the term "union" in their names would place them within the purview of negative legal sanctions. There were, in addition, numerous national organizations in this sector, such as those of the employees of the educational system, of the health services, and others, which in fact constituted some of the most important and influential labor organizations in the country.

At the very top of the union organizational chart there were three confederations—the Central Unica de Trabajadores (CUT), the Confederación de Empleados Particulares de Chile (CEPCh), and the mostly insignificant Acción Sindical Chilena–Confederación Cristiana de Trabajadores (ASICh-CCT)—although all unions were not necessarily members of these organizations. The most important of the three was the CUT, since about 65% of all union organizations were affiliated with it either directly or indirectly around 1970. However, the CUT was in fact primarily a national sounding board for the various political and ideological factions which were active in Chilean unionism to express their overall programs for the working class. The CUT, always greatly underfunded and understaffed, acquired legal recognition only during the Popular Unity government.

Chilean union leaders tended to affiliate or associate themselves explicitly with a political party, and there was keen competition between the various resulting political and ideological groups at all organizational levels. Although there were minor groups both of the extreme left and of the center competing for union leadership, the basic forces were those of the Communist, Socialist, and Christian Democratic parties. Their levels of support were not distributed evenly across the board, but when aggregated at the national level each could be said to command up to roughly a third of all the preferences of the rank and file, with a slight advantage accruing to the Communist party. The president of the CUT has been, in fact, a member of this party since the early 1960s.

Chilean unionism had both a remarkably low level of bureaucratization and consequently of union leadership careerism, as well as great responsiveness to rank-and-file demands. The first attribute was mostly a function of the fact that unions were too weak financially to hire large staffs; in fact, the great majority of union presidents continued to put in a full schedule at their regular jobs even after assuming their leadership positions. And the second was primarily a result of the competition between different ideological and political tendencies at all levels of the union structure. Such competition meant that each leadership group had to make an effort to be maximally receptive to the rank and file's aspirations, since it otherwise ran the risk of losing the next round of union elections. Naturally, in such a setting there was a constant escalation of demands as each one of these competing groups sought to minimize the achievements of the leadership sector that held a majority in the union board. And given the highly decentralized nature of collective bargaining in Chile, the relative smallness of each unit engaged in the process meant that the rank and file could follow the bargaining process closely and judge in a very immediate and direct way the capacity of the leadership to obtain optimal results. In sum, given these structural reasons Chilean unionism was highly permeable to rank-and-file pressure, which bound both leaders and members into a set of expectations which were not to change overnight with the military coup. In other words, Chile's new military rulers were not to face a union movement like that in Brazil, where union leaders had little contact with workers at the plant level, and where the success of a union leader's career depended to a large extent on having a good relationship with Labor Ministry officials. The significance of this point will become clear later on.

According to official figures, union members constituted 24% of the total economically active population in 1970, and 35% in 1973. However, the official statistics greatly underestimate the actual extent of the labor movement, since they do not provide figures for the alegal organizations; and at the same time, they overestimate slightly the numbers of individuals who were members of legal unions, since they do not take into account the overlapping affiliations which could occur between industrial and professional unions. For these reasons, it is in fact difficult to ascertain the exact density of Chilean unionism. In any event, either by right or de facto all the employees of large industrial establishments (those with over 500 workers) and of the state enterprises as well as administration (both centralized and decentralized) were unionized. Beyond these, the proportion of unionized workers fell to perhaps a slight majority in the medium-sized plants (those between 50 and 500 employees), and to a minority in the small enterprises, in commerce, and in the agricultural sector.

Repression and Restrictions after the Military Coup

With the state of internal war which the authorities declared against the left, union leaders who were associated with the various leftist tendencies were particularly hard hit. It is not possible to determine the number of leaders who were killed, imprisoned, exiled, or just simply fired, but the result undoubtedly was that the union movement lost many if not a majority of its most experienced cadre.

The first wave of repression affected not only individual union leaders, but was also extended to disband some of the state sector associations as well as the federal and confederal organizations which were controlled by leaders linked to the Popular Unity coalition. The headquarters of the CUT and of its affiliated federations and confederations were occupied militarily in Santiago as well as in the provinces the very day of the coup. The CUT's legal recognition was abrogated, and all of its property confiscated. The same confiscatory measures were taken against the union of the employees of the educational system (the Sindicato Unico de Trabajadores de la Educación), whose property in this case was transferred to an organization for teachers without union-like objectives which was created by the government and whose leaders are appointed by it. Two of the three agrarian sector confederations were also disbanded and had all their properties taken over by the state; together they represented 61.5% of all agricultural unions.

Despite the severity of the repression, most organizations—even the great majority of those led by leaders of the left—were spared from dissolution and confiscation of their assets. Nonetheless, the new authorities, intending to completely change the characteristics of labor movement organizations and to impose new demand-restrictive economic policies while preventing the expression of any opposition to such policies, enacted a series of decrees whose effect was to eliminate the unions' capacity to represent and defend the rank and file's interests. The first measure (Bando 36, of 18 September 1973) led in practice to the suspension of collective bargaining because it banned the presentation of union demands (*pliegos de peticiones*). The same Bando 36 also suspended the right of union leaders to leave their work in order to tend to union affairs. The next measure was contained in Decree Law 32, which modified previously existing legislation to make it easier for employers to fire workers; among the new clauses was one which allowed the dismissal of workers who had led illegal strikes in the past or who do so in the future. This meant a wholesale authorization to fire union leaders and militants, since for what amounted to legal technicalities the great majority of all strikes in Chile during the previous decades had been classified as illegal.[4] A third measure (Decree Law 43) suspended all agreements regarding salaries, benefits, and other forms of remuneration, and all automatic adjustments of pensions to compensate for inflation. Finally, Decree Law 198, published on 10 December 1973, authorized unions to hold meetings only for internal administrative or informational purposes, and directed them to inform the police in advance of their agenda and scheduling (which had to be after working hours). The same decree law suspended all union elections, thereby extending the mandate of union leaders who remained in place and causing the many vacancies in leadership positions to be filled by an automatic process of appointing the workers with the greatest seniority to them.

All of these measures were adopted, it should be remembered, in a context of internal war, curfews, and suspension of civil rights, with arrests and firings on the slightest accusation or suspicion, either true or false. There was, therefore, no possibility of mounting an effective opposition to them, and the authorities unquestionably succeeded in restricting union activities to a bare minimum. And yet, as we have noted, despite the fiercely anti-union character of the new government, the non-leftist union leaders were initially rather receptive to it. It is only with time that they moved clearly to an opposition stance.

From Dialogue to Opposition: The Evolution of Nonleftist Union Leaders

Given an affinity produced by a shared rejection of the left, the centrist labor leaders became the new authorities' labor movement interlocutors in the wake of the military coup. With the benefit of hindsight, it is clear that the resulting dialogue favored the authorities, since it confirmed the debilitating ideological fragmentation of the labor movement and reinforced the political isolation of its leftist factions. Furthermore, the dialogue helped to diminish the international wave of denunciations aimed at the new Chilean regime by showing that leaders of union organizations independent of the regime agreed partially with it (especially in rejecting the "excessive politicization of unions") and could express themselves openly while making specific criticisms of the government (particularly over the effects of the new economic policies). The most noteworthy public manifestations of this dialogue were the active participation of union leaders with General Pinochet and other authorities in the traditional May first celebrations of labor day beginning in 1974, and the "informational" meetings the union leaders were occasionally invited to attend, with great publicity, at the government building. The external ramifications of this internal dialogue were the participation of union leaders as part of the official Chilean delegation to the Fifty-Ninth General Conference of the International Labor Organization (June 1974) and their intervention as witnesses for the government in the special hearings held by a committee of the same organization on union liberties and rights in Chile. To select the delegation for the conference, the government asked the unions to furnish it with lists of names, from which it selected some and added others.

Nonetheless, the benefit the authorities derived from the initial dialogue proved to be short-lived. Given the severe restrictions imposed on unions and the application of economic policies which were highly detrimental to the interests of the salaried labor force, the nonleftist union leaders could not retain their moderate position of issuing only mild and punctual criticisms of the government indefinitely. Indeed, the very leaders who had been characterized by their early public acceptance of the military regime soon formed the kernel of a growing labor movement opposition to it, leading *pari pasu* to an increasing coincidence of views between all major union leadership sectors, sectors which had previously been so bitterly divided. As a result of the early dialogue, however, the government had already implicitly accepted the existence, even if with restrictions presented as temporary, of the union leaders' organizations and, by extension, of unionism itself. Moreover, by seeking to turn the nonleftist union leaders into their principal interlocutors, the authorities unwittingly placed the union leaders frequently in the news as journalists began to turn to them for reactions to every economic and labor policy initiative. This represented a convenient way for reporters to fill space with commentaries which could no longer be obtained from the then highly denigrated politicians, but be this as it may, the consequence was that union officials greatly increased their visibility in the media. Therefore, as the attitudes of union leaders began to change, these leaders used their ready access to the media to publicly raise the tone and content of their criticisms of government policies. The growing labor movement opposition to the regime thus came to express itself through a succession of declarations to the press rather than through industrial actions made impossible by government restrictions and a lax labor market.

The change from acceptance, dialogue, and punctual criticisms to confrontation and opposition developed quite slowly, however, and it was greatly advanced by the government's own intransigence in not paying any attention to the grievances presented to it by the union leaders. Furthermore, this growing opposition was stimulated by the failure of an attempt by the Ministry of Labor to set up a new mechanism for discussions by worker, employee, and state representatives about wages and working conditions and by the reactivation of base-level union leaderships—in other words, the resurgence of the leaders who are closest to the sentiments and demands of the rank-and-file. These two elements which stimulated the development of the labor movement opposition merit a brief discussion.

THE FAILURE OF TRIPARTITE COMMITTEES OF COLLECTIVE BARGAINING

Let us return for a moment to the situation which prevailed in the country in the months following the military coup. At that point, while condemning the excesses of the repression directed against the left, the nonleftist union leaders had a unique opportunity to speak publicly for the whole labor movement, and thus what they could take to be a chance to extend their influence to those sectors of unionism, now bereft of their usual leaders, which had provided the left with the bulk of its support. However, in order to successfully take advantage of this opportunity, it was necessary for these leaders to do more than merely remain immune from the government's repressive arm. It was also indispensable for them to prove a capacity to channel the demands of the rank-and-file to both the authorities and the employers, and to show that such a brokerage role resulted in at least minimal concessions in favor of working-class interests. Naturally, no negotiations are possible without establishing a bargaining relationship, which is one of the reasons why the initial dialogue with the military regime was established. But once the bargaining relationship was set in motion, the union leaders had to retain some distance from the regime, for too close an identification with the circles of power could lead to the perception among the rank and file that the leaders were merely pawns in the government's labor containment strategy. The union leaders had to strive to be truly representative of the worker's aspirations and interests, for to do otherwise made them run the risk of turning opportunity into defeat, in other words, of losing rather than gaining ascendancy within the labor movement. This risk was especially significant given the characteristics of Chilean unions before the 1973 coup, in particular their great responsiveness to rank-and-file demands and the high degree of competition between the different union leadership factions. The Chilean labor movement was, to repeat, very different from the one in Brazil.

Consequently, it was particularly important for the nonleftist union leadership sectors to retain some space for negotiations over issues of concern to workers. However, the initial policies of the military government contemplated only restrictive and punitive measures towards the unions. It was only during the tenure of the regime's second labor minister,

Air Force General Nicanor Díaz, that the government began to articulate a positive labor policy with mechanisms for labor leadership participation in proto collective bargaining boards. It therefore appeared that the government was to create an institutional framework wherein labor leaders could represent rank-and-file demands, and that this new arrangement could be a first step towards a restoration of union rights.

It should be noted that there is a significant coincidence between General Díaz's tenure in the Labor Ministry and international pressures on the Chilean government over its labor policies. General Díaz assumed his position in July 1974, a significant date, since the International Labor Office's inquiry into the violations of union rights in Chile was scheduled to begin during the first week of that same month. The ILO's Committee of Investigation conducted its inquiries in Chile from 28 November to 19 December of that year, and concluded its report in May 1975.[5] Minister Díaz left the Labor Ministry in December 1975.

As if to confirm the fact that the government would attempt to preempt international criticisms, one of the first measures announced under Díaz's tenure was the establishment of the proto-collective bargaining mechanism. It consisted of tripartite committees of worker, employee, and state representatives for each sector of industry or parts thereof. These boards were to meet to discuss wages, benefits, and working conditions in the sector they covered, but they were not entitled to draft actual collective bargaining agreements; rather, they could only recommend that the Ministry of Labor issue a special decree containing the provisions over which there was unanimous agreement. Both the state and nonstate representatives on the boards were to be chosen by the Ministry of Labor, although the latter were in principle to be selected from lists furnished by employer and worker organizations.

The tripartite committees did not, however, live up to the expectation that they would be a first step toward a restoration of union rights, nor to the hope that they could become a significant forum for representation of worker interests. Only twenty committees were created, covering an insignificant proportion of the industrial and service sectors (one of the twenty was even set up only for elevator installers and repairmen), and by late 1977 only thirteen of these had even held their first, constituent meeting.[6] The principal reason for their failure lies in the fact that neither the government nor the employers were really willing to allow the committees to expand into forums for genuine worker interest representation and collective bargaining negotiations; this was particularly the case after General Díaz, with whom the labor leaders had a mostly good relationship, left the Labor Ministry. The committee mechanism did not allow workers to pressure employers effectively, since the committees were to meet without the possibility of calling union assemblies for rank-and-file debates over the issues at hand and without the right to strike. In addition, the government often selected worker representatives who had no union leadership experience and therefore no rank-and-file support. Such a policy was justified by a deputy labor minister in mid-1977 who asserted that "the rank-and-file worker can be more representative because he is not contaminated"—presumably by past political affiliations.[7] In other words, the tripartite committees turned out to be mere window dressing for international consumption in which, as an analyst pointed out in 1976, the government tried to "consolidate a form of purely superstructural unionism."[8] The committees therefore eventually became a failed attempt by the authorities to supplant all existing union leaderships rather than an opportunity for the existing nonleftist unionists to occupy a newly generated collective bargaining and worker representation space. The government itself did away with the committees when it drafted its radically different labor policy in 1979.

THE REACTIVATION OF BASE-LEVEL UNION LEADERSHIP

After the military coup and through the end of 1974, the combination of severe repression and restrictions placed on the labor organizations forced most of the base unions into inactivity and disarticulated the normal process of contacts among local union leaders and federal as well as confederal ones. Under these conditions, the officials of the peak organizations were free to develop a strategy of contacts with the government guided only by their sense of the sentiments and aspirations of workers in local unions and in the absence of specific demands and pressures from union leaders most closely tied to the rank-and-file. If a reactivation of local union leaders and militants were to occur, with a resurgence of contacts between the peak and the base organizations, the top leaderships would be bound to reflect more clearly the felt aspirations and sentiments of the bases. This is particularly the case given, again, the Chilean context of fundamentally decentralized labor organizations, which reduced the peak leaders' possibility of excercising vertical authority over local ones. Beginning in 1975, just such a process of reactivation of local union leaders and of reassertion of contacts within labor organizations took hold, thereby adding significant pressure on the nonleftist leaders of peak organizations to adopt a more forceful attitude towards the government.

It is not easy to find good indicators for the process of reactivation and rearticulation of unionism in this period. Official statistics, which refer only to legal unions, help little. In terms of union membership, these statistics show the paradoxical result that while Chilean unionism suffered the most severe repression and the greatest restrictions of its entire history, the number of union members continued to increase, from 934,400 in 1973 to slightly over one million after 1975.[9] This point is important in the sense that it probably aided rank-and-file workers in keeping a sense of identification with the union even if the union did virtually nothing for several years, but it cannot be taken as an indication of the vitality of unionism.

Official statistics also include a classification of unions according to their "active" or "inactive" status. And as can be appreciated from Table 7.1, the percentage of unions classified as "inactive" increased to slightly over a third of the total after 1974. However, these figures in fact are not, again, a good indicator of the vitality of unionism, since to be classified as "active" a union merely has to show some "sign of activity," which normally means that the union secretary has either simply met with the legal obligation of forwarding a yearly set of documents on union finances and other matters to Labor Inspectorate officials or that the union has been legally incorporated during the year. A union which held an assembly every week as well as one which did not meet at all but whose secretary communicated with the proper officials would both be entered in the same "active" column. Consequently, it is necessary to find a better indicator for the reactivation of base-level leaders than can be obtained from the official figures.

Given on the one hand the severe restrictions imposed on unions and on the other the increased attention of the press to union leaders' opinions, press declarations became, for lack of a better alternative, an important channel for labor leaders to exert public pressure on the government and on employers. As a result, by examining the daily press it is possible to obtain some sense as to which level of union leadership, whether federal or local, is the source of information to the press on issues concerning workers and therefore which level of the union hierarchy is actively pursuing the public opinion pressure strategy. For this purpose, this research chose the most salient issue for workers, the problem of layoffs, and coded the source of the union reactions to them in the Santiago press reports over a five-year period. The results can be examined in Table 7.2. The table shows a sharp reduction in the percentages of news items which had no reaction from the worker organizations as well as a diminution in those in which the only

TABLE 7.1   Percentage Distribution of Unions according to Their Officially Designated State of Activity, 1970–1977

	1970	1971	1972	1973	1974	1975	1976	1977
Active	84.3	83.5	78.2	71.2	64.5	61.3	62.9	62.9
Inactive	15.4	16.2	21.4	27.6	33.4	35.9	34.8	35.9
Cancelled or being dissolved	0.3	0.3	0.4	1.1	2.1	2.9	2.3	1.2

Source: José Isla et al., Estadísticas sindicales chilenas, 1970–1977 (Santiago: Facultad de Ciencias Económicas y Administrativas, Seminario de Título, 1979), table 4.2.

TABLE 7.2   Type of Organization Reacting to New Items on Worker
Layoffs (October 1973 to December 1978, in percentages)

	1973–74	1975–76	1977–78
Nonunionized workers	—	5.0	8.9
Unions of the same enterprise or line of production	38.2	51.6 ⎫	49.2 ⎫
Local unions or workers together with a union federation or confederation	—	16.7 ⎭ 68.3	17.9 ⎭ 67.1
Federation or confederation	19.0	13.3	7.5
No worker reaction recorded, or organization which reacts is not one of workers	38.2	11.7	15.0
	100.0	100.0	100.0
	(21)	(60)	(67)

Source: Press clipping service of the Chilean National Congress Library, which
covers the following: *El Mercurio, La Tercera, La Tribuna, La Patria, Las Ultimas
Noticias, La Segunda, El Cronista,* all of them dailies, and *Ercilla,* the weekly magazine.

labor reaction was that of federal or confederal officials. It also reveals a
marked increase—from 38.2% in the first years to 68.3% and 67.1% in the
following—in the percentage of items in which local organizations are on
record as reacting to the layoffs. In the latter four years a part of this
increase—16.7% and 17.9%, respectively—can be attributed to a joint reaction by local and higher level union officials, coordination which is not in
evidence in the first period.

   This is admittedly a rough indicator, but it does show that even if
unionism could not revive its activities owing to the weight of state-
imposed restrictions, at least by 1975 local union leaders were in most
reported cases willing to register publicly their protest. Such willingness to
go on record should not be taken lightly given the overall political context,
in which no protests were allowed and in which any statement by labor
which did not fully accept the official line was suspect of having a link to
the leftist political opposition and was therefore not without risk. In the
face of this reactivation of base-level leaders, the nonleftist leadership that
had pursued the initial dialogue with the government without obtaining, in
return, any benefits for the rank and file, could only continue to pursue that
policy at the risk of losing ascendancy over the labor movement. This was
particularly the case given the drastic reductions in real purchasing power
which the salaried labor force suffered with the anti-inflationary policy of

the government, especially in 1975, when wages and salaries reached the low point of 66.2% of their 1970 level.[10] Under these conditions, it was inevitable that the nonleftist leaders would eventually turn to expressing publicly their disagreement with the government, moderately at first, but eventually in strident and unambiguous terms.

THE TURNING POINT: THE FORMATION OF THE "GROUP OF TEN"

The first step toward the development of an organized opposition stance on the part of the labor leaders who had participated in the early dialogue with the authorities came in December 1975. At that point, ten of the most prominent openly active figures in the Chilean labor movement decided to form an ongoing group to discuss and coordinate their positions. Most of them were linked to the Christian Democratic party, and all but one were top officials of either union confederations or federations. In a sense it was the government itself that brought these leaders together, since during the course of 1975 Labor Minister Díaz had repeatedly requested the reactions of the labor movement to several projects which, in addition to the tripartite committees, the ministry had drafted. These included a so-called Social Statute for Enterprises, a new Statute for Worker Occupational Training, a Preliminary Proposal for Labor Code Reforms, and a Preliminary Statute Laying the Basis for the Social Security System.[11] While each labor organization had analyzed the various projects independently, all had for various reasons reacted negatively to them; by the end of 1975, the ten leaders felt that the time had come to voice their opinions as a group. For want of a better name, or perhaps to avoid a more provocative label, they were simply designated as the Group of Ten. The December 1975 date coincided with the replacement of General Díaz by Sergio Fernández, the first civilian to hold the office of labor minister. Fernández took over with what promised to be—and in fact turned out to be—a far less favorable and open relationship with labor leaders.[12]

The Group of Ten's first public salvo against the government was fired on 28 May, 1976, in the form of a lengthy (over 5,000 words) open letter addressed directly to the members of the military junta. Although written in a very respectful tone, the letter complained bitterly that after an initial phase of "paralyzing" the union movement through a series of restrictive measures for national security reasons, the government's policy had since been one of attempting deliberately to "desintegrate" it. And as if to confirm their concern over their standing and ascendancy as leaders of the labor movement, the leaders made a point of noting that a policy aiming at the desintegration of the labor movement would only benefit the "totalitarian" groups within it, an outcome they would deeply deplore because they shared the "democratic and humanistic principles of the Western world." This result would stem naturally from the fact that a weakening of labor organizations was bound to generate a highly conflictual and tense atmosphere in the enterprises given the workers' inability to find adequate satisfaction to their demands for welfare and security, which would only confirm the validity of the "class struggle thesis." The letter also noted, citing various statistics, that the government's economic policy had resulted in a sharp drop in workers' incomes and in a decline in the national economy. It complained, in addition, that worker's representation in various state-level institutions had been discontinued, and it proposed that the mechanism of the tripartite committees be strengthened by permitting labor confederations, federations, or national unions to present formal petitions before them while the regular collective bargaining mechanisms remained suspended.[13] Naturally, such a measure would strengthen the hand and the visibility of the top union leaders, who, because of the purges of leftist leaders from the labor movement, were primarily either Christian Democrats or nonpartisan but nonleftist figures.

The answer to this letter came, not from the military junta, but, on the express instructions of General Pinochet, from Labor Minister Fernández. In his brief response the minister simply asserted that the labor leaders did not understand "national reality" and that they were unaware of "all the facets of the government's labor policy favoring the workers." He also called into question the right of the Group of Ten leaders to speak for the "labor sector" by labelling their influence within it as "partial" and "restricted." To this the labor leaders responded vehemently that they were duly elected representatives of the labor movement, noting that the government itself had recognized this by naming them as part of Chilean delegations to the ILO; the minister in turn retorted by repeating his earlier terms.[14] The open letter and its sequel of curt responses signalled clearly the end of the nonleftist leaders' attempt to seek an accommodation with the government. Given the authorities' instransigence and the consequent impossibility of negotiating any advantages for working-class interests, there was clearly no other alternative for the Group of Ten than the pursuit of a confrontational and oppositionist course in order to retain a place among the leading sectors of Chilean unionism. Although this new stance by the mostly Christian Democratic leaders ran parallel to a similar change from accommodation to confrontation within the bulk of the top leadership of the party, the labor leaders' attitudes unfolded from their own experiences and were not subordinated to party decisions. In fact, Christian Democratic militants at all levels underwent a similar evolution from an initial willingness to compromise with the government in an attempt to preserve positions of power and influence, to an oppositional stance in the face of the government's intransigent and inflexible pursuit of its own, clearly different policies and its continuing violations of the most basic human rights.

The Development of the Labor Movement Opposition and the Formation of New "Groups"

The definitive break of the nonleftist union leaders with the government signalled an important turning point for the development of the labor movement opposition to the military regime. Once these union leaders began to denounce the government in unambiguous terms in order to retain the very viability of their organizations and positions of leadership, they obviously began to express publicly views that were in considerable agreement with those of leftist sectors within the labor movement. Consequently, the various political and ideological factions of the labor movement, until recently so bitterly divided, began to draw closer together rapidly on the basis of a commonly shared opposition to the military regime's economic and labor policies. And since the nonleftist leaders had been allowed by the regime to become the public voice of labor, they continued to occupy that space, but in a totally different manner; soon after its open break with the authorities, the Group of Ten became, much like the tip of an iceberg, the most visible sector of a broad opposition consensus of union leaders located at all organizational levels rather than simply one political and ideological segment of the labor movement. Therefore, the public space that the regime had granted to labor leaders with the intention that they aid it in a crusade against Marxism became the tribune for a revitalized labor movement which sought to express its common rejection of the authoritarian government.

The best example of the Group of Ten's newfound role was an open letter of 30 August 1977 to the military government drafted in response to General Pinochet's "new institutionality" speech. The letter was signed by 852 union officials representing 479 organizations—confederations, federations, and unions—and was particularly interesting because it did not restrict itself to the by-then familiar denunciation of the government for abridging union rights and freedoms, but spoke to the larger issue of the future political order for Chile, the theme of the Pinochet speech. The union leaders rejected the general's call for a "protected and authoritarian democracy," noting that it should simply be "representative and pluralistic." They also indicated that the timetable which Pinochet gave for the process of "normalization" was too drawn out and that the drafting of the new political institutions should be accompanied by a broad process of consultations with the citizenry. The open letter ended by asserting that the greatest of Chilean national values, a notion invoked frequently by the regime's representatives, was its traditional democratic system—which the regime had singled out as an unworkable cauldron for leftist demagogues. Eduardo Ríos, the leading figure of the Group of Ten, presented the union document at a news conference in which he eloquently repeated and

He noted, for instance, that one of the principal obsta-
ıtization of the Chilean political system lay in the fact
ses had benefited enormously from the military govern-
ı the government's economic policy to a funnel which
ı liberty for the industrialists, the large retailers, and the
for the workers? strict control by the state." He went on to
workers could only take so much, and that their patience
ıre not be tried.[15]

The found preeminence of the Group of Ten leaders within the labor movement as a whole was not to last very long, however. Beginning in 1977, and certainly by 1978, other so-called groups began to multiply the public voices of the labor movement. The government itself tried to stimulate the formation of new top labor organizations in order to counter the influence of the Group of Ten, although without much success. One of the organizations it sponsored in 1978, the Unión Nacional de Trabajadores de Chile (UNTRACh), which has included well-recognized leaders of the copper, banking, airline, and shoe and leather industries, in a relatively short period of time took on an independent and even critical position towards the government, moving in fact close to the Group of Ten. A second, more loyal organization formed by the authorities, the Comando Nacional de Trabajadores, has not existed beyond its own stationary except for the participation of its leading figures in official ceremonies. The government's failure on this score has been partly a function of the fact that its attempt has been half-hearted. The military regime has been unwilling to orchestrate an organizational basis, either a party, a union, or both, from which to manipulate a broader process of mass mobilization, and this stifles even the minimal impact that the Comando Nacional could conceivably have.

The most important additional groups to become publicly active during 1977 and 1978 were oppositional in tone and in character. Two of them, the Confederación Nacional de Empleados Particulares de Chile (CEPCh) and the Frente Unitario de Trabajadores (FUT), had existed before the 1973 coup, the CEPCh having been formed in 1949 and the FUT during the Allende government, but neither had taken, openly at least, a leading role during the first years of the military government. The CEPCh's top leadership is generally centrist and has taken positions which approximate those of the Group of Ten, while the FUT is animated by individuals of a generally Christian background and leftist coloration.

The third and most significant organization to add its public voice to the labor movement opposition, the Coordinadora Nacional Sindical (CNS), was formally created in 1978 by union leaders who generally identify with the left of the Christian Democratic party as well as with the major and minor parties of the left. It therefore represents a fusion between, on the one hand, leaders who left the Group of Ten as a result of disagreements over the extent to which there should be collaboration on an equal footing with labor leaders of Communist and Socialist affiliations and, on the other, some of the latter who had reemerged as a result of the reactivation of the contacts and discussions within the labor movement. The president of the CNS, Manuel Bustos, a Christian Democratic official of the Textile Workers' Federation who had been among the original figures of the Group of Ten, represents the first element, while its secretary general, Alamiro Guzmán, a member of the Communist party and leader of the Mining Federation, is indicative of the second.

In a way, the multiplication of these labor groups resulted from the very success of the Group of Ten as well as from its change to a clear-cut oppositional stance. Success, since while the Ten stimulated widespread discussions among labor leaders to forge common positions to use in confronting the government, it also fostered the reestablishment of old links and the creation of new ones that underlay the alignment of the labor leaders into the different groups. And change to an oppositional stance, since this altered the status of the nonleftist leaders in view of the government, with polarizing consequences in labor movement circles. With their new confrontational attitude, the Group of Ten leaders ran the risk of expending their initial immunity from government repression given the shared anti-Communism which made most of them wary of too close an identification with the left. At the same time, since the Group of Ten was to lose its special position, the convenience which the leftist leaders earlier saw in sheltering the public activities of the labor movement as a whole under the cover afforded by the Group of Ten was thereby lost, and they would no longer see any reason to grant the Ten the limelight in the oppositional struggle. If the Group of Ten were henceforth to be placed on an equal footing with the other labor leaders—all disfavored by the authorities but each able to maneuver in an environment which, though far from free, had lost the ruthless and brutally repressive characteristics of the initial years—then there was no reason to allow the Ten to occupy the preeminent role in leading the opposition. Therefore, both the nonleftist as well as the leftist leaders had reasons to seek a clearer division between different peak organizations despite sharing a common rejection of the military government's policies, and it is this dynamic which produced the divisions, particularly between the Group of Ten and the CNS, in mid-1978.[16] Indeed, as if to confirm their desire to distance themselves from the left, the Group of Ten finally decided to change, in April 1981, its innocuous name to Unión Democrática de Trabajadores (UDF); the use of the term "democratic" in this label connotes a rejection of both the positions they see in the left and those they see in the government.

And yet, despite this organizational fragmentation at the top, the various organizations have continued occasionally to draft common declarations on specific and general matters. A notable example of the latter was the hard-hitting document jointly suscribed to by the Group of Ten, the

.he CEPch, and the FUT and issued for the May first labor day com-
,oration in 1979. Entitled "The Workers in Today's Chile," the text
ounces what it calls the "revanchist, rancorous, and spiteful spirit
which the capitalist and powerful classes exhibit today" as they have taken
advantage of the authoritarian government in order to "reconquer all their
privileges" during what has turned out to be a "profound revolution for the
benefit of the rich." The labor leaders then buttress this assertion by
noting that in all areas of policy the government has opted for the "hardest,
most inhuman course, considering workers as objects, things, numbers,
but not as persons." The text turns next to the "crimes" that have been
committed, asking rhetorically where the workers and leaders that have
been killed by the security apparatus are, why so many are forced to live in
exile without ever having been condemned by a court of justice, why so
many have been fired from their jobs, and why labor organizations have
been deprived of their assets without any compensation—all of which
reveals that "workers are currently managed with repression and the fear
of unemployment." The labor leaders then note the sorry state of Chilean
political institutions, given the lack of democracy and the abridgement of
all the liberties and rights which the citizenry enjoyed, concluding that the
present generation of Chileans cannot remember a government that has
produced "greater penury, injustice, abuses," even if—following a pattern
which the labor leaders claim is typical of authoritarian regimes—the government surrounds itself with individuals who sing its praises and orchestrate its favorable publicity in the mass media, and then deludes itself into
believing in its own popularity. The leaders next call on the armed forces to
return to the barracks. They assert that even though the authorities may
remain in place while "fear and terror reigns" in the long run "a nation is
always able to resume its course and to impose its personality." The text
then concludes that for a return to democracy it is necessary to reestablish
the electoral registers and to convoke a Constituent Assembly.[17]

The Government Changes Its Strategy: The Call for Union Elections and the New Labor Legislation

By late 1977, the relations between the regime and all of the nation's labor
leaders were extremely curt and tense. The government knew that virtually none of the important labor leaders would support it, and it consequently began to assert more and more frequently that they were simply
individuals motivated by political concerns and not representative of the
majority of the rank and file. The authorities would probably have preferred to simply ignore the labor leaders, except that two new developments in late 1977 and 1978 made this impossible. The first was the
reemergence of labor actions, especially in the large copper mines—in
other words, in the one sector of Chilean unionism where workers are a

significant force whatever the state of the economy—and the second was the mounting threat of a boycott of Chilean exports and imports which could be called by the Regional Inter-American Labor Organization of the International Confederation of Free Trade Unions, which is best known by its Spanish acronym of ORIT.

The first of the large copper mines to see labor unrest was El Teniente, where in November 1977 an obviously concerted wave of worker absenteeism—an undeclared, passive form of strike in which up to 32% of the workers participated—disrupted production. Meanwhile, and through 1978, workers in the El Salvador mine logged a series of protests against supervisory personnel, accusing them of arbitrariness and of acting in a high-handed manner. And for a full two months, August and September of 1978, the miners of Chuquicamata staged what came to be known as the *presión de las viandas*, since they refused to use the company's cafeterias while arguing that they could no longer afford to do so, resulting in a virtual hunger strike during the working day. In addition, there were strikes and protests among textile, port, and metal workers in this period. In all of these cases the reaction of the authorities was a repressive one; in El Teniente, for instance, sixty workers were fired, and four union leaders were arrested and banished to remote locations in the country. In Chuquicamata there were numerous arrests and banishments and a declaration of a state of siege, none of which broke the movement until the authorities agreed to concede to some of the workers' demands; however, seventy were fired. *El Mercurio,* the leading Chilean newspaper, drew the lesson from this particular conflict by noting in an editorial that while labor actions in the copper industry are inadmissible given their repercussion on the economy, it is not realistic to think that they can be resolved simply with "states of siege and other forceful measures."[18] As implied in this statement, the regime confronted the necessity of generating some form of institutionalization of labor management relations in order to channel labor discontent through a more regular and predictable course.

The idea of calling a boycott of Chilean external trade to protest the abridgement of union rights arose in inter-American labor circles in the early part of 1978. During much of that year it was no more than a rumored possibility, but it was certainly one which was cause for great concern in government circles given its possibly deleterious economic consequences, especially if the U.S. longshoremen joined the movement.[19] It should be remembered, in addition, that during 1978 the Carter Administration was calling attention to human rights violations. This adverse publicity contributed to placing the Chilean regime on the defensive even in terms of its labor policies, since those policies were widely viewed as a further example of the authorities' disregard for basic rights of citizens. The necessity of staving off the possible boycott and of muting international criticism over the human rights issue constituted, therefore, a further incentive for the regime to attempt to introduce some semblance of normalcy in union life and some regularity in labor management relations.

However, the government tried to defuse the crisis in a way that would also reduce the influence of the existing union leaders who were causing them so much trouble. The authorities suddenly decided to call union elections, thereby appearing to concede to long-standing internal and international demands on this matter, but they did so in a manner explicitly designed to create a completely new set of leaders at the local level—leaders who were to be exclusively recognized as representatives of the rank-and-file. Similarly, although the new labor legislation drafted at the beginning of 1979 permitted the reemergence of union assemblies and granted the right to strike, it also laced the collective bargaining system and the right to strike with such limitations that workers would find themselves without a significant capacity to pressure employers through the legally established channels.

But the union elections produced labor leaders who turned out to be just as opposed to the regime as the previous set, and even if the new laws limited worker actions they nonetheless rekindled the participation of workers in union assemblies and affairs, allowing the unions to become an important forum for rank-and-file discussions of issues large and small, from demands to be made of employers to the government's economic policies. Let us examine the elections and the legislation more closely.

THE UNION ELECTIONS OF OCTOBER 1978

The call for union elections took all of the labor leaders completely by surprise. Issued on 27 October, it stated that the elections were to be held in just four days, on the thirty-first, in a total of 1,060 industrial and professional unions. In contrast to the usual practice in Chilean union elections, these were to be held without printed ballots containing the names of the various candidates proposed in the union assemblies (lists which workers were free to disregard in favor of write-ins if they wished). Instead, each worker was simply to vote for any of his or her peers, victory going to those who garnered the largest numbers of votes, providing that they had not held union office before and had no record of partisan political affiliation in the previous ten years. The surprise announcement, the speed with which the electoral process was supposed to take place, the absence of formal candidacies, and the prohibitions placed upon the winners were clearly designed to prevent the various ideological and partisan networks from placing their members in positions of leadership.

With these prohibitions, the government forced the formation of a completely new group of local union leaders. And yet, while the individuals may be different, labor leaders interviewed by the authors of this paper agreed in noting that the overwhelming majority of the new generation of leaders are opponents of the military government, that they retain partisan affiliations or at least identities and sympathies, and that the relative weight of the different ideological and political leanings among them remains mostly unchanged from the previous period. Indeed, soon after the elections the various labor "groups" began campaigns to contact the new leaders, with much success; Manuel Bustos, the president of the CNS, has repeatedly noted, for instance, that the organization's first national convention, held in 1980, claimed the participation of close to 600 leaders—all of them generated according to the regime's new rules.[20]

There is as yet no hard count of the breakdown of union leaders by group or by tendency. Such a count would, in any event, be difficult to obtain under the present circumstances, since it is obviously against the interests of the union leaders to produce it. But firm evidence does exist regarding pro- or anti-government votes in a limited set of very important enterprises and state offices. This breakdown can be examined in Table 7.3. Aside from the truly overwhelming level of support received by individuals who oppose the government, what is particularly noteworthy is that even in the state bank and in the television station, where there is a high level of political control and where workers are a relatively privileged group, the government cannot muster more than a third or a fifth of the vote, respectively, in the union elections.

TOWARD THE NEW "LABOR PLAN": THE BOYCOTT THREAT

Two weeks before calling for the union elections—on 19 October to be exact—the government had issued decrees dissolving seven large union

TABLE 7.3   Pro- or Anti-Government Votes of Newly Elected Union Leaders in Selected Enterprises, 1980

	Total votes	Pro- govern- ment	Anti- govern- ment	Independent
State bank	17,735	32.1%	67.9%	0.0%
Railways	6,295	0.0	98.0	2.0
Chuquicamata (industrial union)	3,112	0.0	100.0	0.0
Chuquicamata-Tocopilla (professional unions)	522	0.0	89.7	10.3
Valparaíso port	2,079	7.4	82.6	0.0
National Petroleum Enterprise	n.d.	4.5	81.8	13.6
Television channel 13	707	20.9	79.1	0.0

Source: Jaime Ruiz-Tagle, "Perspectivas del sindicalismo chileno," in *Mensaje,* no. 294 (November 1980): 617. The data were collected from reports given by the labor leaders themselves.

federations, declaring the illegality of all associations or groups of persons who pretend to represent workers before the state, and permitting the authorities to remove civil servants at will. The first two of these measures were clearly designed to undercut the influence of the existing labor leaders, particularly those associated with the so-called groups. It was largely for this reason that the summoning of union elections toward the end of the month was perceived so clearly and directly as a government ploy to displace the existing labor leaders by all those concerned.

This perception undoubtedly also prevailed in the ORIT, whose Executive Council, meeting in Lima on 26 November, called for a boycott of all merchandise moving to or from Chile, Nicaragua, and Cuba. The most important decision, that of whether or not U.S. longshoremen would participate in the boycott, was still to be made. Nonetheless, the Chilean government became greatly concerned that the AFL-CIO would request the port workers to do so. As a result, General Pinochet dismissed the minister of labor, Vasco Costa, who had followed his predecessor's intransigent policies, and replaced him with José Piñera, who was charged with the task of drafting new labor legislation and of attempting to convince the AFL-CIO not to press for the boycott. Since Piñera confronted both tasks simultaneously, this gave the appearance that the Chilean government had not only told American labor officials that it would lift the prohibitions over union actitities but had also negotiated with them over the content of the new legislation. This impression was reinforced by the fact that the AFL-CIO never called for an implementation of the boycott.

Whether or not there were specific negotiations over the content of the new labor laws remains unclear. There clearly was one face-to-face meeting between an official of the Chilean government, Sergio de Castro, and the late George Meany. However, Michael Boggs of the AFL-CIO's International Department, who was present at the meeting held in the early part of January 1979, says that the discussion did not cover matters of substance. Sergio de Castro simply gave the then president of the AFL-CIO a lecture on twentieth-century Chilean history. The intention of such a presentation was probably to gain Meany's sympathy by playing on his well-known anti-Communism; de Castro noted in essence that Chilean institutions had been infiltrated by Communists, that the military was obliged to intervene against Allende in order to save the country, and that the government was introducing a series of reforms to insure future democratic stability. Even if that was the intention, Meany was by no means impressed: slumped to the side of his chair, eyes closed, he seemingly paid no attention to what therefore turned out to be a lengthy monologue. When de Castro finished, Meany defiantly asked, "And?" meaning in fact "So what!" and the interview promptly came to an end.[21]

The threatened boycott was never called for reasons that had no relation to the de Castro interview. Despite Bogg's assertion that there wer negotiations between the AFL-CIO and the Chilean government over specifics of the new labor laws, José Piñera did in fact keep George Meany informed of his legislative projects through the very private channel of a mutual acquaintance who shuttled between the United States and Chile in his private airplane.[22] One can only conclude from this that Meany either felt that the new labor laws were satisfactory, or at least that they did not warrant calling for a boycott against the Chilean economy. In fact, Piñera could and probably did argue that his labor legislation has many points in common with that which exists in the southern United States, where "right-to-work" laws are common. Moreover, and again according to Michael Boggs, Meany insisted that the AFL-CIO would not join the boycott unless Chilean labor leaders publicly requested it, but the prominent Group of Ten leaders, with whom he also met in Washington, were unwilling to do so. It should be noted that as soon as a boycott became a possibility, the Chilean media castigated local labor leaders for their international connections, accusing them of lacking patriotism. The labor leaders therefore probably—and understandably—feared reprisals in Chile were they openly to request the boycott.[23] Relations between the AFL-CIO and the Group of Ten soured for a time after this episode. There was a widespread rumor in Chilean labor circles that a group of Chilean businessmen had paid a large sum of money to leaders of the U.S. longshoremen, to prevent them from carrying out the boycott. Whatever the facts surrounding the failure of the AFL-CIO to call for the boycott, what is evident is that the pressure the government felt from the threat of a boycott was the fundamental reason for its drafting new labor legislation.

THE NEW LABOR LEGISLATION

The bulk of Piñera's new labor legislation, or (as it is commonly known) "Labor Plan," appeared in a series of five decrees dated 29 June 1979.[24] This discussion will focus on its new provisions for labor organizations and for collective bargaining.

The Labor Plan does away with the previously existing distinction between industrial, professional, and agricultural unions. In their place, it calls for the establishment of four different types of unions: the plant-level union, the inter-enterprise union, the union of independent workers, and the union of construction workers. Only the first of these can engage in collective bargaining. The last one is designed primarily to function as a labor exchange.[25]

Affiliation with any union is made completely voluntary (which therefore formally ends the automatic membership which the industrial unions had), and no worker may belong to more than one union (which eliminates the occasional double affiliation of workers in industrial and professional unions). Only employees of the private sector and of state enterprises are permitted to unionize, the right to do so being again expressly prohibited for all public servants and military and police personnel.

A minimum of twenty-five workers are needed to form a plant-level union, provided that this number constitutes at least 10% of the total employed; in plants of fewer than twenty-five workers, eight can form a union provided they constitute more than 50% of the total number employed. Unions of occasionally employed workers require seventy-five members as a minimum. For the purpose of forming unions in the agricultural sector each property is considered as equaling one plant unless—in what was a later modification—a single owner works different but adjacent properties, in which case they are all considered one plant.

Unions are created by an assembly of workers; at the same time this assembly should elect its leadership and approve its statutes through a secret ballot in a process overseen by a nonunion witness, generally a labor inspector. To obtain official recognition, the new union must simply send to the nearest office of the labor inspectorate two copies of the minutes of the constituent assembly and of its statutes, both of which should be certified as authentic by a labor inspector, who then must make sure that they do not run counter to existing laws.

Depending on its size, a union must elect from three to seven members to its executive board; as was the case during the October 1978 elections, no formal candidacies are to be established beforehand, except that to be elected union leader, an individual must not be under indictment or have served a sentence of more than three years, must not be sanctioned with a temporary (three-year) prohibition of assuming a leadership position due to a prior violation of labor laws (such as that which prohibits anyone from interfering with the right to work), must know how to read and write, and must have at least two years of employment in the plant and six months of membership in the union. If a worker who is ineligible to be a union officer is chosen, the labor inspectorate must require a new election to fill the vacant seat within ninety days. Union leaders are elected for two years, may be reelected indefinitely, and cannot be fired from their jobs for up to six months after they cease to be leaders, unless they abet illegal acts or prevent workers from entering the place of work. The leaders are allowed four hours of the normal working week to tend to union business, which should be paid by the union itself.

Unions are to be financed exclusively through membership dues, the level of which should be decided by the assembly. All union members have a right to review the organization's accounts. The labor inspectorate itself has the "broadest right of inspection"[26] and can at the slightest suspicion of any irregularity condition the drawing of union funds from the bank on its prior authorization. Unions may join federations or confederations, whose purposes are confined in the law to mutual aid, cultural activities, and educational actitivies, and are explicitly forbidden from participating in collective bargaining.

The attributes and characteristics which the Labor Plan establishes for the plant-level union organizations are in many respects a continuation of the legal strictures laid down in the 1931 Labor Code for industrial unions. In both the earlier and the present regulations, these unions are given collective bargaining rights, leading to a highly decentralized union structure composed of many small units; in both, unions are supposed to renew their leadership periodically (formerly every year, now every two) through elections with a secret ballot overseen by an officially accepted witness; in both, unions are subjected to extensive controls of their statutes and finances by the labor inspectorate, although the new legislation does not specify the controls in as many details (insuring the survival of past practices) nor require unions automatically to request authorization to withdraw their funds from the bank; both charge the union assembly with an important voice in running the organization; and so on.

However, there are some very significant differences. The Labor Plan forces all unions that are authorized to bargain with employers to conform to a plant-level organization, whereas in the previous system both the professional and the agricultural unions could involve a broader set of workers. The new regulations also facilitate the process of forming a union and make union membership completely voluntary, with the latent intention of multiplying the number of unions at the workplace; the authorities claim that this change increases workers' freedom of choice. The mechanisms for the union election have also been changed. As already noted, there no longer are formal nominations of candidates in the union assembly; workers simply vote for whomever they wish. In addition, although workers still have to vote for several names (formerly five, now between two and five, depending on the size of the union board), they can no longer accumulate their votes; in other words, while it used to be the case that a worker could, say, by voting for one person give that individual the full five preferences, now a ballot with fewer names than positions to be filled represents a waste of votes. And most importantly, the unions no longer enjoy a legally prescribed participation in the profits of the enterprises, which leaves them only with the resources they can muster from dues collections.

Clearly, these changes are generally designed to weaken the unions, and in the case of the voting procedure reforms, to curtail the possibility of organized political networks to control the elections. However, some of the expected effects have not occurred. There has been no rush to form new unions as a result of the change to voluntary membership, which is not surprising where there used to be only one industrial union. Moreover, no matter what the electoral procedure, unless there is direct and forceful intervention by the authorities in the process, the organized groups at the plant level will prevail. In fact, the new electoral mechanisms can be said to favor these groups even more than was the case before, despite the impossibility of accumulating votes, since workers who are not in touch with any informal network will inevitably disperse their choices to a much larger degree than those who are.

The new provisions for collective bargaining go further and are more effective in weakening the unions.[27] The Labor Plan limits the areas over which workers and employers can bargain only to the various elements that affect workers' incomes. No agreements can be made, therefore, over matters which may limit the right of employers to "organize, direct, or administer the enterprise," or curtail their capacity to determine at will the size of work crews, the hiring of non-unionized labor, the cadence of production, the use of machinery, or the mechanisms for internal promotions. These provisions make it virtually impossible for unions to address questions of working conditions. Moreover, unions may not interfere in any matter relating to non-union workers or workers who are not allowed to negotiate, and may not interfere at any point with individual, direct negotiations between employers and workers, even if the latter are members of the union. In addition, collective bargaining may not refer to any measure which would oblige employers to pay workers for days lost on strike (including employer shares of social security and pension plans), and bargaining cannot lead to any provisions calling for employers to help pay for union activities or social funds (unless the latter are organized under different, officially recognized entities).

The collective bargaining process begins with the formal petition of a union for a new agreement. Such a petition can only be made within forty-five days before or forty days after the expiration of the existing agreement, if any. The employer may not refuse to accept the collective bargaining petition; the law stipulates that management must sign a copy of the union's request and send it within five days of its receipt to the labor inspection office. This formality initiates the negotiation mechanisms. (In order to stagger the beginning of the first round of collective bargaining after the military coup, the Labor Plan stipulated in a transitory article the dates within which the process could start. It did so by assigning the letters of the alphabet to different five-day periods spaced by a month, allowing negotiations in each of these only by those enterprises whose name begins with the corresponding letters; the resulting collective bargaining agreements were, in addition, peremptorily determined to last either for one or for two years with the same alphabetical assignment mechanism. Through this artifact, the authorities prevented the occurrence of collective bargaining in widespread waves, which could have aided workers by temporarily flooding the labor market with claims by organized groups.)

During the discussions between the parties, the employer is obliged to answer each union proposal within ten days with a counterproposal written in the format of a collective bargaining agreement. At any point both parties may request the services of a mediator, who merely suggests avenues of solution, or they may demand an arbitrator from an officially designated list; although the arbitrator's decisions are binding, those decisions may be appealed once to higher authorities. The honoraria and expenses of mediators and arbitrators must be shared equally by both parties to the negotiation, but an appeal in arbitration cases must be fully paid by the party that formulates it.

If at the expiration of the existing agreement there still is no new one ready, the union can call a strike if a majority of all its members agree through a secret vote to do so; the strike cannot begin until three working days after it has been approved. At any point during the strike 10% or more of all the unionized workers can request a new secret ballot to decide whether or not to call it off. If the strike involves more than 50% of the work force or if it results in an important reduction in production, employers have the right to lock out all workers. Employers may also hire non-unionized labor to replace those on strike. After thirty days of strike, workers may disaffiliate themselves from the union, and employers must rehire them, negotiating the terms of a new contract individually; the employer obligation to rehire workers in these cases is the only one of its kind to appear in the new legislation. After sixty days the striking workers will automatically be considered to have resigned their positions; at that point they would simply have to either accept the employer's latest offer—if it is still available to them—or look elsewhere for a job. The president of the republic may at any point decree a ninety-day period of resumption of work if the national economy or the health and safety of the population so require.

As can be readily appreciated, this legislation places great limitations on the ability of workers to negotiate on favorable terms with employers. The strictures governing strikes are designed above all to decrease the capacity of union leaders to mobilize the work force in collective actions, and to favor purely one-to-one negotiations between individual workers and employers. The Labor Plan attempts to prevent workers from insulating themselves from the leveling effects of the labor market; the purpose of collective bargaining is to permit the parties to agree to the wage levels that represent the going rates in the market, plus whatever value the workers may force employers to assign to their plant-specific training and experience.

The previous legislation on collective bargaining and on strikes also contained many limiting provisions and bogged the whole process of negotiations down in a field of legally prescribed procedures and deadlines; but it did not deny workers the right to negotiate over such basic aspects of working conditions as the rhythm of production, scheduling, manning, or promotions, and to hold out for compensation for time lost during labor conflicts. Moreover, it certainly had no specific clauses allowing employers to hire strikebreakers; it did not provide incentives for workers to disaffiliate from the unions with provisions such as an obligatory reinstatement in the job for those who leave the union after thirty days of strike; and it did not predetermine, as the Labor Plan does, that strikes should not last longer than sixty days lest workers lose their jobs altogether. In no area of economic life is the association between the attempt to produce a fully free market (in this case, the labor market) and the authoritarian imposition of norms and regulations by the state—the link, in other words, between liberal capitalism and the Chilean dictatorship—more apparent than here.

AMENDMENTS TO THE LABOR PLAN AND THEIR EFFECTS

Further legislative limitations on workers' collective bargaining rights and capacity were enacted after Piñera left office in late 1980. In particular, law 18,018 of 14 August 1981 eliminated virtually all of the special benefits which various categories of workers had won through legislation over a period of several decades, and authorized employers to fire at any one time as many workers as they wished (mass firings were previously prohibited without government approval) without having to furnish any explanations whatsoever.[28] Law 18,032, which completely reorganized the ports, eliminated the rights of longshoremen and other relevant unions to control job assignments, forcing these workers, who for decades have had special labor relations practices and legislation, into the framework of the Labor Plan.[29]

But the most devastating of these new laws has been law 18,134 of June 1982.[30] It eliminated all automatic increases in wages and salaries after a 10% increase in the cost of living index for workers benefiting from this provision. Moreover, it eliminated the guarantee established in the Labor Plan that each collective bargaining process began from the minimum base established by the wages and benefits of the expiring contract. This guarantee was implicit in the Labor Plan, since at any point during their negotiations with the employers workers could demand the extension of the previous contract, with its wage and benefit levels adjusted to compensate for the increase in the cost of living index. The new law established a new minimum (or so-called "floor"): the wages and benefits which existed on 6 June 1979 or the levels established in the first contract for those employed after that date (plus cost of living increases for all). Therefore, law 18,134 denied workers the possibility of continuing to receive the real wage increases they had obtained during the first two rounds of collective bargaining after the application of the Labor Plan, increases which averaged approximately 14% for all unionized workers.[31] Consequently, the new law gave employers the possibility of reducing wages and benefits, while a continuation of the Labor Plan provisions would have allowed workers to maintain the real gains they had made. Finally, law 18,134 also diminished significantly the value of indemnities for termination of employment; workers were entitled to receive one month's salary for each year on the job, but the new provisions froze these values to 1979 levels (plus the cost of living adjustment).

The effects of the application of the Labor Plan were mixed during its first years. On the one hand, as we have seen, workers appear to have gained higher real wages, but it is not clear whether these exceeded possible increases in productivity, and in any event, the higher wages were still below the real levels reached before the military coup. The wage increases were granted without workers resorting to strikes, since of the 3,654 negotiations which occurred between 1979 and 1981, there were only 102 strikes.[32] In other words, it is highly probable that the rise in wages was a result of an increase in economic activity rather than of workers' pressures on employers, pressures which, given the Labor Plan's provisions, workers could hardly exert effectively. The peculiar sequence of economic expansion until 1981 followed by a sharp 14.3% drop in the GNP during 1982 therefore revealed an advantage of the Labor Plan for workers regardless of their capacity to pressure employers: the legislation permitted a freezing of the higher wage and benefit levels of the expansionary period, carrying them over to the recession. Hence, the government enacted law 18,134, thereby eliminating one advantage which the legislation unwittingly had for workers.

The Labor Plan also permitted the resurgence of participation by rank-and-file workers in union affairs. The frequent union assemblies turned into channels for the expression of workers' opinions over a broad range of local and national questions. Consequently, there has been not only a reactivation of local leaderships (which had already occurred, as we indicated, prior to the Labor Plan), but also of the rank-and-file. The few strikes that have occurred were promoted by rank-and-file majorities (given the labor legislation, it could not be otherwise), and it appears that many were carried out more as a means to express generalized discontent than to obtain a better contract. This expressive use of the strike was favored by the fact that each one was considered a newsworthy item.

Finally, although the Labor Plan led to a reconstitution of the unions as union leaders sought to adjust their organizations to the new legal framework, it did not lead to a significant fragmentation of unionism. In the few instances where more unions have been created than existed previously, they have nonetheless decided to negotiate together. Moreover, since the legislation restricts the benefits of collective bargaining to those who are members of the negotiating unions (in contrast to legislations in other countries, such as France, which extends collective bargaining agreements to the whole labor force in the respective enterprise or even industrial branch), the Labor Plan has inadvertently raised the cost of nonunionization. It therefore prevents free ridership among workers to a certain degree; the benefits of unionism can only be obtained if its costs are assumed.[33] This and the inevitable peer pressures which exist in such situations explain the success of the reunionization drive which the Labor Plan imposed on the labor movement. According to a 1980 survey by the Sociedad de Fomento Fabril, an association of industrialists, 85.61% of the workers in the sample preferred unionization. There have even been cases in which workers have taken the initiative to form a union in order to be able to negotiate with employers.

The Development of Generalized Protests against the Regime

Beginning in May 1983, there have been national protests against the military regime practically every month. Occasionally these protests have been accompanied by calls for partial or general strikes and have included street demonstrations, public gatherings, marches, and, during the evening hours, pot banging as well as barricades in the lower-class areas. Hundreds of thousands have participated in one way or another in these manifestations of opposition to the government. More than one hundred deaths have been registered as a result of police and military repression of the protests. Few governments have faced such generalized and widespread expressions of opposition.

The inception of these generalized protests is linked directly to decisions taken by the labor movement leadership. The spark that lit the fire was law 18,134. Its terms were discussed in a convention of the Confederation of Copper Workers (CTC), which is undoubtedly the most important union organization in Chile, at the end of July 1982. The convention decided to demand that the government repeal the law, threatening a general strike in the copper mines if it did not do so.

Following its characteristic attitude of not bowing to pressures, the government let the law stand. At the next CTC convention, in April 1983, the delegates decided that they had no alternative, in light of their previous agreement, but to follow up on their threat to call a strike. They chose to call it for 11 May, selecting that day since it corresponded to that of the military coup in September 1973.

Once the date had been decided, other labor organizations began to join the strike call of the copper workers. However, as the day for the strike approached, the labor leaders reconsidered the advisability of staging it at a moment at which unemployment was at a record 32% level (including the individuals participating in minimum employment programs run by the government). Moreover, a general strike had never been attempted in the decade of military government and had very rarely been successful in Chile's history; the labor leaders were therefore uncertain of the response. Consequently, almost at the last minute, the labor leaders decided to change the course of the movement from a strike to a "protest," calling for the participation of all popular organizations and even of the public at large.

The objectives of the movement were generalized to appeal to all sectors, the principal one being a call for the return to democracy. The protest would be carried out by abstaining, if at all possible, from using public transportation, not sending children to school, not buying anything, working slowly or taking a sick day off, and turning the lights off while banging pots and pans from eight to ten o'clock in the evening. The tactic of banging pots and pans had first been used in Chile by opponents of Salvador Allende's government, and had already been used against the military regime in the Chuquicamata copper mines in 1977.

The success of the day of protest greatly exceeded the labor leaders' most optimistic expectations. They had thought that the movement would be felt basically in the mining camps and in the working-class neighborhoods of major cities. However, the decrease in the use of public transportation, the low level of school attendance, the decline in retail sales, the demonstrations by university students, and the widespread banging of pots all indicated a massive participation in the protest activities. The labor movement therefore unexpectedly gave direction to a generalized desire to manifest publicly an opposition to the military regime from the most varied quarters of the society. Authoritarian governments have a great capacity to atomize the population, since they abrogate the institutions (such as elections and normal party activities) that permit the articulation of demands; what occurred in Chile beginning on 11 May 1983 was the almost unexpected discovery of a strategy for generalized and concerted mobilization against the government that overcame in part that fragmentation.

The success of the first protest led to new movement toward the unification of the labor movement. Thus, on 1 June the National Workers' Command (CNT) was formed in order to bring together all the labor and professional organizations that wished to participate in planning new days of protest. The CNT did not substitute the existing "groups," but became an on-going meeting ground for the different groups to coordinate protests against the government and to demand democratization. The Confederation of Copper Workers became part of the CNT as if it were one more labor group, and its youthful president, Rodolfo Sequel, has also been the CNT's most characteristic leader.

The CNT called for a second national protest on 12 June 1983. It attracted even more participation than the first one, and its success led the labor leaders finally to decide to call a national strike beginning 29 June. Practically all the labor associations in the country joined the call for the strike, although the truckers, having reached a favorable agreement with the government just days before the strike was to take place, withdrew from it. The strike was, generally speaking, a failure. It was effective principally in the copper mines, where the government countered by firing numerous striking miners. The copper leaders spent the next months requesting the authorities to rehire the fired miners, but to no avail. Given this disheartening turn of events, the labor leaders turned to the political party leaderships and asked them to take over the task of calling for new days of national protest. The labor movement adhered to these calls, but assumed a secondary role in initiating them. However, by the end of 1983 the labor leaders once again took over the principal role in calling for national protests.

As long as the unity and repressive capacity of the armed forces is maintained, it is very improbable that these protests, however widespread, will in themselves put an end to the dictatorship. Authoritarian regimes in the last analysis do not require civil support to retain power. And yet the constant agitation produced by the protests may render civil society ungovernable, leading both Chilean and foreign observers to think that the government cannot elaborate and carry out long-term policies. This perception of instability surrounding the country can lead to a further drop in long-term investments by local and foreign capital, seriously undermining the prospects for future economic growth. Violence will no doubt also increase.[34]

General Conclusions

1. Four phases may be distinguished in the relations between the military government and the labor movement. During the initial phase, the labor movement was deeply divided, and there was a high level of repression of the left while the nonleftist leadership sectors held a dialogue with the government. The second phase, which began with the change in the labor ministry from Díaz to Fernández, saw the centrist labor leaders break off their dialogue and assume an opposition posture. They were led to this new attitude by the instransigence and inflexibility of the government itself, which did not allow them to pressure it into accepting any worker demands. As a result, there was an increasing convergence between the different ideological and political strands in the labor movement as they joined forces in opposition to the military regime. However, toward the end of this phase the divisions reappeared through the creation of different labor "groups." The third phase began as the government changed its strategy vis-à-vis the labor movement in response to internal and international pressures. It called for new union elections and enacted new labor legislation which permitted a resurgence of rank-and-file participation in unionism but did not permit unions to exert effective pressures on employers. Each labor group began a campaign to reach out to the new union leaders, competing to gain their allegiance, but there was a general consensus over rejecting the content of the new labor legislation and its subsequent modifications. The fourth phase began as the labor movement called for national protests against the government. It has been characterized by

considerable unity of action among different labor groups, and by massive mobilizations against the regime, which has responded with ever-increasing repression.

2. The relations between the Pinochet government and the labor movement will inevitably continue to be characterized by tension and confrontation, for a return to the early years of a dialogue with significant segments of the worker leadership is by now not even remotely possible. Moreover, since the Chilean labor movement has always been characterized, overall, by a close identification of leaders with the sentiments and demands of rank-and-file workers, there is no chance that the government will be able to build a subservient cadre of leaders with more than a minimal following even if it attempted to do so. The government will therefore remain on a labor containment course which relies on curtailing the bargaining capability of worker organizations and occasionally using high-handed measures to repress labor leaders. And the labor movement will try to express itself as best it can by using the spaces the regime leaves open to it and by developing new forms of protest.

3. As occurs most often under authoritarian regimes, the labor movement has taken a central place in the overall constellation of oppositions to the military regime. All authoritarian regimes are by definition ones which eliminate the institutions through which political parties normally exert their influence in a democracy (particularly independent legislatures and free, regularly scheduled, competitive elections), which means that the organizations of civil society (referring here to what can be called the *Zivilgesellschaft* rather than to Marx's *bürgerliche Gesellschaft*) can no longer use party channels as one of their means to protect or further their interests. As a result, they must do so by relying on their own resources, which can be identified as a capacity to mobilize their members towards concerted goals and an ability to control important societal institutions. Civil organizations differ in terms of their ability to muster these resources; the labor movement, however, is relatively powerful on both counts, since on the one hand it groups individuals on the basis of a strong common interest reaffirmed most often by a sense of shared identity and tradition of struggle, and on the other it is potentially able to disrupt both production at the workplace and peace in the streets. Questions of labor policy are therefore always among the most delicate for authoritarian regimes, and in one way or another all must attempt to generate institutional mechanisms in order to try to contain labor conflict by permitting its partial expression. This opens officially sanctioned spaces which labor leaders can then occupy and converts those leaders into central actors in the relatively impotent oppositions to these regimes.

Since political parties have little to offer unions in the authoritarian setting (aside from the assistance of a few professionals, or some militants for solidarity campaigns with striking workers, etc.), and since they are prime targets for repression by the regime, the parties which normally associate with the unions generally cease to exercise any significant directive influence over the labor movement as a whole. Labor leaders will therefore stress, and they have repeatedly done so in Chile, the independence of their organizations from the parties. This does not mean that authoritarian regimes can enduringly transform the characteristics of labor movements where, as in Chile, they were distinguished by a particularly strong connection between parties and unions. The party activists who are workers will immerse themselves in labor activities as a means of retaining the parties' touch with mass bases, and the top party leaders recognizing the importance of a presence in the organizations of civil society, will publicly (if possible) or clandestinely (in any case) support any demands made by its militants for the unions—even those they would not accept were they in government. Militants with party affiliations or clear-cut sympathies will also invariably end up with most positions of union leadership. This is because they are tied to a network that provides them, within the union, with an organized nucleus which constitutes an important resource during the elections as well as for controlling union assemblies and, from without, with support by lawyers, economists, and engineers; the latter can give union leaders the necessary assistance to make their leadership more effective at virtually no cost. Moreover, once unions are traversed by different political tendencies, there is virtually no way that an "independent" group can take over the field. This is due to the fact that the independents must in every case establish their bid for leadership by differentiating themselves from the rest of the leaders, and they can do this only by adopting in part the very political and ideological criteria they profess to avoid. In the end, therefore, successful independents become only one more politically identifiable tendency within unionism, confirming thereby the importance of partisan and ideological identifications.

Finally, it should be noted that the relationship between unions and parties in the labor movement will in the end reassert itself if the nation moves back to an enduring democratic regime. The parties in this case would recover their ability to channel—and therefore also to control, however partially—the demands of the organizations of civil society with which they associate. The links between parties and the labor movement in authoritarian situations therefore recede into the background only reassert themselves when the moment is ripe, if, to repeat, they were strong to begin with.

4. Authoritarian regimes can differ greatly in the specifics of their treatment of labor unions. Some—particularly those tinged with populist tendencies—can, in fact, be quite receptive to labor demands, and can

develop good relationships with labor leaders. The perceptions which rank-and-file workers and their leaders have of the regime and of its possible democratic alternative are therefore to a large extent determined by the peculiar nature of the regime itself, and not necessarily by positions of principle.

The Chilean authoritarian regime must certainly be classified as one of the most hostile to the labor movement. Its economic and social policies have meant a drop in real wages, a process of deindustrialization with a consequent increase in unemployment, a limitation of social security bene-fits, a decrease in educational opportunities, a decline in access to health services, a sharp increase in repression, and severe limitations on the capacity of labor organizations to pressure employers and the state. Labor leaders therefore look primarily to a redemocratization of the political sys-tem as the ultimate solution to redress the sharply regressive tendencies that have been imposed by authoritarian rule. Therefore, while a crisis of the authoritarian regime may provoke a sharp efflorescence of labor con-flict as an expression of discontent and opposition, the possibility of a transition to democracy should find such support among labor leaders and even rank-and-file workers that they should be willing to restrain many of their less pressing demands for the sake of insuring that transition. This should give some breathing space to the political elites who oversee such a transition, when and if its time comes.

Notes

A first version of this chapter was written by Manuel Barrera for presentation at the Woodrow Wilson International Center for Scholars conference, "Six Years of Military Rule in Chile," whose papers formed the basis for this book. This version was redrafted and updated by Samuel Valenzuela. Manuel Bar-rera wishes to express his appreciation for the assistance of the members of his research team, Mario Albuquerque and Teresita Selamé, and J. Samuel Valen-zuela his gratitude to José Buscaglia for his aid in locating additional materials. Our names are listed alphabetically.

1. There are a few labor leaders who remain generally supportive of the government. Although they are especially visible, since the authorities make every effort to bolster their position by allowing them frequent access to and coverage by national television, they in fact have an insignificant following in the labor movement. This paper will not discuss these leaders, as it is con-cerned with the development of the labor movement opposition to the regime, a stance which currently encompasses virtually all the labor movement's dis-parate sectors.

2. For a discussion of the period between 1938 and 1970, see Manuel Barrera, *Desarrollo económico y sindicalismo en Chile,* 1938–1970 (Santiago: VECTOR, Centro de Estudios Económicos y Sociales, 1979). A brief overview of

Chilean labor movement history and organizational characteristics may also be found in J. Samuel Valenzuela, "The Chilean Labor Movement: The Institutionalization of Conflict," in Arturo Valenzuela and J. Samuel Valenzuela, eds., *Chile: Politics and Society* (New Brunswick, N.J.: Transaction Books, 1976).

3. These controls, which were mainly over union finances and statutes, are discussed in Valenzuela, "The Chilean Labor Movement."

4. Only legal unions were allowed to strike, and their strikes were classified as legal only if all the complicated procedures laid out in the Labor Code for labor management negotiations had been followed. This meant in practice that workers could strike only once a year at the most (in other words, only after the previously negotiated contract had expired); if a union struck in order to force the employer to abide by some term in the collective contract, that action was still classified as illegal. Between 1961 and 1973 fully 90.7% of all workers on strike participated in strikes which were considered illegal (percentage calculated from statistics of the Departamento de Relaciones del Trabajo y Desarrollo Organizacional of the University of Chile's Facultad de Economía y Administración).

5. The resulting ILO report is one of the basic sources of information on the repression of union leaders and organizations following the 1973 military coup. See Organización Mundial del Trabajo, *La situación sindical en Chile: Informe de la Comisión de Investigación y de Conciliación en Materia de Libertad Sindical* (Genève: O.I.T., 1975). The final report also appears in *Chile-América*, nos. 8–9 (July 1975).

6. See *Ercilla*, 21–27 September 1977, p. 21, for a complete listing of these committees and the status of their activities.

7. Ibid., p. 30

8. Alejandro González, "La situación del movimiento sindical en Chile." *Mensaje*, no. 248 (May 1976): 179.

9. See Dirección del Trabajo, *Memorias Anuales, 1973* on.

10. See Carlos Clavel, "Política de remuneraciones," in *Comentarios sobre la situación económica, segundo semestre de 1979* (Santiago: Departamento de Economía, Universidad de Chile, 1980), table 1. The April 1970 figures are taken as a base (100) for calculating the index, which in 1973 stood at 71.9, in 1974 at 68, in 1976 at 70.8, in 1977 at 88.9, and in 1978 and 1979 recovering to surpass slightly the 1970 level. These figures use the official rate of inflation, and therefore they underestimate the drop in real incomes. For a critical analysis of the official price index see René Cortázar and Jorge Marshall, "Indice de precios al consumidor en Chile, 1970–1978," *Colección Estudios CIEPLAN*, no. 4 (November 1980).

11. The Díaz Ministry also created the Plan de Empleo Mínimo, a program providing work for unemployed workers in exchange for a minimal salary from the government. This program is the only one of the Díaz reforms to continue to this day. The other ones were either never adopted by the government, or were never implemented; similarly, a new Díaz law governing the operation of worker cooperatives was practically made moot by their failure

given the government's economic policy. The Social Statute for Enterprises, still on the books, can be consulted in República de Chile, *Estatuto social de la empresa* (Santiago: Instituto de Estudios Financieros y del Trabajo, Diltec Editores, n.d.), an edition which also includes all of the relevant additional regulations by the Labor Ministry; the Statue for Worker Occupational Training appeared in *el Mercurio*, 24 January 1975, p 28; the Preliminary Proposal for Labor Code Reforms in *El Mercurio*, 3 May 1975, pp. 31–36; and the Preliminary Statute for reforming the Social Security System in *El Mercurio*, 8 November 1975, as a separate undated and unpaginated section.

12. It should be noted that the Díaz program reflected a different, more corporatist, and slightly populist conception of Chile's future institutional blueprint which was prevalent at the time in the air force, Díaz's service. These differences created tensions within the government and military circles; *Latin America* 10 (8 October 1976): 309, notes that Díaz was replaced for "being too soft on the unions" and that since assuming office Sergio Fernández had "refused to consult union leaders or even talk to them." The disagreements culminated in sharp tensions within the military junta which led to the forced removal of Air Force Commander Gustavo Leigh from the junta on 24 July 1978. For Leigh's version of these events as well as for a sense of his more populist conceptions of government, see the interview by Florencia Varas, *Gustavo Leigh: El general disidente* (Santiago: Editorial Aconcagua, 1979), a book that came out in six editions in the space of two months given the high demand for its rarely found view of inner machinations of the military government.

13. The letter appears in Instituto Latinoamericano de Doctrina y Estudios Sociales (ILADES), *Problemas Laborales*, no. 18 (May–June 1976).

14. A report on this exchange of letters may be seen in *Latin America* 10 (8 October 1976): 309.

15. See *Chile-América*, nos. 35–36 (October 1977): 134–41 for the text of the letter and for a listing of all the signatory organizations, and p. 132 for the Ríos quote.

16. *El Mercurio*, in an article written by Blanca Arthur and published 16 August 1981, purports to explain the origins of the CNS as the result of pressures by the AFL-CIO on the Group of Ten. Michael Boggs, who heads the Latin American section of the AFL-CIO's International Department, flatly denied this in an interview conducted on 30 June 1982. It should be noted, in addition, that the International Confederation of Free Trade Unions as well as its Inter-American Regional Labor Organization, in which the AFL-CIO plays a leading role, have relations with both the Group of Ten and the CNS.

17. The text of this declaration can be consulted in *Chile-América*, nos. 54–55 (June 1979): 35–41.

18. Quoted in Francisco Zapata, "Las relaciones entre la junta militar y los trabajadores chilenos, 1973–1978," *Foro Internacional* 20, no. (1979) 214. This paper contains a detailed account of the labor protests in the copper mines (pp. 208–214), from which the description presented here is mostly drawn. Carlos

Ogalde, one of the union leaders of the Chuquicamata mine who was also fired as a result of the *presión de las viandas* won reinstatement to his position after a year of litigation in the courts.

19. This point was forcefully made by Michael Boggs, of the AFL-CIO's International Department. He noted that a boycott by the ORIT would not have been very effective unless the American longshoremen joined in, given the importance of Chilean trade to the United States, especially during the Northern Hemisphere's winter, when Chile exports large quantities of fruit to U.S. ports. Interview of 30 June 1982.

20. See, for one example of this observation, the interview with Bustos in *Análisis* 4 (August 1981): 15. Bustos made this point emphatically because at the time of the interview he was being prosecuted by the government for unlawfully claiming worker representation; the convention had reelected him president of the CNS.

The convention was held at Punta de Tralca, a conference center owned by the Catholic church, which has supported the labor movement's organizing efforts throughout the country and often allows the movement to use its buildings and offices for meetings.

The Punta de Tralca meeting discussed and approved a so-called "Pliego de Chile," which called for the repeal of the government's labor legislation, for revisions of the regime's educational, social security, health, Indian, and foreign policies, and even demanded that the military return to the barracks. It also called on the opposition as a whole to develop a national accord to confront the regime. Bustos subsequently attempted to present the document to Pinochet, who refused to see him. He and another top leader of the CNS, Alamiro Guzmán, were then arrested. The term *pliego*, or writ, is generally used to refer to the document in which unions write their demands at the beginning of a round of negotiations with employers.

21. Interview with Michael Boggs, 30 June 1982.

22. This information comes from an interview with José Piñera conducted in Santiago on 7 July 1983. The mutual acquaintance was Peter Grace, of W. R. Grace & Co.

23. The brutal assassination of Tucapel Jiménez, one of the Group of Ten's prominent figures, in March 1982 served to show that Chilean labor leaders still risk even loss of life. Shortly before his death, Jiménez had issued a very strong statement condemning the government's policies. As of this writing, the crime has not been resolved by the courts.

24. These decrees as well as a series of complementary measures were printed in a popular edition under the title of *Leyes laborales* (Santiago: Empresa Periodística "Aquí Está", 1979).

25. This discussion is based on Decree Law 2,756, entitled "Union Organizations," of 29 June 1979.

26. Ibid., art. 50.

27. Decree Law 2,758, entitled "Collective Bargaining," of 29 June 1979.

28. For a discussion of and commentaries on this law see *Hoy*, 26 August–1 September 1981, pp. 27–33. Eduardo Ríos, the president of the UDT, says in a

column written for this issue of the magazine that "more than the Labor Plan, the law 18,018 will be a monument to the abuse of power." Among a lengthy list of workers affected by this law are restaurant waiters, who no longer can expect to receive a minimum 10% gratuity.

29. For a commentary by Eduardo Ríos, who is a leader of the port workers' federation, see *How*, 7–13 October 1982.

30. For an analysis of its provisions, see *Análisis* 5 (July 1982): 11–13.

31. This figure was calculated by the Confederation of Copper Workers, and we have drawn it from an internal circulation memorandum. Samuel Valenzuela expresses his appreciation to Luis Eduardo Thayer, a lawyer for the confederation, for this information.

32. This information has been obtained by Manuel Barrera's research team from the press clipping service of Library of Congress in Santiago.

33. On the free rider question see Mancur Olson, *The Logic of Collective Action: Public Goods and the Theory of Groups* (Cambridge: Harvard University Press, 1965).

34. As this book goes to press, the government has declared a state of siege, closed opposition news outlets and censored the remaining ones, and conducted large-scale search operations in lower-class sections of Santiago where barricades had become a virtually nightly occurrence. The government has therefore decided to try to end the protest movements with an increase in repression. While it may succeed in stifling the movement in the short term, such measures only prevent the search for lasting solutions to Chile's political crisis.

Old Allies, New Enemies: The Catholic Church as Opposition to Military Rule in Chile, 1973-1979

Brian H. Smith

The Catholic church and the military in Latin America have traditionally acted on the margins of the political system. While both possess important symbolic and institutional resources and have intervened decisively at moments of crisis, except in a few cases neither has exercised a sustained central role in determining the course of political and economic events in any Latin American country historically.

Moreover, both the church and the military have long been allies in regard to some mutually shared concerns, antipathies, and internal organizational dynamics. Both have preferred order, stability, and harmony among social classes, and both have valued the importance of religious legitimation for the state. Each had long-standing fears of radical political movements, especially those with socialist or Marxist orientations. Each prized tradition, discipline, hierarchical control, and institutional autonomy within its respective organization.

Since the mid-1960s, however, each has come to play a more active and central role in many Latin American societies. In some instances this has resulted from an attempt by the church and the military to catch up with rapidly changing events and defend their respective institutional interests. In others it has occurred semi-reluctantly, with each institution drawn into the political arena as a surrogate for other social organizations that have been unable to manage severe societal disruptions.

Vatican II (1962–65) legitimized a more socially active role for contemporary Catholicism, partially as an adaptive strategy to regain lost influence. Medellín (1968) and Puebla (1979) both interpreted this mandate as requiring a close identification by the Latin American church with the needs of the poor. Throughout the 1960s the growing attraction of both Marxism and Protestantism among workers and peasants, a major influx of socially committed clergy and religious from abroad, and the inauguration of social and economic reforms by democratic governments all provided an added stimulus for greater church involvement in societal affairs.[1] In the

1970s severe political and economic repression in many Latin American countries forced the church (as an agent of last resort) to undertake a whole series of humanitarian tasks previously performed by democratic governments, political parties, and labor unions.[2]

Since the mid-1960s the military have also intervened in more systematic and sustained fashion to take control of the state in several Latin American countries. In some cases (Brazil, Peru) this has been due in large part to a new type of training and professionalization that has convinced the military that they better than the civilians can effectively guide the process of development. In other instances (Chile, Argentina, Uruguay) this has resulted from prolonged social and economic disruptions and domestic violence which have led the armed forces to consider themselves the last resort to restore stability. In situations where the military have long played a dominant role in government (Paraguay, prerevolutionary Nicaragua, El Salvador, Guatemala) growing opposition to authoritarian rule in the 1970s precipitated a deepening of their control of the state apparatus.

Regardless of the causes or the motivations, this more active and sustained role in the public domain taken by the church and the military has brought these two traditional allies into direct conflict. Some bishops have denounces abuses of coercive power against real or perceived dissidents, and have publicly criticized what they consider to be disproportionate social and economic costs levied on peasants and workers under military rule. Lower clergy, religious, and lay leaders have become active on the human rights front, offering assistance to many of the opponents of military governments.

The military in many Latin American countries have claimed that the hierarchy is meddling in politics. They also have charged that lower church echelons have been infiltrated by Marxists and are acting as havens for dissidents committed to insurrection. The armed forces in several of these countries maintain a close surveillance on church activities, and in some instances have placed restrictions on church-sponsored programs for reasons of national security.

Suddenly two old allies are at odds with one another. Each has undergone significant changes on behalf of what it believes to be in its own best interest and in the interest of society at large. Each feels betrayed by the other and has taken steps to check the other's new active role in the political arena.

While there has been a significant amount of research on the causes and impact of the expanded role of the military in Latin America since the mid-1960s,[3] thus far there has not been sufficient analysis by social scientists on the new function of the church as counterforce to the armed forces. Some popular reporting (and the statements by some Latin American military leaders) would give the impression that the church is becoming a radical force and a cohesive and formidable foe of military regimes;[4] the reality is far more complex, however. In no Latin American country did the church initially oppose military overthrow of civilian governments in the 1960s and 1970s, and at the official level it has only gradually (and sometimes inconsistently) moved to a position of critical opposition.

Furthermore, divisions exist within the hierarchy and between different social classes of Catholics concerning the proper stance of the church toward the military. The institution in almost every country is badly understaffed and financially weak, which places restrictions on its freedom of action and choice. Its national and international leaders are primarily concerned with keeping the church's energies focused on its religious mission, and will sacrifice other objectives to keep this viable in all types of societies. All of these institutional factors place limitations on the church's capacities as a force of political opposition to military regimes.

What is needed, therefore, is more systematic probing of the causes and the extent of the church's disagreements with military governments and the effectiveness of the strategies it has employed at different levels to pursue its new objectives. For example, under what conditions does a national hierarchy act as a unified moral force to withhold legitimacy from a military government? When a coherent prophetic stance is taken by bishops, what impact does this have on the politics of a military regime? How effectively (and at what costs) can church organizations act as surrogates for political participation and the fulfillment of basic needs when other social structures have been co-opted or suppresed by the military? What is the impact on the church's multiclass membership allegiances when it identifies closely with groups that are marginalized by military governments—workers, peasants, intellectuals, political dissidents? Are international support mechanisms a help or a hindrance to local churches confronting strongly nationalistic military regimes?

Chile offers rich experience with which to explore all of these questions and issues. For a long time both the Catholic church and the military played minor roles in determining the outcome of political and economic events. Each has been thrust into the center of the public domain since Allende's downfall in 1973—the military as government, the church as its former ally turned into a locus of opposition.

To provide a more thorough understanding of the church than normally appears in popular reporting, I shall focus on two different time periods (before 1975 and after 1975) and four different elements in the complex organizations of the church. These are (1) its moral and legitimating influence, exercised primarily by the hierarchy through public statements; (2) its layered institutional network, maintained by lower clergy, religious women, and lay leaders, which acts as a buffer against the state; (3) its transnational linkages, which give it access to foreign sources of personnel, money, and materials; and (4) its multiclass membership allegiances, and how these have shifted since the coup.

Church and Military in Chile Between September 1973 and December 1975

During the first two years of military rule in Chile, the different levels of the church did not act in tandem to oppose the regime. The Episcopal conference granted cautious but definite legitimacy to the new government as soon as it came to power. The conference criticized from time to time thereafter what it considered to be unavoidable and transitory abuses of power, and several bishops individually spoke out in clear support for the junta and its policies.

At lower levels of the church new structures were formed and older ones expanded to offer assistance to those suffering the brunt of repression. This was made possible by large amounts of international financial and material support (including aid from Protestant churches in Europe and the United States). The church also attracted many new adherents from among the lower and middle classes.

Reactions to these new developments at the structural and behavioral levels of the church by upper-income Catholics were negative, and sometimes severely vituperative. The military also exerted strong pressures on the new programs offered by the church, and capitalized on its dependency on the state and on foreign sources of support to limit its freedom of action.

THE BISHOPS

Two days after the coup Cardinal Silva and the Permanent Committee of the Episcopal Conference issued a public declaration decrying the bloodshed, and called for moderation by the military and respect for previous social gains by the poor. These bishops, however, also asked that citizens cooperate with the regime in restoring order, and expressed trust in the prudence and patriotism of the armed forces.[5]

Five days after the coup, at the annual ecumenical service commemorating national independence, the cardinal prayed for those who lost their lives, but explicitly offered the church's "impartial collaboration to those who at difficult times have taken upon their shoulders the very heavy responsibility of guiding our destiny."[6]

On 28 September, after the military regime had been recognized by several Western governments (including the United States), the Permanent Committee of the Episcopal Conference met with the four members of the junta. In return for guarantees that the church's religious ministries would continue unimpaired and an invitation to collaborate in the "work of reconstruction," the bishops expressed their "respect for the armed forces and the police" and thanked them for the "deference which the new authorities have extended to the bishops in every part of the country."[7]

The 28 September declaration of the Permanent Committee of the Episcopate thus reflected the desire of official leaders to preserve the church's freedom and flexibility of action. In exchange for this guarantee, both the cardinal and the Permanent Committee rejected the option of clear and specific denunciation of abuses of power. They feared strong repressive measures against the organizational network of the church (similar to those taken against other major social institutions) which would restrict its pastoral works and prevent the inauguration of humanitarian programs to assist the persecuted. As we shall see in the next section, this cautious approach by the bishops at the symbolic or moral level of the church in the aftermath of the coup provided the conditions of possibility for those at the lower institutional level to begin immediately a whole range of programs in defense of human rights.

Another decisive factor influencing this ambiguous position of the bishops was the sense of relief that the disruption of the final months of the Allende period was over. During my interviews with the bishops in 1975, the overwhelming majority (24 out of 27) indicated that they believed the coup was necessary. A majority of priests, nuns, and lay leaders shared this opinion as well.[8]

Although relations between the church and the Popular Unity government were correct, the bishops and many lower leaders in the church harbored private fears of Marxism and were pleased with the military intervention.[9] This helps explain the official church's openness to the military and the reluctance on the part of many bishops to believe how bad the initial repression actually was.

The final factor which accounted for initial ambivalence by the Episcopal Conference as a whole was the outspoken support given to the junta by several bishops acting on their own. Bishop Francisco Valdés of Osorno offered a public prayer of thanksgiving on the day of the coup, equating the Popular Unity years with darkness and sin and explicitly identifying the new regime with an era of light and salvation.[10] A month later Archbishop Emilio Tagle of Valparaíso stated on television that the armed forces "have taken steps to save the country from falling irrevocably under the power of Marxism." He also remarked that "like a sick person freed from death by a skillful operation, the country has lost some blood, suffered some pains and has some wounds which need to be healed."[11] Several months later, in March 1974, Bishop Augusto Salinas of Linares in a press interview described the coup as a just rebellion against an illegitimate government, and praised the armed forces and police for carrying out their task with "swiftness" and "precision."[12]

However, in the face of continuing repression and mounting pressures on the hierarchy from groups at lower levels of the church working with those being persecuted, in late April 1974 the Episcopal Conference issued its first major criticism of the government. The bishops as a whole expressed concerns about the atmosphere of terror and lies pervading the country and about a range of human rights violations that were becoming institutionalized. In the same statement, however, they said they had no doubts about the "good intentions nor the good will of our government authorities," and praised the junta's recent "Declaration of Principles" for "its explicitly Christian inspiration."[13]

Despite its nuanced tone, the statement drew strong criticism from those closely associated with the regime, and had no significant impact on diminishing the repression. General Gustavo Leigh remarked publicly that, while he respected the church, "like many men, without realizing it, they are vehicles for Marxism." Letters subsequently appeared in several newspapers (all of which by 1974 were in control of those favorable to the regime) attacking the cardinal for his criticism of the present government and for not being harder on the Allende administration. Two prelates (Archbishop Fresno of La Serena and Archbishop Tagle of Valparaíso) distanced themselves from the critical parts of the document and publicly reiterated support for the values and strategies of the military a month later.[14]

For the next year and a half, the Episcopal Conference issued no major statements pertaining to government policies. Private conversations between individual bishops and the military occurred from time to time, and, particularly in provincial areas, these led to leniences or releases from prison on a case-by-case basis.

The only major public event involving the church and the military in 1974 was the dedication of the Shrine of Maipú in November. Bishops and military alike turned out in full dress to commemorate Chile's war heroes from the struggle for independence. The cardinal's homily stressed traditional values of patriotism but also included concern for the present poor. No mutual recrimination occurred at the ceremony as each institution renewed contact with older customs and values which bonded them closely in the past. Many of those who participated in the religious processions and ceremonials, however, were from the working classes. They came as a sign of support for the human rights work underway at lower levels of the church and in defiance of a regime that had outlawed all public demonstrations. Hence, Maipú was a sign of the changing interaction between two old allies, each moving in a new direction but both wanting to maintain correct formal relations based on past allegiances.

By mid-1975 an already institutionalized repression was reaching extremely serious proportions. The secret police (DINA) was by then operating several torture centers in the vicinity of Santiago, one of which was visited peremptorily by a bishop who forced his way in and was horrified at what he saw. The "shock treatment" approach to curb inflation, begun earlier in the year, was inflicting almost unbearable pain on low-income Chileans by 1975, with unemployment reaching 16% by June and purchasing power of workers since the coup having fallen over 60% by September.[15] Graphic accounts of torture, forced disappearances, malnutrition among children, and despair by the unemployed were coming to the bishops from local clerical, religious, and lay leaders (especiaily in major urban areas). Many of these leaders were urging their respective bishops to speak out once more against the new systemic proportions of repression.

In September, therefore, the Episcopal Conference issued its third major statement since the coup, entitled "Gospel and Peace." The document contained both criticism and praise of the military, and reflected the continuing divisions within the hierarchy concerning the performance of the government.

The statement underscored the primacy of certain human rights such as the right to life, to bodily integrity, and to participation in society. It did not claim, however, that torture was actually occurring in Chile nor that the regime was in fact denying genuine, popular input into government decisions.[16] While questioning some of the extremist attitudes and reactions of anti-Marxists, the bishops also thanked the armed forces for "freeing" the country "from a Marxist dictatorship which appeared inevitable and would have been irreversible"[17] (a judgment for which there was no authoritative evidence).

The hierarchy criticized the gains being made by some at the expense of the poor, and expressed concern over the decline in public services that was hurting workers. However, they renewed their confidence in the "spirit of justice of our armed forces to reestablish a fair equilibrium among the competing sections of the economy," praised some of the regime's palliatives for the poor (such as the minimal employment program), and offered glowing praise for the efforts being made by the wives of the junta to aid orphans and the aged.[18]

One major reason for this deference was that some bishops still believed it possible to influence government leaders through private negotiations. A good number continued to maintain warm personal relations with representatives of the government in their provinces. The majority were treated respectfully and cordially by local military commanders, and also felt that they were successful in obtaining lenience or freedom for political prisoners in their respective areas. Hence, many bishops still did not take a systemic view of the deeper structural contradictions that were causing both economic exploitation and political repression, and believed that quiet diplomacy was the best strategy for them to employ in order to alleviate the abuses that did exist.[19]

An added reason for the very cautious and deferential tone that characterized several parts of "Gospel and Peace" was the hierarchy's concern for unity, especially in the Episcopal Conference itself. Many wanted to avoid open disavowal by some of their brother bishops of the general thrust of the document after it was released (as happened subsequent to their April 1974 statement). A few conservative bishops insisted that the new joint declaration contain special words of praise for the military, and although some of the most laudatory paragraphs were not present in the original draft, they were added in the final stages of its preparation to satisfy those who strongly supported the government. While this strategy minimized the possibility of later utilization of episcopal disunity by government sympathizers for their own purposes, it also produced a document that was riddled with contradictions, full of generalities, and openly supportive of the military.

Despite the extremely respectful attitude toward the government expressed in the pastoral letter, however, even the mild criticisms and suggestions it contained had no impact on public policy. In a major speech delivered a week later, on the second anniversary of the coup, Pinochet announced no changes in his political and economic policies. The press made no editorial comment on the bishops' statement, and *El Mercurio* printed it serially over several days, burying it in the back pages of its Santiago edition.

Although "Gospel and Peace" was written partially in response to information and pressure coming from those at lower levels of the church, it was far from prophetic. The fact that lower clergy, religious, and laity wanted a clearer episcopal denunciation of the regime was confirmed in my own interviews, conducted between April and November of 1975. While 90% of the bishops told me that they felt the church should normally adapt to authoritarian regimes so as to maintain its structures and thus continue its sacramental mission, almost one-half of the priests and nearly three-fifths of the nuns and laity in my survey said they preferred church leaders to be more prophetic under such conditions (see Table 8.1).

Throughout 1975, however, the hierarchy as a whole continued to judge otherwise. No form of repression aimed at the Chilean people was sufficient to resolve the internal divisions in the Episcopal Conference, nor to make bishops risk government restrictions on the freedom of the church to perform its religious and humanitarian functions.

CHURCH INSTITUTIONAL NETWORKS

Despite cautious and inconsistent public statements of the bishops during the first two years of military rule, the organizational resources of the church were a significant factor in alleviating some of the most brutal effects of the repression. With the collapse or entrenchment of other major social institutions, local churches became the focal point for those being sought by the police and for those whose family members or friends had been murdered or had disappeared.

Moreover, the acquiescence of the Catholic bishops to military interven-

TABLE 8.1 Opinions on the Prophetic Role of the Church under Authoritarian Regimes: Results of Interviews Conducted between April and November 1975

Question:

Throughout history the church has had to coexist with authoritarian regimes whose ideologies or practices are in conflict with Catholic doctrine (e.g., Nazi Germany, various Communist governments in Eastern Europe and Asia). Leaders of the church frequently have adapted to the situation in such societies rather than publicly confront governments, because they wish to maintain the structures of the church and the possibility of administering the sacraments.

Are you in agreement with this position and strategy, or do you think that the institutional church should be more prophetic under these conditions?

	Bishops	Priests	Nuns	Laity	All respondents
1. *First position*[a]	90% (27)	40.3% (29)	12.1% (4)	29.4% (15)	40.3% (75)
2. *Second position*[b]	10 (3)	47.2 (34)	57.6 (19)	56.9 (29)	45.7 (85)
3. *Combination of both strategies*[c]	0	8.3 (6)	0.0	0.0	3.2 (6)
4. *Don't know; no answer*	0	4.2 (3)	30.3 (10)	13.7 (7)	10.8 (20)
	(N = 30)	(N = 72)	(N = 33)	(N = 51)	(N = 186)

[a] prudence is needed; depends on the situation; church really does not have that much power; church must clarify doctrinal issues; private conversations better than public denunciations; satisfied with present stance of Chilean church

[b] church, including Chilean church, should speak and act more decisively

[c] dialogue and cooperation when possible combined with strong public defense of human dignity and rights

tion made it possible for ecclesiastical leaders at the local level to mobilize immediately to meet these needs. Within a month after the coup Catholic, Protestant, Orthodox, and Jewish leaders joined in an ecumenical effort to coordinate emergency services to the persecuted with the permission of the junta.

A National Committee to Aid Refugees (CONAR) was set up at the end of September, and by February 1974 had helped approximately 5,000 foreigners to leave the country safely. In early October 1973 representatives from these various denominations, led by Lutheran Bishop Helmut Frenz and Catholic Bishop Fernando Ariztía, inaugurated the Committee of Cooperation for Peace (COPACHI) to provide legal assistance to prisoners and those arbitrarily dismissed from their jobs, as well as economic aid to families of both these groups of Chileans in Santiago. Over the next several months, local offices or representatives of COPACHI were established in twenty-two of the twenty-five provinces to provide the same services as in the capital.[20]

Between October 1973 and December 1975 the Committee for Peace initiated legal actions on behalf of more than 7,000 in Santiago alone who had been arrested, condemned, or had disappeared. It defended over 6,000 workers dismissed from their positions for political reasons. It was successful in gaining reduced sentences for many who were actually brought to trial (a small minority of those arrested or disappeared), as well as compensation for countless numbers of those who had been peremptorily fired.[21] During 1974 and 1975 the committee expanded its services to include 126 self-help enterprises managed by workers, 10 cooperatives for small farmers, health clinics in Santiago (where 75,000 patients were treated by the end of 1975), and approximately 400 soup kitchens (the majority in Santiago) for preschool children suffering malnutrition which provided hot lunches to 30,000 youngsters daily.[22]

None of these projects was capable of changing the structures of repression, nor did they reach anywhere near all of those in need. In addition to reducing the sufferings of many, however, the committee established a network of communication. Its nationwide staff of over 300 full-time lawyers, social workers, and medical personnel provided information for almost every area of the country on arrests, disappearances, torture, unemployment, disease, and malnutrition. Such data was channeled to international human rights organizations as well as to national and international church leaders. In such a way, a detailed and comprehensive account of the extent of the repression which acted as a counterbalance to statements of the government was provided to opponents of the regime inside and outside of Chile.

In addition to these expanded social services, the religious activities of local churches also took on added dimensions and a new vitality. Rates of participation in Sunday mass and in weekly Bible study, prayer, and catechetical training programs increased significantly. Moreover, much of what has been described in theory by liberation theologians began to be a living reality in these small base communities in Chile after the coup. A deepening of religious faith coincided with critical discussions of the economic and political structures of repression and of the community's own responsibility to mobilize its resources to meet the basic needs of its members.

Rectories and convents also became places of refuge for those seeking to escape arrest and subsequent torture or execution. With the assistance of those closely associated with the Committee for Peace, many priests, nuns, ministers, and lay men and women helped these persons exercise their right of political asylum and gain entrance into foreign embassies. The story is yet to be told of the countless numbers of lives these courageous men and women saved, risking their own safety to do so.[23]

In addition to these actions on behalf of human rights, the Jesuit-sponsored monthly magazine *Mensaje* provided a balanced but critical viewpoint on public events right from the outset. During the initial period after the coup the journal, like the bishops, expressed cautious acceptance of the regime as the only alternative to civil war. Its editorials early on, however, specifically condemned the widespread use of violence and torture, stressed the need for the reestablishment of traditional freedoms and an early withdrawal of the military from power, and supported the continued desirability of some form of socialism in Chile.[24]

During the period of consolidation of government power in 1974 and 1975, *Mensaje* voiced a concern over the lack of adequate social and political participation. During these two years the magazine also published articles describing the devastating impact of the government's economic policies on the purchasing power and quality of life of workers and other low-income sectors of the population.[25]

While its circulation numbered only 5,000 subscribers, its importance was enhanced by the fact that 80% of the communication media was in the hands of government supporters. *Mensaje* provided one of the few continuous alternate perspectives on public events, and copies were passed by subscribers to many others interested in reading a critical analysis of government policies (including those in jail). It was also circulated abroad among church circles and in the international human rights community and thus provided additional authoritative data on developments inside Chile.

Despite the emergence of new services at the organizational levels of the church, some older ones suffered critical restrictions. Ninety percent of the operating budget of the Catholic university system (and approximately 50% of the finances necessary to operate Catholic primary and secondary schools) were coming from the state by 1973. After the coup the military quickly exploited this institutional weakness of the church so as to consolidate its own control over all branches of education and eliminate what it considered to be "Marxist" influences in schools and universities.[26]

In October 1973 the junta appointed military rectors in all institutions of higher learning, including the three branches of the Catholic university system in Santiago, Valparaíso, and Antofagasta. These men proceeded to exercise the same firing privileges as did their counterparts in state universities, and dismissed numerous faculty and students sympathetic to both the Popular Unity and Christian Democratic parties. Courses in social science, journalism, and fine arts were severely cut back, along with scholarship assistance to students from low-income families. The television and radio networks associated with these university campuses were given over to government sympathizers.

The military also placed restrictions on Catholic primary schools, subjecting them to the same controls imposed on public schools. Books which local military commanders believed an attempt "to indoctrinate students with strange ideologies" were banned, parents' councils were limited in their scope of activities, public subsidies were reduced, and health and nutritional services administered through schools cut back.[27]

The police also harassed local church meetings throughout this period. Informants (usually unemployed workers, desperate for money to feed their children) spied on the activities of small base communities and gave lists of participants to government agents. The DINA regularly carried out search and seizure missions in rectories, convents, and Catholic schools, looking for former union or leftist party leaders and confiscating church documents and files. Periodic arrests of clerical, religious, and lay leaders occurred, the latter remaining incarcerated longer and more brutally treated than priests or nuns.

Beginning in mid-1974 the media inaugurated a continuous campaign to discredit the Committee of Cooperation for Peace, charging that it was infiltrated by Marxists, was giving aid to subversives, and was sending false and disparaging information to Chile's enemies abroad. The members of the junta criticized the committee frequently in the press, and privately urged the hierarchy to close it down. The junta also imposed self-censorship on *Mensaje* in 1974 and carried on behind-the-scenes attempts to get the bishops to withdraw church support for it in 1975 so that they could suppress the journal entirely.

In November 1975, after a group of priests and nuns (some of whom were members of the Committee for Peace) helped four activists in the Movement of the Revolutionary Left (MIR) to gain asylum in the Costa Rican and Vatican embassies, severe pressure was applied on church leaders to dissolve the ecumenical organization. Over a two-week period, eighteen clerical, religious, and lay participants of the committee were arrested. General Pinochet urged the cardinal in a letter to close down the organization, since it was "a means whereby Marxist-Leninists were creating problems threatening the civic order."[28] The fact that Bishop Carlos Camus, the secretary of the Episcopal Conference, had acknowledged in an off-the-record press interview (given in late September and subsequently published) that there were those with Marxist sympathies in the committee also fueled the fire of the committee's opponents.[29] Moreover, the Orthodox and Baptist churches withdrew from the committee out of concern that its activities were becoming too political,[30] and some Catholic bishops (Tagle and Salinas) openly criticized the priests and nuns who had assisted members of the MIR.

Amidst such mounting criticisms and pressures, Cardinal Silva (chairman of the committee) acceded to Pinochet's request and dissolved the organization in December 1975. In granting this concession, however, the cardinal denied that the committee had been "simply an instrument used by Marxist-Leninists to disturb the peace," praised the organization for the humanitarian work it carried out "under very difficult circumstances," and committed the church to continue such activities on behalf of the poor "within our own respective ecclesiastical structures."[31]

This concession gave the hierarchy some added maneuverability with the junta. The same month that the cardinal dissolved the Committee for Peace, the Episcopal conference issued a strong public endorsement of *Mensaje,* expressing a "fervent desire" that it continue its "positive effort of clarification" of crucial public issues.[32] The government subsequently relinquished its pressure on the bishops to close down the magazine, and for a time diminished harassment of local church personnel.

Hence, while the institutional network of the church during the first two years after the coup played an important role in blunting some of the policies of the regime, it encountered serious, and in some cases debilitating, opposition by the military. Under withering pressure new structures less formally part of the official Catholic church (the Committee for Peace) were terminated in order to continue humanitarian efforts and a critical voice through groups considered more integral to the institution (small base communities and *Mensaje*). Moreover, in an area where the church was heavily dependent on the state for the continuance of an apostolate (education), there was almost no room for maneuverability or tradeoff with the government, and it had to suffer the consequence of severe public controls.

INTERNATIONAL LIFE LINES

Of all the forces that enhanced the church's opposition role, the one that was most significant in the first two years of military rule was its access to international resources. Without massive outside help, none of its new institutional commitments to human rights—the National Committee to Aid Refugees, the Committee of Cooperation for Peace, health and nutritional programs—could have been inaugurated or sustained over time.

Catholic organizations in Western Europe and North America (especially Misereor and Adveniat in West Germany and Catholic Relief Services in the United States) donated over US$16 million in money and materials (food, clothing, medicines) to Chile in 1974 and 1975. Various Protestant agencies in Europe, the United States, and Canada also sent considerable financial assistance to church-sponsored projects during the first two years after the coup, much of which was channeled through the World Council of Churches (approximately US$2 million for the Committee for Peace alone). In fact, the major support for COPACHI in its defense of human rights came from Protestant, not Catholic, sources.

Moreover, foreign government aid was also given to the Chilean church, some directly and some channeled through churches. The U.S. Inter-American Foundation donated US$3.7 million directly during 1974 and 1975, and the West German government's program for overseas church development projects (Zentralstelle) administered by the German bishops' program Misereor, sent US$168,699.[33]

Foreign contributions to the church, totalling US$21.7 million, far surpassed the domestic revenues generated by the church through a modified tithing program (*Contribución a la Iglesia*), which amounted to only US$356,347 for 1974 and 1975 combined.[34] Over 98% of the funds and material available to support church-sponsored humanitarian programs in Chile in 1974 and 1975 came from abroad. It also largely originated from international opponents to the Chilean regime, and was dispensed to a very different clientele inside Chile from the beneficiaries of the military's US$824.2 million received from friendly foreign governments and banks.

The military's effort to cut international support for the church was not very successful. In early 1975 the government issued a decree requiring organizations with a private law juridical personality to disclose all currency transactions with groups outside Chile—the main target undoubtedly being the Committee of Cooperation for Peace. The committee was able to ignore this requirement because it was covered by the legal privileges of the Archdiocese of Santiago, which, since the separation of church and state in 1925 has (along with the whole Catholic church) enjoyed a public law juridical personality. Such an exemption did not pertain to Protestant churches, which do not enjoy such a legal personality, and since 1975 they have had to disclose all the assistance they receive from abroad for individual projects.

Since the government was itself concerned with attracting foreign monetary support during its period of consolidation of power, it took no further steps in 1974 and 1975 to cut off international assistance to the church. Some foreign donors (e.g., the U.S. government) were giving money to both the church and the government, while others (private U.S. and West European banks) held church deposits and were already facing ecclesiastical pressures by 1975 for their loans to the Chilean government. Any further action on the part of the Chilean military to cut foreign aid to the Chilean church would have been counterproductive to their own economic self-interest.

While the church was successful in obtaining international financial support, the regime was able to inflict considerable damage by cutting another crucial international umbilical cord: foreign personnel.

In 1973 nearly one-half (48.3%) of the total number of priests serving in Chile (1,202 out of 2,491) were foreign-born, very few of whom were naturalized citizens. Since most had come as missionaries to work among the poor, many had closely identified with the economic and social struggles of workers and peasants during the Allende years. Some had taken political stands through the Christians for Socialism movement, and a few had closely identified with the leftist parties (the Socialist party, the Movement of Popular Unitary Action [MAPU], and the MIR).

After the coup three were killed, some arrested and expelled, and others had their permanent residency permits revoked by the government. Many simply left the country knowing full well that they were marked men and could not continue their function in Chile without serious danger to themselves and their parishioners.

The result was that during the first two years after the coup, the Catholic church suffered an overall decline of 380 priests (15% of the total), the overwhelming majority of whom (314) were foreigners. Consequently, the number of baptized Catholics per priest rose from 3,251 in 1973 to 4,336 in 1975, thereby taxing the sacramental capacities of an already badly understaffed church.[35] This also removed from Chile many priests sympathetic to the left who would also have been in the forefront of opposition to the new regime through their support for the Committee for Peace and other church-related programs.[36]

The mainline Protestant churches also experienced some losses of their foreign-born pastors, who were expelled or left under duress after the coup. Many of these had also been sympathetic to Allende's goals, and some were active members of Christians for Socialism.

The most critical loss among the liberal Protestants was Bishop Helmut Frenz, the German-born head of the Lutheran church and co-president of the Committee of Cooperation for Peace. Frenz was responsible for much of the original Protestant funding of COPACHI upon its founding in 1973. Thereafter, he made frequent trips to Western Europe to collect additional funds and disseminate information about COPACHI. In June 1975, the secular media mounted a major vilification campaign to discredit Frenz for allegedly spreading lies about Chile abroad and for openly defending the Allende government in Europe.[37] As he was leaving the country in September 1975 on a trip to visit friends and family in Germany, his residency permit was revoked.

NEW ADHERENTS AND A SELF-DISTANCING OF TRADITIONAL CLIENTELE

One of the factors that helped to offset the loss of a considerable number of clergy in Chile between 1973 and 1975 was the increase of lay initiatives, especially among those previously alienated from the church or with no close association with it—middle-class Catholics with leftist sympathies and working-class sectors. Upper-class Catholics, those with more traditional religious orientations, and certain reactionary groups, however, all expressed varying degrees of opposition to a church more closely identified with the left and the poor.

In the period following the coup, among those who first volunteered for new church-sponsored organizations to assist the persecuted were those Catholics with leftist leanings. Of the more than 300 professional and clerical personnel who initiated the projects of the Committee for Peace, the majority were identified with parties that supported the Allende government (MAPU and Izquierda Cristiana), and a few included non-Catholics formerly active in the Communist or Socialist parties.[38]

Their new or renewed association with the institutional church did not necessarily entail a return to participation in the sacraments, but it did signal a pragmatic recognition that the church provided the only opportunity for them to alleviate the intense suffering of their fellow Chileans and also oppose the repressive tactics of the military. Among some it also involved a renewal of emotional ties to the institution and a rekindling of religious faith as well, as they witnessed priests, nuns, lay leaders, and Protestant pastors risking their personal safety and security to save lives.

A similar pattern of closer identification with the church occurred among those in the working classes, many of whom had been supporters of Allende. The overwhelming majority of the clientele of the various humanitarian projects undertaken by the Committee for Peace and small base communities after the coup were the poor who were penalized by the military for their former party and union affiliations. Moreover, those administering such programs at the neighborhood level were lay men and women who previously had little formal contact with the church.[39]

These development gave the church a unique opportunity to evangelize sectors who had drifted away from it in the past, or simply had never received much of its attention. After the coup Bible study circles, catechetical leadership programs, prayer groups, and diaconate training projects all blossomed in working-class urban areas.

Advances among these social strata, however, coincided with losses among the church's traditional clientele. Wealthier Chilean Catholics were scandalized by what they considered a betrayal of the church's traditional character. Some were angry at the church's concern for the government's enemies. Others simply found it hard to adapt to a post-Vatican II, post-Medellín church that was finally putting into practice a synthesis of religious faith and a commitment to justice.[40]

There also reemerged after the coup a small but articulate group of reactionary Catholics (most from upper-middle-class families) closely identified with Opus Dei and the Integralist movement, the Society for the Defense of Tradition, Family, and Property (TFP). These groups date back to the 1930s in Chile, and were active opponents of both Christian Democracy and the new social orientation of the Chilean church begun in the 1960s. Although they went underground for the most part during the Allende years (or focused their energies in the militant Fatherland and Freedom movement), they surfaced after 1973 as staunch supporters of the new regime. Moreover, they publicly opposed the official humanitarian position of the church, and even the cautious position of the bishops, on several occasions between 1973 and 1975.[41]

While all of these conservative and reactionary Catholics constituted a relatively small part of the total number of Catholics in Chile (less than

10%), their influence went far beyond their numbers. Several TFP sympathizers were invited by the military into key government positions after the coup, including that of chief legal adviser to the junta (Jaime Guzmán), and leadership in National Secretariats of Youth and Women respectively. They also were very active in the communication media after 1973, and several Opus Dei members replaced Christian Democrats in the administration of the Catholic university system.[42]

Moreover, these were the Catholics most able financially to contribute to the church. Their alienation meant that all the new and expanded social and religious services of the post-coup church had to be supported from outside the country. Any hopes of a financially autonomous church (less vulnerable to state control) were dashed by the further self-distancing of these Catholics after 1973.

Hence, at the fourth level of the institution (multiclass membership allegiances) there were both advances and losses during the first two years of military rule. While the gains among the poor outweighed the losses among the rich from a gospel perspective, the withdrawals of the latter weakened the church economically and politically.

Church and Military in Chile after 1975

After 1975 all four levels of the church worked much more cohesively to enhance the institution's capacities as a force of opposition to the regime. The hierarchy as a group, in defensive reaction to direct attacks on individual bishops and on the Christian Democratic party, took a more prophetic moral stance against the repressive tactics of the government. The institutional network of the church exhibited remarkable resilience after the Committee of Cooperation for Peace was dissolved, and new structures were rapidly created to counter the state apparatus. International monetary support increased during this period, as did commitments of allegiance among low-income Catholics. The military and conservative Catholic sectors continued to harass the church, but with less success than in the former period. International political and economic factors along with creative strategies by higher and lower church leaders limited the options of the church's political and religious opponents.

EMERGING PROPHECY AMONG THE BISHOPS

From mid-1976 through 1979 the public statements of the Episcopal Conference grew more consistent and critical of government policies. Public divisions among the bishops virtually ceased, and as a group they denounced what they considered specific abuses as well as the deeper structural causes of the political and economic repression.

Two major developments precipitated this about-face by the Episcopal Conference: the military's efforts to severely limit the Christian Democratic party, and its permitting the secret police to humiliate several members of the church hierarchy publicly.

In 1976 the government began a series of attacks on the centrist opposition parties, whose leaders protested to the Organization of American States (during its Sixth Assembly held in Santiago in June) the state of siege and arbitrary detentions continuing in Chile. Eugenio Velasco (a Democratic Radical former Law School dean) and Jaime Castillo (a prominent Christian Democrat) were subsequently expelled from the country, purportedly for threatening the internal security of the country.

On 12 August three Chilean bishops attending a meeting in Riobamba, Ecuador, were arrested along with fourteen others from several countries in the hemisphere (including the United States). The military government of Ecuador charged that the seventeen prelates were discussing "subversive themes of a Marxist orientation," and after detaining them overnight, expelled them from the country. The Chilean bishops (Enrique Alvear of Santiago, Fernando Ariztía of Copiapó, and Carlos González of Talca) were greeted at Pudahuel airport upon returning home by a group of pro-government demonstrators (including members of the DINA), who shouted insults, threw stones, and physically mistreated those accompanying the prelates. The media gave the event wide coverage, and several commentators denounced the "leftist bishops" for meddling in politics.[43]

The Permanent Committee of the Episcopal Conference reacted almost immediately, and issued two strong statements on the same day— one criticizing the treatment of the prominent political figures and the other threatening excommunication for those involved in the attack on the bishops. These were the first unequivocal statements by the bishops as a group in almost three years of military rule. In the first, they denounced the arbitrary expulsion of Castillo and Velasco "without a decision about their culpability by a free and impartial judge." They concluded by asking that if this could happen to "two prestigious professional people . . . what could happen to simple and ignorant citizens?"[44] No acknowledgement was made of the fact that thousands of "simple and ignorant citizens" had already been expelled from the country since 1973. In the second statement, the bishops protested the "violence and verbal aggression" against the church by the press and television, and also the insulting demonstrations at Pudahuel airport. They named specific members of the DINA who had taken part in the incident, and reminded them that canon law automatically imposes excommunication on those Catholics who "perpetrate violence against an archbishop or bishop." The hierarchy also took the occasion to address themselves to what they now considered to be systematic repression being imposed by many military governments throughout Latin America.[45]

Hence, the hierarchy as a group were coming to realize that abuses of power by the Chilean security forces were not isolated, transitory, or unavoidable mistakes. However, it took a direct attack on themselves and on prominent individuals, one a Christian Democrat, to make them open their eyes to this fact.

In late 1976 and 1977, after Pinochet had announced that the military would remain in control of the state indefinitely to protect national security, the Christian Democratic party again stepped up its activities against the government. Its members became more involved in legal defense of prisoners and the disappeared, and its radio station (Radio Balmaceda) increased its broadcasts on repressive aspects of the government's political and economic policies. The party leadership, encouraged by Jimmy Carter's election as president of the United States, inaugurated internal discussions on feasible scenarios that would bring an end to military rule and also establish a tactical alliance between the Christian Democrats and moderate sectors of the left.

The junta responded decisively. At the end of January 1977 it closed Radio Balmaceda down permanently. On 12 March Pinochet also announced the dissolution of all political parties, and justified this by claiming that the Christian Democrats had broken the political recess imposed in September 1973 on all non-Marxist parties.

In the wake of these reprisals against the Christian Democrats, the bishops issued another clear denunciation of the regime in late March 1977. The pastoral letter, entitled "Our Life as a Nation," included an analysis of the structural weaknesses of the system as a whole, and placed the church clearly behind those urging an early return to constitutional and representative government.

The statement did not mention the suppression of the Christian Democrats as such, but addressed itself to what the bishops considered a basic flaw in the regime which the dissolution of that party reflected. In accordance with traditional Catholic social teaching about subsidiarity, the bishops argued that intermediate organizations between the state and the individual must not be suppressed. Such institutions, they said, guarantee both social and political participation and a healthy pluralism of ideas, which are essential ingredients in the pursuit of the common good. Using the same line of argument, the hierarchy criticized the economic plan of recovery for not being subject to wider societal debate or allowing for more popular input into its formulation. Finally, the bishops called for an end to government by decree, and urged popular ratification of any future constitution or set of laws.[46]

This was the first time in three and a half years that the hierarchy had implied that the military were not the legitimate representatives of the people. It was the first time that they had acknowledged that inadequate protections for personal, political, and economic rights were due to the absence of accountable government rather than to failures by some individuals within the administration.

The reaction of the government and its supporters was swift and acerbic. *El Mercurio* accused the bishops of having for the first time adopted a "political position in face of the military regime," thus overstepping their "pastoral authority." The minister of justice publicly called the bishops "useful fools, ambitious, bad-intentioned, and resentful" who have "abandoned the care of souls" and have "launched a hypocritical political attack on the government."[47]

Over the course of the next three years the Episcopal Conference continued to issue statements critical of the regime, and for the most part each declaration focused on a specific aberration of public power.[48]

NEW INITIATIVES AT THE LOWER LEVELS

Although the Committee of Cooperation for Peace was dissolved by Cardinal Silva in December 1975, in January 1976 he established a new organization to take its place, the Vicariate of Solidarity. While there were some changes of personnel, the vicariate continued the same services of the former committee. It was, however, made a completely integral part of the juridical structures of the Catholic church along with representatives appointed by the bishops in local episcopal chanceries.

The vicariate quickly established regional offices in twenty of the twenty-five provinces associated closely with chanceries, and over the course of the next four years it provided legal, health, nutritional, and occupational services to more than 700,000 persons throughout the country. In 1979 alone, over 5 million hot meals were served to hungry children, and a whole series of training, credit, and technical assistance programs were expanded in the countryside.

The vicariate also inaugurated the publication of a biweekly bulletin (*Solidaridad*) that has published accounts of the various projects the vicariate has undertaken as well as articles on problems affecting workers, peasants, and students. *Solidaridad* by 1979 had a circulation of 33,000 copies, which were distributed gratis in parishes, small base communities, and social action projects of the church throughout the country. It was also distributed abroad through international church networks.[49]

Hence, while the church had lost a tactical skirmish with the government in 1975, the bishops (under the cardinal's leadership) were shrewd and foresighted in the way they went about replacing the Committee of Cooperation for Peace. The Vicariate of Solidarity was much more closely tied to the official church than its predecessor, making it both easier for the bishops to control and harder for the government to smash without directly attacking the core of the church itself.

At the parochial level of the church, humanitarian and religious activities continued with the same vitality after 1975 as before. Social action committees, prayer groups, and catechetical leadership training all maintained the same services to those with material and spiritual needs. They also continued to provide surrogate forms of social participation and networks of accurate information in the absence of viable secular structures to accomplish these ends.

The security forces and supporters of the government in the media continued their attacks on these local structures of the church after 1975, but with less frequency than before. The bishops not only protested publicly on several occasions, but they also officially removed some of the grounds for previous accusations that small base communities were havens for Marxist political activists. In 1979 Cardinal Silva issued criteria for who and what kinds of activities could be legitimately considered part of the local church. In this statement he acknowledged the danger of the church's being manipulated for political purposes, and explicitly ruled out any type of activity with clearly partisan political goals. He also defended as integral to the church's mission all humanitarian activities to those in need regardless of religious affiliation, and indicated that all lay persons could exercise leadership positions in local church projects provided they were at least open to the religious message of the church and were not militant atheists.[50] In such a way he removed the government's excuses for harassing local church programs by publicly taking upon himself the responsibility of safeguarding the institution's proper mission.

The only area where more forthright words and actions by the hierarchy after 1975 did not gain more protection for the local structures of the church was in the realm of education. The junta maintained firm control of the Catholic university system and continued to reduce state subsidies by more than 10% each year, making it more difficult for all except the wealthy to attend. At the primary and secondary level, government support also continued to decline. By 1977 enrollment in private grammar and high schools had fallen by more than 13% since the coup, and those affected were from families of modest incomes. Such cutbacks have, therefore, continued to make it difficult for the church to carry through on previous plans to train more of the poor in its schools, and have meant that private education (which is predominantly Catholic) has become more selective and elitist since the coup.[51]

With this one exception, the layered institutional network of the church expanded its capacity after 1975 to act as an important counterforce to government policies and propaganda. More forthright statements and shrewd tactics by the hierarchy were major factors in making this possible.

FURTHER INCREASES IN INTERNATIONAL SUPPORT

Foreign financial and material support to church-sponsored humanitarian projects in Chile substantially increased after 1975. The government attempted briefly to block some of the donations, but it had to back off once international pressures were exerted and it realized that its own economic support from private banks and multilateral lending institutions (which had also significantly increased) might be jeopardized.

Between 1976 and 1979 Western European and North American Catholic agencies donated over US$67 million in financial aid or the equivalent in food, medicines, and clothing to various projects of the Chilean church. Protestant assistance also increased substantially during this four-year period, totaling in the vicinity of $8 million just for works of the Vicariate of Solidarity alone.[52] Foreign governments more than doubled their grants to the vicariate and other church-related projects in Chile as well.

The Chilean government in 1977 had become concerned about these substantial increases of foreign aid to the church. In late 1977 Pinochet publicly charged that the World Council of Churches (one of the major donors of aid to the Vicariate of Solidarity) was financing subversion in Africa and was also sending over US%2 million annually to Chile to underwrite similar activities. A subsequent statement issued by the Archdiocese of Santiago rejected these accusations as inaccurate.[53]

The government also ceased expelling foreign priests after 1975. The number of foreign clergy in Chile continued to decline during this period (from 888 in 1975 to 824 in 1979). These men have left on their own accord, however, and have more than been replaced by substantial increases in Chilean priests, who accounted for 1,402 (63%) of the 2,226 priests in the country by 1979.[54]

Hence, during this second period the third critical dimension of the Chilean church—its international support linkages—also acted as a strong reinforcement for its humanitarian and religious programs. The government found it more difficult to undermine this strength owing to international economic pressures protecting the church's access to foreign money.

CONTINUED OPPOSITION OF TRADITIONALIST CATHOLICS AND CONSOLIDATION OF NEW SUPPORTERS

After 1975 traditionalist Catholics associated with the Integralist movement continued to distance themselves from the church. In response, the hierarchy took more decisive action to protect the church from their attacks. Moreover, sectors in the working classes and middle-income Catholics continued their new forms of participation in the church, and some have also increased their financial contributions.

In 1976 the Society for the Defense of Tradition, Family, and Property (TFP) published a book entitled *The Church of Silence in Chile,* printing 10,000 copies for domestic and international circulation. The work claimed to represent the views of all those conservative Catholics in Chile who purportedly had been betrayed by their clergy and no longer had any voice in the church. The book argued that since 1960 almost all the bishops and a decisive number of the priests in the country had been undermining traditional Catholic positions on social issues, especially in regard to private property and Marxism. The authors claimed, therefore, that the leadership of the Chilean church was in heresy, and that Catholics had the duty to resist such bishops and clergy. Opposition, they said, should take the form of condemning these ecclesiastical leaders publicly, preventing them from using their prestige for further damage to the church and Christian civilization in Chile, and severing all spiritual relations with them to the point of refusing the sacraments from their hands.[55]

The reaction of the bishops to such a frontal attack on their authority and upon church unity was swift and decisive. As soon as the book appeared they issued a declaration condemning the movement for setting itself up as a "parallel teaching office" in the church. They reminded Catholics that the church "is founded on Jesus Christ in communion with the Holy Father and the bishops" and that those who "do not accept this doctrine do not belong to the Catholic church." They also clearly implied that members of TFP had automatically placed themselves in a state of excommunication by their activities.[56]

As in the aftermath of the DINA's humiliation of the bishops at Pudahuel airport, the hierarchy's reaction to the TFP's challenge was unequivocal and ecclesiastically punitive.

Some wealthier and conservative Catholics continued after 1976 to remain estranged from the church as in the prior period, 1973–75.[57] Middle-class Catholics, however, increased their participation in the church's social and religious activities, and some substantially raised their financial support for the institution. The revenues from the church's voluntary contribution program (Contribución a la Iglesia, or CALI) rose steadily after 1975, and by 1979 reached US$1.5 million annually, a tenfold increase from the amount given in 1974. While this accounted for a very small part (about 4%) of the total amount of income for the church (96% coming from abroad) between 1976 and 1979, it indicated a growing identification by Chilean Catholics with the works of the church.[58]

Working-class sectors of the population also continued their increased rate of participation in the church's social and religious programs. Many more came forward to take leadership roles in these new activities, especially women. By the late 1970s over 10% of all parishes were being administrated by women (particularly nuns), and these are mostly in rural and urban working-class areas. Both lay and religious women in Chile were administering several of the sacraments and conducting prayer services and leadership training programs and were well accepted as surrogates for priests.[59]

These new forms of participation in the church by middle- and low-income sectors have provided the opportunity for greater mutual understanding and collaboration among persons who in former years were very much divided politically. Christian Democrats and sympathizers of leftist parties over the past few years have worked together in both social and religious programs at the neighborhood level, and as a result some reconciliation has occurred between the two groups. Such a process of practical cooperation is paving the way to greater mutual respect across party lines, respect that was sadly lacking in the last months of the Allende regime.

Conclusions

1. *Prophetic denunciations of the military government by the hierarchy did not occur until core interests of the church were threatened, and even when they were made they had little impact on changing overall policies of repression.*

Although the Chilean bishops have gained an international reputation for exercising a prophetic function in the face of state repression since 1973, this judgment must be qualified. During the first three years of the regime, their moral critique of the principles and practices of the military government tended to be cautious and cast in very general terms and was rarely denunciatory. Furthermore, the style and tone of their public statements provided the government with important legitimacy during the initial transition period and while it was consolidating its power in 1974 and 1975. Only after mid-1976, when the repressive apparatus of the state touched the bishops themselves personally and the Christian Democratic party, were they able and willing as a group to issue clear condemnations of both the underlying ideology and the behavior of military leaders.

This pattern of initial caution and gradual evolution towards more prophetic positions by Catholic bishops in the face of conservative authoritarian regimes has been repeated elsewhere in Latin America—Brazil, Bolivia, Argentina, Paraguay, El Salvador, and Somoza's Nicaragua. While some individual bishops have been openly critical during early stages of repression in these countries (e.g., Dom Helder Camara in Brazil, Archbishop Oscar Romero in El Salvador), the episcopacies as a group have followed the same ambiguous pattern as the Chilean hierarchy at the start.

Although most Chilean bishops maintained correct relations with Allende and articulated public moral values close to many of those his government espoused, they harbored deep-seated private fears about the future objectives of his administration, since it was Marxist in orientation. Such fears, coupled with the promise to restore order after a period of social chaos by an avowedly Christian group of military officers, predisposed the hierarchy at the start to be relatively understanding of the ultimate goals of the junta whatever their misgivings about some of the initial tactics used.

Prophetic positions by episcopal conferences do, nevertheless, occur. When they emerge, however, they are not primarily in response to brutality against the populace as a whole but to specific acts of violence or abuse aimed at those directly engaged in religious work or closely associated with the church. In Chile it was an attack on bishops personally and the suppression of the Christian Democratic party. In Brazil, Argentina, Bolivia, and El Salvador it was mistreatment or murder of priests. In Paraguay it was the smashing of church-sponsored peasant leagues and small base communities. In all of these cases in recent years, the hierarchies as a group have not taken a united prophetic stance against their respective governments until the repression touched the innermost circles of church elites themselves.

Moreover, in Chile as well as in all of these other Latin American countries where Catholic bishops have eventually articulated clear and specific condemnations of both ideological and behavioral aspects of governments, military leaders have not significantly changed their policies. Prophetic episcopal statements may reduce pressures on the church for a time, diminish the moral legitimacy of these regimes, and discredit them further in world opinion, but they do not by themselves precipitate the downfall of such governments, nor even influence basic structural changes in government principles or tactics. The moral powers of the church in comparison to the resources for physical coercion enjoyed by repressive military rulers, while not insignificant, is clearly limited.

2. *The structures of the Chilean Catholic church underwent significant role expansion to perform a variety of resistance functions under the military regime, but they have also been vulnerable to direct and indirect restrictions by the state.*

The institutional resources of the Chilean church were more effective than its moral voice in checking the repressive effects of a military regime. In the absence of other forms of organizational mobilization, the structures of the church expanded rapidly and provided a number of important services—the building of communication networks, the dissemination of accurate information on repression, the delivery of legal and economic services, and the promotion of alternate forms of social participation.

Chile is perhaps one of the best known cases of a national church organization acting as a surrogate for such activities when there are no other viable institutions mediating between the state and the individual. The Chilean church is not, however, the only one to perform such functions in recent years. Paraguay, Brazil, Bolivia, Argentina, and El Salvador are other examples where both Catholic and Protestant churches have set up new ecumenical organizations to offer a whole range of legal, social, and economic services to those being persecuted.[60]

As resilient and inflatable as are the structures of the church in military regimes of purported Christian inspiration, however, the Chilean case clearly indicates that the institutional network of the church is unable to challenge effectively the fundamental structural causes of oppression in these societies. Church-sponsored programs can alleviate some of the worst aspects of brutality, but they cannot effect changes in the dynamics of the economy nor in the apparatus of the state—the two critical structural factors that underlie the repression.

While not subject to annihilation or manipulation as in totalitarian societies, ecclesiastical structures in authoritarian regimes such as that in Chile are vulnerable to some forms of state pressures once they begin to oppose the objectives of government. The Chilean case indicates that there is a whole range of strategies such a government can employ, short of declaring a persecution of the church, in order to hamper the church's effectiveness: harassment and arrest of local leaders, threats against, and censorship of, its media channels of communication, and periodic vilification campaigns against its personnel and programs. When the pressure becomes relentless and adamant (as in the case of the Committee of Cooperation for Peace), church leaders sometimes choose to accede to government demands rather than risk losses in other areas, especially those that relate more directly to its religious activities.

While it is true that the structural weight of the church cannot undermine the power of the military, the Chilean case shows that the church has staying power and is not easily smashed. There is a certain line beyond which Latin American military governments that profess Christian principles and that need foreign support from Europe and North America will not go even when they have begun to mount an offensive against church personnel and programs. The organizational network of the church, therefore, can act as an important holding operation or locus of minimal resistance until other forms of domestic and international pressure can be mobilized.

3. *International support has provided the Chilean church with invaluable resources for its commitments to human rights, but these have also been exploited by the military junta to limit the church's freedom at the local level.*

The Chilean case is a dramatic illustration of how absolutely crucial outside monetary aid is for the rapid expansion of local church roles and structures to defend human rights against state brutality. None of the new social efforts undertaken by the Chilean Catholic and Protestant churches since the coup could have been inaugurated or sustained without massive and immediate increases of financial assistance from Western Europe and North America. The general economic situation of the country and the extreme poverty of those directly benefiting from these new humanitarian programs in Chile make autonomous financing of such efforts, both now and in the foreseeable future, highly unlikely.

Moreover, not all international aid that has flowed into new humanitarian programs undertaken by the Chilean church is ecclesiastical in origin. The United States and the West German governments channel money directly and indirectly into those projects. Hence, church networks can also serve as alternate conduits for democratic governments to transmit change-oriented resources into authoritarian military regimes, thus bypassing the repressive apparatus of the state in these countries.[61]

The Chilean case demonstrates that there are definite limitations on the controls which military governments can impose on international financial aid to churches. Many of the authoritarian governments now in power in Latin America are themselves heavily dependent upon public and private institutions in Western Europe and North America for grants, loans, and credits. If dependent military regimes such as Chile's were to gain more economic self-sufficiency, the state would probably restrict international church financial linkages. Under such circumstances, local church structures that had expanded rapidly in earlier crisis periods with the help of foreign aid would shrink as outside support was cut off unless autonomous local financing was generated.

4. *The Chilean church has experienced an influx of new adherents since the coup among those with previously weak ties to the institution. Such crisis support may be transitory among those with leftist sympathies, however, and could be offset by the permanent loss of more conservative groups.*

Since 1973 the Chilean Catholic church has enjoyed a unique opportunity to reach many who have never had much contact with the institution—workers, peasants, intellectuals, leftist sympathizers—all of whom now are the ones most in need of the church's protection and assistance. Furthermore, the needs of these new adherents are such that emphasis can be given by church leaders to both social humanitarian work and religious evangelization in the same projects—an objective central to newly announced goals in official church pronouncements at Medellín (1968) and Puebla (1979).

One could expect, however, that once the repression subsides and other forms of social participation in society become viable, attendance patterns among the new churchgoers will decrease. Significant withdrawals will almost certainly occur among those engaged in human rights or social action work when the crisis passes and secular structures to accomplish these goals are again functioning. Many Christian Marxists will take with them more positive attitudes about the church and religious beliefs, and this will reduce the possibility of religio-political conflicts in the future, especially between the church and the left. But very little participation in the life of the church by contemporary social activists will be likely once they can achieve their goals more effectively elsewhere.

The Chilean case also suggests that while inflated rates of participation by some new adherents might be reversible once the repression is over, the erosion of the allegiances of more traditional Catholics may well not be a transitory phenomenon. There is no indication that the official position of the church to support social justice and to construct more communitarian lay-directed programs of religious formation will be altered in the foreseeable future, regardless of changes in the political system. Unless there are dramatic changes (as of now unpredictable) in the attitudes and behavior of upper-income Catholics regarding these new emphases in ecclesiastical policy, one would have to expect that their alienation will continue rather than diminish.

While this group is relatively small in comparison to middle- and low-income sectors (and accounts for less than 10% of the Catholic population), their political role in contemporary Chilean society is most significant. They cannot be written off if the post-Puebla church wants to exert influence in policymaking through its most prestigious laity. Furthermore, if the church is going to develop an autonomous base of financial support for its own apostolates, it will have to convince some of these people to shoulder much of the responsibility. Middle-class groups can share more of this burden, but not all of it, given their own limited resources and the large amount of new contributions necessary to make the church self-financing. The exodus from the institution of wealthy Catholics precisely at a time when it is attempting both to develop new lay resources for influence in society and to expand its services to the poor weakens the church considerably, and places serious limits on the possibility of carrying out some of its newly announced commitments effectively in the future.

The Chilean experience in its most recent past highlights both the great potential and the crucial challenges with emergency situations under authoritarian regimes present to churches. Under such circumstances they have unique opportunities to develop new methods of religious socialization and to deepen the internalization of their goals and values among many sectors of their nominal membership. Such opportunities, however, may be temporary, due to the changeable reasons for the drawing near of new members. Given the multiclass scope of allegiances of such institutions, however, a weakening of influence is almost inevitable among other clientele who are adversely affected by new church commitments in these periods.

Such institutional diminishment might very well be the cost of the church's living more authentically its perennial religious mission along the lines envisioned in the Gospel. The church also may very well lose some of its traditional political and economic power in so doing. Such is the paradox of genuine Christianity.

Notes

A longer version of this chapter appears as Chapter 9 of Brian H. Smith, *The Church and Politics in Chile: Challenges to Modern Catholicism* (Princeton: Princeton University Press, 1982).

    1. Brian H. Smith, "Religion and Social Change: Classical Theories and

New Formulations in the Context of Recent Developments in Latin America," *Latin American Research Review* 10 (Summer 1975): 3–34.

2. Smith, "Churches and Human Rights in Latin America: Recent Trends in the Subcontinent," *Journal of Inter-American Studies and World Affairs* 21 (February 1979): 89–127, reprinted in Daniel H. Levine, ed., *Churches and Politics in Latin America* (Beverly Hills: Sage, 1980), pp. 155–93.

3. Among the best-known studies of the Latin American military and their expanded institutional role in politics since the 1960s are the following: Luigi Einaudi and Alfred Stepan, *Latin American Institutional Development: Changing Military Perspectives in Peru and Brazil* (Santa Monica: Rand, 1971); John Samuel Fitch, *The Military Coup d'Etat as a Political Process: Ecuador, 1948–1966* (Baltimore: Johns Hopkins University Press, 1977); Richard Maullin, *Soldiers, Guerrillas, and Politics in Colombia* (Lexington, Mass.: Lexington Books, 1973); José Enrique Miguens, "The New Latin American Military Coup," in Kenneth Fidel, ed., *Militarism in Developing Countries* (New Brunswick: Transaction Books, 1975), pp. 99–123; José Nun, "The Middle-Class Military Coup," in Claudio Veliz, ed., *The Politics of Conformity in Latin America* (New York: Oxford University Press, 1967); Frederick M. Nunn, *The Military in Chilean History: Essays on Civil-Military Relations, 1910–1973* (Albuquerque: University of New Mexico Press, 1975); Nunn, "Military-Civilian Relations in Chile: The Legacy of the Golpe of 1973," *Inter-American Economic Affairs* 29 (Autumn 1975): 43–58; Guillermo O'Donnell, *Modernization and Bureaucratic Authoritarianism: Studies in South American Politics* (Berkeley: Institute of International Studies, University of California, 1973); Philippe C. Schmitter, ed., *Military Rule in Latin America* (Beverly Hills: Sage, 1973); Alfred C. Stepan, *The Military in Politics: Changing Patterns in Brazil* (Princeton: Princeton University Press, 1971); Stepan, "The New Professionalism of Internal Warfare and Military Role Expansion," in Alfred C. Stepan, ed., *Authoritarian Brazil: Origins, Policies, and Future* (New Haven: Yale University Press, 1973), pp. 47–65; Stepan, *The State and Society: Peru in Comparative Perspective* (Princeton: Princeton University Press, 1978); Víctor Villanueva, EL CAEM *y la revolución de la Fuerza Armada* (Lima: IEP Ediciones, 1972).

4. Two recent examples of such reporting by journalists who are convinced that the Catholic church has become a force of consistent opposition to military governments in Latin America are Penny Lernoux, *The Cry of the People: United States Involvement in the Rise of Fascism, Torture, and Murder, and the Persecution of the Catholic Church in Latin America* (New York: Doubleday, 1980), and Alan Riding, "The Sword and Cross," *New York Review of Books*, 28 May 1981, p. 3.

5. "Declaración del Señor Cardenal y del Comité Permanente del Episcopado Chileno," Santiago, 13 September 1973, in *Mensaje* 22 (October 1973): 509.

6. "Homilía del Señor Cardenal en el acto ecuménico de oración por la patria," 18 September 1973, in *Mensaje* 22 (October 1973): 510–11.

7. "Episcopado ofrece colaborar en la reconstrucción," *El Mercurio*, 29 September 1973.

8. In addition to all 30 active Catholic bishops, I also included in my survey 41 priests serving different social classes in 16 provinces, a randomly selected stratified sample of 31 priests in Santiago, 33 religious women doing direct pastoral work in 7 provinces, and 51 lay men and women from all social classes who were active in small base communities (mainly in Santiago).

9. For an account of the relations between Christians and Marxists at the official external level of church and state during the Allende period, see Smith, *The Church and Politics in Chile: Challenges to Modern Catholicism* (Princeton: Princeton University Press, 1982), chap. 7.

10. Bishop Francisco Valdés S. "La oración de Chile nuevo," 11 September 1973, *DOLCA* 1 (September 1973): 20.

11. *El Mercurio*, 14 November 1973.

12. *El Mercurio*, 3 March 1974.

13. Los Obispos de Chile, "La reconciliación en Chile," Santiago, 24 April 1974, *Mensaje* 23 (May 1974): 197.

14. Lester A. Sobel, ed., *Chile and Allende* (New York: Facts on File, 1974), p. 171; Jaime Ruiz-Tagle, "La Iglesia frente a la prensa," *Mensaje* 23 (July 1974): 267; Bishop Juan Francisco Fresno, "Es necesario superar la situación de vencedores y vencidos," *El Día* (La Serena), 19 May 1974; Bishop Emilio Tagle, "Acerca de la reconciliación," *La Revista Católica* 73 (January–April 1974).

15. José Aldunate, S.J., "Salarios y precios: ¿Cómo sigue la situación?" *Mensaje* 24 (May 1975): 186–88.

16. Comité Permanente del Episcopado de Chile, "Evangelio y paz," Santiago, 5 September 1975, in *Mensaje* 24 (October 1975): 465–66.

17. Ibid., pp. 446, 469.

18. Ibid., pp. 470–71.

19. The belief that private conversations with the military were more effective than public condemnations to correct abuses of state power was mentioned by many bishops during my interviews with all of them in 1975.

20. P.N., "Qué hacen las iglesias por la paz?" *Mensaje* 22 (November–December 1973): 561–63.

21. El Comité de Cooperación para la Paz en Chile, "Crónica de sus dos años de labor solidaria" (mimeo, Santiago, December 1975).

22. U.S. Congress, House, Subcommittee on International Organizations of the Committee on International Relations, "Prepared Statement of José Zalaquett Daher, Chief Legal Counsel, Committee of Cooperation for Peace in Chile," *Chile: The Status of Human Rights and Its Relationship to U.S. Economic Assistance Programs*, 94th Cong., 2d sess., 1976, pp. 57–65.

23. For a vivid account of some of the heroic efforts of these local church leaders, see Sheila Cassidy, *Audacity to Believe* (London: Collins, 1977).

24. "Pronunciamiento militar," *Mensaje* 22 (October 1973): 468–70; "Un grito de alerta," *Mensaje* 22 (October 1973): 470–71; "Hacia un nuevo año,"

Mensaje 23 (January–February 1974): 9–10; "Rectificando una línea?" *Mensaje* 23 (March–April 1974): 78–80.

25. Aldunate, "Remuneraciones y costos de vida," *Mensaje* 23 (December 1974): 634–36; Ruiz-Tagle, "El estatuto social de la empresa," *Mensaje* 24 (May 1975): 145–47; Alejandro González Poblete, "El anteproyecto del Código del Trabajo," *Mensaje* 24 (August 1975): 371–75; Sergio Molina, "La encrucijada actual de la política económica," *Mensaje* 24 (October 1975): 439–44.

26. During the Frei and especially the Allende years, all levels of Catholic education made attempts to meet more effectively the needs of low-income sectors of the population. Government subsidies to Catholic schools were expanded to enable them to grant scholarships to students from working-class families, and tuition payments for wealthier students were increased. Additional public aid to the Catholic university system during the Popular Unity period facilitated the establishment of new social science research centers sympathetic to Marxist analysis. Adult education programs at night and on weekends for workers were also significantly expanded with the help of this assistance to the Catholic universities from the Allende government.

27. *El Mercurio,* 10 October 1973, p. 21; Carlos Hurtado E., S.J., "Las subvenciones de la educación particular gratuita," *Mensaje* 24 (October 1975): 447–50.

28. *Chile-América,* no. 3 (November–December 1974), p. 41.

29. "Infiltración Marxista," *El Mercurio,* 12 October 1975, p. 3.

30. The Lutheran church underwent a formal schism in June 1975 because of strong opposition to the Committee for Peace's work among the church's pro-junta German-speaking numbers. A majority of congregations (mainly in the south) split off and formed a second Lutheran church, leaving only a minority of Lutherans headed by Bishop Helmut Frenz (co-president of COPACHI) as participants in this ecumenical human rights organization. Fernando Salas, S.J., "Crisis en la Iglesia Luterana Chilena," *Mensaje* 24 (July 1975): 312–15.

31. *Chile-América,* no. 3 (November–December 1975), p. 42.

32. "Carta de los obispos a '*Mensaje,*'" Santiago, 30 December 1975, in *Mensaje* 25 (January–February 1976): 1.

33. Data from Catholic Relief Services (New York), U.S. Catholic Conference (Washington, D.C.), Inter-American Foundation (Rosslyn, Va.), International Catholic Confederation for Social and Economic Development (Brussels), and Adveniat and Misereor (West Germany). The vast majority of the financial statistics for Catholic Relief Services represent the dollar value of food supplies originating from the U.S. government's Food for Peace Progress (P.L. 480, Title II) distributed by CRS.

34. Mutual Pax Chile, Secretariado del Episcopado de Chile.

35. Oficina de Sociologia Religiosa (OSORE), Secretariado del Episcopado de Chile.

36. In my interviews with all of the Chilean bishops in 1975, I asked their opinions concerning the expulsion of these priests. Of the bishops who had lost clerics from their diocese (19 out of 30), over two-thirds (68.4%) said it was

better that the priests had left the country since they were troublesome persons or former political activists.

37. "Las iglesias de Chile," *El Mercurio*, 24 June 1975, p. 2.

38. This judgment is based upon my own observations and conversations with several persons active in the Committee of Cooperation for Peace in 1975.

39. Allende never discouraged workers from practicing their faith, but low-income sectors in Chile (as in all Latin American countries) seldom attended mass. The church until very recently was not institutionally present in densely populated shantytowns because of a scarcity of clerical and religious personnel and a traditional sacramental focus on middle- and upper-income Catholics.

40. Several bishops and priests whom I interviewed in different parts of the country in 1975 said that they found upper-income Catholics reluctant to volunteer their services for new lay-led religious or social ministries. These Catholics preferred older forms of piety, centered around mass attendance and private devotions.

41. For an account of the tactics of Opus Dei and TFP after the coup, see Thomas G. Sanders and Brian H. Smith, "The Chilean Catholic Church during the Allende and Pinochet Regimes," *American Universities Field Staff Reports*, West Coast South America Series, 23 (March 1976): 18–19.

42. Ibid., p. 16. See also Julio Silva Solar, "El integrismo católico-fascita en la ideología de la junta militar," *Chile-América*, no. 3 (January 1975), pp. 1–13.

43. R.A.H. "Sentido del episodio Riobamba-Pudahuel," *Mensaje* 25 (October 1976): 455–60.

44. El Comité Permanente del Episcopado, "Declaración," 17 August 1976, in *Mensaje* 25 (September 1976): 446.

45. "Declaración del Comité Permanente del Episcopado," Santiago, 17 August 1976, in *Mensaje* 25 (September 1976): 437.

46. Comité Permanente de la Conferencia Episcopal de Chile, "Nuestra convivencia nacional," Santiago, 25 March 1977, in *Mensaje* 26 (April 1977): 167–68.

47. "Posición política de los obispos," *El Mercurio* (editorial), 27 March 1977; Gregorio Meneses V., "Acontecimientos de marzo," *Mensaje* 26 (May 1977): 174.

48. Los Obispos de Chile, "El sufrimiento del exilio," Santiago, 25 December 1977, *Mensaje* 27 (January–February 1978): 84; El Comité Permanente del Episcopado, "Carta del Comité Permanente del Episcopado a cada uno de los Sres. Miembros de la Honorable Junta de Gobierno," Santiago, 30 December 1977, *Mensaje* (January–February 1978): 101; El Comité Permanente del Episcopado de Chile, "Proyecto ODEPLAN contra la cesantía," Santiago, May 1978, *Mensaje* 27 (June 1978): 350–51; El Comité Permanente del Episcopado, "Los detenidos desaparecidos y sus familiares en huelga de hambre," Santiago, 6 June 1978, *Mensaje* 27 (July 1978): 428; Arzobispado de Santiago, "Allanamiento a casa de sacerdotes jesuitas," 8 November 1978, *Mensaje* 27 (December 1978): 821; El Comité Permanente de la Conferencia Episcopal de Chile, "Juramento exigido a nuevos dirigentes sindicales," 9 November 1978, *Men-*

saje 27 (December 1978): 822; El Comité Permanente de la Conferencia Episcopal de Chile, "Detenidos desaparecidos," 9 November 1978, *Mensaje* 27 (December 1978): 823; La Conferencia Episcopal de Chile, "Carta a los trabajadores cristianos del campo y la ciudad," Puerto Montt, 17 November 1978, *Mensaje* 28 (January–February 1979): 79–80; Bishop Manuel Sánchez B. et al., "Evangelización del pueblo mapuche," Temuco, 4 May 1979, *Mensaje* 28 (July 1979): 408–10; La Conferencia Episcopal de Chile, "Carta pastoral a los campesinos," Santiago, 14 August 1979, *Mensaje* 28 (October 1979): 675–79. Arzobispado de Santiago, "Petición de los familiares de las víctimas de Lonquén," 10 August 1979, *Mensaje* 28 (September 1979): 579.

49. *Vicaría de la Solidaridad: Cuatro años de labor* (Santiago: Arzobispado de Santiago, 1980), pp. 60–69, 101–105.

50. Raúl Cardenal Silva Henríquez, "Iglesia y participación de los no cristianos," Santiago, 18 April 1979, in *Mensaje* 28 (June 1979): 229. The auxiliary bishop of western Santiago issued a similar declaration and clarification for those in his sector. See Bishop Enrique Alvear, Vicario Zona Oeste, "Relación de la iglesia con organizaciones no eclesiales," Santiago, 3 March 1979, in *Mensaje* 28 (June 1979): 337–38.

51. Hurtado, "Qué pasará con los colegios subvencionados?" *Mensaje* 26 (August 1977): 432–38; Dr. Luis Bravo, "Cuatro aspectos de la crisis del sistema educacional escolar," *Mensaje* 247 (August 1978): 484–90; Ernesto Livacic G., "Nuevos caminos para la Universidad," *Mensaje* 29 (September 1979): 573–75. The church was able after 1975 to provide support for several dozen professors and scholars no longer able to function in university positions because of their past political affiliations. These included social scientists with Christian Democratic sympathies as well as some with more leftist ideological leanings. The church organization under which these academics have been able to carry out research on contemporary economic and political issues in Chile is called the Academy of Christian Humanism, founded in late 1975. It functions with the aid of foreign church money (especially from West Germany) and publishes a monthly journal called *Análisis*. Francisco López F., "La crítica de la Iglesia chilena al modelo autoritario liberal: Discurso de praxis crítica, análisis de la experiencia" (mimeo, Santiago, Academia de Humanismo Cristiano, July 1980), pp. 61–70.

52. The majority of the support on the Catholic side came from Misereor and Deutscher Caritasverband in West Germany and Catholic Relief Services in the United States. This included not only money for the vicariate but also support (including food and clothing) for all social projects of the church. Exact dollar figures were provided to me by CIDSE in Belgium—a federation of Catholic development agencies—and by CRS in New York. Statistics from the Protestant side are not distributed publicly, but it is estimated that aid from the World Council of Churches and other Protestant organizations just to the vicariate alone was about $8 million between 1976 and 1979.

53. "Declaración del Arzobispado," Santiago, 29 November 1977, in *Mensaje* 27 (January-February 1978): 80–81.

54. *Guía de la Iglesia en Chile* (Santiago: Ediciones Mundo, 1979).

55. Sociedad Chilena de Defensa de la Tradición, Familia, y Propiedad, *La Iglesia del silencio en Chile* (Santiago: Edunsa, 1976), pp. 377–400.

56. "Declaración del Comité Permanente," Santiago, 9 March 1976, in *Mensaje* 25 (July 1976): 316.

57. A survey of religious attitudes and practice of Catholics in Santiago in 1979 confirmed this continuing alienation from the new church by wealthier members. Upper-income Catholics went to mass more often and had a better knowledge of doctrine than did the poor, but they were more critical of the clergy, felt more distant from the church, and were less willing to accept a commitment to social justice as an integral part of Christian life. Renato Poblete B., S.J., Carmen Galilea W., and Patricia van Dorp P., *Imagen de la Iglesia de hoy y religiosidad de los chilenos* (Santiago: Centro Bellarmino, 1980), pp. 156–58.

58. The number of contributors to the program doubled from 78,396 to 160,682 in the same period. This still represented a very small percentage (0.02%) of the Catholic population in the country, however. Information on CALI was provided to me by Fr. José Kuhl of Mutual Pax Chile in the Secretariat of the Episcopal Conference.

59. Sister Katherine Ann Gilfeather, M.M., "Women Religious, the Poor, and the Institutional Church in Chile," *Journal of Inter-American Studies and World Affairs* 21 (February 1979): 219–55, reprinted in Levine, *Churches and Politics in Latin America*, pp. 198–224. See also Gilfeather, "Women and Ministry," *America* 135 (2 October 1976): 191–94.

60. Smith, "Churches and Human Rights in Latin America."

61. Ibid.

Chile's External Relations under the Military Government

Heraldo Muñoz

The accession of the armed forces to power in Chile in September of 1973 marked a profound transformation of Chilean economic and political life. The area of foreign relations, which under previous administrations had been generally treated as a sphere of continuity of the nation, and therefore as a field more or less isolated from partisan political and ideological influences, was radically transformed by the military regime both in substance and style. The result was that the Chilean military government placed itself in a situation of international political isolation[1] although not in a position of international economic isolation.

On the basis of four fundamental explanatory elements—the dominant domestic project, the style of diplomacy, the international context, and the transnational dependency condition—it is asserted here that Chile's political isolation from the world community since September 1973 is the direct outcome of (*a*) the establishment of an authoritarian national project characterized by the curtailment of political participation and human rights, (*b*) the materialization of a highly controversial praetorian-ideological style of diplomacy which contrasts with the civilian-pragmatic style traditional in Chilean diplomacy, and (*c*) the pursuit of a markedly anti-Communist foreign policy in a world context which differs from the rigid bipolar scheme of the cold war era.

The military regime's position of isolation in the political sphere contrasts with a generally positive situation in regard to economic matters. The reason behind this is that the economic model undertaken by the military government signified a rapid reinsertion—after a period of relative withdrawal—in the transnational economic system, and the restoration and strengthening of transnational ties between the local economic groups and the centers. In short, the transformation of the economic structure of Chile brought about improved economic relations with key actors in the advanced capitalist countries. Interestingly, the government sector known as *blandos*[2] viewed the strengthening of economic relations with the world not only as an intrinsic and necessary goal of the domestic project, but also as a possible indirect road to overcoming political isolation and its implications.

Chile's International Relations from World War II to 1973

During the post-World War II period the international system expanded considerably. New independent nations appeared, global and regional organizations were formed, and the rapid development of science and technology permitted noticeable increases in the level of interactions among the growing number of actors in the world system. Politically, the international system began to evolve from a highly centralized, cold war pattern of confrontation between two relatively monolithic blocs—led respectively by the United States and the Soviet Union—to a more decentralized, détente pattern characterized by the emergence of new regional powers, the reemergence of Western Europe and Japan, a progressive disintegration of the ideological-political blocs, and a rapprochement between the United States and the Soviet Union and between the United States and the People's Republic of China.

Throughout the cold war period, Chile was unquestionably aligned with the Western bloc, led by the United States. Chile's subordination to the United States translated into clear limits on Chilean external behavior. However, the administrations of the period occasionally were able to pursue specific independent courses of action, particularly regarding the defense of Chile's position on the Antarctic, on the maritime issue of the 200-mile limit on territorial waters (under the González Videla presidency, 1946–52), and on the renegotiation of a new agreement with the American copper companies (under the Ibáñez presidency, 1952–58.)[3]

During the conservative administration of Jorge Alessandri (1958–64), Chile sustained a position of moderate autonomy with regard to the United States, based on the juridical or "legalist" vein that traditionally characterized Chilean foreign policy. Precisely making use of solid juridical arguments, the Alessandri government joined the majority of Latin American states in resisting a move to expressly condemn Cuba, as Washington wanted, in the Seventh Consultation Meeting of San José in 1960; abstained in the voting that excluded Cuba from the Organization of American States (OAS) in Punta del Este in 1962; and abstained when a proposition was voted in July of 1964 to apply sanctions to Cuba.[4]

The shift in the international context from cold war to détente facilitated the pursuit of a more autonomous external strategy on the part of the Chilean government. Under the Christian Democratic administration of Eduardo Frei, Chile reestablished diplomatic and consular relations with the Soviet Union, Czechoslovakia, Hungary, Bulgaria, Poland, and Rumania. The improvement of relations between Chile and these socialist countries led to the exchange of numerous trade missions and to some cooperation agreements. For example, in 1968 the Soviet Union expanded its sales of machine tools to Chile through credit extension, and loaned US$42 million for industrial development.

During the Popular Unity administration, the intensification of relations with socialist countries accelerated. By 1972 Chile had established diplomatic and consular relations with the People's Republic of China, the German Democratic Republic, North Korea, and North Vietnam; and had restored full relations with Cuba, broken, as already stated, in 1964 in compliance with a sanction resolution of the OAS Foreign Ministers' Conference.

Throughout both administrations Chile further asserted its independent orientation in the New World order by establishing or strengthening relations with African countries like Zambia, Zaire, and Nigeria, and Asian nations such as India and Japan. Chile also played, with various degrees of intensity, a growing role in international economic and political associations like CIPEC (Inter-Governmental Council of Copper Exporting Countries), the Andean Pact, and the Group of Non-Aligned Countries. In the hemispheric context, Chile exercised a leading role in the articulation of a more or less unified Latin America position vis-à-vis the United States, the hegemonic power that until then tended to identify its own political and economic interests with those of Latin American countries; Chile also favored the introduction of major reforms to the Inter-American system. In short, despite its reduced economic resources, small population, and nonstrategic geographic position, the country played a leading role in regional and world affairs. Chile was influential beyond its objective material means because of its democratic political institutions and processes; its moderate style of diplomacy based on a juridical logic, and the quality of the human resources in charge of foreign policy; and the atmosphere of international détente, which facilitated the pursuit of contacts and attitudes considered "disfunctional" in a cold war framework.

The Imposition of the Authoritarian Model and Its International Impact

Following the military coup of September 1973, the economic order shifted from a highly regimented type of capitalism to a laissez faire capitalism, and the import-substitution model of the past was rejected in favor of opening the country to the world economy: public spending was severely reduced, tariff and nontariff barriers were drastically lowered, prices and interest rates were progressively liberalized, exchange controls were largely eliminated, and foreign investment began to be actively encouraged. All of these changes in the economic sphere understandably were well received by foreign bankers and entrepreneurs.

The military, the private economic clans, and a reduced group of conservative technocrats-economists (*el equipo económico*) emerged as the key actors of the new order. The last two were largely responsible for conceiving and overseeing the new socioeconomic project, while the first was mostly in charge of executing the scheme and assuring its stability. The newspaper *El Mercurio* summarized very appropriately the governmental division of labor that materialized between these actors: "The military established public tranquility and ensured the full execution of the norms dictated by the government while the civilians accompanied by the military elaborated and applied an economic scheme of immense projections for the stability and development of the country."[5]

The economic plan of the junta coincided with the orientation of the prevailing U.S. government. Hence, U.S.-Chilean relations during the 1974–76 period were quite warm. Washington backed the rescheduling of Chile's debt in the Paris Club and, together with international financial institutions, allocated significant amounts of foreign aid to the military regime.[6] A number of agreements were made during the second half of 1974 with U.S. companies which had been expropriated by the previous government. Compensation agreements were reached with Anaconda, Kennecott, ITT, and others. The Chilean government's desire to attract external finance was underlined by the introduction, in 1974, of Decree Law 600, a new foreign investment statute which set out very favorable terms for new capital coming into the country.

Chile's withdrawal in October 1976 from the Andean Pact—precipitated by the conflict created between the liberal Decree Law 600 of the military government and Decision 24 of the Pact, which limited profit repatriation on foreign investment in the subregion—demonstrated that during the earlier years of the military regime, the country's foreign relations were subordinated to the requirements of the domestic economic plan. But the success of the new economic scheme depended on more than just realigning external policy with domestic economic priorities: it relied heavily on the absence of local trade union pressure for higher wages and, more generally, on the lack of organized political opposition. The role of the repression that followed the military coup became critical in terms of ensuring the political stability of the new order, but at the same time, it also signified an erosion of Chile's positive image abroad and became the fundamental cause of the international political isolation experienced by the military regime.

Governments of various ideological postures, ranging from Zambia to Belgium, quickly suspended their relations with the Chilean regime or lowered their representations in Santiago. The involvement of foreign citizens, some of them diplomats, in various incidents with the armed forces was a significant factor in the early deterioration of bilateral relations with countries such as Sweden and France. Relations between the government of Chile and the governments of Colombia and Venezuela reached their lowest point in 1974, when, owing to discrepancies over the application of the right to asylum, the Chilean Foreign Ministry delayed the granting of safe-conducts to several leftist congressmen who had sought refuge in the embassies of those two countries. Official links between Colombia and Chile were particularly tense in 1974, when the Chilean foreign minister, Vice-Admiral Ismael Huerta, accused the Colombian ambassador of having close contacts with "Communists and extremists." The following year, the arrest and torture of Sheila Cassidy, a British doctor, for tending a wounded leader of MIR (Movimiento de Izquierda Revolucionaria), motivated the recall of Great Britain's ambassador in Santiago. Likewise, the detention and/or expulsion of journalists from *Le Monde, Newsweek, Corriere della Sera, Dagens Nyheter,* and other news organizations had a direct negative impact on Chile's international image.

In November 1974 Mexico broke relations with the military government following a visit to Chile by Mexican Foreign Minister Emilio Rabasa in which he obtained exit visas for seventy-two Chileans who had taken asylum in that embassy. Rabasa, the first foreign minister to visit Chile after 11 September 1973, had received the safe-conducts in return for a Mexican promise to exchange ambassadors, renew the granting of visas for Chileans wishing to enter Mexico, and renew suspended trade in pharmaceutical products, fertilizers, and sulphur. Mexico automatically cancelled these agreements after the rupture of diplomatic relations. Various other incidents related to the situation of human rights in Chile caused serious damage to relations with Italy, West Germany, and even the United States, among others.

Towards 1976, Chile's relations with the United States—particularly with the Congress—experienced a significant decline. In June of that year, the U.S. Senate and House of Representatives voted to suspend arms sales to Chile and limited economic aid to US$27.5 million unless it could be proven that Chile had made substantial progress in observing human rights.

The election of Jimmy Carter marked a new stage in U.S.-Chilean relations. The military government immediately assumed a rather defensive stance, especially considering that, during the presidential campaign, Carter had publicly criticized the Chilean human rights situation. On 17 and 18 November 1976, shortly after Carter's election, the government of General Augusto Pinochet released more than 300 political prisoners. The releases came amid a growing debate within government circles on how to respond to international pressures and to the new Washington administration. Carter's commitment to a policy of human rights translated into a deterioration of the relations between Chile and the United States. The Carter Administration, for instance, voted in international organizations to condemn the Chilean government's record on human rights, it officially received in Washington opposition leaders like Eduardo Frei and Clodomiro Almeyda, and it pressured the military regime to improve local human rights conditions.

Without a doubt, the most sensitive event in U.S.-Chilean relations after the military coup was the murder of Orlando Letelier and Ronni Moffit in Washington, D.C. in September 1976, involving Chilean military officers, former DINA (National Intelligence Directorate) agent Michael Townley, a U.S. citizen, and Cuban exiles formerly employed by the CIA. Townley, after being extradited to the United States, confessed to having participated in the assassination under the direct orders of DINA's director, General Manuel Contreras, and hence the U.S. Justice Department asked for the extradition of Contreras and the other two military officers. In October 1979, Chile's Supreme Court turned down the U.S. Justice Department request for extradition of the three men and freed them immediately. Consequently, the White House temporarily recalled its ambassador in Santiago and implemented a series of economic and diplomatic sanctions against Chile for failing to conduct a serious investigation into the charges against the Chilean officers. By January of 1982 the Reagan Administration had suspended the sanctions imposed by its predecessor. However, and independently of the specific outcomes of the trials,[7] the "Letelier case" still constitutes a rather delicate theme, although not an obstacle, in the rapprochement between the military regime and the Reagan government.

The international isolation which the military government has suffered owing to its dictatorial and repressive policies has had other concrete expressions. For instance, under the present regime, Chile has been visited by a small number of foreign heads of state: during the six-year period of the Frei Administration (1964–70) Chile was visited by ten heads of state from various parts of the world, while in the eight-year period between October 1973 and October 1981 the country was visited by only four heads of state—all from South American countries.[8] Chile has been consistently left out of the Latin American itinerary of world leaders like West German Chancellor Helmut Schmidt, French President Giscard d'Estaing, King Juan Carlos of Spain, and U.S. President Jimmy Carter. Of course, visits from foreign heads of state are not always a precise indicator of the status of a nation in the international system. What matters is the quality of the external relations of a given country. From this viewpoint, one proof of Chile's political isolation was the unprecedented support gathered by Bolivia in 1979 for its demand to gain access to the Pacific Ocean through Chilean territory;[9] another was the incapacity of the Chilean government to gain international backing when, in February of 1978, Argentina unilaterally rejected the ruling on the Beagle Channel produced by the arbitrator, Great Britain.[10]

Because of these and other circumstances, the Chilean government has invested substantial amounts of financial resources in defense. Chile's military spending jumped from US$177 million in 1972 to US$984 million in 1980, while the size of its armed forces increased from a total of 47,000 men in 1972 to 92,000 in 1981.[11] Yet, in the opinion of independent observers, the national security of the country in the regional context does not appear to have improved sufficiently, owing precisely to the problem of external political isolation which has complicated the normal flow of military supplies far beyond what has been the case with Chile's neighbors. In effect, a study published in 1981 in the journal *Proceedings of the U.S. Naval Institute* concluded that so long as the military government continues to experience political isolation, "there will occur a permanent deterioration of Chile's power and security with regard to its neighbors."[12]

The Style of Diplomacy of the Military Government

From the 1950s to 1973, the predominant Chilean style of diplomacy was what we call a civilian-pragmatic style, which meant an emphasis on strict adherence to international law, the practical recognition of international power realities, the support of democracy both domestically and internationally, and the predominance of career diplomats in the management of foreign policy. The military junta altered this traditional style: in their mediating role between the dominant actors of civil society and the state, the military forces imprinted on Chilean foreign policy their own technical experience and anti-Communist world view, giving rise to what is called here the praetorian-ideological style. This style is direct and highly ideological, it allows little room for negotiating and compromising, and it is associated with military personnel rather than with career diplomats.

One of the main features of the praetorian-ideological style has been the utilization of direct, personal channels instead of the Foreign Ministry and professional diplomats to conduct the government's international relations. This is apparently due to the fact that General Pinochet—who plays a key role in foreign policy—dislikes the cautious, indirect, and compromising ways of the civilian-pragmatic style of diplomacy, and likes to ensure that his emissaries execute assignments according to his stated instructions. Among the individuals sent by Pinochet on such missions are Generals Manuel Contreras and Herman Brady, and civilians like journalist Alvaro Puga (who in July 1974 carried a personal letter of Pinochet to then President Perón of Argentina) and Federico Willoughby, a former press secretary of the junta. Another feature of the praetorian style has been the displacement of quiet and discrete negotiations in favor of passionate public confrontations in the handling of bilateral disagreements with various countries.

It is clear that throughout the first years of military rule, internal consolidation was the top priority of the Pinochet government and of all the dominant social actors. Foreign policy was secondary, and this facilitated the implantation of the praetorian-ideological style of diplomacy. Once the new national project was firmly secured though, the economic advisers and the private economic groups argued for a reevaluation of the importance of foreign policy and pushed for a return to a more pragmatic and "efficient" style of diplomacy that would facilitate the strong external linkages required for the success of the laissez faire scheme.

In November of 1974 *El Mercurio,* echoing the concern of the economic groups and the technocrats, warned, in two separate editorials, that the military government's external policy had an exceedingly anti-Communist ideological orientation and lacked professionalism because of the excessive direct involvement of the military in its management. On the ideological issue the newspaper stated: "There is absolutely no reason why our diplomacy should seek to lead the world anti-Soviet or anti-Communist movement, or to convince the Western countries of the errors of détente." Then it addressed the question of professionalism in the following terms: "Only a strictly professional diplomacy can strengthen the foreign service. The risks and difficulties of Chilean foreign policy require a professional diplomacy . . . the type of habits and discipline of a good diplomatic service demand flexibility, a spirit of conciliation and negotiation, the search for peaceful solutions. The military man is prepared professionally for the stage when the diplomat is no longer needed."[13]

But the most comprehensive critique of the praetorian-ideological style of diplomacy stemming from the economic circles was cogently presented in an extensive April 1978 editorial of *Economía y Sociedad,* a publication sponsored by the Colocadora Nacional de Valores, a financial institution controlled by the Cruzat-Larraín economic group.[14] The editorial stated: "The anti-Communist cause as a fundamental parameter of international relations has lost relevance since the end of the cold war, and today there are few governments interested in publicizing their rejection of the Communist model, even when they may struggle against it domestically. . . . It is time to rethink our foreign relations strategy. . . . It is necessary to elaborate a modern foreign policy as a function of well-defined national interests [and to define] a program of action characterized by an imaginative and pragmatic approach and by a professional execution." The editorial concluded that "a new foreign policy should stress *the economic dimension* of international relations at the expense of ideological factors" (emphasis added).[15]

The growing criticism of the praetorian-ideological style of diplomacy on the part of economic groups was soon joined by a progressive discontent among senior career diplomats. In March 1977 the government sent economist Jorge Cauas, a former minister of the treasury of the military regime, as its ambassador to Washington. The designation represented a more direct involvement of technocrats and of the economic sector in foreign policy making, and a slight turn towards a modified civilian-pragmatic style that could effectively address some of the external political obstacles to the Chilean economic model. According to Cauas, his plan of action—which he called "low profile"—in Washington consisted in "rebuilding the image of Chile, avoiding the exaggerated visibility that the country showed in recent years," and in making efforts to "maintain and increase the good image attained by Chile from the economic viewpoint because of the multiplying effect that this could have in other areas."[16]

The critical shift towards a more civilian-pragmatic foreign policy approach occurred one year later, in April 1978, when Hernán Cubillos, a civilian of the private business sector, was named foreign minister. In addition to the criticisms stemming from economic circles, there were four key reasons behind the shift: first, the December 1977 U.N. General Assembly vote condemning the continuing violation of human rights in Chile, after which Pinochet ordered a "national consultation" and declared that the government "would henceforth pursue a more aggressive and pragmatic foreign policy";[17] second, the deterioration of relations with Argentina, following her rejection on 25 January 1978 of the arbitration ruling on the Beagle Channel, which awarded the islets of Picton, Lennox, and Nueva to Chile; third, the breakdown of diplomatic relations with Bolivia that occurred on 17 March 1978; and fourth, the increasing tension between Chile and the United States over the Letelier case (only one week before the designation of Cubillos as foreign minister, the Chilean government, pressed by Washington, had expelled Michael Townley to place him in the hands of the U.S. Justice Department). In other words, the delicate international situation and the requirements of the economic scheme produced the reinstatement of several retired career diplomats and a softening of the praetorian-ideological style of diplomacy.

Nevertheless, the civilian-pragmatic style that emerged during Cubillos' tenure was significantly different from the classical civilian-pragmatic style that characterized Chilean diplomacy in the past: while the latter was founded on respect for the democratic values of the country and on a juridical logic, the former was to be based on the predominance of the economic dimension in Chile's foreign relations. Moreover, the designation of Cubillos by no means signified the total replacement of the praetorian-ideological style by a new version of the civilian-pragmatic style: what developed was an uneasy coexistence between two different approaches to the management of Chile's external affairs. The contradictions between the two styles were already apparent in two decrees (Supreme Decree 161 of 1978 and Decree with Force of Law 53 of 1979) which reorganized the

Ministry of Foreign Relations. On the one hand, the decrees unified and strengthened the role of the economic sector in foreign relations, but, on the other hand, they also created the special post of vice-minister, with the rank of minister of state, a position originally assigned to a tank expert, Colonel Enrique Valdés. The post was clearly conceived as a military counterbalance of the civilian minister.

One concrete example of the strain in military-civilian relations in the conduct of Chile's external affairs occurred in December 1978, when four Chilean diplomats and three military officers were expelled from Peru, while the ambassador to Lima was declared *persona non grata,* on charges of spying for Chile. Foreign Minister Cubillos openly accused the military personnel attached to the Chilean embassy in Lima of meddling in foreign policy matters, while the Chilean ambassador explained that the whole incident was due to "unfortunate actions of Chilean functionaries who did not belong to the civilian personnel of the embassy, personnel over which the ambassador had no direct authority."[18] Despite this information, General Pinochet—in a policy decision typical of the praetorian style of diplomacy—sent off General Herman Brady as his personal emissary to mend things directly with the Peruvian defense minister. Although Brady knows several of Peru's top generals, he was unable to prevent the breakdown of diplomatic relations that followed.[19]

Another example of the military-civilian tension had occurred in early January 1978, when the Chilean Foreign Ministry instructed its ambassador in Buenos Aires to invite the Argentine government to resort to the International Court of Justice to resolve their differences over the Beagle Channel arbitration issue; at the same time, General Pinochet was sending—without the knowledge of the Foreign Ministry—General Manuel Contreras to Buenos Aires to invite Jorge Rafael Videla to a special presidential meeting. The invitation of the Chilean Foreign Ministry was never answered, and on 19 January 1978, Pinochet and Videla met in Mendoza, Argentina, in what was reported as "a strictly military session" attended also by Chilean Admiral Luis de los Ríos, Air Force General Fernando Matthei, and a legal adviser from the foreign minister. Six days later Argentina declared that the arbitration produced by Great Britain was "null and void."[20]

The "Philippines incident"—the abrupt cancellation by the Marcos government of a visit of General Pinochet to the Philippines in August 1980, when he and a high level delegation were on their way to the Asian country—produced a clear setback for the civilian-pragmatic style in the formulation and conduct of Chilean foreign policy. The removal of Cubillos as foreign minister, and his replacement by René Rojas, a rather obscure official in the diplomatic bureaucracy, signified a noticeable weakening of the position of those who preferred a pragmatic foreign policy approach based on maximizing economic links. The shift in style was evidenced in

March of 1981, when General Pinochet named General Enrique Morel, one of his closest collaborators, as ambassador-at-large in his representation, to visit embassies abroad and to become a direct link between the head of state and the diplomatic corps.

In mid-1981, the new foreign minister announced that Chile would begin to implement a more aggressive foreign policy "so as to be present, if possible, in all international events, to show that Chile is a progressive country, a lively, creative, imaginative country."[21] The rapprochement that the Chilean government initiated with respect to several regimes in Central America, particularly with El Salvador, was, in part, a concrete outcome of this more aggressive foreign policy. In any case, the changes registered after the removal of Cubillos did not signify that the economic dimension of foreign policy had also declined radically. At least this aspect of Chile's external relations maintained the relevance it had under Cubillos, owing, in great measure, to the continued global orientation of the country according to the priorities of the economic model.

Transnational Insertion and the Strategies of the Military Government to Overcome Political Isolation

The methods used by the government to minimize political isolation through noneconomic means have achieved little success. The information offensive of the first years ("Operación Verdad"), the publication of paid advertisements in the foreign press, and other similar actions have yielded scarce positive results, and in some cases, they have had a negative impact. Similarly, the Chilean government's search for closer relations with African countries has been frustrated by the very warm and special relationship that the military regime has with South Africa. In the case of the Middle East, the cordial economic-military relationship between Chile and Israel could explain, at least in part, the lack of dynamism in the interactions between the Pinochet government and the Arab countries. With respect to the nations of the Asia-Pacific region, which Chile cultivated vigorously, the government has made progress mainly in the financial and commercial spheres.

The transnational bonds that normally exist between the private sectors of the periphery and their counterparts of the centers as a consequence of the structural coupling of developed and underdeveloped economies have solidified considerably in the case of Chile from 1973 onwards. The Chilean economic model has been able to project until now (1982) a positive image of the country in international business circles so that, at least economically, the military government is not isolated. The ease with which local economic groups have obtained external credits, particularly from private instead of public sources, illustrates the good relations that exist between Chilean bankers and entrepreneurs and transnational banks. Evidently, these cordial relations have been stimulated by the high international liquidity of recent years, produced by an overabundance of petrodollars and by the subsequent eagerness of bankers to extend loans. In 1980, Chile's foreign debt reached the record sum of US$11,239 million; it was estimated that in 1981 this amount would increase to US$15,250 million.[22]

The volume and service of Chile's external debt, as well as the recent financial collapse of the CRAV-CRAVAL conglomerate and the government's intervention of eight private financial institutions to impede their falling into bankruptcy, have created doubts about the future solvency of the Chilean economic model. Similarly, although the country's economic image in the transnational business circles is positive, there still appears to exist some apprehension on the part of foreign investors about becoming too deeply involved in a politically sensitive country like Chile. For example, the actual inflow of direct foreign investment capital under the aegis of Decree Law 600 has been surprisingly low throughout the last eight years, despite the large number of projects approved by the Committee on Foreign Investments (CIE). According to this state entity, authorized direct investments between August 1974 and October 1980 reached US$4,398 million, but materialized investments represented only 19.2% of that sum, that is, about US$847 million.[23] Most of the investments authorized in the 1973–80 period concentrated in the mining sector, and according to law, they may become effective in a period up to twelve years. However, a significant portion of the investments already materialized corresponds to simple purchases of already existing enterprises instead of new productive activities.

Notwithstanding the situation described above, the Chilean authorities are well aware of the existence of transnational channels and the relatively positive image that Chile enjoys in foreign business circles. Hence, and given the outward orientation of the economic scheme, the military government has sought, progressively, to overcome political isolation through economic contacts.

The goal of international political legitimization through the economic route is being pursued at two different levels: (1) at the governmental level, where the task is to convince foreign governments critical of the regime's authoritarian rule that the economic position of Chile merits a reassessment of bilateral relations on the basis of "objective," mutually advantageous considerations, and (2) at the private level, where the aim is to strengthen ties with bankers, corporations, and other nonstate actors, particularly of the developed nations, so as to compensate for possible deteriorations of public bilateral relations and so as to earn direct access to the official circles of the corresponding countries.

Private economic groups in Chile have played a fundamental role in the military government's effort to deal with the problem of political isolation.

For example, on multiple occasions, the heads of private business associations have acted as unofficial ambassadors of the regime participating in overseas missions coordinated by the Ministry of Foreign Relations. In many instances these businessmen have reported directly to General Pinochet upon returning from their visits abroad. One basic function of these trips has been, in the words of a local industrialist, "to present a true picture of Chilean reality abroad and to clear up many doubts about Chile's economic growth."[24] With regard to some countries, the Ministry of Foreign Relations has yielded to the private sector in the maintenance of Chile's presence.

Bilateral chambers of commerce, integrated by local and foreign businessmen, have also played an increasingly important role in Chile's foreign relations. These business committees have multiplied rapidly in recent years; from September 1973 to June 1981 committees were created between Chile and Egypt, Canada, Spain, France, Japan, South Africa, Israel, South Korea, Brazil, and Peru. In some instances, these entities have discreetly replaced the Foreign Ministry in hosting visitors from sensitive countries. This was the case with the Chilean-South African Chamber of Commerce, which, on one occasion, managed the visit to Santiago of an important delegation of South African members of Parliament.

The private economic route has been employed particularly in reference to countries that are hostile or distant toward the Chilean government, as is the case with Mexico, Italy, and even some socialist nations. However, in practically all of these instances Chile has managed to increment its commercial relations with those countries, without affecting political ties to any significant degree. Thus, for example, until January of 1982, diplomatic relations between Chile and Italy continued suspended at the ambassadorial level, despite the commercial boom registered between the two nations in the previous two or three years.

The Military Government and the International Context, 1973–1981

The accession of the military to power in 1973 and its implementation of a style of diplomacy founded on a militant anti-Communism clashed with the prevailing world context characterized by a relaxation of tensions between East and West. In the view of one author, détente constituted a "systematic obstacle" to the foreign policy orientation of the military government.[25] There was, therefore, a high degree of incongruence between Chile's national position and the concrete international political reality.

One of the first foreign policy decisions of the military junta after it came to power was to expel Cuban diplomats and sever relations with Cuba. Subsequently, several socialist nations broke relations with the Chilean government, including the Soviet Union, North Korea, North Vietnam, the German Democratic Republic, Poland, Czechoslovakia, Hungary, Bulgaria, Yugoslavia, and North Vietnam.[26] Soon after, in January 1974, the military regime broke relations with Cambodia, alleging that the Asian country had attempted to introduce political propaganda into Chile.[27] Moreover, in March 1974, Chile renewed diplomatic links with the former Republic of Vietnam (South Vietnam); shortly before the fall of Saigon, in May 1975, the Chilean government even made a public declaration on the political situation of Southeast Asia, accusing North Vietnam of violating the human rights of the Vietnamese people.[28]

More importantly, the new Chilean government launched from the outset an international campaign against détente, with the intention of informing the United States and other Western nations about the disadvantages and dangers of "political ambivalence" and "comfortable neutralisms."[29] The immediate target of the military government's campaign to transform the international order was, naturally, the Soviet Union. In October 1976, in a speech before the General Assembly of the United Nations, then foreign minister Vice-admiral Patricio Carvajal denounced the USSR as the number one enemy of world peace and added that the Soviets utilized détente "as a disguise for their expansionist policy."[30] In the opinion of this high military officer, détente had assumed the form of "a drug, an anesthesia that [was] hiding true reality from the countries of the world."[31]

In light of Washington's negative reaction to the idea of a global offensive against détente and the specific political postures of the Carter Administration, the military government also began to condemn the "soft and hesitating" attitude of the West towards Communism. In 1976, Foreign Minister Carvajal recognized openly that "the position of Chile, based on the values of Western Christian civilization, was contrary to Communism and could not be well received by the supporters of détente à outrance."[32] In unequivocal terms, General Pinochet traced a parallel between "Soviet imperialism" and "American imperialism," and condemned the United States for attempting to export its own political system to other countries, applying its human rights doctrine in a selective fashion, and not fulfilling its natural role as anti-Communist world leader.[33]

The Soviet invasion of Afghanistan in December of 1979 and the tensions between the United States and the USSR over Poland throughout 1980–81 deeply eroded the international context of détente and, hence, produced a conflictive global environment more functional to the interests and perspectives of the Chilean military regime. The election of Ronald Reagan as president of the United States in November of 1980, together with the previous election of a conservative government in Great Britain, brought about the most positive change of recent years in the foreign relations of the military government. The victory of Margaret Thatcher in England permitted the renewal of diplomatic ties at the ambassadorial level between London and Santiago in January 1980, which had been suspended in 1976 because of the Sheila Cassidy incident.[34]

Similarly, in February of 1981, the Reagan Administration lifted the prohibition imposed by the Carter Administration on extending subsidized credits from the Export-Import Bank to finance U.S. exports to Chile, and sent an invitation for the Chilean navy to participate again in the hemispheric naval exercise "Unitas." The official visit of Chilean Foreign Minister René Rojas to Washington in 1981 and the later visit to Santiago of U.S. Ambassador to the U.N. Jeane Kirkpatrick and of several delegations of U.S. congressmen ratified the upward turn registered in the public ties between Santiago and Washington. Recently, the White House pressured Congress into suspending the embargo of the sale of weapons to Chile imposed in 1976 through the Humphrey-Kennedy amendment; the new decision of Congress, however, includes a clause that requires a certification by President Reagan showing that there has been no deterioration in the local human rights situation.

In conclusion, the progress that the Chilean government has made in the sense of minimizing its international political isolation has not been the result of specifically designed strategies or of a reevaluation of the domestic human rights situation on the part of the world community but, rather, a result of temporary changes of attitude in the international context towards regimes like those of Chile. To the extent that Chile's foreign relations are basically dependent upon given changes in the external context, the military government is also subject to the political oscillations that democratic systems experience periodically, and that may signify the arrival of governments hostile to authoritarianism and of new moments of crisis in the external ties of the country. Thus, the election of François Mitterrand as president of France in May 1981 provoked a rather strong shock in the Chilean government.[35] Given the opposition of Mitterrand and of the French Socialist party to Chile's military regime, diplomatic ties between Paris and Santiago became less than cordial.

Conclusion

The critical issue of the authoritarian domestic order remains as the fundamental obstacle to the military government's efforts to overcome political isolation. In this respect, the U.N. voting record on the Chilean human rights situation from 1975 to 1980 reveals no significant improvement in the international assessment of Chile's internal order. (See Table 9.1.)

In sum, it would appear that even the combination of a more pragmatic style of diplomacy, the pursuit of economic growth through private channels (oriented to take advantage of Chile's closer ties with the transnational economic system), and certain changes in the international context will not suffice to put an end to the political isolation still experienced by the military government. More transcendental than the prevailing style of diplomacy or the global environment is the nature of Chile's domestic

TABLE 9.1   U.N. Voting Record on Condemnation of the Chilean Human Rights Situation

	For	Against	Abstaining	Total
1975	95 (73.6%)	11 (8.5%)	23 (17.8%)	129 (100%)
1976	95 (71.9%)	12 (9.0%)	25 (18.9%)	132 (100%)
1977	96 (71.1%)	14 (10.3%)	25 (18.5%)	135 (100%)
1978	96 (68.1%)	7 (5.0%)	38 (27.0%)	141 (100%)
1979	93 (73.2%)	6 (4.7%)	28 (22.0%)	127 (100%)
1980	95 (67.0%)	8 (5.6%)	39 (27.4%)	142 (100%)

Sources: Compiled from Keesing's *Contemporary Archives* and *El Mercurio.*

order. The notoriety of the country on the world scene may temporarily pass to a secondary plane, but every time the government accentuates authoritarian measures, its negative international image will be reactivated, and political isolation will continue to characterize the foreign relations of the Chilean military regime.

Notes

1. The use of the term *isolation* should not be understood simply as the lack of international contacts, but rather as the incapacity on the part of a state to establish or maintain positive and dynamic external ties. Political isolation, when it affects a given country, implies a deterioration of the factor "national prestige," an intangible element of power of special importance to countries which, like Chile, do not have great military and/or economic resources. In the case of Chile, then, isolation means that the present government is not able to satisfy national objectives in the world with the same ease and success as its predecessors.

The relationship between the real external position of a country and the international community is mediated by the image that the country projects in various spheres of that community. The image of a nation-state is important because decision makers respond or act not only according to the objective features of a situation—that is to what is commonly perceived as reality—but also according to the meaning that individuals attribute to such situations. In short, the international image of the Chilean government—like that of any other government—is as important as its objective external position. On this point see Ole R. Holsti, "Cognitive Dynamics and Images of the Enemy," in John C. Ferrell and Asa P. Smith, eds., *Image and Reality in World Politics* (New York: Columbia University Press, 1967), pp. 16-39.

2. The pro-military government forces have divided into at least two major factions: the *blandos* and the *duros*. The first group favors the rapid institutionalization of the military regime, backs all policies of economic liber-

alization, and has close contacts with private economic groups. The duros, by contrast, lean towards a corporativist conception of the state, generally oppose the institutionalization of the military regime emphasizing the importance of goals instead of datelines, reject the laissez faire economic model, oppose the progressive privatization of the Chilean economy, and criticize the existence of ties between some blandos and the conservative Catholic group Opus Dei.

3. See Manfred Wilhelmy, "Hacia un análisis de la política exterior chilena contemporánea," *Estudios Internacionales,* no. 48 (October–December 1979): 457–58.

4. Afterwards Chile broke relations with Cuba in compliance with an agreement of the OAS which, even though it had not supported, it believed had to be respected. On this matter, see Otto Boye S., "Chile y el interamericanismo en las dos ultimas décadas," *Mensaje* 20 (September–October 1971): 494–501.

5. "La semana política: Civiles y militares en el régimen," *El Mercurio,* 16 March 1980, p. A3.

6. Detailed data on U.S. foreign assistance to Chile from 1964 to 1976 may be found in Heraldo Muñoz, "Autoritarismo y política exterior: El caso chileno, 1973-1981" (mimeo, Instituto Relaciones Internacionales, Universidad de Chile, Santiago, May 1981), p. 9.

7. There have been several public and private trials conducted in Chile and the United States around the assassination of Letelier and Moffitt. For a detailed description, see Muñoz, "Autoritarismo y política exterior," pp. 21–23.

8. Ibid. pp. 80–82.

9. The resolution of the Ninth General Assembly of the OAS, approved by a vote of 21 to 1 (Chile dissenting), recommended that the states involved initiate negotiations to consider granting to Bolivia territorially sovereign access to the Pacific Ocean and creating a port developed and managed multinationally without territorial compensation on the part of Bolivia. In November 1980 the OAS approved another resolution recommending that the parties involved initiate direct conversations to find a satisfactory solution to the problem. The Chilean government considered the second resolution a significant improvement over the previous one. The approval of the 1980 resolution was made possible, in great measure, by the extreme international unpopularity of the Bolivian military regime of Luis García Meza, who had just overthrown the democratic government of Lidia Gueiler.

10. Even countries like Uruguay, Paraguay, and Guatemala, considered friends of the present Chilean government, kept silent on the Argentina decision. The silence of Guatemala contrasted with the earlier attitude of the Chilean Foreign Ministry, expressed through its vice-minister, supporting Guatemala in its dispute with England regarding the now independent state of Belize.

11. Data taken from reports of the International Institute of Strategic Studies and the Stockholm International Peace Research Institute. For additional details, see Muñoz, "Autoritarismo y política exterior," p. 72.

12. Document cited in *El Mercurio,* 13 March 1981, p. A12.

13. *El Mercurio,* 1 December 1974, p. 49.

14. For a detailed description of the principal Chilean economic groups and the process of concentration and centralization of capital under the military government, see Fernando Dahse, *El mapa de la extrema riqueza* (Santiago: Editorial Aconcagua, 1979).

15. "Reflexiones para una nueva política exterior," *Economía y Sociedad,* no. 2 (April 1978): 1-2, 8-9. At this time, the journal was edited by José Piñera, an economist who later became minister of labor and minister of mining.

16. Cauas quoted in *Qué Pasa?* 28 April 1977, p. 6.

17. Pinochet quoted in *Latin American Political Report,* 13 January 1978, p. 13.

18. Quoted in *Hoy,* 31 January–6 February 1979, p. 6.

19. On 10 April 1981, Chile and Peru renewed diplomatic relations at the ambassadorial level. The armed conflict between Peru and Ecuador over the El Cóndor border region was apparently the key factor that facilitated the normalization of relations between Santiago and Lima, since the Chilean foreign minister backed the Peruvian thesis for the resolution of the conflict. This, not surprisingly, caused a deterioration of bilateral relations between Chile and Ecuador.

20. See *Hoy,* 5–11 November 1980, p. 19.

21. Rojas quoted in *El Mercurio,* 28 March 1981, p. C9.

22. Calculations of the Banco Hipotecario de Chile (BHC) cited in *El Mercurio,* 23 September 1981, p. C1.

23. Data gathered by the author from official documents of the CIE. The designation in May of 1981 of a former minister of mining of the military regime as ambassador in Washington was apparently motivated by the government's desire to attract U.S. investors to the Chilean mining sector. The ambassador, who had never before occupied a diplomatic post, was supposed to publicize the new mining code among his numerous contacts in the U.S. mining industry.

24. Manuel Valdés quoted in *El Mercurio,* 5 July 1980, p. C7.

25. Wilhelmy, "Análisis de la política exterior," p. 467.

26. Rumania and the People's Republic of China did not suspend diplomatic relations with the military government. Apparently, the close commercial ties between Rumania and Chile and Rumania's nonaligned international posture influenced the former's decision to stay in Santiago; in the second case, the common identification on the part of Chile and China of the USSR as the principal enemy, as well as Peking's fear of being replaced in Santiago by Taipei, was responsible for China's decision to maintain normal relations with the Chilean military regime.

27. *El Mercurio,* 20 January 1974.

28. *El Mercurio,* 6 April 1975.

29. Pinochet quoted in *Qué Pasa?* 10 June 1976, p. 7.

30. Carvajal quoted in *El Mercurio,* 6 October 1976, p. 21.

31. Carvajal quoted in *El Mercurio,* 7 October 1975, p. 8.

32. Speech by Vice-admiral Patricio Carvajal, "Algunos aspectos de la política mundial y chilena durante 1975," *Diplomacia,* no. 9 (January–May, 1976): 8.

33. See "Texto del mensaje del Presidente Pinochet," *El Mercurio,* 12 September 1979, p. C6.

34. According to a London newspaper, the normalization of relations was possible thanks to the economic interest of British entrepreneurs in the Chilean market, and thanks to "an official apology from the Chilean government for the torture of Dr. Sheila Cassidy" (Julia Langdon, "Envoy to Chile Reinstated 'after Apology,'" *The Guardian,* January 18, 1980, p. 1).

35. The Chilean government has feared that, if Mitterrand nationalizes the weapons and space industry, France—which became Chile's alternative supplier of armaments after the U.S. Congress imposed limitations on the sale of weapons to the military regime—could interrupt the sale and delivery of important war equipment like AMX-30 tanks, Mirage jets, Puma helicopters, and Exocet surface-to-surface rockets. In fact, the Mitterrand government has already interrupted a previously agreed-upon delivery of arms to Chile.

List of Contributors

Genaro Arriagada Herrera is a Senior Researcher at the Instituto Chileno de Estudios Humanísticos and the Corporación de Investigaciones Económicas para América Latina. Among his numerous books are *De la Vía Chilena a la Vía Insurreccional* and *El Pensamiento Político de los Militares*. He has been a Fellow at the Woodrow Wilson International Center for Scholars.

Manuel Barrera is Director of the Centro de Estudios Sociales and author of numerous studies on the Chilean labor movement, including *Desarrollo Económico y Sindicalismo en Chile, 1938–1970*.

Ricardo Ffrench-Davis is a Senior Researcher at the Corporación de Investigaciones Económicas para América Latina. He has held numerous visiting appointments and served as a consultant to the United Nations, the World Bank, and other organizations. An expert on international economics and stabilization policies he is the author of, among other works, *Políticas Económicas en Chile 1952–1970* and *Economía Internacional: Teorías y Políticas para el Desarrollo*.

Alejandro Foxley is the Helen Kellogg Professor of Economics and International Development at the University of Notre Dame and President of the Corporación de Investigaciones Economicas para América Latina. He has held numerous visiting appointments, including at the University of California at Berkeley. Among his books are *Latin American Experiments in Neo-conservative Economics* and *Para una Democracia Estable*.

Manuel Antonio Garretón is a Senior Researcher at the Facultad Latinoamericana de Ciencias Sociales in Santiago. Among his many books are *El Proceso Político Chileno* and *Análisis Coyuntural y Proceso Político: Las Fases del Conflicto en Chile (1970–73)* with Tomás Moulian. He has held the Tinker Chair at the University of Chicago and been a Fellow at the Woodrow Wilson International Center for Scholars.

Heraldo Muñoz is Director of the Centro de Estudios de la Realidad Contemporánea of the Academia de Humanismo Cristiano and Senior

Researcher at the Instituto de Estudios Internacionales, University of Chile. He is the author of works on foreign policy and development issues including *From Dependency to Development* and *Crisis y Desarrollo Alternativo en América Latina.*

Brian H. Smith is Associate Professor of Political Science at the Massachussetts Institute of Technology. He is the author of numerous articles on religion and politics as well as *The Church and Politics in Chile.*

Arturo Valenzuela is Professor of Political Science and Chairman of the Council of Latin American Studies at Duke University. He has been a Fellow at the Woodrow Wilson International Center for Scholars and held visiting appointments at Oxford University and the University of Sussex. Among his books are *The Breakdown of Democratic Regimes: Chile* and *Political Brokers in Chile.*

J. Samuel Valenzuela is Associate Professor of Sociology at Harvard University and the President of the New England Council of Latin American Studies (1984–85). He is the author of *Democratización por Reforma: La Expansión del Sufragio en Chile* and co-author and editor of *Chile: Politics and Society.*

Pilar Vergara is Associate Researcher at the Facultad Latinoamericana de Ciencias Sociales in Santiago. Among her studies are "Apertura Externa y Desarrollo Industrial en Chile: 1974–78," and "Estado, Ideología y Politicas Economicas en Chile 1973–78," with Tomás Moulian.

Index

The Development of the Labor Movement Opposition
and the Formation of New "Groups"

The definitive break of the nonleftist union leaders with the government
signalled an important turning point for the development of the labor movement opposition to the military regime. Once these union leaders began to
denounce the government in unambiguous terms in order to retain the very
viability of their organizations and positions of leadership, they obviously
began to express publicly views that were in considerable agreement with
those of leftist sectors within the labor movement. Consequently, the various political and ideological factions of the labor movement, until recently
so bitterly divided, began to draw closer together rapidly on the basis of a
commonly shared opposition to the military regime's economic and labor
policies. And since the nonleftist leaders had been allowed by the regime to
become the public voice of labor, they continued to occupy that space, but
in a totally different manner; soon after its open break with the authorities,
the Group of Ten became, much like the tip of an iceberg, the most visible
sector of a broad opposition consensus of union leaders located at all organizational levels rather than simply one political and ideological segment of
the labor movement. Therefore, the public space that the regime had
granted to labor leaders with the intention that they aid it in a crusade
against Marxism became the tribune for a revitalized labor movement
which sought to express its common rejection of the authoritarian government.

The best example of the Group of Ten's newfound role was an open
letter of 30 August 1977 to the military government drafted in response to
General Pinochet's "new institutionality" speech. The letter was signed by
852 union officials representing 479 organizations—confederations, federations, and unions—and was particularly interesting because it did not
restrict itself to the by-then familiar denunciation of the government for
abridging union rights and freedoms, but spoke to the larger issue of the
future political order for Chile, the theme of the Pinochet speech. The
union leaders rejected the general's call for a "protected and authoritarian
democracy," noting that it should simply be "representative and pluralistic." They also indicated that the timetable which Pinochet gave for the
process of "normalization" was too drawn out and that the drafting of the
new political institutions should be accompanied by a broad process of
consultations with the citizenry. The open letter ended by asserting that
the greatest of Chilean national values, a notion invoked frequently by the
regime's representatives, was its traditional democratic system—which the
regime had singled out as an unworkable cauldron for leftist demagogues.
Eduardo Ríos, the leading figure of the Group of Ten, presented the union
document at a news conference in which he eloquently repeated and

expanded its terms. He noted, for instance, that one of the principal obstacles to a redemocratization of the Chilean political system lay in the fact that the upper classes had benefited enormously from the military government. He likened the government's economic policy to a funnel which produces "ample liberty for the industrialists, the large retailers, and the financiers. And for the workers? strict control by the state." He went on to assert that the workers could only take so much, and that their patience should therefore not be tried.[15]

The newfound preeminence of the Group of Ten leaders within the labor movement as a whole was not to last very long, however. Beginning in 1977, and certainly by 1978, other so-called groups began to multiply the public voices of the labor movement. The government itself tried to stimulate the formation of new top labor organizations in order to counter the influence of the Group of Ten, although without much success. One of the organizations it sponsored in 1978, the Unión Nacional de Trabajadores de Chile (UNTRACh), which has included well-recognized leaders of the copper, banking, airline, and shoe and leather industries, in a relatively short period of time took on an independent and even critical position towards the government, moving in fact close to the Group of Ten. A second, more loyal organization formed by the authorities, the Comando Nacional de Trabajadores, has not existed beyond its own stationary except for the participation of its leading figures in official ceremonies. The government's failure on this score has been partly a function of the fact that its attempt has been half-hearted. The military regime has been unwilling to orchestrate an organizational basis, either a party, a union, or both, from which to manipulate a broader process of mass mobilization, and this stifles even the minimal impact that the Comando Nacional could conceivably have.

The most important additional groups to become publicly active during 1977 and 1978 were oppositional in tone and in character. Two of them, the Confederación Nacional de Empleados Particulares de Chile (CEPCh) and the Frente Unitario de Trabajadores (FUT), had existed before the 1973 coup, the CEPCh having been formed in 1949 and the FUT during the Allende government, but neither had taken, openly at least, a leading role during the first years of the military government. The CEPCh's top leadership is generally centrist and has taken positions which approximate those of the Group of Ten, while the FUT is animated by individuals of a generally Christian background and leftist coloration.

The third and most significant organization to add its public voice to the labor movement opposition, the Coordinadora Nacional Sindical (CNS), was formally created in 1978 by union leaders who generally identify with the left of the Christian Democratic party as well as with the major and minor parties of the left. It therefore represents a fusion between, on the one hand, leaders who left the Group of Ten as a result of disagreements over the extent to which there should be collaboration on an equal footing with labor leaders of Communist and Socialist affiliations and, on the other, some of the latter who had reemerged as a result of the reactivation of the contacts and discussions within the labor movement. The president of the CNS, Manuel Bustos, a Christian Democratic official of the Textile Workers' Federation who had been among the original figures of the Group of Ten, represents the first element, while its secretary general, Alamiro Guzmán, a member of the Communist party and leader of the Mining Federation, is indicative of the second.

In a way, the multiplication of these labor groups resulted from the very success of the Group of Ten as well as from its change to a clear-cut oppositional stance. Success, since while the Ten stimulated widespread discussions among labor leaders to forge common positions to use in confronting the government, it also fostered the reestablishment of old links and the creation of new ones that underlay the alignment of the labor leaders into the different groups. And change to an oppositional stance, since this altered the status of the nonleftist leaders in view of the government, with polarizing consequences in labor movement circles. With their new confrontational attitude, the Group of Ten leaders ran the risk of expending their initial immunity from government repression given the shared anti-Communism which made most of them wary of too close an identification with the left. At the same time, since the Group of Ten was to lose its special position, the convenience which the leftist leaders earlier saw in sheltering the public activities of the labor movement as a whole under the cover afforded by the Group of Ten was thereby lost, and they would no longer see any reason to grant the Ten the limelight in the oppositional struggle. If the Group of Ten were henceforth to be placed on an equal footing with the other labor leaders—all disfavored by the authorities but each able to maneuver in an environment which, though far from free, had lost the ruthless and brutally repressive characteristics of the initial years—then there was no reason to allow the Ten to occupy the preeminent role in leading the opposition. Therefore, both the nonleftist as well as the leftist leaders had reasons to seek a clearer division between different peak organizations despite sharing a common rejection of the military government's policies, and it is this dynamic which produced the divisions, particularly between the Group of Ten and the CNS, in mid-1978.[16] Indeed, as if to confirm their desire to distance themselves from the left, the Group of Ten finally decided to change, in April 1981, its innocuous name to Unión Democrática de Trabajadores (UDF); the use of the term "democratic" in this label connotes a rejection of both the positions they see in the left and those they see in the government.

And yet, despite this organizational fragmentation at the top, the various organizations have continued occasionally to draft common declarations on specific and general matters. A notable example of the latter was the hard-hitting document jointly suscribed to by the Group of Ten, the

CNS, the CEPCh, and the FUT and issued for the May first labor day commemoration in 1979. Entitled "The Workers in Today's Chile," the text denounces what it calls the "revanchist, rancorous, and spiteful spirit which the capitalist and powerful classes exhibit today" as they have taken advantage of the authoritarian government in order to "reconquer all their privileges" during what has turned out to be a "profound revolution for the benefit of the rich." The labor leaders then buttress this assertion by noting that in all areas of policy the government has opted for the "hardest, most inhuman course, considering workers as objects, things, numbers, but not as persons." The text turns next to the "crimes" that have been committed, asking rhetorically where the workers and leaders that have been killed by the security apparatus are, why so many are forced to live in exile without ever having been condemned by a court of justice, why so many have been fired from their jobs, and why labor organizations have been deprived of their assets without any compensation—all of which reveals that "workers are currently managed with repression and the fear of unemployment." The labor leaders then note the sorry state of Chilean political institutions, given the lack of democracy and the abridgement of all the liberties and rights which the citizenry enjoyed, concluding that the present generation of Chileans cannot remember a government that has produced "greater penury, injustice, abuses," even if—following a pattern which the labor leaders claim is typical of authoritarian regimes—the government surrounds itself with individuals who sing its praises and orchestrate its favorable publicity in the mass media, and then deludes itself into believing in its own popularity. The leaders next call on the armed forces to return to the barracks. They assert that even though the authorities may remain in place while "fear and terror reigns" in the long run "a nation is always able to resume its course and to impose its personality." The text then concludes that for a return to democracy it is necessary to reestablish the electoral registers and to convoke a Constituent Assembly.[17]

The Government Changes Its Strategy: The Call for Union Elections and the New Labor Legislation

By late 1977, the relations between the regime and all of the nation's labor leaders were extremely curt and tense. The government knew that virtually none of the important labor leaders would support it, and it consequently began to assert more and more frequently that they were simply individuals motivated by political concerns and not representative of the majority of the rank and file. The authorities would probably have preferred to simply ignore the labor leaders, except that two new developments in late 1977 and 1978 made this impossible. The first was the reemergence of labor actions, especially in the large copper mines—in other words, in the one sector of Chilean unionism where workers are a